COURTROOM

COURTROOM

THE STORY OF SAMUEL S. LEIBOWITZ

By QUENTIN REYNOLDS

"I hear many people calling out, 'Punish the guilty,' but very few are concerned to clear the innocent." Samuel S. Leibowitz, summation to the jury, *People vs. Scutellaro*.

FARRAR, STRAUS AND GIROUX

NEW YORK

The author is indebted to D. Van Nostrand Company for permission to quote from THE POWER IN THE PEOPLE by Felix Morley, copyright 1949 by D. Van Nostrand Company, Inc.; and to Sidney Kingsley for permission to quote from his play, *Detective Story*.

For the protection of those concerned, a few of the names —but none of the facts—have been changed in this book.

Manufactured in the United States of America by H. Wolff Book Manufacturing Company, New York. Designed by Stefan Salter.

First Printing, May 1950
Second Printing, June 1950
ISBS 0-374-52743-2

To Ginny and Joanie, of course.

CONTENTS

PREFACE

In 1941, when, at the age of forty-seven, he retired from the turbulent give-and-take of the criminal courts, there was no one to challenge Samuel S. Leibowitz as the nation's No. 1 criminal lawyer.

This book is in part a study of the technique used by Leibowitz during his life in the criminal courtroom. It is in part a series of vignettes of the lives of the men and women he defended, most of whom are walking the streets free today because of the mastery he exerted in their behalf.

Detective Story, by Pulitzer Prize Winner Sidney Kingsley, was one of the hits of the 1949 theatrical season. In the play, Kingsley created the character of Endicott Sims, the criminal lawyer. The sadistic detective, Lieutenant James McLeod, is annoyed with Sims because the lawyer has objected to McLeod severely beating a prisoner who is Sims's client. The beaten prisoner almost dies. Sims tells the detective he is lucky he isn't facing a murder charge.

McLeod. I could always get you to defend me.
Sims. And I probably would. That's my job, no matter how I feel personally.
McLeod. As long as you get your fee.
Sims. I've defended many men at my own expense. Every man has a right to counsel, no matter how guilty he might seem to you or to me. Every man has a right not to be arbitrarily judged, particularly by men in authority; not by you, not by the Congress, not even by the President of the United States.
McLeod. He's guilty! you know it as well as I do.
Sims. I don't know it. I don't even permit myself to speculate on his

innocence or guilt. The moment I do that I'm judging—and it is not my job to judge. My job is to defend my client, not to judge him. That remains with the courts.

"Sims" is expressing the legal philosophy of the ethical trial lawyer. Leibowitz never felt that he, the district attorney, or the public had any right to prejudge a defendant, no matter how guilty he appeared. Leibowitz took the statute which says that an accused man is presumed to be innocent with deadly seriousness.

2

The reader may be puzzled as to what qualifications a former sports reporter, foreign correspondent and fiction writer has to write a book dealing with the intricacies of criminal law. The answer to that is to remember the comic who wanted to play Hamlet. There have been many lawyers who were frustrated writers; as far as I know, I am the only writer extant who is a frustrated lawyer.

I had always wanted to be a lawyer, and while I was working on the *New York Evening World* I stumbled through law school at night. During my senior year I was assigned by Jack Rainey, city editor of the *Evening World*, to cover the trial of a motion picture projectionist named Harry Hoffman. He had already been convicted of murder and sentenced, but he had been given a new trial and Samuel Leibowitz was his latest counsel. I watched Leibowitz tearing prosecution witnesses to bits; I watched as he made even the District Attorney squirm with impotent rage, and I saw him take over the courtroom, making his opponent fight his fight.

He was slim and tall then. His hair was smoothed back from his forehead and his fair complexion made him seem younger even than he was. His face colored deeply in anger. He could also blush. He still can. His hands are quick at gestures but one feels that he is restraining a tendency to wave them. He likes to point, and back of the leveled finger the eyes can seem very grim. His voice has great range and his timing is that of an actor reading a line. He leads up to a point, whether it is violent or witty, with care and he can pounce on it or throw it away with a neat dry crackle. I noticed that he was wearing a quietly cut blue suit and a bright, plain red tie.

Gene Tunney was heavyweight champion of the world then, and his pugilistic eminence was based on his genius as a counterpuncher. Leibowitz reminded me of Tunney. You couldn't afford to make a mistake when in the ring with either, or you'd be countered to death.

In those days, when you covered a trial for the *Evening World* you wrote a play-by-play story in the courtroom and then, when the session was over, you wrote an "overnight" for the first edition of the next day's paper.

The trial of Harry Hoffman, chiefly because of the sensational attacks on the prosecution by defense counsel, had attained the dignity of a big story, which meant that the reporter covering it had to write a large number of newspaper columns per day. One night I approached the understanding professor who was teaching our course in Real Property II, a nightmare of every law student. I asked him not to call on me that night as I just wasn't prepared. He was sympathetic to those of us who had to work our way toward a legal sheepskin, and he asked me what it was that was keeping me too busy to spend the requisite two or three hours a day for classroom preparation. I told him I was covering the Hoffman trial.

"That's all right," he said. "Watch that man Leibowitz in action. You won't learn anything about the law of real property but you'll learn more about how to try a case than anyone in the law school can teach you."

I covered many trials later in which Samuel Leibowitz was the defending lawyer, and I never tired of watching his unpredictable and often unorthodox defense tactics. One day in the winter of 1948, I picked up an old book of *New Yorker* profiles (it was published in 1934) and found a brilliant portrait of Leibowitz written by Alva Johnston. I went to the newspaper clips and through them followed his career from the day he first stepped into a courtroom. Why not a book on Leibowitz?

I went to see him. He was Judge Leibowitz now, senior jurist of the Kings County Court, one of the busiest criminal courts in America. No longer slim, sitting behind the desk he gave an impression of brawn and force. The hair is gray, still back from the forehead, the complexion still florid. He thought the idea of a book to be rather silly. "You might at least wait until I'm dead," he said, smiling.

"But you've been involved in more dramatic trials than any lawyer of our time," I said. "You've defended everyone from the Scottsboro boys to Al Capone."

"I don't like to think of another book about a criminal lawyer," he said. "There have been so many books written about the Howes and Hummels, the Fallons and McGees, that the public has been given the impression that these tinseled *Police Gazette* fabricators of evidence and jury-fixers are typical of the profession."

"That's true enough," I admitted.

Then Judge Leibowitz talked some time, telling me his ideas about the public's conception of the criminal lawyer.

"The American people," he said, "are poorly informed about what happens in their criminal courtrooms. Perhaps I should say they are misinformed. Some primitive races know more about their superstitious ritual trials than our people do of the workings of their judicial institutions. For the most part the public has a sham conception of what goes on in the course of a criminal trial. They are constantly exposed to portrayals of phony trial scenes in our motion pictures; and more of the same over the radio and television. This has helped jell the public misconception. The average person's idea of a criminal trial is exclusively a synthetic Hollywood product. The public has contentedly decided that practically everyone who is arrested for a serious crime stands trial in an attempt to defeat justice, whereas in fact only about 15 per cent do, while the remaining 85 per cent plead guilty immediately. For the most part, the public also thinks trials run to set form. Theatregoers know what to expect next in the way of legal fireworks and when to anticipate some breathtaking, out-of-the-hat rabbit-pulling maneuver by the attorney for the defense, who is generally depicted as a slick, sleazy, glib-tongued shyster. These deceptive pictures are enjoyed by the public, but the false notions they get by hearing and seeing so many garbled courtroom scenes piled one on top of the other are downright distasteful to the legal profession.

"The average American has come to regard the criminal court as a perfectly suitable stage for the exhibition of perjury, trickery and dishonesty. Yet he is totally unacquainted with the civil courtroom, even though so much of its business is settled at trial. Why are people so uninformed about the civil courts? Largely because such courts lack human interest and appeal. What goes on during a ponderous trial concerned with a railroad's right of way cannot possibly arouse the same sort of interest as a criminal trial in which the issue at stake is no mere property matter but a human life. Because the civil court is seldom if ever dramatized, the public misses the occasional picture of sharp manipulation and cunning maneuvers by high-priced corporation lawyers in such courts. They do not realize the extent of human damage sometimes done by some legal retainers of multimillionaire corporations.

"Of course, every profession and every business, too, has its share of quacks and charlatans and the criminal law is no exception. My experience as a lawyer and judge, however, convinces me that lawyers who practice in our criminal courts are for the most part high-minded, honest and decent people. Also I am fully convinced that our criminal courts offer the cleanest and most challenging battleground for the testing of legal knowledge and wisdom. It is not easy, I admit, to convince the public of this. They are traditionally suspicious of the whole legal profession. 'Let's kill all the lawyers,' an opinion spoken by one of Shakespeare's characters, may well be as correct an interpretation of the public's feelings today as it was hundreds of years ago."

"For twenty-one years you battled in courtrooms," I said, as he paused. "You saw the mistaken witness and the occasional perjurer. You saw the earnest, hard-working district attorneys and you saw prosecutors who wanted a conviction at all costs. You saw the dark prejudices of the Alabama jury in the Scottsboro case. You saw . . ."

"If you'd write a book that would not only be revealing to the public but helpful to law students and also to lawyers, it might be worth your effort," he said slowly. "If you'd not only tell the human stories of the trials, but also point out changes that can be made to improve the administration of criminal justice, the book might have some value."

4

My job of research was made easier by the fact that the trial record of every important case in which Leibowitz had participated was available. I used the trial records as a basis and then supplemented this by newspaper reports and by interviewing witnesses, district attorneys, newspapermen and jurors who were still available. In some cases I located men and women who had once been familiar figures to the public when they were being prosecuted for murder. Sometimes they had changed their names and begun new lives in communities which never knew their past histories.

Occasionally, research revealed that the dead victim was actually the one who precipitated the violence and who was primarily the "guilty" one. The conversations outside the courtroom between principals in the various cases are not manufactured bits of dialogue. Except where otherwise noted, the conversations are as accurate as participants or witnesses can recall.

When unresolved doubts arose, I sometimes went to Judge Leibowitz and asked him to tie some of the loose, dangling ends together for me. For obvious reasons some of the characters are referred to by names furnished by me. The events related are absolutely true.

"The usual criminal trial is like an iceberg," Judge Leibowitz told me when I began to work. "Only one-fifth of it can be seen; the remaining four-fifths is hidden. Yet the hidden four-fifths which, to the untrained eye, is never evident in the courtroom, is often the most important and most interesting part of the whole trial."

In the main, this book concerns itself with that hidden four-fifths.

COURTROOM

1. THIS THING CALLED JUSTICE

"The law, wherein, as in a magic mirror, we see reflected
not only our own lives, but the lives of all men that
have been!"

MR. JUSTICE OLIVER WENDELL HOLMES

The career of even a great criminal lawyer would hardly be worth
considering if no importance were attached to his profession. A criminal lawyer who by trickery and corruption manages to free the
guilty criminal is not worthy of our attention. Before we consider the
story of the greatest criminal lawyer of our time, suppose we present
a few pages of evidence to prove the worth of Leibowitz' own statement, printed in the Harvard Law School *Record*, "Only an alert
criminal lawyer can safeguard these inalienable rights to the defendant. The good criminal lawyer is to crime what the physician is to
disease." What happens when an innocent defendant is poorly represented by counsel? Is the ethical criminal lawyer necessary in our
modern society?

2

Edmond Fitzgerald is a brown-eyed, redheaded Irishman with a
quick smile and a suggestion of brogue in his soft voice. He is
chief probation officer of the County Court of Kings County which
has a population of nearly three million. Judge Leibowitz says very emphatically that Fitzgerald is the best man in the country at his job.
New York City's Mayor William O'Dwyer, who was once a judge

3

of this court, says, "Do I know Fitz? I appointed him and once when he tried to resign, I practically got on my knees to beg him to stay."

Fitzgerald's work usually begins when the trial is over and the defendant has been found guilty and is awaiting sentence. He and the men under him then find out everything there is to be known about that defendant, and, if occasion warrants it, everything about the complainant. Fitzgerald is not bound by any technical rules of evidence. In many ways he is the eye, the ear and the conscience of the court; the judges of the County Court of Kings County never sentence a defendant until they study the reports made by Fitzgerald.

His reports are masterly documents. When a judge has read his analysis of a defendant, he knows whether or not the man is capable of reform. Fitzgerald has interviewed members of his family, his employer, his neighbors, his priest or minister if he is a churchgoer, and has talked to his parents and to his teachers. Fitzgerald admits that he has a fervent faith in the inherent decency of people and he always does his best to find out something favorable to the man who has been adjudged guilty and is awaiting sentence. Often a defendant insists that he could prove his innocence if he could locate some witnesses who have disappeared or who, because of the incompetence of his legal defenders, were never summoned to the witness chair; often the defendant is in no position to hire anyone to locate such witnesses. Fitz takes notice of the defendant's plea and hunts such missing witnesses with the tenacity of a bloodhound. Usually, of course, they turn out to be mythical characters.

More often than not he discovers that the defendant is guilty as charged, that there are no extenuating circumstances and that the defendant and witnesses who testified in his favor had told nothing but lies. Fitzgerald is always sad and a bit disillusioned when he has to make out such a report, for his respect for the oath taken by witnesses is so great that he is reluctant to believe that any human being made in God's image could deliberately lie.

4

Fitzgerald was not smiling when he entered the chambers of Judge Leibowitz one morning in September, 1944. He was frowning unhappily, and he only nodded in answer to the cheery "Good morning, Fitz" that Judge Leibowitz threw him.

"What's on your mind, Fitz?" Judge Leibowitz had no idea that Fitzgerald was about to toss a legal time bomb on his desk.

"The Goldman case. I'm not satisfied with it, Judge," Fitz said sadly.

"The Goldman case?" the Judge questioned. "Why Fitz, it's completely open and shut. That man deserves the limit and I'm going to give it to him. Goldman is guilty of attempted rape in the first degree and he's going to get ten years."

"I'm sorry, Judge," Fitzgerald's brown eyes were mournful, "I've been investigating. There's a very good chance that there was a lot of lying going on during Goldman's trial."

Judge Leibowitz looked at Fitzgerald in amazement. He was perfectly satisfied with the verdict, but he knew that Fitz had a sixth sense and that time after time he had unearthed startling and hitherto undisclosed facts about principals in criminal trials over which the Judge had presided.

"You're wrong this time, Fitz," Judge Leibowitz said, shaking his head. "But go on and let me have it . . ."

The Judge folded his arms, and tucked his legs under the desk. When he is intent on new evidence, his concentration is complete. He looks then almost Buddha-like, the eyes masked, the unusually expressive full lips quiet, the whole figure relaxed yet somehow tense, for Judge Leibowitz is never so quiet or relaxed that one does not feel he might suddenly spring into the middle of the room shouting.

Fitzgerald sat down across the desk. "If you don't mind," he said almost apologetically, "I'd like to review the case from the beginning. You remember that Goldman was picked up by the police at noon on July 1. He was brought . . ."

4

Anne Brewer at thirty-one was a nurse's assistant in the Brooklyn State Hospital. She was tall, slender and attractive, although the rimless hexagon-shaped spectacles she wore gave her a prim appearance. She looked like a spinsterish schoolteacher. In 1943, hospitals were desperately short of nurses and assistants and when she applied for a job at the Brooklyn institution they were glad to accept her. She was merely one of the nearly eight million New Yorkers, living her life and doing her work in relative anonymity. But on the morning of July 2, 1943, she emerged from the anonymous mass to find her name spread on the front pages of every New York newspaper. The papers screamed that she had been the victim of a brutal attempt at rape. She had fought off her attacker with vigor and courage and he had finally fled. Alert police had caught the would-be rapist and he was being questioned by the district attorney's office.

As a story this one had everything, and the newspapers, quite understandably, played it for all it was worth. Newspaper readers, weary of reading about the war, devoured everything that was written about the case. Anne Brewer seemed bewildered by the spotlight which had so unexpectedly revealed her to the public gaze, but she told a straightforward story which had a complete ring of truth to it. It was impossible not to feel sympathy for the nurse's attendant.

She was rather shy but self-possessed when she told her story. She was from the Midwest, she said. It was there that she had met and married her childhood sweetheart, Fred Brewer. He enlisted in the Navy the day after Pearl Harbor. When he was sent overseas as a Seabee, she came to New York, thinking that the chances of occasionally seeing her husband would be better if she were living on the seaboard. On her arrival she had registered with the U. S. Employment Service and had been immediately offered the job in the Brooklyn State Hospital. She began work there on May 25. She had been living in a room in the nurses' dormitory on the hospital grounds since then.

She was on night duty, and she said that on the morning of July 1 she had finished work, taken a shower, donned a nightgown and gone to bed at 10:00 A.M. She had been awakened by a knock on the door. The night before, Anne had suggested to another of the attendants, Margaret Visi, that they go to the movies the next afternoon, and when she heard the knock, Anne assumed that this was Margaret waking her up. She went to the door, still half asleep, opened it, and there to her horror stood a burly man with brown hair—a complete stranger to her. He pushed his way into the room and shut the door behind him. Terrified, she had managed to gasp, "What do you want?"

"You know what I want," he had said, and then he had reached for her. She told of how she had tried to fight him off. She had screamed, but no one heard her cries, or if they did they assumed them to be the cries of a patient, for Brooklyn State Hospital is an institution for the mentally unbalanced, and cries which might be unusual at most hospitals are common in such an institution. The stranger forced her back upon the bed while she resisted with every bit of strength she had. But she was getting weaker and weaker and then there was a sharp knock on the door. The knock was repeated, and the stranger whispered to her that if she cried out now he would choke her to death.

"I told him that it was undoubtedly the supervisor knocking on the door and that she knew I was in the room," Anne said. "He told me to open the door and speak to her but not to let on that he was in the room. He said he would kill me if I said he was there; he would hide behind the door when I opened it."

Anne went to the door, opened it, and there was Margaret Visi ready for the movies. Margaret looked at her friend and sensed that something was wrong. Anne motioned silently to the door. The resolute Margaret stepped into the room, pulled the door aside, saw the man, seemingly grasped the whole situation at a glance and ran from the room to raise an alarm. The intruder wasted no more time. He, too, ran from the room and hurried to the street. There was a bus stop outside the hospital. By now several nurses and attendants, alerted by Margaret, were looking for policemen. Margaret herself ran after the man. She caught up with him and he pleaded with her to forget that she had seen him. He went so far as to offer

7

her presents if she would forget it, but Margaret Visi indignantly refused. A moment later a prowl car came along and two cops hopped
out to nab the sex criminal.

They took him back to the nurses' living quarters. Anne identified
him, told her story, and a few moments later the assailant was on
his way to the district attorney's office, protesting his innocence. His
name, he said, was Murray Goldman. In describing him, the papers,
with their usual fine sense of restraint, used the good old time-
honored expressions "sex maniac," "fiend," etc. The whole story was
one which had been told a hundred times before. It was not the
first time that an unbalanced psychopath had invaded a women's dormitory. It followed the familiar pattern of sex crimes. No one at
the hospital had ever seen Murray Goldman before. Apparently he
hadn't come seeking Anne Brewer. He was merely following some
perverted sexual urge that drove him to seek any woman. It was
sheer chance that led him to the door behind which Anne Brewer
was sleeping. When reporters asked Anne if she had ever seen him
before, she looked at them with astonishment. Of course she hadn't
seen him before. As a matter of fact, she'd been in New York only
about six weeks. Outside of the workers at the hospital she knew
practically no one in New York.

Murray Goldman told a weird and unconvincing tale. He was a
burly man with a moon face and uneasy eyes. He was thirty, had
separated from his wife and was living in a furnished room. He
had received his draft notice and was waiting Uncle Sam's summons.
He said that he had met Anne Brewer on May 25, on a New
York subway station while on his way home from work (he was employed by the American Express Company). She had asked him the
best way to get to the Brooklyn State Hospital. Goldman told her
he lived in Brooklyn; if she wished to go with him to his apartment, he would get his car and drive her right to the door of the
hospital. She went with him. When they reached his rooming house,
he said he'd like to change his clothes. Perhaps she wouldn't mind
coming inside with him? No, she didn't mind at all. She not only
went inside with him but, according to Goldman, within a few
minutes was in bed with him. He saw her several times after that,

he said. He'd take her for a drive, they'd stop somewhere for a drink and then they'd go to his room. Yes, she always went willingly.

On July 1, he had phoned and made an appointment to meet her at a cafeteria a block from the hospital. He arrived a bit late, he said, and she wasn't there. He thought she had grown tired of waiting and had returned to the dormitory. He went to the dormitory. There was a desk in the lobby but there was no one behind it. A girl passed through, he said, and he asked her where he could find Anne Brewer. The girl said that her room was on the floor above. He went up the stairs and called Anne's name. She opened her door and he went in. She told him that he shouldn't have come to her room; she would be fired if he were discovered.

Then came the knock on the door. Margaret Visi walked in, saw him and he hurried out. He admitted that he had tried to persuade Margaret to keep quiet about finding him in Anne's room, and he added weakly that he did this because he didn't want Anne to get into any trouble. This was his whole defense—this rather fantastic story. He couldn't name anyone who had ever seen Anne and himself together. In fact he couldn't verify even one single portion of his story and he was quickly indicted for attempted rape in the first degree. The trial took place in September, with Judge Leibowitz presiding and with Assistant District Attorney John E. Cone prosecuting.

The stories told by Anne and by Murray Goldman on the stand were substantially the same stories each had told on the day of the arrest. The jury was presented with two versions. It was obvious that the story one of them told was a complete fabrication. Anne had no apparent motive for lying. Besides, she just didn't look like a girl who was capable of lying. Goldman stumbled nervously and unconvincingly through his testimony. To the jury it seemed obvious that he had concocted this improbable story on the spur of the moment and that having told it, he was stuck with it. Not a soul in the courtroom believed a word that Goldman said, and when the jury brought in a verdict of guilty everyone was satisfied that justice had been done. The spectators cheered the verdict and gazed with admiration at Anne Brewer. The newspapers took the opportunity of patting American womanhood, as represented by Anne Brewer, benignly on the head. Goldman was led away to Raymond Street Jail to await sentence, and gradually interest died down. Everyone forgot the case except Edmond Fitzgerald and his assistants. And then Fitzgerald walked into the chambers of the Judge to drop his bomb.

5

"Now let me tell you about this lady who looks like an old-fashioned schoolteacher, Judge," Fitzgerald said. "Two weeks before Goldman's arrest, Anna Mardorf, the supervisor of female attendants at the hospital, made a written complaint against Anne Brewer to Dr. Clarence Bellinger, superintendent of the institution, charging Mrs. Brewer with lewd and improper conduct in the presence of male attendants. The hospital was desperately understaffed and instead of firing her, Dr. Bellinger reluctantly kept her on but he transferred Anne Brewer to night duty, where chances of contact with male attendants would be lessened. About a week before Goldman's arrest, Anne Brewer had accused another attendant of attempted rape upon her person, but Dr. Bellinger on investigation found that the charges were completely false. Judge, I have found that Anne Brewer frequented bars and grills in the neighborhood, and on more than one occasion picked up men. Her reputation in these places is bad. I have found," Fitzgerald went on tonelessly, "that Mrs. Brewer has been carrying on an affair with one of the male attendants at the hospital— a sixty-one-year-old ex-convict—and that she had sexual relations with him at least twice in an alleyway on the hospital grounds. His wife, incidentally, learned of this and is divorcing him, naming Anne Brewer as co-respondent.

"You have statements from witnesses as to the truth of all this?" Judge Leibowitz was stunned at the revelations.

"Of course," Fitzgerald nodded. "There are a great many discrepancies in the story told by Anne Brewer. She said that she kept screaming for help during the twenty minutes she fought Goldman off. I now have a witness who occupied the room next to Anne Brewer's. She is Margaret Belford, another nurse's attendant. She was in her room during the alleged attack. Her door and her window were both open, yet she heard no sounds at all. The walls are quite thin, and, as a matter of fact, if you are in Miss Belford's room you can hear ordinary conversation by people in Anne's. Had there been any screaming at all, Miss Belford surely would have heard it. In my opinion, Judge, it was the Brewer woman who did all the lying and it was Goldman who was telling the truth."

"Well, tell me, Fitz, what motive had she for lying?" The jurist was thoughtful now, going over in his mind the cross-examination of Goldman.

"There is a strict rule at the hospital that no visitors are allowed in the rooms of the attendants," Fitzgerald went on. "A moment after Goldman entered Anne's room, Margaret Visi knocked on the door, came into the room and saw Goldman. Anne was afraid that Margaret would report his presence and that it might lose her her job. So she made up that story of the attempt at rape right on the spur of the moment. Another thing, Judge. Dr. Bellinger is, as you know, one of the finest psychiatrists in America. As soon as the police brought Goldman back to the dormitory, he was notified. Dr. Bellinger hurried to Anne's room, thinking perhaps that after such a harrowing experience she might need some medical attention. To his surprise, instead of finding a hysterical girl who might be expected to show some signs of having fought a twenty-minute battle against a powerful sex-crazy man, he found, to use his own words, "a calm, collected, complacent and smiling" Anne Brewer who showed no outward marks of having been engaged in a desperate fight for her honor. Dr. Bellinger listened to her story, concluded that it was a complete fabrication and returned to his office. As superintendent of the hospital it was his responsibility to make a complaint against anyone who had entered a hospital building and attempted to commit a crime. However, this eminent psychiatrist, a trained judge of people, realized that the Brewer woman was lying and he washed his hands

11

of the whole matter. He says that he was completely unimpressed by her story. He did not even appear in the courtroom while the Goldman trial was going on."

"But, Fitz, there wasn't a bit of evidence to corroborate Goldman's story."

"If you'll pardon me, Judge, I think if the defense counsel or D.A. had only half tried they could have found plenty of such proof," Fitzgerald said solemnly. "You remember that Goldman testified that he asked a girl in the lobby where he could find Anne Brewer. She told him that Anne's room was on the floor above. I have located that girl—her name is Elizabeth Connolly, a waitress in the nurses' dining room—and she says Goldman was right. But to be on the safe side," Fitzgerald continued, "let's give Goldman a lie-detector test."

Evidence which is the result of such a test is not as yet admissible in court. The lie detector is still a stepchild in all forty-eight states, but many judges—Judge Leibowitz is one—have complete faith in it. There are several types of "lie detectors" and Judge Leibowitz likes the pathometer, invented by the late Father Summers of Fordham and perfected by Professor Kubis of Fordham's Department of Psychology. The pathometer measures the electrical changes in the sympathetic nervous system of the human body that takes place under questioning. Goldman agreed to the test and was asked eighteen questions. He repeated his story of having met Mrs. Brewer on a subway platform and of the intimate relationship into which they had subsequently entered. Judge Leibowitz and Assistant District Attorney Cone, too, were satisfied now that Goldman had been telling the truth right along. A few days later the prosecution made a motion to set aside the jury's verdict of guilty and to dismiss the indictment.

"The District Attorney's office," Assistant District Attorney John Cone said, "took cognizance of the court's misgivings as to the defendant's guilt and interviewed several of the men with whom she is said to have consorted. Their statements demonstrate the testimony of the complainant as being absolutely worthless and brand her as a lewd character. After I had apprised the complainant of the statements made by these men, she admitted that many of these statements were true, and then she made a statement to me that she did know Goldman before the date of the alleged attack on herself. She now admits that she did meet him on a subway station, as he said, and that he did later drive her to the hospital. I move for the dismissal of the indictment of attempted rape against Murray Goldman."

In granting the dismissal, Judge Leibowitz paid a tribute to the young prosecutor who, once doubt had arisen as to the justice of the verdict, had investigated assiduously to bring out the facts as they were and not as Anne Brewer had said them to be.

"This woman almost succeeded in railroading the unfortunate defendant to State Prison for a term of ten years," Judge Leibowitz said. "Her perjury in my opinion was a crime that is second only to murder."

Murray Goldman walked out of court a free man. Once again the sanctified system of having twelve good men and true decide the guilt or innocence of a defendant had failed. Once again the law had been mocked by a clever liar. Eventually justice had triumphed, but not because it received any help from the law. It triumphed because redheaded Edmond Fitzgerald, who isn't even a lawyer, is a conscientious and brilliant investigator who has a "sixth sense."

There is no doubt that the jury system is the best method yet devised to determine the guilt or innocence of an accused person, but juries, being composed of human beings, are not infallible. The Goldman case jury believed every word uttered by Anne Brewer, but then so did Judge Leibowitz and alert Jack Cone, and so did every spectator in that courtroom who saw her and heard her as she sat on the witness stand. But was the jury to blame for this almost tragic miscarriage of justice? What of the defense counsel? Why hadn't he made the necessary investigation before the trial began? Why hadn't he discovered the character and reputation of the apparently prim complainant? Why hadn't he found Elizabeth Connolly, the girl Goldman had spoken to in the lobby of the building? Why hadn't defense counsel brought out the fact that the walls between the rooms were so thin that ordinary conversation, let alone violent screams, could easily have penetrated into the next room?

13

6

Judge Leibowitz has been on the bench since 1941, and during that time he has disposed of more than four thousand cases. Murray Goldman is not the only one found guilty in his court and afterwards cleared. Sometimes defendants have to be protected even against themselves, against their own fear of the police. More than one such fear has prompted a man to confess his guilt to a crime that he never committed.

In 1942, a jury found Harold Jackson guilty of sodomy on the complaint of a fourteen-year-old girl. She had accused him of this crime and also of having raped and impregnated her. On arrest he had confessed the sodomy to the police but had denied the rape charge. At trial, the confession was admitted in evidence and (in addition to the girl's direct testimony) was the principal factor leading to the verdict of guilty of sodomy. The rape charge had to be thrown out because there was neither a confession nor other corroborating evidence of the complainant's allegation with regard to it, as is required by statute. Throughout the case, however, the girl had stated frequently and unequivocally that both the sodomy and rape had occurred on a specific day. Her story was to the effect that the defendant, a boarder in her home, had taken advantage of the absence of her parents on the afternoon of this particular day and had induced her to submit to both natural and unnatural relations with him. She was quite insistent that Jackson was responsible for her pregnancy, inasmuch as she had never had relations with any man before or after that day.

Her story was pertly and convincingly delivered before the jury. All the lurid details stood up under vigorous cross-examination. As soon as the guilty verdict was returned, Jackson was remanded for sentence. His record of previous convictions (none involved sexual violations) made a twenty-to-forty-year sentence mandatory. Once again Judge Leibowitz was assailed by doubts; although all the evidence was against the unsavory Mr. Jackson. Somehow, the girl's story was too letter perfect—too good to be true. Fitzgerald's investigation revealed that on the date and at the time of the alleged offense Jackson was at his bench in the machine shop where he was employed. There was incontrovertible evidence of this both in the records of the employing concern and in the independent recollection of the employer (a responsible business man) and of several of Jackson's co-workers. Furthermore, on the very same date and at the very same time, the girl was in her classroom at school. The school records and her teacher verified this. It developed that it would have been physically impossible for the pair to have met on the fateful day during the time that the girl's parents were absent from the home. Further investigation by Fitzgerald revealed the unhappy fact that the fourteen-year-old complainant had a reputation as an habitual liar. An examination by a physician from the Children's Society led to the disclosure that she was already pregnant at least a month before the defendant came into her life. Faced with this new information, the girl acknowledged that she was in fact pregnant by another man at the time of the alleged crime. She had sought escape from her panic and from the wrath of her parents by contriving to pin criminal responsibility on the convenient Jackson and her whole story was a fabrication.

Why did Jackson deny the rape charge (of which he was innocent) to admit a sodomy charge (of which he was equally innocent)?

On a previous occasion he had been badly beaten by the police for protesting his innocence on a felony charge. Apprehensive that he was in for another beating unless he admitted his guilt, he decided to confess, but he had a twisted idea that sodomy was a lesser crime than rape—so he confessed to sodomy. The police and the District Attorney were well content to accept the confession, and but for Fitzgerald's investigation an innocent (if worthless) man would be spending the rest of his life behind prison bars.

A great majority of those charged with crime in New York City are paupers. The court assigns defense lawyers to them and those lawyers, except in first-degree murder cases, work without compensation. Many young lawyers are glad to accept such cases without compensation merely to get the experience. Quite often they get the experience, and the defendant gets a longer sentence than his crime called for, or occasionally he finds himself in jail for a crime which he never committed at all. The lawyer is the only active participant in a trial in whom ignorance of the law and proper trial technique is excused.

Criminal law is one course which many students enter with happy sighs. It is considered a "snap" course at most law schools. You study the Code of Criminal Procedure, you learn the Penal Law, you read a handful of cases illustrating the operation of both, and you can pass your criminal law examination without drawing a nervous breath. Of course they're always apt to throw a trick question at you such as, "What is the difference between murder in the first degree and murder in the second degree?" but usually you can count upon being asked to consider more conventional problems such as, "Distinguish between a felony and a misdemeanor."

It is quite different when you are tested on your knowledge of equity, corporation law or real property. These are considered important subjects and are treated seriously by law professor and student. But it is seldom that a man graduates from law school with anything but the most perfunctory knowledge as to methods of protecting the rights of a man accused of crime. Any time a case involving a substantial sum of money is argued in a civil court, you can be sure that both sides will be represented by eminent and highly skilled counsel. When a man's life or liberty is at stake in the criminal courts, it sometimes happens that his defense will be conducted either by some youngster who doesn't know his nolle prosequi from a hole in the indictment, or by some older incompetent.

A few years ago, a Massachusetts district attorney made a speech in which he declared, "Innocent men are never convicted. It is a physical impossibility." This statement so enraged Edwin M. Borchard, professor of law at Yale University, that he promptly wrote a book which he called *Convicting the Innocent*. In it he discussed the cases of sixty-five defendants who were found guilty of crimes and whose innocence was later established. In a majority of these cases witnesses lied or were mistaken, but were believed by the jury.

However, to create the impression that our prisons are filled with innocent men is absurd. Mr. Bumble in *Oliver Twist* was certainly overcritical when he snorted, "The law is an ass—an idiot," but it is a fact that in the criminal courts of our land injustice is an occasional visitor. Innocent defendants have been convicted and men are serving longer sentences than they deserve because they were poorly represented when they were tried.

Are resourceful, conscientious criminal lawyers necessary so that those arraigned before the bar of justice are accorded their day in court? In the April 13, 1949, issue of the Harvard Law School *Record*, Leibowitz answered the question.

"The need for capable criminal lawyers was never greater than it is today. Only the talents of the criminal lawyer can save the occasionally accused innocent man or woman. Each year the Supreme Court of the United States is flooded with petitions alleging that the applicant has been deprived of due process of law and other legal rights. In far too many cases the Supreme Court finds the allegations to be true. This is sometimes the result of carelessness, disinterest, or downright incompetence on the part of defense counsel in the court of original jurisdiction. Only an alert criminal lawyer can safeguard these inalienable rights of the defendant. The good criminal lawyer is to a defendant accused of crime what the physician is to a patient affected with disease."

The history of jurisprudence is studded with the names of great criminal lawyers, and all of them combined the knowledge of the law and the insight into the complexities of the psychological factors that go to make up the human being. All, according to their individual methods, were great salesmen—salesmen not of tangible articles but of ideas, of causes. The great criminal lawyers of history championed not only the rights of their clients but, incidentally, the rights of all free men.

Thomas Erskine, even to this day, is regarded as the greatest courtroom genius the English bar has ever known. We are told that, "As a lawyer his strength lay in the keenness of his reasoning faculty, in his dexterity and the ability with which he disentangled complicated masses of evidence, and above all in his unrivalled power of commanding the attention of juries."*

When Thomas Erskine successfully defended Captain Thomas Baillie, who was accused in 1778 of criminal libel, he not only

* Encyclopaedia Britannica.

17

freed an innocent man; he exposed the corrupt way in which the agents of the Admiralty were handling pensions and veterans' homes, and thus a reform was inaugurated that has lasted until today. Yet, at the time Erskine won his case for Captain Baillie, his thought was not primarily on instituting reforms in the social structure of England. He was merely interested in guarding the legal and fundamental rights of his client. Later he would be known as the defender of liberal causes, he would be made a peer and finally be named Chancellor of England—but he made his reputation and his livelihood as a criminal lawyer.

No one was ever more zealous in the safeguarding of the basic rights of man than a criminal lawyer who, as a small child in his native Roumania, was known by the name of Samuel Lebeau. Like Erskine, he had three children, and during his early career he was seldom able to bring them more than the necessities of life. But his skill as an advocate developed and was recognized, and soon his services were in great demand. Today he is moored in the comfortable harbor of the judicial robe, but only a few years ago he was acknowledged to be the nation's leading criminal lawyer, an advocate in the tradition of Thomas Erskine.

He was better known as Samuel S. Leibowitz.

2. THE NOVICE

"If there would be no bad people, there would be no good lawyers."

CHARLES DICKENS

The newspapers of March 17, 1897, were filled with exciting news and stirring editorials, so they can be pardoned for omitting to mention the arrival on that day of three visitors from Roumania. The arrivals were Isaac and Bina Lebeau and their four-year-old son Samuel. Their first impression of New York was that of a gay, music-filled city where crowds gathered on street corners to sing what seemed to be haunting, old-world songs. As they made their way crosstown from the North River dock, where the good ship *Kensington* had berthed early that morning, this impression was strengthened. When they reached Fifth Avenue they found it filled with men who marched ten abreast behind bands which blared forth such fine old American folk songs as "The Wearing of the Green" or "Kathleen Mavourneen."

They were getting their first glimpse of New York's annual saturnalia held each March 17 in honor of the good Saint Patrick. In the 1890's, the day perhaps was more festive than it is now; it is a fact that there was more whiskey drunk on that day than on any other during the year, and although there were more riots, fights and fires, there were seldom any arrests, for members of New York's finest were far too busy marching and drinking to bother arresting anyone. It would, in fact, have been almost sacrilege to apprehend a man on the natal day of Saint Patrick, an affront to the memory of the worthy saint. And so a hundred thousand Irishmen marched

19

and three times that many celebrated the glorious day with unrestrained and uninhibited enthusiasm.

The city seemed filled with gaiety and friendliness, an atmosphere far different from that of their native town of Jassy in Roumania. Roumania had anticipated the Germany of Hitler by many years. In Roumania, Jews were allowed only one privilege—they were permitted to pay taxes. They could not vote, own land, nor were they accorded any of the civil rights permitted their Aryan neighbors. Isaac Lebeau owned a dry goods store in Jassy, and although he had no particular desire to own land or vote, he did writhe under the indignity of being arbitrarily classified as inferior. When he had saved enough for passage money, he took his wife and child to the new world. Now, as he heard the glorious music and sensed the spirit of friendliness, he knew that he had made a wise choice. In the years ahead Isaac Lebeau was to undergo occasional hard times and sometimes find injustice, and prejudice too, in this new world, but nothing ever diminished the love for New York which came to him on Saint Patrick's Day, 1897.

He settled his family in Manhattan in a tenement just a few blocks from where the Williamsburg Bridge was to be erected, and it was here in the dark jungles of New York's lower East Side that his son Samuel grew up. "Lebeau" was a strange-sounding name on Essex Street in New York. Kindly neighbors told Papa Lebeau that he'd never get anywhere with that foreign name; he should find himself a good old American name, then automatically his status would change from that of newly arrived greenhorn to that of American citizen. Papa Lebeau didn't much like the idea of changing the name that his forbears had always worn, but another ingenious neighbor resolved his indecision.

"You don't have to change your name," he urged. "Just Americanize it. Your name is pronounced Lee-Beau. Just add an i-t-z to it and you get Lee-beau-itz, which is the American version. You spell it L-e-i-b-o-w-i-t-z."

So Isaac Lebeau became Isaac Leibowitz, and his young son became Samuel Leibowitz. He played and was educated on the lower East Side, during the days when organized gangs had developed in the Leibowitz neighborhood and on the nearby Bowery and Chinatown. By 1910, Monk Eastman's gang had been taken over by Big Jack Zelig, Jack Sirocco and Chick Tricker. Zelig grew in importance as a gang chief, moving in his influence farther uptown, and on the lower East Side were still the gangs captained by Dopey Benny Fein. Soon after, across the crime horizon moved Lieutenant Charles Becker, head of the Vice Squad, and the four gunmen, Dago Frank, Leftie Louie, Gyp the Blood and Whitey Lewis. These five died in the old death house at Sing Sing for the murder of Herman Rosenthal, shot on the sidewalk in front of the Hotel Metropole in midtown Manhattan. The cops working out of the East Side precincts carried important clubs in those days and they often had to use them, but it is not of this phase of their activities nor of the grim side of the neighborhood that Leibowitz talks when he reminisces.

There were diversions, too. Not far off, Miner's Bowery Theatre still flourished. Thomashevsky's People's Theatre, at Bowery and Delancey Street, was at the height of its glory. There Gordon's heavy drama, such as *God, Man and the Devil*, were being played. At the Cafe Royale one could see the brilliant and renowned gossiping: Boris Thomashevsky, Jacob P. Adler, David Kessler of the Second Avenue Theatre, Abraham Cahan, founder of the Jewish *Daily Forward*.

Back in the home streets Leibowitz remembers the cops as the patron saints and general confessors and advisors to the neighborhood in semi-legal matters. As he recalls it, there wasn't a thin cop on the force; they had bellies like balloons and their handle-bar mustaches and huge gray helmets were impressive to a boy. "Maybe there was a cantankerous one, now and then," he says. "But they were versed in diplomacy. Why not? They were all Irish—oh, maybe a German or two." His eyes twinkle as he adds that they couldn't run very fast; that he fancies they delivered more babies than the police force does today, with all its squad cars; and that he thinks his particular avuncular copper was called Brannigan.

The incredible truth is that although the East Side was a jungle, it produced more fine, public-spirited citizens than almost any section of New York. And even in those far-off days, organizations like the Boys' Club, the Grand Street Boys and the Police Athletic League were coming into being and influencing the life of the community. Some of the finest statesmen, eminent priests and rabbis came out of the East Side. The early environment in which these men flourished gave them a sympathy for the underprivileged and the poor, but left no evil marks on them.

3

Sam's father prospered and bought a store in the then lovely, tree-shaded East New York section of Brooklyn. The jungles were not so dense here; life was not so violent, and survival less of a fierce struggle. There was nearby Highland Park, where you could play baseball all day with no fear of blasting a ball through a window.

Sam made absolutely no impact upon the scholastic traditions of Jamaica High School. The only course he showed much interest in was elocution. In elocution you not only had to read the Declaration of Independence and the Gettysburg Address—you had to memorize them. And then you recited them in class.

Sam found that he had a gift for memorizing and he found, too, great exhilaration in declaiming before his classmates. He had discovered the excitement and satisfaction of performing before an audience.

It was his father who insisted that he study law. Sam was interested only in baseball or in reciting memorized pieces. But the father was boss in a first-generation family, and Sam dutifully accepted the command. Cornell University was a background against which Sam Leibowitz played many parts, and by a happy coincidence each part helped form the personality that was later to emerge in the criminal courts. He made the Dramatic Club in his freshman year. Dramatics and debating, baseball and track were his passions at Cornell. He found debating a fascinating pastime. A subject for debate would be assigned and you would be handed either the affirmative or the negative. It was your job to make out the best case possible for the position you defended. That position might be virtually indefensible, but if you were clever enough you could make it prevail. It was a magnificent exercise in co-ordinated thinking and dramatic presentation so that the blend of the two would convince an audience that your position was tenable. Sam studied the masters of argument. He especially admired the tenacity of Demosthenes, who had to overcome a speech impediment before he became acknowledged as the greatest of Athenian debaters. College debating was in the tradition of Demosthenes. Apparently the doughty Athenian never bothered much about the justice of his argument. He would make out a persuasive case for either side. It was Dinarchus who said that Demosthenes was more interested in rounding a period than in preserving his country. Sam was intrigued by Phillip's comment that "Demosthenes could make the worse appear the better cause." That was truly the real art of debate—to make the worse appear the better cause.

Debating was a game. Instead of a bat and a ball you used your mind, your tongue and your personality. It was exhilarating to win a contest with no weapons other than those. Sam moved easily enough through his law courses, and gradually he began to think of the law, too, as a profession in which you used your mind, your speech, your personality.

And now the law began to fascinate the young student, and when he was about to graduate he told Professor Edwin Hamlin Woodruff, Dean of the Law School, that he intended to specialize in criminal law. The reaction of the Dean was not unlike the reaction one would expect from the dean of a medical school who has been informed by a graduating student that he intended to specialize in abortions. Criminal practice was hardly in the tradition of the Cornell College of Law.

Leibowitz had none of the dedicated qualities of a Clarence Darrow; he had no fierce hatred of capital punishment. He was no crusader entering the lists to joust against injustice. He was dominated by only one driving force, a heritage of his early poverty—the will to survive.

"I have no business connections in New York," he told Dean Woodruff. "My parents are poor. I'd never get a chance to represent big corporations or railroads or real estate holders. Criminal law is the only way for a man to get a foothold in a large city. Once I'm well-known, then maybe I can attract worth-while clients."

"You've got it all figured out," Dean Woodruff smiled.

"I've got it all figured out, Dean," Leibowitz said gravely.

So he stuck his sheepskin under his arm, took time out to pass his bar examinations, and then exchanged his well-developed dramatic and debating talents, plus just about the best legal education that could be obtained in the country, for a job as law clerk—for the sum of five dollars a week.

The dreary business of looking up precedents and of furnishing lawbook ammunition, which the established lawyers would use to break a lease or foreclose a mortgage was not for Sam Leibowitz. This was altogether too tame. This was drudgery. He switched jobs and eventually established himself in the offices of Michael F. McGoldrick, a generous man who paid his young clerk thirty-five dollars a week. But after two years, Sam felt that he wasn't getting anywhere. Damn it, you can't practice law in a law office, he stormed, ignoring the fact that most of the best paid and most highly respected lawyers in New York had literally never been inside a courtroom. You "rehearsed" the law in your office; you "practiced" it in the courtroom. And he wanted to practice law. The sooner he got into the active battleground of the courtroom, the sooner he would become known. Then perhaps clients would follow.

He became a lawyer in search of a client—any client. He felt that he was a craftsman who had to learn how to use the tools of his profession, and he knew that he could develop his skill only where it was practiced—in the courtroom. Moreover, he was anxious to start making some money. As often as not, defendants accused of felonies can't afford a lawyer so the court appoints counsel to take care of their legal rights. Only if the charge is murder is the defense lawyer paid for his services, but such cases usually go to the experienced criminal lawyer. Eddie Reilly, Stephen Baldwin, Frank McCaffrey, Abe Levy, Martin Littleton and Max Steuer (who had emerged from obscurity with his successful defense in the Triangle Fire case) were some of the lawyers who got the plums in criminal cases in the early 1920's. They had experience, ability, and above all they had reputations. Bill Fallon (the Great Mouthpiece) and McGee, his partner, were making the fast dollars, and clients were lined up in front of their office. They were later disbarred. It was hard for a young lawyer to break in, but Leibowitz—self-assured and cocky—was not one whit troubled by any lack of confidence. Cornell had given him smoothness, but beneath, the lanky, red-cheeked young lawyer was still a tough, hard, East Side kid.

4

Young Leibowitz was like a stage-struck actor willing to accept any role just to get on the stage. He took his courage in both hands and went to see Judge Howard P. Nash in his chambers. He told the Judge that he had time on his hands and that he'd like to volunteer his services as counsel to any penniless defendants who might be appearing before the Judge. Judge Nash noted his name. A few days later Samuel Leibowitz had his first client.

Judge Nash assigned him to defend a character named Harry Patterson, who was charged with having broken into a saloon in the early morning hours and extracting seven dollars from the cash register. He had also lifted a bottle of stimulant which he immediately applied internally to such good purpose that a few hours later he was picked up in a drunken coma. In his befuddled state and prodded by a few well-directed blows in the back room of the detectives' quarters, he was happy to oblige with a confession. Sure, he'd rifled the cash register. How had he entered the saloon? Why, he had a skeleton key right here in his pocket. They tossed Mr. Patterson in jail to await the formality of trial. Patterson was

25

an enthusiastic and devout drunkard. For years, drinking had been his hobby, his avocation, his only interest in life. When Leibowitz met his client he winced. The client was barefooted; he didn't even own a pair of shoes. He looked like a bum and he was a bum. But now he insisted that he was innocent; the cops had framed him, he said.

Leibowitz spent two solid weeks trying to figure out a defense for a man who, the prosecution said, had no defense. The lawbooks he had studied were no help. Kindly Michael McGoldrick advised him to have his client plead guilty. The poor devil would be better off in a nice warm jail, McGoldrick said. But a conscientious lawyer doesn't plead a man guilty who insists he is innocent. Leibowitz (except incidentally) was not representing Patterson; he was representing Leibowitz. Leibowitz, as well as Patterson, was on trial, and if Patterson went to jail, Leibowitz would suffer a defeat. This he was not prepared to do. So he studied the case as thoroughly as nearly twenty years later he would study the case of the Scottsboro boys. And he resolved to risk everything on a bold and unorthodox maneuver.

Louis Goldstein was the Assistant District Attorney in charge of the case. Today he is Judge Goldstein of the Kings County Court, and his chambers are located on the sixth floor of the Central Court Building, just above those of his colleague, Judge Leibowitz. Today they are "Louie" and "Sam" to each other and they are very good friends indeed, but on the morning of March 2, 1919, Leibowitz looked at Louis Goldstein with smoldering eyes. This was his enemy. Louis Goldstein, ten years older than Leibowitz, smiled affably at this intense rookie. Goldstein assumed (as any rational district attorney would have assumed) that Leibowitz would enter a plea of guilty and throw the defendant on the mercy of the court. Judge Nash called Patterson in front of the bench and asked him how he pleaded.

"Not guilty," Leibowitz said with great confidence. Judge Nash peered down over his glasses and Goldstein looked puzzled. This derelict appeared to be as guilty as a man could be; he'd even confessed and produced the key he'd used to open the door. Then

26

Goldstein had to scurry around to get his police witnesses. In short order they gave the facts. Leibowitz put Patterson on the stand and questioned him about the confession.

"Is it true," Leibowitz asked sharply, "that the police beat you with a rubber hose and that you signed the confession to make them stop beating you?"

"Sure," the amiable Patterson said. He wasn't a man who wanted any trouble. Hell, he'd agree to anything. If any thought at all was able to penetrate his rum-soaked brain, it was probably to the effect that this fresh young lawyer was a bit crazy going to all this trouble.

And then Leibowitz took up the question of the skeleton key found in Mr. Patterson's pocket.

"The District Attorney," he said scornfully, "says that Patterson used this key to gain entrance to the saloon. But he has offered no proof that this key will in fact open the door of the building." He paused and looked up at the astonished Judge Nash. "If Your Honor please, I request that you direct the jury to visit the scene of the burglary and see for themselves whether this key will open that door. If the key does not open the door, I shall ask that the case against my client be dismissed."

Louis Goldstein stared, open-mouthed. He had a long list of "Harry Pattersons" to try. If he sent the jury to the scene of the burglary to try the key, it would waste a whole day. And then, Goldstein pondered, suppose the damn key didn't open the lock on the door. He hadn't bothered to try it. Good heavens, the man had confessed, hadn't he? And he'd produced the key and admitted that it was the one he'd used. But it would be mighty embarrassing if Goldstein were to march the jury all the way out to the scene of the burglary only to find that the key didn't fit. He thought quickly and made up his mind.

"I would not think of wasting the time of the court and of the jury by agreeing to any such demonstration," he said firmly. "The State rests."

The twelve good men and true went into the jury room, deliberated four minutes, and returned with a verdict of not guilty. Patterson shuffled out into the street, a bewildered but free man, and

Leibowitz strutted happily out of the courtroom. It was he—not Patterson—who had been acquitted. In the corridor he said to the Assistant District Attorney, "Mr. Goldstein, may I see the little skeleton key?"

"Sure," said Goldstein, handing over the key.

It was a fine key. Leibowitz proceeded to try it out on a dozen locks in the courthouse. It opened every one. It would, in fact, open any ordinary door. It would undoubtedly have opened the lock on the saloon door—a Shetland pony could have opened that lock with its teeth. And now the little key had opened the door to a fabulous career which has never been equaled in the history of American criminal jurisprudence.

It would be eight years before he would be recognized as the most noted criminal lawyer in America, but nothing would ever happen to him as important as the successful defense of Harry Patterson. He learned a great deal while conducting the defense of the down-and-out derelict and all of this knowledge would pay off huge dividends later.

The case was so unimportant that it wasn't even mentioned in the *Brooklyn Daily Eagle* the next day. It wasn't even important to poor Harry Patterson. It was important only to Leibowitz. Coldly and analytically he reviewed his preparation for the defense. For days he had tried to conjure up some feat of magic that would upset the District Attorney's case against Patterson. But what was the District Attorney's case? Leibowitz had prepared that just as he thought Goldstein was preparing it. He had in fact prepared and mentally presented Goldstein's case before he had determined upon his own defense.

Every night he had taken the case to bed with him. Every night he lay awake searching for a weak spot in the prosecution's armor. The case looked hopeless. And one night he thought of swinging the wild punch that might win if it landed in the right place. Would the District Attorney bother to investigate the key? It was such a picayune case; would the D.A. be bothered to try the key in the lock? If he had in fact fitted the key to the lock, Patterson was a dead pigeon. If he hadn't, the wild swinging punch might land in a vital spot. The punch had landed in a vital spot.

The more Leibowitz considered the case, the more convinced he became that he had won it in bed. During the next twenty years he would win a hundred acquittals lying in bed. That's when you could think best—when the rest of the city was asleep and the shrill sound of traffic was muted. After that he always kept a notebook and a pencil on a bedside table.

He learned another thing during that brief hour of the trial. He learned that juries have a deep-rooted suspicion of confessions obtained by the police in police stations or jails. If you raised the cry of police brutality or frame-up or third degree, and presented evidence to back it up, you had twelve receptive listeners who had been conditioned by the movies and by the crime magazines to expect such tactics from the police. When, exuding confidence, he had cried out, "I request that you direct the members of the jury to visit the scene of the burglary and see for themselves whether this key will open that door," his voice had trembled with emotion. The jury had been impressed, not with Patterson—but with Leibowitz. They hadn't been impressed with his knowledge of law but with his sincerity. Leibowitz never forgot that lesson.

There was one thing that annoyed him. As he had left the courtroom, Assistant District Attorney Louis Goldstein had smiled and said, "Congratulations, kid." As he walked down the corridor toward the elevator, one of the spectators had nodded to him and said, "Nice going, kid." Leibowitz didn't like that "kid" business. How could he attract substantial clients if he was considered to be a kid? Actually his complexion and slightness made him look younger than his years. He'd have to do something about that. How could he make himself appear older? He went to a shop and for a dollar and a half bought himself a pair of pince-nez spectacles fitted with ordinary glass. He attached a heavy black ribbon to them. When they rested on the bridge of his nose, he felt that ten years had been added to his appearance. Then, too, the glasses made a good prop. You could express amazement, bewilderment, anger, disgust, by means of the glasses. And if a cross-examination took an unexpectedly bad turn, you could take your glasses off, hold them between thumb and forefinger, polish them and gain a few precious seconds during which you could figure out a new method of attack.

Next he bought what he always called a "Court of Appeals" coat. It was a long, shiny black frock coat that he felt added dignity to his appearance. This was the way Edward Reilly, the Beau Brummel of the bar, was always dressed. Now he felt he was ready for the big adventure. He would cut adrift from kindly old Michael McGoldrick and open his own office.

A week later a sign painter stepped back from the door to a little hole-in-the-wall office on Court Street, Brooklyn and admired the lettering he had just finished. It read: SAMUEL S. LEIBOWITZ, ATTORNEY-AT-LAW. It was May, 1919. Leibowitz was on his way. He had spent every cent he had in the bank ($260) to furnish his tiny office with some secondhand furniture, but he was in business.

His success in the Patterson case had not gone entirely unnoticed. Lawyers who practiced in the criminal courts chuckled over the brash confidence of the newcomer. It was discussed in one of the finest postgraduate law schools in the world—the Raymond Street Jail. The hardened professional criminal is usually something of a catch-as-catch-can lawyer, and although he couldn't give you the Rule in Shelley's Case, he could tell you a dozen ways of making "the worse appear the better cause." The lads waiting trial or sentence in the Raymond Street Jail have the same interest in new criminal lawyers that baseball scouts have in new rookies. They appraise them with experienced professional eyes. They noted with approval the way Leibowitz handled Patterson's case and they decided to keep an eye on him.

During his first years Leibowitz would take almost any client. If the client could pay—so much the better. Leibowitz had learned something which many older, more experienced lawyers never learn. He had learned that you can't perfect your technique as a spectator. Many experienced lawyers had given him well-meant advice, telling him to frequent the courtrooms to watch the veteran lawyers in action. This was the standard advice to young lawyers, but Leibowitz soon realized that it was completely unsound. You couldn't learn courtroom technique merely by watching others practice it any more than you could learn to play the violin by watching Jascha Heifetz perform.

The only way you could master your profession was to engage in it actively. To do that you had to have clients. The client wasn't important except as a means of getting you into the courtroom. He spent more and more of his time in the criminal courts. Most of his clients were paupers, but gradually his success began to bring him to the attention of the more affluent defendants. Each case brought him closer to a complete mastery of his profession.

He soon realized that he didn't need the doubtful help of a pair of spectacles and a long frock coat. Actually his youthful appearance was no handicap at all. Juries were only too willing to believe that "nice-looking young fellow" who seemed so sincere.

Leibowitz realized that he had to prove himself more skillful than his colleagues in the criminal law to get his share of clients. Unlike them, he was prepared to give all of his time to perfecting himself in his profession.

5

During the 1920's, many renowned criminal lawyers spent a great deal of their time in the gilded speakeasies of the upper East Side. Lawyers often met their clients at George Lamaze's beautiful Park Avenue Club (decorated by Joseph Urban), Sherman Billingsley's lively, well-run Stork Club, the Club Napoleon or the Club Guinan, presided over by the flamboyant Texas. Lamaze was proud of the fact that there were always four or five judges, a handful of prominent lawyers and at least a dozen potential clients in his Park Avenue Club. It gave the place tone. The gang lords were as a rule the best-behaved customers in the place. You'd see quiet, good-looking Owney Madden in one corner, the equally quiet, unobtrusive Big Frenchie (George Fox) at another table. As often as not they'd be accompanied by their lawyers, and on occasion they'd be joined by a thirsty and friendly judge or assistant district attorney.

When a city editor told a police reporter to get a statement from some beer baron, wholesale entrepreneur in homicide, gang leader or criminal lawyer, the reporter always made the rounds of the plush speakeasies and the chances were he'd meet up with his man.

But you'd never find Leibowitz in the speakeasies. He had nothing in common with the men he defended and he had no social contacts with them at all. Spectacular in the courtroom, he was a quiet, home-loving Brooklyn citizen once the judge banged his gavel to signify adjournment. In those early years, he had only one extra-curricular passion—baseball. On Saturday and Sunday afternoons he was back of first base at Ebbets Field rooting for Zack Wheat, George Cutshaw, Ivy Olsen, Babe Herman, Casey Stengel and the incomparable Dazzy Vance. Then he'd go home, have dinner, see a movie with his lovely young wife Belle and then be off to bed—not to sleep but to study possible ways of frustrating the district attorney on Monday in court.

Leibowitz always prepared two cases; the district attorney's and the defendant's, and he learned to anticipate any tactic that a D.A. might attempt. Leibowitz was seldom surprised by witnesses whom the D.A. had kept under cover to spring at a psychological moment. He had an uncanny knack of exposing shoddy maneuvers; and prosecutors acquired a wholesome respect for this truculent young counsel for the defense.

New York City was a free and easygoing community during the 1920's. It was the era of wonderful nonsense, and the cynical political leaders of New York were putting judicial robes about the shoulders of men whose chief qualities for the judgeship were acquiescence and party regularity. When Leibowitz appeared in front of such a judge, he had no trouble dominating the courtroom. He had one terrific advantage over the judge and a lazy district attorney. He had prepared his case and he knew the law. Leibowitz was not the prototype of the fictional Perry Mason or a Mr. Tutt. His strength did not rest upon trickery. He lived with a case twenty-four hours a day, and when it came to trial there was little about defendant or witnesses that he did not know.

As his amazing record of acquittals mounted, the newspapers pictured him as a legal magician, a reputation which the public accepted. He was always good copy for Walter Winchell, Ed Sullivan, Danton Walker, Louis Sobol, Dorothy Kilgallen and others. In a Sunday supplement article, the *Daily News* called him "The Miracle Man of the Criminal Courts." Only Leibowitz himself knew how spurious the picture was. Actually he was a plodder, and what the public mistook for intuitive brilliance was nothing but the result of thorough, painstaking investigation resulting in evidence presented and interpreted dramatically in the public forum of the courtroom.

He became renowned as a "cop fighter" who handled police witnesses with brutal sarcasm, and although they looked at him with sullen, hate-filled eyes, when they themselves got into trouble they ran to him for help. Before he had been in practice many years, he had defended cops for everything from petty larceny to murder. He was the sternest foe of police brutality, and Grover Whalen, who spent a brief period as Police Commissioner, delivered a wonderful weapon into his hands when he cried to his cops, "There's a lot of law at the end of a nightstick." (Much earlier, in the 1870's, Inspector Alexander S. Williams, prettily known and reviled as "Chubber" Williams had observed, "There is more law in the end of a policeman's nightstick than in a decision of the Supreme Court.") Again and again, Leibowitz convinced juries that there was no law at all at the end of a nightstick. Somehow he managed to make a juror feel that police brutality could happen to him, too, no matter how exemplary his life was, and they turned out defendant after defendant just because Leibowitz had convinced them that the police had substituted the nightstick for the law.

The greatness of Leibowitz as a criminal lawyer stemmed from his fervent belief in the profession he had embraced. When he entered a courtroom it was to fight with every legal and dramatic weapon he had learned to use.

The fact that a man pulled the trigger and was found standing over the body of his victim with the gun in his hand did not make him guilty per se in the eyes of Leibowitz. He asked himself a hundred questions. What was the provocation? What was the mental state of the defendant at the time he committed the act?

33

What were his early family background, his education, his medical history? There are those who say that Leibowitz often hypnotized himself into believing in the innocence of his client. He certainly "hypnotized" hundreds of juries to believe in it.

District attorneys, smarting under the lash of defeats administered to them by Leibowitz, were understandably discomfited. They often said bitterly that because of him murderers and thieves who should have been behind bars were walking the streets, free to kill or rob again. Leibowitz always answered such criticism by reminding them that only an inefficient, bungling prosecution would allow a guilty man to escape the consequences of his crime. Leibowitz seldom received credit for freeing men who had been wrongly accused of a felony, yet his career is studded with such cases.

Leibowitz seemed to delight in tearing circumstantial evidence to shreds. Dozens of times when prosecutors had woven the tightest net of circumstantial evidence around a defendant, Leibowitz destroyed the net with a few snips of his legal shears. And more than once he managed to extract entirely innocent defendants from the strangling webs of such nets. The case which today is considered to be the classic example of how circumstantial evidence can convict a completely innocent man is that of *The People vs. Hoffman.* The evidence against Hoffman seemed to be complete and conclusive, even though circumstantial. When a jury found him guilty of the murder of Maude C. Bauer, not a dissenting voice was heard. Only two people in the world knew that Hoffman was innocent—Hoffman himself and the man who actually did the killing. And Hoffman disappeared behind the gray prison walls, there to spend the rest of his natural life. Then one day the desperate, broken prisoner wrote a note on a penny postcard to a man he had never met. And that postcard started a chain of circumstances that made legal history.

3. THE FLY SPINS THE WEB

"To him who is in fear everything rustles."
SOPHOCLES

By 1929, Leibowitz was already the most spectacular criminal lawyer in New York City. He had defended dozens of men and
women accused of first-degree murder and not one of them had
gone to the chair. He was a master of his craft and he had far
outdistanced the defense lawyers who had been such shining lights
when he began practice. He could pick and choose clients now, and
he fought tooth and nail for every client he represented. Each case
seemed to him to be a personal challenge that sent him into a courtroom in the same mood that another man might enter the boxing
ring. But like a champion fighter he didn't depend upon uncontrolled fury to stop his opponent; he went into a trial as well trained
and as well prepared as any good boxer goes into the ring. In
the language of the ring he had developed into a great counterpuncher. Let a district attorney make a careless move, let a hostile
witness relax and lower his guard, and Leibowitz would attack un-
mercifully with the bludgeon of his cross-examination.

It was the Hoffman case perhaps more than any other which
brought him to national notice and solidified his position as the
leader of the criminal bar. It is the Hoffman case which earned
him the respect of his fellow lawyers, for in that case he per-
formed what to them seemed to be the impossible.

One morning he arrived at his office and began to go through
the mail. He had just finished a long arduous murder trial and he
had been toying with the idea of a Florida vacation. There was

35

nothing urgent on his calendar and as he thumbed through the mail and looked at the snow swirling against the windows of his office the idea grew more attractive. He idly fingered a penny postcard that lay among the letters on his desk, looked at it casually, and dropped it back on the desk. Almost as an afterthought he looked at the signature. It was "Harry L. Hoffman." That name seemed familiar. He remembered that a Harry Hoffman had been tried and convicted of murder. He picked up the card again. It read:

> Dear Mr. Leibowitz, I am writing this as a last desperate appeal. I do not know you personally and of course you don't know me. I am accused of murder but I am an innocent man. I was sentenced to from twenty years to life in Sing Sing. I have fought for five years to win my freedom. My friends raised a fund for my defense but that is gone. Will you help me?
>
> HARRY L. HOFFMAN

To this day Leibowitz doesn't know what prompted him to go to the Raymond Street Jail to see Hoffman. He had no feeling at all that an innocent man had been wrongfully sentenced. Hoffman's protestations of innocence meant nothing to Leibowitz; for years he had heard the same protestations from patently guilty men. When it came to known criminals and racketeers he was a complete skeptic, and his attitude toward them was one of contemptuous cynicism. He knew that lying was an occupational disease with most criminals; his own clients had seldom told him the truth about themselves, but Hoffman was not an habitual criminal. Hoffman by his own admission wouldn't even be a paying client. But for some inexplicable reason he went to see the convicted prisoner.

He found Hoffman to be a thin, nervous, intent-eyed, desperate man. In 1924, Hoffman had been tried and convicted of the very brutal murder of a Staten Island woman named Maude C. Bauer. He had been indicted for first-degree murder, but the jury had brought in a verdict of second-degree murder and this had saved him from the chair. It was as though the jury had said to the district attorney, "We're pretty sure you're right, but there is a slight chance that this man is innocent, so we'll find him guilty of second-degree murder."

36

The district attorney wasn't very happy with the verdict. Neither was the press. Practically no one really thought that Hoffman was innocent, but his old associates in the Motion Picture Machine Operators Union, Local 306, out of a sense of loyalty, raised a fund to finance an appeal. The union retained a battling defense lawyer, Leonard Snitkin, a former municipal court judge, and he was successful in having a new trial granted. He took advantage of a slim but useful technicality. He said that the original first-degree indictment had been improperly drawn. It charged that Hoffman had killed Mrs. Maude Bauer while engaged in a felony; that is, while attempting to commit the felony of rape he had "without design" killed the young woman. But the jury had brought in a verdict of second-degree murder and second-degree murder is homicide "with intent to kill." In short the verdict was a contradiction of the indictment. Attorney Snitkin, a capable practitioner, presented this argument to the Appellate Division of the New York Supreme Court, his argument prevailed and a new trial was ordered. By the time the court had made up its mind, two and a half years had passed, during which time Hoffman was not Harry Hoffman at all, but Sing Sing Convict No. 75990.

And so Hoffman was tried again. Now grim District Attorney Albert C. Fach made sure that the indictment was in order. Again it was for common law first-degree murder, and this time if Hoffman lost, it would mean the electric chair. Hoffman was willing to take the chance.

2

It was not until March, 1928, that the new trial began. It terminated abruptly after two weeks, when Attorney Snitkin collapsed with a heart attack while examining a state witness. A mistrial was ordered. Snitkin partially recovered to argue for a change of venue on the ground that Hoffman could not obtain a fair trial before a Staten Island jury and the third trial was transferred to Brooklyn. This opened in November, lasted three weeks and resulted in a disagreement by the jury. The twelve men had deliberated twenty hours and then reported that they were hopelessly deadlocked. Attorney Snitkin made a motion for bail but it was denied, so Hoffman went back to the Raymond Street Jail. Snitkin immediately requested a fourth trial, but before his request was granted, death removed him from the case. Hoffman was desperate now. Snitkin had believed in his innocence and now he was gone. The defense fund of twenty-five thousand dollars was exhausted and Hoffman was penniless. His wife had written him off and had married another man, and his two children had been sent to an orphan asylum. It is something of a miracle that Hoffman was able to retain his sanity at all.

Of course his fellow prisoners took his sometimes hysterical protestations of innocence as seriously as they took similar outbreaks on the part of themselves. To insist upon your innocence was a traditional pretense indulged in by all prisoners.

"If you could only get Leibowitz," they'd tell him, "he might spring you."

Again and again he heard this, and then one day he picked up a pencil and made his appeal. No one was more surprised than he when a jailor unlocked his cell one morning and said, "Sam Leibowitz, the lawyer, is in the counsel room to see you."

Leibowitz listened to his whole story. Because the newspapers had featured the trial in 1924, Leibowitz was generally familiar with it. But Hoffman told him a few things that hadn't been brought out at any of the three trials. As he listened, Leibowitz couldn't help but feel that the case against Hoffman wasn't as clear-cut and overwhelming as the newspapers had reported.

Leibowitz told Hoffman that he'd look up the records of the case and then let him know whether or not he'd undertake his defense. Leibowitz studied the case against Hoffman thoroughly. There was little in the testimony of prosecution witnesses to give comfort to Hoffman or anyone considering taking over the job of defending Hoffman. The case as presented by District Attorney Fach was as follows:

Maude Bauer, at thirty-five, was a good-looking brunette whose

38

only interest was her family. On March 25, 1924, she decided to take her three-year-old daughter Helen to visit a married sister who lived some five miles away. Mrs. Bauer asked her mother, Mrs. Catherine Pero, to come along. It began as a pleasant, ordinary day in the lives of two pleasant, ordinary women and a vivacious child. They began the trip in Mrs. Pero's car with Maude driving. They were within a mile of their destination when an incident happened that resulted in the death of Maude Bauer and the imprisonment of Harry Hoffman. The car skidded and it was that which brought tragedy to two hitherto happily obscure Staten Island families. It wasn't even a dangerous skid. A large truck was approaching, and Maude, wishing to allow it plenty of room, hugged the right side of the road. The front wheel slipped off the concrete onto the soft shoulder of the road. It had snowed the week before and although the road itself was clear, some snow and ice still clung to the shoulder and the car skidded to the right. When Maude stopped it the two right wheels were imbedded in the mud and snow. The wheels only spun ineffectually when she tried to drive away from the shoulder.

The skid had occurred on Merrill Avenue, just 150 feet away from the intersecting highway known as South Avenue. This was a heavily wooded, sparsely settled neighborhood, and Maude quite sensibly decided to walk to the nearest house and phone a garage to send a wrecker. Her mother said she'd take care of the restless young Helen, and Maude started off for South Avenue. As she reached the intersection, a Model T Ford sedan stopped. Maude talked to the driver briefly and then called to her mother that the driver of the Ford was going to take her to a garage. That was the last time Mrs. Pero ever saw her daughter alive.

Mrs. Pero waited for nearly an hour and then a motorcycle drove up, and Patrolman Thomas Cosgrove asked her what she was doing there. She explained, and the cop told her that a badly injured young woman had just been found on a lonely road about a mile away. It might possibly be her daughter. It was. But she was not injured; she was dead. She had been shot twice, once in the chest and once in the neck.

Death stripped the anonymity which Maude Bauer had preserved through thirty-five pleasant years. Her picture stared at practically every reader of the New York newspapers the day after her body was discovered. When the body was found it was obvious that she had put up a fierce struggle. Her clothing was torn and disarranged and there were bruises on her body. The papers said that she had died defending her honor, and this time they were right. The blameless character of the dead woman, her good looks, the tragic figure of her three-year-old child and the brutality of the attack all contributed to making this one of the most avidly read newspaper stories of the year. Staten Islanders were aroused. It seemed apparent that there was a murderous degenerate loose in the community, and men who took the ferry each morning bound for their Manhattan offices didn't feel easy until they had returned home to find their wives and daughters alive and well. Civic organizations and public-spirited citizens spurred the hunt for the criminal by offering rewards which finally totaled eighty-five hundred dollars.

A shadowy picture of the murderer began to emerge. To begin with, he drove a Ford sedan; Mrs. Pero was sure of that, and she was sure that he wore a brown coat and hat. Two other witnesses had seen him. One was thirteen-year-old Barbara Fahs. She had been running an errand for her mother and she had arrived at the intersection of South and Merrill Avenues as the Ford sedan had stopped. She had heard Maude Bauer ask the driver if he had a rope with which he might haul her out, off the shoulder. He didn't have one, he said, but he'd drive her to a garage where she could get one. Young Barbara said that the driver of the car was wearing a brown overcoat, a brown hat and tortoise-shell glasses. He was dark-complexioned and he had thick brown hair. A description of the murderer was issued by the police. Maude had been killed by a bullet from a .25-caliber Colt automatic.

Now they began hunting for a man who wore a brown hat and overcoat, who owned a .25-caliber Colt, who drove a Ford sedan, who had thick brown hair, a dark complexion and wore tortoise-shell glasses. They scoured the neighborhood where the crime was committed. They found men who owned Ford sedans but who had no brown overcoats or Colt automatics. They found men who kept Colt automatics but who owned neither Ford sedans nor brown coats and who were bald. And then on April 17, nearly a month after Maude was killed, they accused Harry Hoffman of the crime. He owned a brown overcoat, the police said, drove a Ford sedan, owned a .25-caliber Colt automatic, and had a dark complexion. His hair was brown but it had been closely cut three days after the crime. On April 25, Hoffman was indicted and went to trial before Judge J. Harry Tiernan in the Richmond County Courthouse, St. George, Staten Island.

3

Harry Hoffman, who stood before his neighbors as a friend who had attacked a decent and defenseless woman and who had become so filled with maniacal rage at her resistance that he had shot her, looked very guilty indeed. Outwardly, at least, he was the proto-type of the average man. He was short (five feet six) and plump (198 pounds) and he had the jolly amiability of the fat man. At thirty-two he was happily married and had two children, one-year-old Dorothy and five-year-old Mildred whom he called Beanie. He and his wife Agnes seemed a devoted couple. Hoffman operated a motion picture machine in the Palace Theatre, just about the best movie house in Port Richmond. For recreation he played a trombone and was proud of the fact that he was good enough to play with the Grace M. E. Church orchestra. His life seemed to be normal and complete. He had no pronounced political views, and when the boys, sitting around Symonds Drug Store up the street from the Palace, began to argue about the League of Nations or other absorbing topics of the day, Harry usually sat there smiling, peering at them a bit nearsightedly through the rimless spectacles he wore outside the projection booth. He kept a pair of tortoise-shell glasses in his eight-by-ten coop and wore them while he worked. "They stayed on better," he said. Outwardly Hoffman was as harmless as the trombone he played, and if strange, unnatural passions existed under his placid, chubby exterior they were never evident to his neighbors.

Captain Ernest L. Van Wagner of the Staten Island Detective Bureau, who had questioned Hoffman for three days, painted an entirely different picture of the amiable, good-natured Hoffman, and District Attorney Fach presented that picture to the jury. But Staten Island, for all that it is an integral part of metropolitan New York, is in reality a chain of small communities. The private lives of the residents are as much the public property of all the neighbors as they would be in a country town. Tongues began to wag and the chorus began to swell. "You never know about those quiet fellows." "Remember the old saying about the man who is an angel abroad and a devil at home." Perhaps Mrs. Jones, hanging the wash in the back yard, resurrected a long forgotten tiff between Hoffman and Agnes and related it to her neighbor. The neighbor added a detail or two in passing it along. Any chance Hoffman might have had to excite community sympathy vanished with the ballooning revelation that he was not only capable of being, but was a domestic tyrant.

Hoffman was on trial for murder, and relentlessly the evidence piled up. There was a lot of it (Leibowitz had to read through 3,600 pages containing 750,000 words before he knew it all). To begin with, Hoffman had absolutely no alibi for the crucial hours of March 25, 1924, when the murder was committed. He said that he had gone to Manhattan to see his broker, but the broker didn't recall having seen him in the office on that afternoon. Hoffman said that he had lunched at a Chinese restaurant on Sixth Avenue, but none of the Chinese waiters remembered him. He had met no one on the ferry boat that plies between the Battery, at the lower tip of Manhattan, and Staten Island. Hoffman did say, almost as an afterthought, that he had dropped into the Liberty Theatre at three-thirty on the day of the crime and that he had remained there chatting with his friend Racey Parker until about four-thirty. Parker operated the Liberty Theatre motion picture machine. If this alibi stood up, Hoffman would be cleared, because it had been established that the murder had taken place during that hour.

The alibi sounded convincing until Captain Van Wagner went to work on Racey Parker. Parker said that Hoffman and he were chatting a few days after the description of the murderer had been posted. Hoffman was nervous, Parker said, because the description fitted him. He explained how he had sat in his broker's office watching the ticker, how he had lunched at the Chinese restaurant and how he had returned by ferry without meeting anyone he knew. Hoffman said glumly that the police were questioning every man in the neighborhood who owned a Ford sedan, and when they came to him he wouldn't be able to produce an alibi. Now if good old Racey would say that he, Hoffman, had dropped into his booth at the Liberty Theatre just to pass the time of day (as he often did), why the police would be satisfied. Good old Racey, who couldn't imagine his plump friend attacking anything more substantial than a trombone arrangement of "Rock of Ages," laughed and said he'd be glad to be Hoffman's alibi.

Why had he disowned the alibi? Well, when he heard that Hoffman owned a .25-caliber Colt automatic and that he had mailed the gun to his brother immediately after the killing, he was convinced that Hoffman might actually be the murderer, and he, Racey Parker, wanted no part of him now.

Hoffman protested that he had never been in the lane off South Avenue where the murder took place. William Whittet, a reel boy at the Palace Theatre, discredited that statement when he said that a few days before the murder Hoffman had asked him, "Do you know any lonely road where I can take a girl?" Whittet, a lad who was up on his lonely roads, told him about the lane off South Avenue. (The newspapers, of course, henceforth referred to this as Lover's Lane.) Harry Edkins, another reel boy, said that he had been riding one day with Hoffman along South Avenue and that they had passed Lover's Lane.

Hoffman's story of having spent several hours at the office of Hutton and Company, the firm that handled his tiny market account, fell to pieces when George McCabe, a customer's man, took the stand. A few days after the murder Hoffman phoned McCabe to ask if he remembered seeing him in the office on the day of the murder. He tried to jog McCabe's memory, but the broker said he had no recollection of seeing Hoffman on that day. And now Hoffman's alibi was proven to be a clumsily fabricated edifice that collapsed miserably at the impact of the first contrary winds. Had Hoffman merely stated that he had no alibi for March 25, it would have been embarrassing, but not necessarily fatal. The fact that he had attempted to fake an alibi proved damning.

The gun? Well, Hoffman did own a .25-caliber Colt and a few months before the murder, a clerk testified, he had bought a holster for it at the sporting goods store of Abercrombie & Fitch. The alert clerk remembered the sale. He went to the police with the information. When Captain Van Wagner confronted Hoffman with the incident (it could as yet hardly be called evidence), the harassed trombone player broke down and admitted ownership of a .25-caliber automatic. He had a right to own the gun, he protested, because he had been made an honorary deputy sheriff. He had a badge and everything. He said miserably that he had been panicky after he read the description of the murderer and he had burned the holster and mailed the gun to his brother Albert who lived in the Bronx. When queried, brother Albert produced the gun and also a note that had arrived with it. The note read, "Hold this. Keep it in a safe place. If you hear of my being in trouble give it to my attorney."

Sergeant Harry F. Butts, renowned ballistics expert, testified that Hoffman's gun was the murder weapon. Only one of the two bullets had been recovered. He said that he had fired fifty bullets from the gun and that the markings on them corresponded to the markings on the bullet which had been found in the chest of Mrs. Bauer. That evidence put Hoffman just a step from the electric chair. If a clincher were needed, it was supplied by Patrolman Matthew McCormack, who had been on Victory Boulevard about a mile from where the crime was committed at 4:25 that fatal afternoon. He was on his way home and was thumbing a ride. A Ford sedan approached at about twenty miles an hour. It did not stop but McCormack said that he obtained a good look at the driver. Who was the driver? Why, Hoffman, of course; there was no possibility of a mistake, the patrolman testified calmly.

44

This then was the case against Hoffman. He had been identified and placed near the scene of the crime by young Barbara; he owned what seemed to be the murder weapon and he had tried to fake an alibi. He owned a Model T Ford sedan. A week after the murder he asked a man to repaint it for him; he owned a pair of tortoise-shell glasses. No one had seen him fire the fatal shots, but that was the only bit missing in the picture of guilt which District Attorney Fach showed to the jury. It was all good solid circumstantial evidence. Most of it, of course, had been deliberately manufactured by Hoffman himself. It isn't often that a defendant goes out of his way to manufacture circumstantial evidence that will be used against him, but Hoffman had done this almost as though he had wanted to make things easier for the D.A. His phone call to the broker, his mailing of the gun to his brother and his attempt to manufacture an alibi with the help of Racey Parker were not ordinary pieces of circumstantial evidence—they were manufactured circumstances. Only a guilty man, Fach thundered, would go to such lengths to avoid the appearance of guilt.

"The consciousness of guilt," he told the jury, "pursued this defendant from the time he killed Maude Bauer."

When the jury brought in a verdict of guilty there was hardly a person in the courtroom who didn't nod with satisfaction—except Hoffman. When Judge Tiernan sentenced the defendant to twenty years to life, the spectators felt that Hoffman had cheated the chair. As he was led away Hoffman turned toward District Attorney Fach and screamed, "Go split up the rewards with your lying witnesses. You know I'm as innocent as you are."

And they took Hoffman to Sing Sing and put number 75990 on his gray shirt.

4

Leibowitz studied the court records of the two succeeding trials but found nothing new in them. The case interested him as a legal problem that he wasn't sure had been properly solved. He didn't

45

think much of the identification by the thirteen-year-old Barbara Fahs or the patrolman Matthew McCormack. He decided to see Hoffman again, and once more he visited the Raymond Street Jail. As he greeted Hoffman he was struck for the first time by the incongruity of the man's appearance. For two days and two nights Leibowitz had been reading about a fat, placid fellow. This Hoffman who looked up so eagerly as he entered the counsel room was a shrunken wisp of a man.

"How much do you weigh?" he asked Hoffman.

"About a hundred and twelve," Hoffman told him. "I was close to two hundred back in 1924, but . . . well, I guess I worried about eighty pounds off."

"What were you worrying about?" Leibowitz asked coldly. As far as he was concerned Hoffman was a convicted murderer and he, Leibowitz, was talking to him only because he was a minor figure in an interesting legal chess game.

"If you were in jail for a crime you had nothing to do with, you'd lose weight too," Hoffman said. "If I were guilty I'd accept the verdict. I'd figure I was lucky not to get the chair. But I'm innocent—you hear me, I'm innocent—and I've spent five years cooped up like a wild beast. Why, damn it, Mr. Leibowitz, it's a wonder I haven't gone mad."

"You're innocent? Come now, Hoffman, could anyone be innocent and do as much lying as you did concocting that silly alibi?"

"I had to build an alibi." Hoffman's eyes were blazing now and he was shouting. "I was afraid they'd lynch me. Sure, the way they did Leo Frank. That's all I could think of—Leo Frank."

"Leo Frank?" Leibowitz was understandably puzzled. There had been no mention of anyone named Leo Frank in the testimony. "You don't mean the Leo Frank who was lynched in Georgia?"

"Sure I do," Hoffman said eagerly. "There was nothing against him but circumstantial evidence. But he was a Jew, just as I am, and they lynched him. And then ten years after he was dead another man confessed to the crime. I met a man who knew Leo Frank. He told me all about the case, and that's all I could think of when I read the description of the man who murdered that

46

Bauer woman. The description fitted me. I owned a .25-caliber gun and a Ford sedan. I had no alibi for the time of the murder. I was afraid. Don't forget I was a Jew living on Staten Island. I knew what it was to be called a dirty Jew by my neighbors. Sure, they were just waiting to lynch me. Like they lynched Leo Frank. That's what I told my brother too when I sent him the gun."

"But your brother never mentioned that?" Leibowitz now was beginning to feel the start of a tiny doubt.

"I guess it wasn't important," Hoffman shrugged his shoulders.

"You said you didn't know the South Avenue neighborhood at all. That was an especially stupid lie," Leibowitz said. "Those two reel boys both testified that you knew where Lover's Lane was."

"The two reel boys!" Hoffman exploded. "You mean Whittet and Edkins. You know what Whittet is? He's a thief and a peeping Tom and he was convicted of both crimes. And then after I was sentenced he was put on probation. Why? They were paying him off for that lying testimony he gave against me. And that poor kid Edkins was beaten up and made to testify."

"This was never brought out," Leibowitz said, and now the tiny doubt was crystallizing. "Sit down, Hoffman, I want to ask you some questions."

He began by asking Hoffman where he was born, and his questions led Hoffman all the way through his youth, through his nine years on Staten Island, through the three trials and right up to the present. He used every device he had ever learned in cross-examining a thousand witnesses to trip Hoffman, but he was unable to make the sweating but eager prisoner contradict himself once. Then suddenly Leibowitz stood up.

"Do you realize that if you go to trial again it means the electric chair if you are found guilty?" Leibowitz said. "As it is, you only have another fifteen years to serve and then you'll walk out of Sing Sing a free man."

"Only fifteen years," Hoffman cried. "My God, Mr. Leibowitz, I'd rather get the chair than spend another fifteen years in jail. I tell you, I'm innocent. I don't look for any compromise. I'll take my chances on being freed or . . . well . . . or fried," he said grimly.

47

Leibowitz looked at him thoughtfully. He had defended so many men and women accused of murder. Some he believed were guilty. That hadn't prevented him from insisting that each one of them be given the full measure of his constitutional rights before the law. But there was something about Hoffman that set him apart from the many miserable malefactors whom he had represented. Leibowitz found himself liking the thin, haunted-eyed, nervous prisoner who had once been a laughing, amiable fat man. He liked Hoffman's courage too in gambling for his life. Something stirred within him (perhaps it was the "Give the kid a break" philosophy of the East Side), and he found himself saying, "I believe you're innocent, Harry. I'm going to get you off."

5

The trial opened on May 6, 1929, before white-haired, dignified Justice Burt Jay Humphrey in the Supreme Court in Brooklyn. Leibowitz had been meticulous in picking the jury. Some of his questions to the talesmen puzzled the crowded courtroom. Again and again Leibowitz asked, "Do you know Horatio J. Sharrett?" When jurors shook puzzled heads, Leibowitz added, "He is the brother of Clinton J. Sharrett, political leader on Staten Island."

"I object," Fach roared, and then in a snarling aside to Leibowitz, "Stop playing politics."

"We will get along nicely," Leibowitz said in the tone of a patient teacher chiding an unruly pupil, "if you will address your objections to the court and not to me and the jury."

The fight was on. At first the blows were light, tentative left jabs, exploratory taps designed to harass an opponent rather than hurt him; designed to puzzle and confuse him. Leibowitz was smiling with satisfaction when the last juror had been picked. It was a good jury and among them were three engineers and one contractor. Leibowitz improvised tactics only when unexpected developments made it necessary. As always, he had planned his whole defense down to the last detail before the trial opened, and his insistence on the presence of technical brains in the jury box was a calculated maneuver. He was going to demonstrate something later on and he wanted at least four of the jurors to have the technical background that would enable them to understand his demonstration.

The jury picked, Leibowitz made an audacious opening address which aroused District Attorney Fach to fury. Leibowitz said bluntly that the prosecution in previous trials had deliberately held back facts that would have cleared Hoffman.

Fach in his opening address said heatedly, "We will produce Horatio J. Sharrett and show that he was not the slayer of Mrs. Bauer, as defense counsel has intimated."

"I intimated no such thing," Leibowitz interrupted blandly. "However, Sharrett was seen in the neighborhood of the murder just after Mrs. Bauer was killed, he answers the description of the man who drove Mrs. Bauer away and he certainly acted in an extraordinary manner."

Fach objected strenuously, and the court sustained him. But Leibowitz wasn't talking for the court record—he was talking to twelve men in the jury box. And by now, human nature being what it is, the twelve men were wondering who Horatio J. Sharrett was, and what if any was his connection with the murder. He was beginning to lay the foundation that would eventually (he hoped) result in establishing reasonable doubt in the minds of the jurymen.

The *Staten Island Advance*, furiously pro-Sharrett and pro-Fach, paid Leibowitz a reluctant tribute the next day when it said, "The pink-cheeked prodigy who presides over the defense table plays his legal basketball with his sleeves dangling down, and he has many things up those sleeves. Leibowitz was a star basketball player at Cornell. (The Judge demurs. "I played *some* basketball," he says.) In the courtroom he keeps shooting for the legal basket from the center of the floor, a smart but rather hazardous stunt. The very confident schoolboyish orator with his schoolboyish complexion and manner promises a real defense. There will be no pussyfooting in this trial."

There was no pussyfooting in the trial. It developed into a grim, bitter battle between Fach and Leibowitz. Leibowitz had the ad-

49

vantage in that he knew just what to expect from Fach's witnesses, all of whom had testified in previous trials. Fach never knew what Leibowitz was going to spring. Leibowitz faced four difficult problems, and he had to solve each one of them before the jury would be justified in believing that a "reasonable doubt" existed as to Hoffman's guilt.

(1) He had to demolish the identification made by Barbara Fahs and Patrolman Matthew J. McCormack.

(2) He had to convince the jury that Whittet and Edkins had both lied.

(3) He had to show that Harry F. Butts had erred in testifying that the fatal bullet came from Hoffman's gun.

(4) He had to convince the jury that Hoffman, although innocent, had been actuated by a frantic and compelling fear complex that prompted him to manufacture the futile alibi.

There were a dozen other collateral problems, but they would solve themselves if these major issues could be resolved. He began by showing that Barbara Fahs (now eighteen years old) was mentally dull and completely hazy about things on which she had been quite certain at the original trial five years earlier. He questioned her gently, with almost fatherly concern. Barbara didn't even remember the school she had attended as a child. She didn't remember her street address or how many rooms there were in her house. Leibowitz asked her about identifying Hoffman at the station house. She remembered Captain (now Inspector) Van Wagner.

Q. When Hoffman first walked into the room at the station house and Inspector Van Wagner asked, "Is that the man?" did you answer, "No, that is not the man?"
A. Yes.
Q. Later Hoffman was brought into the room again, and did you again say, "That is not the man?"
A. Yes.

Leibowitz brought out the fact that Barbara had only identified Hoffman after several subsequent conferences with Van Wagner and other detectives and after she had been shown his picture in a newspaper. When he had finished, not one juryman believed that her identification had been genuine.

Now came burly Patrolman Matthew McCormack, scowling at the suave Leibowitz. Leibowitz dropped his gentle air of fatherly concern. The murder took place on March 25. The rewards, totaling eight thousand dollars, were posted during the second week of April. McCormack knew, of course, that everyone was eager to lay hold of the murderer but not until April 25 did this police officer reveal that he had seen Hoffman near the scene of the crime.

Q. That was one month after the crime. Do you mean to say that you carried the image of Hoffman in your mind for an entire month before telling anyone about it?

A. Yes.

Q. You made the identification of Hoffman in the Sheriff's office on April 25. Did the District Attorney send you there to make the identification?

A. No sir. I went there myself.

Q. Let me refresh your memory. On page 750 in the minutes of the second trial I read this: "Question Now then, who told you to go to the Sheriff's office? Answer Mr. Fach." Do you remember that?

The flustered patrolman continued to deny that Fach had sent him to the Sheriff's office to identify Hoffman, but finally Fach himself, red with embarrassment, conceded that the testimony given by McCormack in the previous trial had been correct and that he was lying now. McCormack stepped down, and now Leibowitz had solved his first problem. He had demolished the two identifying witnesses. Now for Whittet and Edkins, the two reel boys.

It took him five minutes to dispose of Whittet. First he established the fact that Whittet had been convicted of grand larceny. Whittet said virtuously that he had never been convicted of being a peeping Tom.

Q. What was the nature of the offense which you were convicted?

51

A. Watching a lady disrobe.

Q. You were in the street and she was in her home?

A. That is right.

Leibowitz made the unhappy, perspiring witness admit that he had never mentioned the conversation with Hoffman about a "lonely road to take a girl" until after being convicted of nocturnal spying. He didn't mention it until he applied for probation. Leibowitz dismissed him contemptuously, and he left the stand completely discredited. Harry Edkins was next.

Q. Do you remember a big black ruler that was on the desk in the District Attorney's office in 1924?

A (shouted). Yes, Fach hit me with it when I refused to change my story about Hoffman's glasses.

He explained that on the afternoon of the murder he had seen Hoffman's tortoise-shell glasses hanging on their accustomed hook in the projection room of the Palace Theatre. Fach had tried to make him admit that he was wrong. Edkins added that the police had urged him to change his story. It had been considered an important point because Hoffman had pretty well established even before the first trial that he owned only two pairs of glasses, one rimless, the other tortoise shell. Edkins testified further that he had been beaten by a cop because he refused to give testimony unfavorable to Hoffman.

Fach tried to salvage something of the wreckage, but Edkins, sullen and defiant, stuck to his story. He "didn't remember" driving past Lover's Lane with Hoffman at all. After thirty minutes of it Fach gave up in disgust. Leibowitz smiled understandingly at the jury and the jury smiled back.

Fach aparently felt that Leibowitz was going to involve Horatio Sharrett, and, trying to anticipate this, he put Robert Ferguson, a delivery boy, on the stand. In previous trials he had testified that he had stopped his truck near the spot where the body was found and that a motorist had driven alongside. Fach knew that Ferguson had told his boss he thought the man was Sharrett, but that later he felt he had been mistaken. Perhaps Fach felt he could spike Leibowitz' guns by making Ferguson his own witness. When he was finished, Leibowitz cross-examined.

Q. Did you not maintain for weeks after the murder that it was Horatio Sharrett you had seen?
A. I thought I'd seen him.
Q. Didn't you tell detective Lewis, the night after the murder, that it was Sharrett you had seen?
A. Yes.

A motorcycle cop, Thomas S. Cosgrove, put Sharrett within 1,500 feet from the entrance to Lover's Lane. He had stopped Sharrett's car, talked to him briefly telling him of the murder, and then let him go.

Q. Did you search Sharrett to see if he had a pistol?
A. No.

From Captain Van Wagner, Leibowitz drew the following:

Q. Did Mr. Fach tell you he had interrogated Mr. Sharrett and that Mr. Sharrett was okay?
A. Yes.
Q. Did Mr. Fach tell you to lay off Mr. Sharrett, that he, Fach, was giving Sharrett a clean bill of health?
A. Yes.

Fach, obviously disturbed by the line of questioning, asked Leibowitz in a low voice, "Are you suggesting that Sharrett had something to do with this?"

"I'm suggesting no such thing. I'm merely pointing out," the lawyer said in an equally low voice, "that because of your faith in Sharrett and because of your friendship with him you didn't investigate him as thoroughly as the circumstances seemed to indicate."

Every time Sharrett's name was brought into the case, the men in the jury box became alert. Gradually Leibowitz was drawing attention away from Hoffman and concentrating it on Sharrett. Finally Fach knew that he would have to put Sharrett on the stand. It was the only way to combat Leibowitz' line of questioning. The harassed Sharrett took the stand. The courtroom expected Leibowitz to take off the gloves and start slugging. Instead he was courteous, gentle and gracious. He established the fact that Sharrett and Fach had been good friends for twenty years. Sharrett readily admitted that he had been near the scene of the crime in a Model T Ford sedan just after it had been committed. That was just about all that Leibowitz wanted to establish. He smilingly told Sharrett to step down.

Only the legal minds in the courtroom realized how tactful Leibowitz had been. He hadn't intimidated or browbeaten Sharrett. He had merely put him near the scene of the crime. Leibowitz was establishing a "reasonable doubt" in the minds of the jurors. That disposed of problem number two. The third problem was the toughest of all. Sergeant Harry Butts was a highly respected ballistics expert. He had testified in a hundred trials and was quite at home in the witness box. Reporters sitting at the press table wondered how Leibowitz could ever discredit his testimony.

If Fach could convince the jury that Hoffman's gun had fired the shots that had killed Maude Bauer, they would be compelled to find him guilty. The demonstration that Leibowitz had arranged climaxed the trial, and Leibowitz took full advantage of his sense of the dramatic in setting the scene for it. He presented three qualified ballistics experts to support his contention that the bullet had not been fired from Hoffman's gun. First was the elderly Captain William A. Jones, official firearms expert for the New York Police Department for thirty-two years. Second was Merton Robinson, ballistics engineer for the Winchester Repeating Arms Company. Third was Albert Foster, general manager of the Colt Company which had made the gun. The four technical men on the jury understood the language used by these experts. Later on in the jury room they would explain anything in the testimony which businessmen on the jury might find a bit difficult to grasp. Weeks before, while lying in bed late at night, Leibowitz had decided to seek technical

54

men for the jury, and now the soundness of his tactics was to be demonstrated.

Leibowitz turned the courtroom into a laboratory. He had a comparison microscope mounted on a table, and that was wheeled into position before the bench. He had easels set up, and mounted on them were charts, diagrams and blown-up photographs of shells and bullets. Then Leibowitz introduced his two star witnesses—the two tiny shells found alongside the body of Maude Bauer. When an automatic is fired it leaves its "fingerprints" on both the lead bullet itself and on the shell. At the instant of firing there is a tremendous repercussive pressure, and the breechblock of the gun (a small steel block at the beginning of the chamber against which the face of the shell recoils when the explosion occurs as the gun is fired) invariably imprints its markings on the face of the shell.

Captain Jones testified that he had fired fifty bullets from Hoffman's gun and that he had the shells of those bullets with him. The microscope had twin stages. Leibowitz put a test shell on one stage and one of the shells found by Maude Bauer's body on the other. If the microscope showed identical markings he would grant that Hoffman's gun had fired the shots; he would admit that Hoffman was guilty.

Leibowitz asked the members of the jury to file past the microscope and decide for themselves. Judge Humphrey allowed the request, and one by one they peered into the glass. It was obvious that the two shells had entirely different markings. Both Jones and Robinson testified that the shells from bullets they had fired from Hoffman's gun all bore the same marks—and that these marks were completely dissimilar to marks on the shells introduced by the prosecution. The jury might not have believed the witnesses, but they believed what they saw with their own eyes. The two technical witnesses merely corroborated what the jurors already had seen and knew to be true. Leibowitz always believed that the eye is a more receptive organ than the ear. A jury might not believe something it heard; it would most certainly believe something that it had seen.

Expert Robinson went on to say that the bullet which killed Mrs. Bauer had been fired from a gun which had a rough or rusty bar-

55

rel. Test bullets fired from Hoffman's gun showed no well-defined scratches or rust marks. The expert then testified bluntly that the markings on the fatal bullet did not coincide with markings found inside the barrel of Hoffman's gun.

There was one more bit of evidence disconcerting to Fach. The State claimed that after Hoffman had fired the two bullets he had then cleaned the gun. Fach introduced a small wire "brush" with which he claimed Hoffman had oiled and then used to eliminate any evidence inside the gun barrel that would show the gun had been fired. Leibowitz countered this by producing a chemical analysis of the wire gun cleaner which showed that no oil had ever touched the brush; that it was in exactly the same condition as when it left the factory.

Fach was unable to make any of the defense experts give any ground. They were qualified technical men and they talked calmly, objectively, as technical men will, and the engineers and the contractor in the jury box were impressed. Thus problem number three was also resolved.

Then Harry Hoffman took the stand. Under the adroit questioning of his counsel, he articulated the fears that had gripped him during the days after the body of Maude Bauer was found; he told unemotionally of the mass hysteria that had gripped the community. He told of his frantic search for witnesses who had seen him in Manhattan or on the ferry boat; of his despair when no one remembered seeing him. He had been an invisible man that day. As Hoffman warmed to the story, Leibowitz stepped back, letting him tell it to the jury in his own way. Without interruption for questions, the story took on a substance and continuity that it might otherwise have lacked. He told of a friend, Oscar Yager, who kept a candy store in Richmond. Yager, too, owned a Ford sedan and in general answered the description of the murderer. The police had taken him and questioned him and he, Hoffman, had been told of the horrible bruises on Oscar's body after the "questioning" was over and Oscar was released. He was afraid of the same kind of treatment. When he walked down the street he was sure to meet some-

one who'd say jokingly, "Say, Harry, you look a lot like that murderer they're after. Why don't you give yourself up?"

And so in desperation he had fixed the alibi. He had lied and
lied, but each lie had come back to torture him. Oh, he had been
wrong to lie—he admitted readily—but he'd been punished. He'd
been caged like a wild animal now for more than five years. That
seemed a severe penalty for the telling of a lie. And the lies had
hurt no one—except himself.

Now Leibowitz took over. He handed Hoffman the .25-caliber
gun.

Q. Did you ever fire that gun?
A. Never in my life, so help me God. I could not have fired it.
Q. Why not?
A. It had a right-handed safety catch. I'm left-handed. It was awk-
ward for me to handle it. So after I bought it I put it in a drawer
and forgot about it.

Everyone in the court (except Leibowitz) was surprised. Fach was
more than surprised. He was stunned. It was the first time that
Hoffman's left-handedness had been brought out. When Hoffman
stepped down Leibowitz proceded to establish his left-handedness by
evidence of other witnesses, and then he proved that Mrs. Bauer
had been shot by a right-handed man. He had charts ready to show
the path of the bullet. It had entered the chest two and a half
inches left of the median line and had lodged in the spinal region
two inches to the right of that line. It would have been virtually
impossible for a left-handed man to have fired a shot that would
(after entering the body) travel four and a half inches to the right
as this bullet had done.

Leibowitz ended his defense and made his summation. He began
conversationally, going over the flaws in the State's case. He told of
how the circumstantial evidence against Hoffman had been created by
himself, prompted by his frenzied fear. He reminded the jury (for
the benefit of the four technical men) of the testimony given by

the firearms experts. When he had summarized the evidence in Hoffman's favor, he changed. That had been Leibowitz the lawyer. Now
Leibowitz the artist took over. His appeal now was frankly emotional,
and within five minutes reporters noted that tears were streaming
down the face of Hoffman. Members of the jury were looking intently at Leibowitz as he addressed them.

"I do not believe any jury would convict a dog on the evidence
presented here," he cried.

In charging the jury, Judge Humphrey said, "When evidence is
chiefly circumstantial, it must not only be consistent with guilt but
must exclude to a moral certainty every reasonable hypothesis of innocence."

The jury filed out and the reporter for the *New York Journal*
wrote, "The corridors were filled with men who looked upon this
murder trial as a sporting contest. When the trial opened they were
giving six-to-one odds that Hoffman would get the chair. After
Leibowitz had displayed his legal magic and after his brilliant summation, the contest had become an even money proposition. Those
who said that Hoffman would be acquitted and who backed their
opinion with money were not betting on Hoffman—they were betting
on Leibowitz."

Those who bet on Leibowitz were right. The next day every
newspaper in New York (including the staid *Times*) screamed the
acquittal in headlines. The jury had believed the evidence that
Leibowitz had presented. The jury had realized how treacherous circumstantial evidence could be.

Harry Hoffman left the courtroom a free man. The Motion Picture Machine Operators Union, Local 306, took Hoffman under
its wing and got him a job. He returned to the anonymous
obscurity which had been his before the death of Maude Bauer.

Horatio J. Sharrett went back to his real estate business in Staten
Island.

6

"I'd like to ask you a question or two about the Hoffman case."
"You may cross-examine," Judge Leibowitz grinned.
"Why did you drag Horatio Sharrett into your case?"
"The District Attorney thought I was bringing in Sharrett as a
red herring. I wasn't. I wanted to show that the testimony of the
witnesses (regarding a Ford sedan, a brown hat and overcoat and
tortoise-shell glasses) fitted another man as well as my client; that
furthermore it fitted a man whom other witnessess had placed within
a stone's throw, figuratively speaking, of the scene of the murder.
My point was not to accuse Sharrett. I would have had no more
reason (or evidence) to do so than Mr. Fach had in accusing Hoffman. It was very necessary to drive this point home to the jury. In
short, my objective was to demonstrate the unreliability of certain
kinds of circumstantial evidence."
"At what point in the trial did you win the case?"
"I won the case a month before the trial opened," the Judge
said. "Cases aren't always won in courtrooms. In the Hoffman case I
made up a list of the things which were against Hoffman. These
were: his resemblance to the killer, the gun he owned, the identification by the girl and the policeman and the evidence of the reel
boys, Hoffman's own suspicious actions and his apparent "consciousness" of guilt, and the fact that he had no alibi.
"Then I listed things in his favor. I could prove by experts that
the State's ballistics witness, though sincere, had been in error, that
this gun of his had not fired the fatal bullets. I could destroy the
identification by showing that the girl was mentally deficient and that
she had undoubtedly been coached before she named Hoffman, and
of course I could impugn the credibility of the cop and the reel
boy. I could prove that Hoffman's years of watching moving pictures
had instilled in him a sense of the dramatic and a fear complex
which would account for his clumsy attempt to arrange an alibi.
When I went into the courtroom I had an answer for every bit of

evidence the D.A. would use against me. This involved a great deal of work and plenty of sleepless nights."

"The toughest evidence to overcome seemed to be the evidence of Sergeant Butts regarding the gun," I suggested.

"It was," he nodded. "At that time I had never fired a gun in my life. I knew nothing about firearms. During the three months before the trial I made a study of ballistics. And when I had learned at least the fundamentals of the science, I realized that the identification of Hoffman's gun as the murder weapon was not complete and irrefutable. No two guns ever leave the same markings on the shells. There I saw a ray of hope. I took the shells found near the body of Maude Bauer, and had a qualified expert examine them. He said bluntly that they could not have been fired by Hoffman's gun. And he and two other really great ballistics experts testified to that effect during the trial. The prosecution experts had been guilty of honest error."

"Reading the testimony of the trial, I felt that you were very severe on Patrolman Matthew McCormack, who said he had seen Hoffman near the scene of the crime."

"You bet I was severe on Patrolman McCormack," Leibowitz snapped. "McCormack said that he had been standing on Victory Boulevard at 4:25 on the afternoon the crime was committed. He said he was thumbing a ride, that a Ford sedan had passed at twenty miles an hour and that Hoffman was at the wheel. I had a hunch, and I followed it up. I found out from the Weather Bureau that March 25, 1924, the day on which the murder was committed, was a bright, clear day with a dazzling sun. I waited for a day on which climatic conditions were exactly the same as they had been on that March 25, and then I took the ferry to Staten Island and drove to Victory Boulevard. I stood in the exact spot where McCormack testified that he had stood at the hour he said he had been there. McCormack had said that this Ford sedan had come from the direction of Lover's Lane; that is from the east.

"I stood there watching cars approach and pass me. The sun was still dazzling at 4:25 and it hit the windshield of every car that came from the eastern direction. At that time the windshields of

60

automobiles didn't slant as they do now; they were perpendicular to the floor of the car. When the sun hit that glass it was reflected or deflected to such an extent that I, standing there, could not tell whether the person behind the wheel of an oncoming car was a man or a woman. I could not distinguish features at all. I couldn't tell if the person behind the wheel was black or white.

"And incidentally, this was an open, uncrowded highway. Automobiles were buzzing by at much faster than twenty miles an hour. No driver would hold his car down to that speed on such an inviting road. I stood there for an hour, and then I was satisfied in my own mind that Patrolman McCormack was—let us say—mistaken in his identification. That is why I was rather severe on him when he was on the witness stand. I won that case by studying ballistics for three months and by spending a sunny afternoon on Staten Island."

"You'd done a lot of preparing," I said.

"Exactly," he replied. "And the Hoffman case is a good example of how cases are won by plodding. Check! Check! Check! The so-called brilliance you hear and see in the courtroom is the end product of the lime, the cement and the brick of weeks, sometimes months, of grinding and often boring work.

"It is really ludicrous to read some of these books that 'in ten easy lessons' are guaranteed to teach the practitioner how to become a courtroom lawyer. Whenever you hear of a defense lawyer who acquits clients by the sheer brilliance of his personality," Leibowitz smiled, "or who gets not guilty verdicts by pulling one bit of legal legerdemain after another, you can be sure you're hearing of a moving picture lawyer. The trial lawyer who knows his law and who is willing to work his head off to prepare his facts and is able to interpret these facts in a pleasing and forceful manner, is the one who makes the best record. A trial lawyer must have the capacity and the will to study and master subjects entirely remote from the law. In my time I've had to study and thoroughly understand every conceivable scientific subject from ballistics to serology. Consider a murder case. You see, people may kill and still not be murderers. In defending clients whom I believed to be mentally irresponsible, I had to make

61

an intensive study of psychiatry. If you're interested, you might study the case of Alvin Dooley. The trial record is available and perhaps most of the witnesses are still alive. No reason why you can't interview them. That was an interesting case. I remember discussing it one afternoon with a group of law students . . ."

4. DOOLEY WAS A COP . . .

"Who shall decide when doctors disagree."
                    ALEXANDER POPE

1

Leibowitz had been invited to speak to the students at New York University Law School. When he finished, the professor who had introduced him asked if he would answer questions. Leibowitz was happy to do that. Questions came flying at him from the eager students. Here was a man who dealt not with the abstract theory of the law but with its practice, and he had been phenomenally successful at it.

"In our study of criminal law," one student said, "it seems apparent that almost all defendants in murder cases are congenital criminals; that is, they were born criminals. You have defended more than a hundred men accused of murder. Did hereditary, physical or mental characteristics make it inevitable that they embrace a life of crime? In short, were most of your clients born criminals?"

"As far as I know," Leibowitz said, "I never met or defended a man who was born a criminal. I don't believe there is such a thing as a "born" criminal."

"But," the student protested, obviously quoting from a textbook, "when you say that, you are disputing the theory of Franz Joseph Gall, that criminal tendencies are innate and can be detected by the conformation of the skull."

"Gall was a Viennese doctor who had nothing but a theory. I believe his theory is complete nonsense."

"When you say that," the student said hotly, "you are implying that the positive school of Lombroso is also nonsense, and yet most European police forces respect the Lombroso doctrine."

63

Leibowitz smiled again. He remembered how he too had discovered Cesare Lombroso when he had been a law student. He recalled a line from the writing of the Italian criminologist: "The criminal is a special type, standing midway between the lunatic and the savage." "I believe that Lombroso was wrong," Leibowitz said. "To him the criminal was a subhuman anthropological freak marked by definite anatomical characteristics, such as the shape of the ear or the slope of the jaw, or angle of the chin. He believed that such a man was doomed by nature to a criminal career. In short, he considered man as though he were a beast without free will or a soul."

It was evident that some of the students had studied and had been influenced by Cesare Lombroso and his disciples, Raffaelo Garfolo and Enrico Ferri. Several of them questioned his criticism of the Italian school of criminology.

One said, "What about Capone, Lepke, Luciano, Abe Reles, Vincent Coll, Dillinger, Two Gun Crowley, Baby Face Nelson, Alvin Karpis? They were criminals from the day they were able to walk. How can you deny that they were *born* criminals?"

"I represented some of the men you've mentioned," Leibowitz said. "I know their backgrounds. Not one of those men was born a criminal. Men embrace criminal careers for various reasons—some because of poverty, some because they feel working for a living is a sucker's game, some because mental disease (which has nothing to do with their physical characteristics) robs them of all conception of right and wrong. These latter belong in hospitals—not prisons. Circumstances force many into criminal careers. I doubt very much if any man in this room contemplates committing a crime. But it is entirely possible that any one of you might one day find yourself charged with first-degree murder."

"That is absurd," a student said angrily. "You might as well say that there are eight million potential murderers walking around the streets of New York."

"That's exactly what I do say," Leibowitz said calmly.

"You say that ordinary, decent, law-abiding men are capable of murder?"

"Under certain circumstances," Leibowitz said. "And I'm not talking in abstract terms. I'm talking now as a practicing lawyer. I could give you possibly fifty examples of how circumstances made killers out of decent, ordinarily law-abiding, even deeply religious citizens. It is natural for us to show restraint in dealing with our fellow men. Occasionally something happens to snap this restraint, something we can't control.

"Occasionally a man who is ordinary in every way will find himself on trial for murder," Leibowitz said. "Circumstances over which he has no control force him to kill, yet society in its ignorance treats such a man exactly as it treats a professional murderer-for-profit. Why, I only have to go back two months to give you an example of a killer, who, in my opinion, was not guilty of murder. Remember the case of Alvin Dooley? Let me tell you about Dooley, and you decide whether or not he was a born murderer.

2

Alvin Dooley was a cop. Even as a kid, he had wanted to be a cop. It was a rather surprising ambition, because he had been a sensitive, shy child whose health prevented him from joining in the rugged sports of the neighborhood. He was the sissy of the block, and when the kids refused to let him play with them, he'd run home crying to his mother. Only she understood him.

She knew that he had been a "seven months" baby and that his life had hung by a thread during the first year of his existence. Every day she had to bathe him in oil and swathe him in cotton batting. When he was two, he weighed only eleven pounds and there was not a sign of a tooth in his head. He was subject to convulsions which puzzled the doctors until they discovered that his teeth, instead of growing through the gums, decayed within them and poisoned his whole system. He didn't enter grammar school until he was nine. He was backward in every way, and the doctors attributed it all to his illness as a baby.

He was big but flabby. He was always the oldest but least important boy in his class. The others could run faster, throw a ball more

65

accurately, hit a ball farther. Young Alvin was always left out of things.

There is a mechanism deep in the interior of the human which automatically endeavors to make up for deficiencies of any sort, whether they be perceptual, physical or social. This compensation is often automatically and unconsciously accomplished. Mozart and Beethoven were deaf, but hidden in their minds was an overwhelming urge to create beautiful music. The sculptor Gonnelli, who became blind at twenty, left masterpieces. It was inevitable that Alvin, unconsciously or instinctively, comparing his own with the physical and mental equipment of his playmates, should acquire a strong feeling of inferiority, and it was inevitable that the mechanism in his mind should strive to give him some comforting compensation. This was his desire to be a cop. A cop is a symbol of the strong. A cop is one to whom the rest of society shows respect.

By the time he was twenty, Alvin had outgrown the physical illness of his childhood. Nature now seemed to treat Alvin in a benign mood of compensation. His body lost its flabbiness and hardened. And finally he passed his physical examination for the police force. He became a cop, and no prouder man ever wore the shield. It was as though his early years had been a nightmare out of which he had only just emerged. Now he had the respect which he had never been able to command as a schoolboy. Men, who as kids had bullied him at school, passed him now and said, "Hello, Al," and they were flattered when he recognized them. His old teachers would see him in his blue uniform with the brass buttons on it and they would smile and say, "Hello, Officer," and Alvin would feel a deep sense of pride.

Alvin got along well with his fellow patrolmen. His record was excellent in a community where corruption was usually taken for granted. Alvin Dooley was a member of the police force of the smallest city in New York State—Long Beach, which is on Long Island. Long Beach was founded by Senator William Henry Reynolds. In 1924, Senator Reynolds was found guilty of larceny in connection with the sale of municipal bonds. The newspapers said that Long Beach was to New York what notorious Cicero of the Al Capone days was to Chicago. They were right, in view of the fact that gambling and prostitution were two industries which operated fairly openly in both communities. Long Beach hibernated during the winter (its permanent population was five thousand), but when the warm weather came there was a great influx of visitors from New York, and Long Beach, in those days, always did its best to give its summer visitors everything they wished in the way of amusement. Political scandals were then as much a part of Long Beach as the white sands and cool breezes that are its chief attractions.

Alvin Dooley, a self-respecting cop, was never involved in even the most minor scandal or infraction of rules. When he joined the force, a Police Benevolent Association had just been organized to help support the widows and children of policemen who died in the line of duty. Alvin took a great deal of interest in this organization. Dances and ball games were held each year to raise money, and Alvin was always the one who sold the most tickets.

He had been on the force seven years when his fellow cops elected him president of the Benevolent Association. This was the first honor that had ever come to Alvin Dooley. There were forty-eight men on the force and every one of them voted for Alvin Dooley. Life could never hold anything like this for Alvin again. The "compensation" for this unhappy, unhealthy childhood had finally been fully accomplished. He looked upon his new position as a sacred trust. There was only about a hundred dollars in the treasury when he took over, and he resolved to increase this. Each year, the balance grew. Three years later, one of his fellow cops was killed. Alvin was right there with a check for the funeral expenses and another check for the family of the slain policeman.

The Police Benevolent Association of Long Beach gradually became more than an organization to raise funds. If one of the cops got what seemed to be a bad deal, the boys would talk it over and ask Alvin to go to bat for him.

"Someone is always complaining about a cop," Sergeant Bertram Wolff, who was Dooley's immediate superior, recalls. "Well, often the cop is completely innocent but he can't make out a good case for himself. When this happened the men would ask Al Dooley to 'front' for them. Dooley would then go to the Police Commissioner and present the cop's case. Al Dooley was a quiet, peaceful, decent man who had everybody's respect."

He had married pretty Mary McCarthy, and their neighbors were shocked when they separated after five years of wedded life. They had seemed very happy. One day, he took young son Joseph and walked out. No psychiatrist would be surprised by the fact that he went to his mother's house and made his home with her. Mary took Joan and Alvin, Jr. Their separation was a friendly one and Alvin was liberal in his support of them.

Alvin developed into a completely happy, well-adjusted man living with his mother, for whom he had a great love, his sister and his younger brother Wilbur, who worked on the *New York Herald Tribune* as a pressman. Wilbur was about thirteen years younger than Alvin.

"We were closer than brothers," Wilbur says, looking back. "Al was not only my brother—he was my best friend. Al was the kind of guy you just naturally went to for advice. And he certainly worshipped Mother. I never knew a fellow so crazy about his mother as Al was. She was his guide, his idol, his whole life."

The Dooley family had a nice old-fashioned frame house with a garage in back of it. Alvin was a great one for tinkering with things. If something went wrong with the family car, he insisted upon fixing it himself.

"Alvin was always working around the house," his sixty-three-year-old mother, Emma Dooley, says. "We had an oil burner in the cellar. If that went wrong, Alvin fixed it. If a pipe was stopped up, Alvin wouldn't let me call a plumber. He would fix it. He spent most of his spare time at home, and spent all of his money on the house. Every night he'd help his little Joe with his homework. Joe had trouble with arithmetic, and Alvin sometimes worked with him so long that I'd say, 'Alvin, it's time for the child to go to bed.' And Alvin would laugh and send Joe to bed and then he'd go to work on his books. Almost every night he'd work on those books."

He kept the records of the Police Benevolent Association at home.

68

He had studied the operation of such organizations in other cities and he had discovered new ways to raise funds. He wrote out a set of bylaws which were unanimously adopted. He took care of the funds too, and the disbursements, and when a brother cop would kid him about his preoccupation with the association, Alvin would grin and say, "One of these days some hood may knock you off and your wife will be glad I worked on these books."

Alvin lived with one fear, and he expressed it often at association meetings. "We got to keep our association out of politics," he'd say earnestly. "Once these politicians get their dirty hands on the association they'll take it over. Now we've got almost twelve thousand dollars in the kitty. They never bothered with us when we had a hundred dollars in the till, but now we've got to watch out. They'll try to move in sooner or later, and we've got to stick together to protect ourselves."

But it didn't look as though Alvin's fears would ever be realized. Major Charles Gold was an easygoing man who was proud of his police force and who left it pretty much alone. The P.B.A. was an organization run by the cops for the benefit of the cops, and even men like Sergeant Bertram Wolff and Sergeant Francis Donnelly never spoke at meetings or tried to dictate election of the officers by the rank and file. Besides, Dooley was running it so well. Dooley was a good cop, a good citizen, and he was the only one on the force who'd spend hours over those tiresome books making them balance to the penny. "This was Dooley's baby," the men chuckled. "Why, he'd brought it up all by himself." To Dooley, that Police Benevolent Association was the most important thing in the world. He had a feeling of dedication to it.

Another honor came to Alvin Dooley. The various Police Benevolent Associations of Long Island had a parent organization which they called the Police Conference of Nassau County. Problems that affected the police as a whole were discussed at the meetings of the Conference. Because of the great record Dooley had made in strengthening the Long Beach P.B.A., he was elected secretary-treasurer of the Conference. Henceforth, he would not only keep an eye on the funds of his own small association, but of the larger organization as well. It was great to be trusted not only by your own neighbors but by outsiders who hardly knew you.

Alvin had as happy a five years as a man can have. He had been assigned to motorcycle now (one of four in the force) and he was almost as proud of that motorcycle as he was of his neatly kept association ledgers. He could go home for lunch now and be back on the job in an hour. Usually he, his mother and young Joe had lunch together. That was probably the happiest part of the day for all three of them. Alvin would always have some tale of a speeder he had caught or of a robber one of the boys out of Headquarters had brought in, and young Joe would listen popeyed at the stories of what to him was stirring adventure. Alvin could play the piano a little, and after lunch he'd play songs that Joe was learning at school and Alvin and his mother would sing them for Joe. Then Joe would run back to school, Alvin would kiss his mother goodbye, mount his motorcycle and roar down the street. Here was a decent, law-abiding, religious man who had the good cop's hatred of criminals and crime.

3

In 1937, they elected a new mayor in Long Beach. His name was Louis F. Edwards. Edwards had been in the paint business in Altoona, Pennsylvania, and then he had moved to Long Beach where he had established a similar enterprise. It was rather difficult for a Long Beach businessman to stay completely out of politics, and Edwards gradually drifted into a fairly influential position in local political circles. In 1937, he defeated Mayor Gold in the primaries, and then in a bitterly contested general election he won over Lorenzo Carlino, the opposition boss. Edwards had been a crusading candidate who promised a reform administration; he swore to make an end of the "twenty gay years" which had given Long Beach such an unsavory reputation. He would make Long Beach the "Miami Beach of the North"; he promised "a first-class coastal town, a health resort." He was out to make Long Beach a "class resort," and he established a beach club and built cabanas on the sand. The first thing he did on becoming Mayor was to ban the wearing of suspenders by boardwalk promenaders.

There was nothing easygoing about Edwards. He was a strict disciplinarian, and you had to do things his way—or else! He had a police booth built across the street from his home and he ordered Edward J. Begly, his new police chief, to assign a man to that booth. The cop in the booth had orders to cross the street each morning when Mayor Edwards emerged from his house, stand at attention and salute him. The men didn't like this much; they kidded about Edwards being a Long Beach local dictator, but they obeyed all right.

Alvin Dooley and his fellow cops were uneasy. Edwards had promised to effect municipal economies, and one of his first moves was to cut the four-man motorcycle squad to a two-man squad. Dooley was one of the two men put back on a beat. His beat was a lonely, uninhabited stretch of sand north of the little city. Now for the first time in years the old uncertainties returned. The sense of inferiority which had apparently vanished had actually been hiding somewhere in the dim recesses of his subconscious mind. Now it began to emerge. They had taken his motorcycle away from him. What would they take next? His Benevolent Association? His uniform? These fears tortured Dooley.

A woman said that he had been discourteous to her and she complained to Mayor Edwards. Shortly thereafter the woman, her momentary flash of annoyance forgotten, refused to appear against Dooley. The woman pleaded that she had no real grievance, that in fact she had been unreasonable in her complaint. Nevertheless, the Mayor insisted on holding a hearing. Dooley was exonerated. But he felt he had been unnecessarily humiliated by Edwards. Dooley now felt that the Mayor had it in for him. Petty though it was, this was the first black mark against him in his twelve years as a cop. He no longer felt secure. He never played the piano at home any more. He never helped young Joe with his homework.

Then Alvin heard disquieting rumors that threatened to destroy his

71

whole existence. He heard that Mayor Edwards was working behind the scenes to oust him as president of the Benevolent Association. Edwards had his own candidate, Detective James Horan, who had been assigned as the Mayor's bodyguard and chauffeur. Horan had run for president in a previous election against Alvin but he had received only one vote—presumably his own.

Alvin had good friends on the force and they kept him informed of the campaign Edwards was waging. Sergeant Francis Donnelly told Alvin that he had been approached to vote for Horan. The Mayor hadn't approached him directly; he had sent Alfred Von Brock, a political leader in the second district.

"I was in the back room at Headquarters," Donnelly told Alvin. "Von Brock came in and said, 'The Mayor sent me to tell you he wants you to vote for Horan for president of the P.B.A.' I asked, 'Why is the Mayor so interested in the P.B.A. all of a sudden?' He said, 'I don't know or care. He just sent me to tell you how to vote.' Then he left, and outside I ran into Chief Begly. The Chief said to me, 'Every man on the force should vote for Horan if they know what's best for them.'"

"Horan was never interested in the P.B.A.," Dooley said. "The boys would never elect him."

"You don't know how much heat Edwards is putting on," Donnelly said gloomily. "My own father-in-law, John Glynn, came to me and told me I'd better vote for Horan."

"Glynn isn't even a cop," Alvin protested.

"He's on the city payroll," Donnelly said. "The Mayor could fire him. It's the old story, Al, you can't beat City Hall. I know I'll blow my job if I don't vote for Horan."

Sergeant Bertram Wolff, filled with indignation, came to Al with substantially the same story.

"Ben Bergman came to see me," Wolff said. "He's a court attendant and a good friend of Edwards. He asked me about the election and I told him that Horan didn't have a chance. Bergman told me to go see the Mayor and I did. The Mayor had a list on his desk of all the men, and he checked those who were for Horan and those who were for you. He had question marks after some of the names. He said to me, 'If Horan is beaten, it will reflect on my office, because Horan is so close to me. See what you can do amongst the boys to elect Horan.' After that the Chief called me in to see if I could persuade you to withdraw. He said if you pull out he'll give you your motorcycle back."

"If I withdraw I'd feel like I was selling the boys out," Dooley said. "This is what I always warned the boys about. I knew these damn politicians would try to grab our association. But the boys won't stand for it."

"I hope not, but they're putting lots of pressure on them," Donnelly said. "Take Herman now; he's a good friend of yours. Well, the Mayor did him some favor and now he has to pay off by voting for Horan. And Mulligan, he . . ."

So it went. One man after another came to Dooley. These were honest, decent men who liked Dooley, but they were insecure men; their future depended upon the good will of Mayor Edwards and Chief Begly. As the election drew near, Edwards intensified his efforts. He'd have Horan drive him around the city and he'd have the car stop and he'd chat with cops on the beat. He talked to Sergeant Doris and he said, "Remember when you gave a ticket to Mr. Hooven's chauffeur and Hooven came to me and wanted you fired? Well, I didn't fire you, Doris, did I? You ought to show your appreciation by voting for my man Jim Horan." He stopped and told Patrolman Ryan to vote for Horan and Ryan looked at him with contempt and said, "Dooley has done a great job. Why should we throw him out in the gutter?" But there weren't many like Ryan. All this and more was reported back to Dooley. The whole department was jittery now. Every bit of pressure was put on the men. Men who had been lifelong friends looked at each other suspiciously as they walked into Headquarters to check in each day.

"Horan is in a spot to make you or break you," was the whisper that insinuated itself into their consciousness. They had to think of bread and butter for their tables, of second payments on cars and electric iceboxes, of brothers and sons who were on the city payroll. Al Dooley was their guy—but, God Almighty, a man had to think of his family, didn't he? And, after all, they weren't throwing Al down so bad; the presidency of the P.B.A. was an unsalaried job, wasn't it? So if Al lost the job, it would only mean he'd lose a lot of grief. What the hell, the job was nothing but a headache anyhow. Right? They'd gather at the Baldwin Harbor Inn or some other Nassau County bar and tell that to each other. If Al walked in they'd slap him on the shoulder, say, "Hiya, Al," avoid his eye and then walk out.

Alvin finally realized that all the cards were stacked against him. He didn't have a chance and he knew it. At night he would lie on his bed and stare for hours at the ceiling. His mother tried in vain to comfort him. What difference would it make if he lost the election?

"We got twelve thousand dollars in the kitty, Mom," he'd say in a flat, dull voice. "If Horan wins, the politicians will get their hooks on that money, and it's goodbye widows and children."

Once he threatened to kill himself by taking gas, and his mother tried to soothe him.

"Don't think like that, Al," she pleaded. "Live for me. Think of me. If you can't stand it, Al, we will walk out into the ocean, just you and me."

"I wouldn't mind getting licked if it was on the up and up," Al said, "but they're making my best friends vote against me. I'm a failure, Mom, I'm a failure."

"Now, Al . . . now." His mother put her arms around her sobbing son and did her best to comfort him, just as she had done years before when he'd run home sobbing because the kids called him a sissy and wouldn't let him play baseball with them.

The election was held on November 1. Detective James Horan was elected president of the Long Beach Police Benevolent Association by the narrow margin of three votes. Alvin, white-faced and shaking, congratulated him and then left the meeting. He walked down to the lonely beach, deserted now that the summer visitors had all left. He walked and walked, and then at 5:00 A.M. he went home. His mother was waiting for him.

"I got beaten," he said simply, "by three votes."

"I know, Al, I know." They sat down on a couch in the living room. Large tears rolled down Al's face. He kept repeating, "They beat me . . . they beat me," and then he lost all control. His big body shook with sobs. This time, his mother couldn't comfort him. His loss was too great. Finally she persuaded him to go to bed. Then she undressed and knelt beside her own bed with a rosary in her hand. Emma Dooley was a frightened mother now. She could do nothing but pray. And she knelt there praying until the gray dawn lightened and the street noises told her that the world was awakening and it was time to get breakfast for her family.

4

The afternoon newspapers of Wednesday, November 15, all carried large headlines on their front pages. Purchasers of the *New York Journal-American* read the following story:

MAYOR OF LONG BEACH
SLAIN BY POLICEMAN

A long-smouldering feud in the tangled police-politics of Long Beach, L. I., erupted today as Mayor Louis F. Edwards, 47, was shot to death by a disgruntled member of the town's police force.

As the Mayor stepped from his home at 15 W. Beech St., accompanied by his bodyguard, Detective James Horan, Patrolman Alvin Dooley, gun in hand, suddenly confronted them.

Neither Horan nor the Mayor had a chance. Five shots mowed them down, killing Edwards and critically wounding the detective.

A few seconds later, as the Mayor's wife and horrified neighbors rushed to the street, Dooley, smoking gun still in his hand, cried at them:

"I just shot that ———— Mayor and his stool-pigeon Horan, and I hope they both die."

Mayor Edwards, the father of five children, died at 10:30 A.M. on the way to Long Beach Hospital. Three bullets entered his body on the right side.

Horan, shot in the left kidney, was in a "very very critical" condition at the hospital.

Dooley—in the pocket of his uniform was found a half-pint of whiskey from which he had taken two drinks—was boastful and defiant as police questioned him at City Hall.

75

Police Chief Edward Begly said the man was "faking a drunk because he needs an alibi." A doctor who examined Dooley immediately after his arrest said he was not intoxicated, Chief Begly declared.

Taken to Chief Begly's office at City Hall for further questioning, Dooley bellowed at the Chief:

"And I'm sorry I didn't get you, too."

With understandable solicitude for the sensibilities of its readers, the *Journal* did not publish the next sentence, which was, "I just shot that Jew son-of-a-bitch of a Mayor and his God-damned stool pigeon." The Long Island newspapers did publish it, however, with a bit of editing. They replaced "son-of-a-bitch" (Presidents had not as yet given that expression the dignity that would allow it to be printed) and "God-damned" with inoffensive dashes.

Dooley was held without bail while District Attorney Edward Neary went before the Grand Jury and asked them to return a first-degree murder indictment. Meanwhile, flags in Long Beach were all at half mast and the dead Mayor was eulogized by civic and political leaders. Funeral services two days later were held at the Temple Israel, and Rabbi David I. Golovensky delivered a glowing tribute to the slain man. "He was patriotically American and proudly Jewish," the Rabbi declared. "He was a valiant emissary of brotherhood, a missionary for justice, a champion for charity and a richly endowed public servant."

Father John A. Cass, pastor of St. Ignatius Martyr Roman Catholic Church, addressed a meeting of grieving neighbors and suggested that a permanent memorial be established to honor this man who had worked so "diligently and sincerely for the welfare of the city." From his hospital bed Jim Horan cried out, "He was a wonderful man. I wish I, not he, had been killed."

Feeling ran high against Dooley in Long Beach. Edwards had left a widow and five attractive children. It was impossible not to feel sympathy for the bereaved widow and children, and this sympathy generated a violent antipathy toward Dooley. Two psychiatrists, Dr. Joseph H. Shuffleton and Dr. Richard A. Hoffman, were quoted in the papers as declaring that Dooley was sane.

The *Long Island Independent* and the *Nassau Daily Review Star* were bitter in their denunciation of Alvin Dooley. The *Review Star* said that there was plenty of evidence to prove premeditation, and the *Independent* fanned the embers of hatred that the shooting had ignited among the Long Beach citizenry. When Dooley was brought into court to be arraigned, hundreds jeered at him. There were cries of, "Lynch him . . . Let's get him now." In the minds of the people Dooley was guilty of a vicious, premeditated murder and he deserved the electric chair. The electric chair is just what District Attorney Neary demanded.

Leibowitz was retained to defend Dooley.

5

It was a difficult, almost impossible assignment. To begin with, where in Nassau County could you find twelve unprejudiced, open-minded citizens to form a jury? Only the cops and his family sympathized with Dooley; they knew of the provocation, but they were disqualified from serving on the jury. By publishing the reports of physicians who said that Dooley was sober at the time of the murder, and of psychiatrists who said he was sane, the props had apparently been knocked from under any possible defense based on temporary insanity. By now, Edwards had assumed the status of a martyr. Each day his memory grew more sacred as additional tributes to his character filled the local press. This, Leibowitz knew, would be a tough one.

He interviewed dozens of men who had known Dooley well. He talked to members of the family and to the cops who had been Dooley's friends. He talked to teachers in whose classes Dooley had sat as a young boy. He talked to doctors who had treated Alvin years before. Through them he got to know Dooley and to understand his fanatical devotion to his Police Benevolent Association. He talked to Dooley for hours on end and finally he felt that he knew as much about Alvin Dooley as any man alive; he certainly knew a lot more about Dooley than the prisoner himself knew.

It seemed fairly obvious to Leibowitz that the tactics employed by

Mayor Edwards had literally driven Dooley mad. But this would be difficult to prove. Dooley had no past record of obvious mental illness; his childhood illness had been organic. He had been normal and decent and trustworthy. Neary, Leibowitz reflected, had a good case and he was an able prosecutor who would know how to make the most of it. Leibowitz, hoping to find medical authority to back up his own belief that Dooley was insane at the time of the killing, retained Dr. Clarence H. Bellinger, superintendent of the Brooklyn State Hospital for the Insane, and Dr. Thomas S. Cusack, prominent Brooklyn psychiatrist. After thoroughly examining Dooley in his cell and after talking to his mother, brother and several policemen, both psychiatrists agreed that there was no question that Dooley was insane when he shot the Mayor and Horan.

Leibowitz and his two psychiatric experts had dinner together. They discussed the killing and Leibowitz presented what he felt would be Neary's case. The big problem was that of interpreting the facts to a jury in a manner that would convince them that Dooley had in fact been insane when he pumped the shots into his two victims.

"The fact that Dooley kept shooting Edwards after the Mayor lay there on the ground," Cusack said, "convinces me that he was actuated by some force within him that was beyond his control."

Leibowitz nodded. "Last year I went to Mexico City, and while I was there I saw a few bullfights. Occasionally the bull would knock the cape out of the hands of the matador. Then the bull would gore the cape, attacking it again and again in a blind, senseless fury. Was Dooley like that?"

Dr. Cusack nodded. "That's right."

"Yes, Dooley was like a mad bull," Leibowitz said thoughtfully. "That's something a jury will understand. Now, Doctor . . ."

For an hour they discussed methods of translating the technical language of psychiatry into terms of the bull ring. When they had finished, Leibowitz was ready for trial.

The trial opened on January 22, 1940, before Judge Cortland A. Johnson, an experienced, capable jurist. Neary and Leibowitz nodded to each other, not with hostility, but with mutual respect, and the trial was on.

Never had Leibowitz exercised more care in the selection of a jury. To begin with, he made it plain that he would not allow a Jew on the jury. He felt that Dooley's remark, "I just killed that Jew son-of-a-bitch of a Mayor," would hardly endear him to any Jewish juror. Incidentally, it was the only anti-Semitic remark Dooley had ever uttered in his life. The newspapers were filled with atrocity stories from Europe, and a strong wave of sympathy for the Jewish victims of Hitler was sweeping the country. "Jew hating" was not popular in 1940, and Leibowitz knew that Dooley's unfortunate intemperate statement would be in the minds of the jurors.

The panel consisted of 175 men and women, all residents of Nassau County. Judge Johnson wisely barred all residents of Long Beach itself. Leibowitz had sent two of his assistants to examine the records of each of them. They found that some who had served on juries before had reputations as habitual "convicting jurors." They found that others had expressed opinions against capital punishment. This pre-trial investigation of jurors is entirely legal, though very few defense lawyers bother to do it because of the tediousness of the research involved. But when the trial opened, Leibowitz knew exactly how many times each member of the panel had served on a jury in a criminal case during the past twenty-three years (the county court records extended back exactly that far). He knew how each former juror had voted. He knew whether or not the prospective juror had any relatives who had been put on the city payroll by Mayor Edwards. In short, Leibowitz knew just about everything there was to know about those 175 unsuspecting talesmen, who had been quite unaware of the investigation.

Discomfited district attorneys, excusing their failure to convict an accused man defended by Leibowitz, often said in disgust, "What could I do? Sam had the jury in his pocket from the beginning."

There was nothing sinister in this observation; it was merely a tribute to a lawyer who knew how to present a defense in human and plausible terms. He talked the language of the average

79

juryman; he never patronized or antagonized a jury. His mastery over juries is best shown by the fact that never while defending a client in a murder case was there a "'hung" jury (eleven for conviction—one for acquittal). Even district attorneys admitted that the "friendly" juries so often found in the courtroom when Leibowitz was defending a client were the result of nothing but careful, legitimate investigation. The backgrounds of the talesmen who now paraded before the bench were all familiar to Leibowitz.

The *New York Times* reported:

Leibowitz was full of surprises. Some jurors he examined for more than an hour before accepting or rejecting them. One he took without asking a single question. Others, he challenged almost before Neary had gotten under way with his own questioning.

He would unhesitatingly accept a juror like Francis M. O'Laughlin, an electrician, without asking a single question because his investigation had revealed that O'Laughlin was an amiable, kindly open-minded man, uninterested in Nassau County politics. He would spend an hour questioning Joseph D. Mero, painter and decorator, because Mero was a Catholic and Dooley, despite his Irish ancestry and his Catholic mother, had embraced his father's Lutheranism and had become a member of a Masonic lodge. Then, convinced that Mero had no prejudice against Lutherans or Masons, Leibowitz accepted him. He'd accepted John S. Mulcare, insurance salesman, another Catholic, but rejected a dozen others who perhaps without knowing it had revealed a bias against members of Masonic organizations.

He indicated the nature of his defense by asking talesmen such questions as:

"Have you ever known a man to become a wild man under the influence of liquor?"
"Do you believe that a man can be insane about one thing and perfectly sane about everything else?"
"Have you ever heard of a persecution psychosis, a form of insanity in which a man believes that he is being persecuted?"

It took four days to fill the jury box, but Leibowitz was reasonably satisfied. It would not be a friendly jury, he knew, because these people had looked up to Louis Edwards as a leading citizen of the county, but he felt the twelve men would at least try to be fair.

Neary opened for the prosecution by demanding the death penalty for Dooley. He told the story of what had happened on the morning of November 15. He told of the confession Dooley had made after the shooting. He didn't reveal what the confession said. Leibowitz hadn't seen the confession. This would be one of Neary's heaviest guns, but he was saving it for later. It was an excellent opening speech in that it outlined the case without giving too much of it away. These tactics were good. Leibowitz was given no chance to see the weakness (if any) in Neary's case. His manner was informal, ingratiating, and it was obvious that the jury was impressed.

Leibowitz arose to open for the defense. He began quietly, almost conversationally. He told of how the men had elected Dooley to run the P.B.A.

"Dooley is a simple sort of fellow. Long Beach never had a more honest policeman than Alvin Dooley. The presidency of the P.B.A. was the biggest thing in this ordinary cop's life.

"Now about two years ago," Leibowitz began to show his claws, "a politician by the name of Edwards got to be Mayor. This man immediately started to dominate everything. Tammany Hall in its palmiest days under Tweed never sought and obtained such absolute control over the bodies and souls of those who came in contact with politics in Long Beach, including the poor little Benevolent Association of the police. This man Edwards deliberately started undermining Dooley. Edwards personally browbeat policemen into voting for his stooge to supplant Dooley as the president of the P.B.A. I will prove this up to the hilt.

"You shall hear from witnesses to what extents Edwards went; the threats he made; the intimidation he and his Police Chief Begly applied in order to railroad poor Dooley out of his little honor of being president of the Police Benevolent Association.

"I shall produce witnesses who will tell how the Mayor and his crowd were out to get Dooley; how Dooley felt his job slipping away from him; how Dooley's mind started to crumble, slowly, slowly, until finally it was smashed into pieces. This tragedy occurred on a Wednesday. But Dooley had seen Edwards on the preceding Friday night at the railroad station; he could have killed him a hundred times before that fatal day, if he had

81

had murder in his heart as charged by the prosecution; if he had harbored any intent to kill the Mayor, he could have killed him right then and there. If he had intended to kill him he could have killed him at night, when nobody would have seen it; not in broad daylight in the presence of witnesses."

Leibowitz was talking without referring to notes. His voice rang with sincerity and, when he mentioned Edwards, with indignation. The jury sat enthralled, but it was hard to tell whether they were impressed with the facts which Leibowitz was presenting or with his amazing performance. Finally he neared the end of his opening remarks.

"You heard Mr. Neary's opening speech. It was moving; it was dramatic. After such an address it is not easy for a juror to keep his mind open. But I pray that you will keep your minds open until you have heard our side of the case.

"We have an honest defense here, gentlemen, as honest a defense as was ever presented in a courtroom. We say that Edwards brought about his death by his own tyrannical conduct; by his ruthless methods; by browbeating helpless little people who have to work for a living; by tearing from them that which was theirs.

"Gentlemen, Edwards drove Dooley insane. Our defense is that when he shot the Mayor, this unfortunate man on trial was so intoxicated and so bereft of reason that he didn't know that what he was doing was wrong; that everything he did was done while he was in a maniacal furor. We say further that under our law this man is not responsible for what he did. We say that Justice under law cries out for a verdict of not guilty."

6

The crowded courtroom seemed stunned by the harshness of the attack on Edwards. It was a negation of everything that Rabbi David Golovensky had said in his tribute at the funeral; this was not the Edwards of whom Father Cass had said, "He was a man who worked diligently and sincerely for the welfare of the city." And Leibowitz had promised that he would prove his accusations by testimony of witnesses. Members of the jury looked puzzled but (Leibowitz noted) not resentful. They had entered the courtroom that morning, understandably convinced that Edwards was the hero of the story and that Dooley was the villain. It would take them some time to get used to the idea that the case wasn't that simple; it was not all black and white. They didn't know it but this lawyer was beginning to do their thinking for them.

Neary looked thoughtful. He, more than anyone else in the courtroom, realized what Leibowitz was attempting to do, and he had to give grudging approval to these daring tactics. Strip Leibowitz' opening of all dramatics, take the sugar-coated verbiage away from the legal skeleton which it covered, and this is what remained. Leibowitz was saying in effect, "Dooley was completely insane when he fired the shots. Some weeks before the killing Dooley began to go mad. It was a progressive growth which culminated in the killing of Edwards." This was a complex defense, because Leibowitz would have to produce witnesses who could testify as to Dooley's gradual mental degeneration. If some of his fellow cops (Neary knew by now they were all for Dooley) testified that they knew Dooley was acting irrationally days, even weeks, before the actual shooting, Neary could impeach them by saying that they should have reported this irrational conduct to their superior officers; he would accuse them of dereliction of duty in allowing an insane man to walk a beat in uniform and with a gun in his holster. Yet, because of the facts, Leibowitz was committed to this defense.

Were there weak points in this defense? Well, Neary might say, "If Dooley went completely berserk, explain his excellent marksmanship. He fired five shots; four of them hit vital spots. If he was in a maniacal frenzy and drunk in addition, explain how he was able to shoot so well. Only a cool, calm man could handle the heavy police gun with the deadly efficiency Dooley displayed."

Leibowitz worried about another point which Neary might be able to make. Neary might say, "After Dooley shot Edwards, his wounded victim ran. Dooley pursued him. The first shot might conceivably have been the result of an emotional crisis contributed to by his monumental brainstorm, but the pursuit and subsequent shots showed grim determination to kill Edwards. Dooley knew what he was doing, all right."

83

The case might well hinge on the interval between the first and fifth shots fired by Dooley. His first shot had hit Edwards in the chest, his second had struck Horan. Then there was an interval of a few seconds before Dooley had fired three more shots at the dying Edwards, who lay on the sidewalk. Neary would claim that this interval showed cold-blooded premeditation. Leibowitz would contend that these additional three shots were evidence of his "mad bull" theory. A tortured, suffering bull who gores and kills a matador will still be dominated by his wild rage and will blindly continue to attack his already lifeless victim. It became evident that the jury would have to accept one of these interpretations, and Dooley's life would depend upon whether Neary or Leibowitz could persuade the jury that his viewpoint should prevail.

Neary presented his witnesses one by one, and Leibowitz, to the amazement of the reporters at the press table, only gave them perfunctory cross-examinations. Leibowitz was courteous with Michael Kreger, a gardener who had heard the shooting; he treated Judge Charles Zimmerman, another witness, with great respect, and when Claire Edwards, widow of the Mayor, finished testifying, he merely said gently, "No questions, Mrs. Edwards." Then Detective James Horan, just out of the hospital, took the stand. Under the adroit questioning of Neary he told the story of the shooting and told it well. Pale, obviously weak and shaky, his voice faltering when he spoke of the slain Mayor, Horan created a fine impression. Then Leibowitz went to work. His cross-examination was pitiless, and within five minutes he had Horan writhing with embarrassment and anger.

He made Horan admit that he was in fact the Mayor's stooge; he drove his car, ran errands for him, bought cigars and cigarettes for him. He admitted that he had never been interested in the P.B.A. until a few months before the election in which he had ousted Dooley. He had only attended a few meetings during his twelve years on the force.

"Then the Mayor put you in that job to act as his stooge, didn't he?" Leibowitz thundered. Neary objected and the court sustained.

"Did you talk to the Mayor about the twelve thousand dollars in the P.B.A. treasury," Leibowitz asked. Horan denied that he had ever mentioned the amount in the treasury.

Horan at first denied that Edwards had done any active campaigning, but finally, under Leibowitz' relentless questioning, he admitted that Edwards had finally come into the open as his supporter. The questioning was merciless, but Horan, trying desperately to preserve the good reputation of his late boss, had been foolish enough to fence with the cross-examiner and to tell half-truths. Leibowitz finally made him admit that Edwards had brought the cops into his office one by one and had told each of them that if Horan were elected he (Horan) would be in a position to "help the boys."

"Help them protect the gambling joints?" Leibowitz asked, but Neary objected to that. Neary in fact complained bitterly to Judge Johnson that Leibowitz was virtually making Horan his own witness (which is exactly what Leibowitz was doing). Leibowitz hammered away at Horan for another hour, and before he was finished, it was apparent that pressure had been put on the cops to force them to oust Dooley. Leibowitz, through a hostile witness, had been able to generate considerable sympathy for Dooley. In addition, he had prepared the minds of the jurors for the testimony of cops who would later be defense witnesses and who would testify to the hounding of Dooley by the Mayor and Chief Begly. Horan finally collapsed on the stand and had to be excused.

"I am sorry if I have said anything to bring you to tears, Mr. Horan," Leibowitz said.

Neary introduced the interrogation of Dooley by detectives and an assistant district attorney. After the shooting, Dooley had given himself up and he was taken from the Long Beach station house to the Mineola jail. During that drive the detectives questioned him and a stenographer took down the conversation. Many of Dooley's answers were incoherent. He blasted Edwards and Chief Begly in the most vile language imaginable. He characterized Begly as a "Philadelphia pimp" and Edwards as a "Jewish Hitler." He expressed satisfaction at having killed Edwards. Why had he done it?

"His Royal Highness came out of the house and said, 'Hello, Alvin,' or some such to me, and then Jesus, I just went whacky. I don't know what the hell I said. He didn't have any use for a cop," Dooley rambled on, "and he didn't have use for me in particular, so I just went nutty and let him have it. I didn't mean to shoot Horan, I only wanted to shoot the ——— Mayor. I'd rather die in the chair than take this continual hounding."

Q. When did you decide to shoot the Mayor?
A. When he gave me that phony "hello." I was no dog. I was with the men. I was president of the P.B.A. I never got anything out of that except the honor. That's all I wanted. That was enough.
Q. Did the Mayor say anything to you after you shot him?
A. Yes, he lay there and he yelled at me, "You son-of-a-bitch."

Nathan Birchall was the police stenographer who took down the questions and answers as the car sped from Long Beach to Mineola, the county seat. Dooley did not know that his answers were being recorded and he laid bare in the most violent and profane language (language no one had ever heard him use before) his feelings toward Edwards and Begly and how they had hounded him. When Birchall finished reading his transcribed notes and had been turned over to Leibowitz for cross-examination, the defense lawyer handed him a newspaper photograph taken of Dooley as he was leaving the Long Beach police station. This was about forty minutes after the slaying. The picture had been taken by Joseph Costa, ace photographer of the *New York Daily News,* and published in that paper. The photograph showed Dooley with staring, empty eyes and horribly contorted face.

"This is how Dooley looked that morning?" Leibowitz asked.

Birchall studied the picture, considered a moment and answered, "No, I wouldn't say he looked like that."

Leibowitz introduced another picture taken by Jesse Strait, crack lensman of the *Daily Mirror.* Birchall denied that it was a good likeness of Dooley as he had appeared on that fatal morning.

Neary then ended the people's case. He had not called his two psychiatrists, Shuffleton and Hoffman. It was obvious that he would save them to use as rebuttal witnesses after Leibowitz had put his de-

86

fense psychiatrists on the stand. Neither Neary nor Leibowitz was missing a trick in this courtroom battle. Each was at his brilliant best, and Judge Cortland Johnson, knowledgeable, completely fair, supervised the legal duel the way a really great boxing referee handles a championship fight. The fairness of the court and the brilliance of the two opposing antagonists is evident in every one of the 1182 pages of the trial record. No trial lawyer could read that record without learning something about his profession he didn't know before; no law student could read it without the excitement one must feel at watching two champions in action.

Leibowitz moved for a dismissal of the murder in the first degree indictment on the ground that the prosecution had failed "as a matter of law to prove premeditation and deliberation as required by the statute defining first-degree murder." He asked that the charge be reduced to murder in the second degree. Judge Johnson denied the motion and then Leibowitz began his parade of defense witnesses. He began by calling photographer Joe Costa, who testified that the picture he had taken was a perfect likeness of Dooley as he was forty minutes after the shooting. Now Leibowitz had opened the door for the introduction of the picture as evidence, and he passed it to the jury box. The men (there were no women) examined the picture intently. To a layman it certainly looked like the picture of an insane man.

The picture had been shot through the window of the car in which Dooley was taken to Mineola. Neary tried to make Costa admit that there is a certain distortion when a picture is taken of a subject who is behind a glass window. Costa was on firm ground now. He had been a photographer for twenty years and there was little about the technical side of the craft he didn't know. He explained that there was no distortion, "that is how Dooley looked."

Emma Dooley, the sad-faced mother of the defendant, was the next witness. She testified as to the great love that existed between herself and her son. Never in her life had she ever heard Alvin swear, she said emphatically. He must have been completely out of his mind when he had used that awful language in his confession. She told how Alvin had changed as the campaign to oust him as president of the P.B.A. gathered momentum. He began to drink heavily, something he had never done before. He had always been a happy-go-lucky extrovert. He became a sullen, quiet, suspicious man, tortured by fears and insecurity. Leibowitz led her gently through the weeks preceding the murder and finally brought her to the early morning of November 15. She was worried about Alvin. She couldn't sleep until he was in the house.

"I waited for him," Mrs. Dooley said softly. "About half-past four in the morning, I heard a voice outside saying, 'You are all right now, Al.' I was on the second floor at the head of the stairs. I heard Al go into the downstairs bathroom and then I heard a fall and then nothing else. I woke my husband and my daughter and told them about it. They went to help Al. I didn't go because I knew Al wouldn't want me to see him in that condition."

"What happened then?" Leibowitz asked gently.

"They helped him up and then started getting him upstairs to his room, and Al kept saying, 'I am no good, Pa. I am a failure. Let me go. I'm a failure.' Finally they got him into his own room. It was about five o'clock now and Al had to check in at eight. I lay on my bed, clothed, and waited, and then at five I got up. I went to Al's room and tried to get him up. I shook him to wake him and he said, 'Get out of here. Get out of here.' Then he turned on me and said, 'You are all to blame. You are all to blame.' I said, 'Oh, Al, I ain't to blame.' I went to the kitchen to get breakfast and then I heard Wilbur—that's my youngest son—talking to Al. I went into the living room where they were talking."

"What did Alvin say to you?" Leibowitz asked.

Emma Dooley put a handkerchief to her eyes. "He said, 'Get out of here. I'll kill you.' I ran to my bedroom and knelt down and prayed to the Sacred Heart. I said, 'If you ever helped me, help me, dear dear Lord.' Then I went into the living room and I said, 'Stay home today, Al,' and then Al came at me with his hands outstretched, clawing at me. It was like he was going to kill me, as if he wanted to choke me. His hands. His hands."

"What happened then?"

88

There wasn't a sound in the courtroom. Even Neary was listening sympathetically as this mother, made eloquent by her sincerity, went on.

"I ran away," she sobbed. "I was afraid of him—my own boy. He was crazy. The drink had made him crazy. He went into his own room. He had a lot of bottles there; hair lotion and tonic and things on his dresser. I heard glass breaking. Al had smashed the bottles against the wall and made a big hole in the wall and the plaster had fallen on his bed."

"Look at this picture taken two days later," Leibowitz said. "Is that how Al's room looked after he had smashed the bottles?"

Emma Dooley looked at the picture and nodded. The picture which Leibowitz had ordered taken showed the bedroom in great disarray, with a gaping hole in the wall where the plaster had crumbled. As often, pictures were an integral part of Leibowitz' defense tactics, as he always believed that a jury could see better than it could hear. A picture was worth a thousand words of testimony. The jury could not disbelieve this picture. It brought up a vision of a madman, intent only on senseless destruction.

"Finally Al ran out and got into his car," Emma Dooley continued. "My boy Wilbur tried to stop him but he got away. He drove off and Wilbur and my daughter Hortense got into her car and went after him, but they lost him in the traffic."

By now the jury was getting a new conception of the defendant. It was impossible not to believe this mother when she told of the gradual disintegration of her son under the hounding of Mayor Edwards. Nothing Neary was able to do on cross-examination caused Mrs. Dooley to change a word in her testimony. She had told the truth as she saw it and she answered every question freely—but changed nothing.

Wilbur Dooley merely strengthened the impression his mother had made.

"He knew he was being railroaded out of his job as president of the P.B.A.," Wilbur said, "and he brooded about it. He became a different man. It got so he looked at his own son like he was a stranger."

"Did Al ever use vile, profane language at home?" Leibowitz asked.

"Never," Wilbur said emphatically. "Even when he and I went out to have a few beers he might say 'damn it,' but that's all. And at home he never even said that. Not in front of Mother. He worshipped Mother."

Wilbur worked on the night shift at the *Herald Tribune*, and he had reached home about seven on the morning of the shooting. He had fallen asleep only to be almost immediately awakened by hearing Al "stumbling around." He tried to quiet his brother.

"He kept repeating, 'It's all gone, it's gone. I'm crazy, Bill,' and he sat on the sofa beating his head with his hands," Wilbur testified in answer to Leibowitz' questions. "I said to him, 'Al, you got a load on. You'll get over it,' and then Mother walked in and Al raised his hands and rushed toward Mother as if he was going to hit her, and I grabbed Al from behind and we both fell onto the sofa. Then I motioned Mother to get out of the room. Al suddenly said, 'I'm a cop and I got to get to work,' and he went to his room. Before I could stop him he had smashed all the bottles and then hurled his cop's billy at the wall. I told him I'd go and tell them at Headquarters that he was sick and couldn't check in, but he wouldn't listen to me."

"Would you say he was drunk?" Leibowitz asked.

"Either stone blind drunk or crazy," Wilbur said bluntly.

Neary couldn't do much with Wilbur on cross-examination because, like his mother, Wilbur only had to tell the truth. Leibowitz then put three policemen on the stand in quick succession. They completely corroborated the charges which Leibowitz had made against Edwards in his opening address. They testified that Edwards and Begly had put pressure on them to oust Dooley. They told of how Dooley had changed. They testified as to his strange behavior at the Police Conference meeting on the night of November 14, and of the great amount he had drunk.

"His eyes were glassy and stary," Sergeant Bertram Wolff testified. Patrolman Christopher Hannon said, "A few days after the election that Horan won, Dooley and I were assigned to a patrol. We were together for eight hours and he never opened his mouth. I'd say something to him and he'd look straight ahead and not even answer me." Patrolman Lincoln Murphy said he was talking to Dooley two days before the shooting, and when he offered his condolences about Dooley losing the election, Dooley began to cry. "I couldn't imagine a man like him crying," Murphy said thoughtfully. "His eyes were sort of wide open. He wasn't rational."

"Didn't you think it your duty to report this irrational behavior of Dooley's to your superior officer?" Neary asked on cross-examination.

"I did not," the witness said calmly.

Joseph Dooley, aged ten, was the next witness. He was dressed in his Sunday clothes, and his dark hair was slicked down—but he had a black eye. He explained that he had gotten that the day before when one of his playmates had made a derogatory remark about his father. He had taken a punch at the kid and the kid had punched back. The jurors looked with sympathy at this attractive youngster who seemed so small in the big witness chair.

"I wouldn't be surprised if Leibowitz gave him that shiner," a reporter wisecracked to his colleagues at the press table.

"He didn't have to," another said. "This is typical Leibowitz luck."

Young Joseph told of how wonderful his father had been to him. Judge Johnson, kind and understanding, occasionally prompted the boy.

"He played with me and helped me with my homework," the boy said. "And he always fixed my bike when it broke. Then something happened and he acted different. He didn't play with me any more. He wasn't happy any more."

Leibowitz asked him what had awakened him on the morning of November 15.

"I heard a lot of glass breaking," the boy said. "Like bottles being thrown. I was afraid and I stayed in bed."

Leibowitz excused the boy. Alvin Dooley, who up to now had

managed to control himself, broke down completely. Tears rolled down his cheeks and Leibowitz pressed a sympathetic arm around him and soothed him. None of this was lost on the jury.

Dr. Clarence Bellinger was the next defense witness. He said he believed that Dooley was the victim of a "paranoid trend coupled with pathological intoxication." Leibowitz propounded a lengthy hypothetical question in which the witness was asked to assume that all the evidence as presented by defense witnesses was true.

"Based on that assumption, can you state with reasonable certainty whether or not Dooley, at the time he shot Mayor Edwards and Horan, was suffering from a defect of reason?" Leibowitz asked.

"In my opinion, yes," the physician answered.

"Would you say he was crazy when he attempted to strike his mother?"

"I would."

Anticipating the cross-examination that would follow, Leibowitz asked the psychiatrist if it were possible for a man in such a pathological condition to "turn into a wild animal and run amok and still be able to remember things that had happened." The witness said that was quite possible.

Neary cross-examined for three hours, but Bellinger stuck to his guns. He insisted that if the story of the events of the early morning of November 15, as told by the defendant's mother and brother, were true (and he said he believed them to be true), then Dooley was most definitely insane and "laboring under such a defect of reason as not to know the nature and quality of his acts and not to know they were wrongful."

"Why wasn't this killing a simple matter of revenge?" Neary asked—and this was one of the few mistakes Neary made in the entire trial. He forgot that Leibowitz always anticipated questions to be asked on cross-examination and that he discussed such possible questions with his own witnesses. Bellinger's answer was a severe blow to Neary's whole concept of the murder.

Bellinger answered, "If he had merely wanted to injure Edwards out of a feeling of revenge, he hardly would have picked a time when Edwards was accompanied by his bodyguard in broad daylight."

Several members of the jury nodded in agreement. Neary said curtly, "That is all," and then Dr. Thomas S. Cusack took the stand.

Cusack was a large, florid-faced man with a heavy Irish brogue and a friendly smile. He had the knack of apparently taking the jury into his confidence, and no jury was proof against his expansive charm. He never used difficult medical terms. His conclusions, he said, were the same as those of his colleague. Dr. Cusack lectured to the jury as though they were a class of students and he their professor. At times the spectators chuckled as he explained the psychiatric terms in laymen's language, and even Judge Johnson smiled appreciatively. Neary didn't smile at all. Cusack was making an excellent impression on the jury by his avoidance of overtechnical terms.

"When the Mayor greeted Dooley with a smile and a 'Hello, Alvin,' Dooley interpreted this as a sneer," Cusack said, "and the door of his mind became unhinged. He was like a wild bull then, the mad bull going after the red cape. After the shooting he entered into a twilight state—not a complete return of sanity. At the station house he attacked the man in charge and then, during the drive to Mineola, he was in a state of exaltation. The alcohol in his system was being oxidized by now. The obscenity, the scurrility, are well-known symptoms. He had peaks and valleys of degrees of insanity that morning. At times that morning he acted as an automaton. He knew he had to report for work. He did that even though he was drunk. He went to the police booth automatically; as a cop he had done this sort of thing hundreds of times, and it was a habit with him. When a bull kills a man he keeps goring him, and then he steps back and wags his tail. Dooley was like that after his insane killing of Edwards. He stepped back and looked for someone who would take him to the station house. This is like the bull stepping back and wagging his tail."

On cross-examination, Neary showed an astonishing technical knowl-

93

edge of insanity, but he found it difficult to trip the calm, perfectly composed physician. Neary quarreled with his description of Dooley as a wild bull, and he asked sarcastically if Cusack had ever seen a bullfight.

"Many many times," Cusack answered calmly. "In France and in Spain."

Neary asked him some questions about bullfighting, and, nothing loath, the doctor launched into a dissertation on bullfighting which fascinated the spectators and the jury. Leibowitz sat at the defense table, smiling contentedly. This jury was liking Cusack; like a man and you are apt to believe everything he says. Cusack was putting on a splendid show for the jury, all of which would react in Dooley's favor. In his opening speech Leibowitz had stressed the "mad bull" which Dooley had become. He had used the expression "mad bull" a dozen times while questioning witnesses, and had cleverly led them to use the same expression. He had learned at dinner that night that Cusack happened to be a real *aficionado* of the bull ring. Leibowitz had hoped that when Cusack got on the stand to make his analogy, Neary would question his competence to discuss the psychology of the bull. Neary had fallen neatly into the trap, and now all of Leibowitz' strategy was paying off. Cusack was vastly entertaining as he explained what it was that so enraged a bull in the ring.

"The picadors and the matadors wear bright red coats," Cusack said. "This attracts the bull's attention. He sees red, to use the colloquial expression. The color scheme has that effect on the bull. It enrages him."

Neary interrupted to ask sarcastically, "Do you mean to tell us that the bull has a sense of color?"

"Certainly I do," Cusack said blandly. Neary, realizing that further questioning along these lines might only generate more sympathy for Cusack, dropped the subject.

When Dr. Cusack stepped down, Leibowitz raised his hand to the bench and said, "That is our case, Your Honor."

"The defendant rests?" Judge Johnson asked.

"The defendant rests," Leibowitz said.

Dr. Joseph Shuffleton, assistant superintendent at the Kings Park Insane Asylum, stepped up as a rebuttal witness. He said that although
Dooley was intoxicated at the time of the killing he was nonetheless
in full control of his faculties. Dr. Shuffleton disputed the defense
testimony (Bellinger and Cusack) that Dooley had been in a state of
insanity during the furor at his home on the morning of the killing.
"He knew it was time to report for work," Shuffleton said. "He
knew enough to put on his uniform, including his gun, and drive
to the station house. And he knew enough to drive to the booth to
which he had been assigned."

Leibowitz was scathing in his cross-examination. But first he asked
Shuffleton what he thought of Dr. Bellinger. The witness said that
Bellinger's reputation was that of an honest, capable psychiatrist. Shuf-
fleton also approved of Cusack as a fellow physician.

"There is apparently a difference of opinion between you and
these two doctors on the case?" Leibowitz asked.

"That is true."

"You do not believe that their opinions are motivated by dishonesty, do you?"

"No, sir, I do not."

"They each got $150 to examine Dooley and testify. Do you
think that either of them would commit perjury on this witness
stand for $150?"

"I do not," Shuffleton smiled.

He stopped smiling when Leibowitz began to probe into how he
made his income. It developed that Dr. Shuffleton had testified in
Nassau County criminal cases thirty-three times during the past seven
years. Leibowitz inquired if he considered himself a "professional
testifier." Shuffleton protested furiously, but Leibowitz handed him a
paper listing each case in which he had testified and the substantial
fees he received.

Leibowitz shifted now to the evidence he had given as to
Dooley's state of mind on the morning of the murder. He drew an
admission from the witness that insane patients even in the violent

ward at Kings Park Asylum were able to dress themselves, to tell time and report for work punctually; other patients there drove cars and acted as clerks behind the counter in the hospital general store. Shuffleton stepped down and Neary must have known that the doctor hadn't helped his case any.

Dr. Richard Hoffman was Neary's next witness. Urbane, handsome, educated, a wily veteran of the witness chair in many sensational trials, he was to be the "clean-up hitter" in Neary's psychiatric batting order. He would be asked only a few simple questions by Neary on direct examination, and each he would answer in the affirmative: Was Dooley sane, in Dr. Hoffman's opinion? Did Dooley know what he was doing? Did he know at the time of the slaying that to shoot Mayor Edwards was wrongful? Neary expected that on cross examination Leibowitz would step into the trap of asking the doctor "the why's and wherefore's" of his conclusions. But he reckoned without his adversary.

Leibowitz knew that Dr. Hoffman was a clever, articulate man who would hardly blunder into a damaging admission and who could hold his own in a battle of wits. To tangle with a Dr. Hoffman or with any astute expert witness on technical or theoretical issues might be playing with dynamite. Leibowitz believed all the time that he could break down the doctor's conclusions, since he was quite confident the facts were on his side and could be made to stand up against the witness's opinions. But to put the issue to test would mean giving Dr. Hoffman an opportunity and a forum to display his erudition. His demeanor alone might impress the jurors. Worse still, it might obscure the vividness of the Shuffleton debacle. Leibowitz had pitched to Dr. Shuffleton and "struck him out." Why pitch to the heavy hitter? Wouldn't it be better to give Dr. Hoffman his "base on balls" and leave him stranded on first?

The wise trial lawyer always *lets well enough alone.* There is an art in knowing when *not* to cross-examine. Leibowitz' strategy, therefore, called for serving up "four wide ones." The four questions he threw in the direction of the witness had utterly no relevancy to the subject of psychiatry and in a second or two the witness was waved off the stand. As far as the jury was concerned, the brilliant Dr. Hoffman might as well have not wasted his time and erudition.

96

Leibowitz spent four and a half hours summing up. The *Nassau Daily Review Star* reported it this way:

Employing a startling change of pace varying from a whisper inaudible the width of the courtroom to a shout rising sometimes almost to a scream, Leibowitz slashed at some of the state's witnesses, took statements of others that he considered favorable to the defense and wove them into a pattern that he told the jury could indicate only one thing, that Dooley could not be held responsible for the crime.

Leibowitz turned, walked over to the defendant, and placed his hand on his shoulder.

"There's a man, gentlemen," he shouted. "There's a man, a decent man sitting in that defendant's chair, a fine decent American. That man sitting there is not the Alvin Dooley who fired the shots that killed Mayor Edwards—that was another Dooley, a man changed by forces over which he had no control."

The lawyer discussed the political situation.

"Do you wonder why Long Beach in the past has been a stench in the nostrils of every decent citizen? Peddling pull! Peddling corruption! Mr. Neary didn't dare put Chief Begly on the witness stand; he didn't dare bring him into this courtroom. Do you know why? Because he would have been torn apart. They would have carried him out on a shovel."

He then went on to the insanity theory.

"It is hard for us here to figure out how a person could lose his mind over a little picayune thing like the presidency of the P.B.A. It is true that one with a strong, healthy mind would have survived it. But people do go crazy over disappointments, don't they? The asylums are full of them. If some of them hadn't found their way into institutions they might be sitting right in the same chair where Dooley is sitting now.

"Blow, blow, blow, blow, blow." Leibowitz accompanied each word with a rap with his fist on the rail of the jury box. "That was the way this continuous persecution wore down Dooley's mind. It was just like sandpaper rasping back and forth across human flesh until it was worn raw." The lawyer's voice rose. He paced back and forth in front of the jury box, rubbing the palm of his hand back and forth across his forehead. "Can't you see that sandpaper of mental torment rubbing against this man's mind until it finally wore through?"

Nearing the conclusion of his summation, Leibowitz took three two-foot-high enlargements of the pictures taken by newspaper photographers showing Dooley following his arrest at Long Beach police headquarters and pinned them on an easel facing the jury. One picture showed Dooley

97

with a contorted face, another laughing as police escorted him out of the station house, another scowling.

"If he looked like that two hours after the crime, I'll leave it to you gentlemen how he looked when he committed the crime," he declared.

In ending, Leibowitz said, "We don't want a compromise. A man may as well be dead in the electric chair as suffer living death in jail. I ask for a verdict of not guilty by reason of insanity."

Neary took two and a half hours to sum up. He demanded the electric chair for Dooley, contending that Shuffleton and Hoffman had been right in declaring that this was a murder for revenge and that the drinking Dooley had done was merely to bolster up his courage.

Judge Johnson gave the jury a fifty-five minute charge which was a brilliant capsule statement on the whole law of insanity and its effect on the responsibility of a defendant. He said that the jury could find any one of six different verdicts: first-degree murder, second-degree murder, first-degree manslaughter, second-degree manslaughter, not guilty, and not guilty by reason of insanity.

"You must not compromise, you must carefully consider the facts and see which of them fits the crime," the court said. "You have been called upon to determine what the truth of this situation is. You have been awarded the highest privilege given any man, that of sitting in judgment on the fate of another man. You must weigh the facts carefully and above all apply the common sense which you would exercise in your everyday affairs into the jury room with you."

The jury deliberated eleven hours and came in with a verdict of first-degree manslaughter. Dooley was saved from the chair. The jubilant Leibowitz thanked the court and jury for "its splendid treatment accorded me and the defendant," and he expressed appreciation to Neary for the manner in which he had conducted the State's case. Outside the courtroom, he gave fervent thanks to photographer Joseph Costa of the *News* and Jesse Strait of the *Mirror*. 'If it hadn't been for your pictures, the jury never would have believed that Dooley was insane that morning," he said gratefully.

It was obvious that the jury had believed his version and not Neary's. The verdict of first-degree manslaughter left the sentence to the discretion of the court. If the court wished, it could give Dooley a suspended sentence. It could also give Dooley the maximum—ten to twenty years. Public opinion, which had been so strongly against Dooley when the trial began, had now switched completely. The reporters who had covered the trial gathered in the same courtroom two days after the verdict of the jury to hear the sentence. Most of them thought Dooley would get a suspended sentence. No one felt that the court would be very severe.

Judge Johnson, however, sentenced Dooley to a term of ten to twenty years for the manslaughter, plus an additional five to ten years for being armed with a dangerous weapon (as is permitted by the New York State statute).

8

That is the story (not in such detail) Leibowitz told to students at New York University Law School.

"I say that Alvin Dooley, until he shot the Mayor, was a decent, law-abiding citizen, who in ordinary circumstances was no more capable of cold-blooded murder than any one of you in this lecture hall," Leibowitz said.

"It seems to me that the verdict contradicted the evidence in the Dooley case," a student said. "Why didn't that jury acquit him?"

"I was not in the jury room with the jurors when they deliberated. Therefore, I can't say. I can only surmise. Perhaps it was because of subconscious loyalty," Leibowitz said. "Each of us as we reach maturity acquires a great many deep-rooted habits. We may be unconscious that we have these. One of these is a respect for authority. Another is a desire to be respected by our neighbors and fear of criticism. To members of the jury, Edwards was the Mayor of Long Beach; he represented elected authority, and, as such, he had a right to absolute security. Edwards was not a vicious, evil man by any means. He was just an amateur politician, and, when circumstances put him into a position of some power, it went to his head. He was captain of the team and he wanted not only to call the plays but also carry the ball all the time. He failed lamentably in dealing with men who were under him, although he succeeded brilliantly in establishing human relationships with his family, his neighbors and members of his synagogue. But to the jury he was neither the arrogant tyrant who tried to dominate every municipal activity, nor was he the kindly husband and father, or genial club member he appeared to others. To the jury he was civic authority, and when Dooley killed him, Dooley was outraging one of their strongest feelings—respect for elected authority. Had Edwards been a businessman for whom Dooley worked, and had he persecuted Dooley in an effort to make Dooley quit his job and had Dooley broken under the tension, run amok and shot his employer, that jury, in the face of the evidence we presented before them, might have brought in a not guilty verdict. But Edwards was not an ordinary employer; he was the Mayor. I believe that the jury wanted to free Dooley but it didn't want to take the responsibility for putting a stamp of approval on his reaction to tyranny in an elected official. Always remember that at heart we are a law-abiding people who have a horror of killing, and who find it difficult to justify the taking of human life. The jury sympathized with Dooley; the verdict showed this sympathy. But I believe that the men on the jury just couldn't completely override their respect for the office of the man who was slain."

"You mentioned respect of the neighbors. How does that come into it?"

"The neighbors, too, had that same feeling toward authority," Leibowitz said. "Subconsciously perhaps, members of the jury were thinking of what Mr. Smith, next door, might say after the trial. Suppose they freed Dooley. Neighbors would chide them, 'So you allow drunken cops to go around killing mayors. It's a wonder you didn't give him a medal.' The desire to conform is a strong one among us Americans. Members of this jury had heard their neighbors attack Dooley before the trial, and these jurymen wanted to conform to general standards. That's another possible reason why they didn't bring in a not guilty verdict."

"Why didn't you put Dooley on the stand?"

"What could he have contributed?" Leibowitz smiled. "There is always a danger that even an innocent defendant on cross-examination will become confused and make an error damaging to himself, thus casting suspicion on his whole defense. Mind you, Dooley was completely cured by the time the trial opened. He was calm, rational, repentant. In fact, he was horrified at what he had done. But if he took the stand the jury would see a calm, healthy man, and it would have had trouble reconciling that Dooley with the irrational, maddened creature who had killed the Mayor. Dooley wouldn't have been able to explain his mental state on the day of the shooting nearly as well as the doctors could."

"If I were on that jury, I would have been convinced by Dr. Bellinger and Dr. Cusack," a student suggested.

"Perhaps," Leibowitz smiled. "The trial produced an excellent stage for a display of forensic psychiatry. As a rule defense and prosecution psychiatrists cancel each other out as far as the jury is concerned. Juries are suspicious of paid expert witnesses. One set says 'sane,' the opposing set says 'insane,' and the jury says, 'Oh, the devil with it, we'll use our own common sense.' A jury always has a 'show me' attitude. A juror can see an X ray of a broken bone, but he can't see a broken, twisted and distorted mind and he is hesitant to believe what he can't see. The jury did see the picture of a drunken, drooling Dooley and was impressed by it, but not impressed enough to free him.

"However," he added, "Dr. Cusack's lucid, down-to-earth explanation of the mad bull theory did have an effect on the jury and did, I believe, save Dooley from the chair—which of course was my primary object. Dooley's life may have been saved the night Cusack, Bellinger and I sat around the dinner table and by a happy chance started to discuss bullfighting."

Another student said, "There has been so much odium cast upon these courtroom spectacles where the plea is insanity, and one set of hired men bat for the prosecution and another set for the defense! What do you suggest as a remedy?"

"In these situations," Leibowitz replied, "there is so much room for honest disagreement as well as chicanery that to do away with the expert witness altogether is perilous. The state of a man's mind at a certain time can't be reproduced in court, like a written contract or a revolver, and that gives rise to honest controversy between opposing counsel and, for that matter, among medical men.

"My suggestion is that the court appoint a specialist, preferably one attached to a city hospital, to examine the prisoner and to testify at the trial subject to cross-examination by either the prosecution or the defense or both. Such an expert could be considered as a disinterested witness. Either side, of course, would have the privilege of calling its own expert witnesses as well.

"Place two painters side by side before the same landscape, and return a day later to see what each has on his canvas. You will find two landscapes so different that it will seem impossible that both painters were viewing the same scene. Yet you cannot say that either painter betrayed the truth. Which is the more faithful reproduction of the landscape? A jury of eminent art critics might disagree violently as to that. Often really qualified experts disagree. Consider Robert Irwin for a moment. I was convinced that he was mad by any medical or legal standard."

5. THE MADMAN . . .

"Tell us, pray, what devil this melancholy is, which
can transform men into monsters."

JOHN FORD, *The Lady's Trial*

Everybody wanted Robert Irwin to die.

The staid *Brooklyn Eagle* said editorially, "Everyone knows that
Irwin is insane but the killer should be wiped out. As we do have
capital punishment, electrocution is certainly indicated." The *Daily
News* presented its readers with a cartoon depicting Irwin with
bloodstained hands saying, "I am murderously insane, so spare my
life." In the cartoon, Justice answers by saying, "You are murderously
insane. For the sake of others I cannot let you live." Clergymen
thundered from their pulpits; doctors dropped scalpel for pen and
(at generous space rates) wrote columns explaining why Irwin should
forfeit his life. Assistant district attorneys, sob sisters of the press,
governors and senators and the man in the street all clamored for
his blood.

Everybody wanted Irwin to die. Had he lived two thousand years
ago he would have been stoned to death. Had he lived in the days
of the Inquisition he would have been torn to pieces on the rack.
Had he lived in the time of the Reformation he would have been
burned at the stake. But this was 1939. Why did everybody want
Irwin to die? Why did it take every bit of legal wizardry that
Samuel Leibowitz could command to keep the obviously insane Irwin
from the electric chair? Well, we have to go back a bit. . . .

The individual has always had a great fear of madness, and because collective society usually reacts in the same fashion as does an

103

individual, this fear has always been expressed in hatred. Throughout the ages anyone who deviated from what society felt to be the norm inspired contempt and hatred—seldom pity. In the early days society justified its attitude toward the insane by insisting that the devil had taken possession of the soul of such a one, and that only death could stop the evil that he or she might spread. The clergy, which heartily agreed, based its attitude on the famous text of the Mosaic law, "Thou shalt not suffer a witch to live," and through the centuries hundreds of thousands who were guilty of nothing but the illness called insanity were tortured and put to death. In the early days of our own country, witch burning had the stamp of approval of such supposedly enlightened scholars as Cotton Mather, who was one of the guiding spirits behind the prosecution of witches in the famous Salem trials of 1692.

Later, authorities on Talmudic lore revealed that when Moses apostulated his famous dictum he did not have in mind the mentally diseased at all. They insisted that the word Moses used and which was translated as "witch" actually meant something else. It was a word which in his day meant poisoner, a dabbler in spells, or a fortuneteller. It really meant a "criminal." In the time of Moses, there were many who trafficked upon the credulity of mankind by pretending to the power of divination. There were many false prophets, glib and persuasive, and they made a very good thing out of it. Some pretended to go into trances or fits and then speak with the voice of God—at so much a word. Some even went further. Some of these charlatans claimed to be able to cast spells and to cause death to an enemy, and if the price was right they could negotiate such a death easily enough and there was no one to order an autopsy to show the poison that dotted the spleen or rotted the intestine. Modern students of biblical lore, law and literature insist that it was these malefactors whom Moses had in mind. But King James VI of Scotland didn't have the benefit of modern interpreters of biblical law, and under his benign rule the trade of witch hunting assumed tremendous proportions. Historians have estimated that seventeen thousand witches were burned in Scotland alone between the years 1550 and 1590. They were accused of all sorts of crime

—real and imaginary—but there is no doubt that most of them were suffering from some form of mental disease.

Society, being afraid of them, hated them—and hating them, decreed torture and death. It wasn't until the nineteenth century that society realized that insanity was a disease that came to man entirely without the aid of the devil, and that it was no more a source of evil than scarlet fever or chickenpox. Hospitals for the mentally ill replaced the wheel, the rack and the stake. But even today, a generation which has had a chance to study Freud and Jung and Adler and Krafft-Ebing still retains a great deal of the prejudice and hatred for the man whose actions show that he deviates sharply from the norm. There is no doubt that hundreds who should have ended their days in asylums ended them instead in the electric chair or on the gallows. Juries hesitate to say that a defendant who has committed some particularly brutal crime is insane and not responsible for his acts, even though a first-year medical student would, without hesitation, certify him as hopelessly insane and not responsible for his acts. Buried deep within the heart of the average district attorney and juror (or ordinary citizen) there seems to be a memory of Moses crying, "Thou shalt not suffer a witch to live."

The law itself seems to suffer from the same deep-rooted prejudice. In English-speaking countries, the law regarding the responsibility of insane defendants was determined back in 1843 by the House of Lords in the McNaughton case. McNaughton, under the delusion that he was being persecuted by Sir Robert Peel, killed Peel's secretary. He pleaded insanity. This was the cause célèbre of the year, and it gave rise to so much discussion and argument that the Peers decided to ask the law lords to clarify the whole question of criminal responsibility. They asked the judges fifteen questions, and the answers to these have always been known as McNaughton's Rules.

In nearly every state (Massachusetts is one of the few exceptions) there are penal statutes based on the rules in that case, and they continue in general to be the law of the land. McNaughton's Case came before the Lords thirteen years before Sigmund Freud was born in Moravia. Freud opened the door to a new world of knowledge and understanding, but the law prefers to remain within the rigid confines of its ancient decisions and statutes. The law is like a man chasing a trolley car that always stays ahead of him. But whereas the man may get close to the trolley car, the law always remains a century or so behind the problems of the day.

In New York State the law, as far as criminal responsibility is concerned, operates within a self-imposed straight jacket called Section 1120 of the Penal Law. This statute was sired by McNaughton's Case, and district attorneys and most judges look upon it as holy writ and consider it sacrilege when defense counsel even suggests that it is not infallible. Section 1120 of the Penal Law of the State of New York says, "A person is not excused from criminal liability as an idiot, imbecile, lunatic or insane person, except upon proof that at the time of committing the alleged criminal act he was laboring under such a defect of reason as (1) not to know the nature and quality of the act he was doing; or (2) not to know that the act was wrong."

The word "wrong" has been interpreted in dozens of court decisions to mean "contrary to the law of the state." In short, the law based on statute and precedent says that a defendant, even though he is in the most advanced state of dementia paralytica, is responsible for a criminal act if at the time he commits the act, he is aware that such an act is contrary to the law of the state. His hopelessly warped and twisted brain may have generated an irresistible impulse to kill, so compelling that no knowledge or memory or man-made laws could stop it, yet he is still as guilty as is the cold, professional murderer who premeditates his act calmly and executes it for profit. In New York State, under the statute, a man who has been committed to an asylum as hopelessly insane, and who escapes from his place of confinement and while at liberty commits murder, can be held legally responsible for his act. Under Section 1120 the responsibility of the defendant is measured by the deprivation of understanding at the time of his act rather than measured by the defendant's general mental condition.

In 1915, brilliant Justice Benjamin Cardozo, realizing that the statute lent itself to ambiguous interpretation, tried to clarify it.

106

"We hold," he wrote in his opinion in the famous Hans Schmidt case, "that there are times and circumstances in which the word 'wrong' as used in the statutory test of responsibility ought not to be limited to legal wrong. If there is an insane delusion that God has appeared to the defendant and ordained the commission of a crime, we think it cannot be said of an offender that he knows the act to be wrong."

Cardozo pointed out that under the statute a defendant could not be excused of responsibility just because he was morally depraved or because he held views that were at variance with those that found expression in the law, unless this variation had its origin in some disease of the mind.

Psychiatrists have conflicting views on the legal responsibility of those who are mentally afflicted, so it is logical enough that judges, and district attorneys, too, don't often find themselves in accord. Many judges ask juries to use their "common sense" in determining the measure of responsibility expected of a mentally ill defendant. Unfortunately, the common sense that would enable a jury to give a fair decision as to ordinary matters of fact is no help at all when it comes to mentally ill defendants. Prosecution and defense counsel invariably call in expert witnesses to help the jury arrive at a decision, but these experts (eminent though they may be) as often as not find themselves in sharp disagreement. And the press and public, confused and afraid, in effect cry out, "Thou shalt not suffer a witch to live."

And that brings us to the case of Robert Irwin.

2

On Monday morning, March 29, 1937, readers of New York newspapers were told by screaming headlines that there had been slaughter on Fiftieth Street over the week end. They read that Mrs. Mary Gedeon, her daughter Veronica Gedeon and a bartender named Frank Byrnes had all been murdered the day before, which had been Easter Sunday. The mother and daughter had been stran-

5 killed

gled; Byrnes had been stabbed five times in the head by a sharp weapon—probably an ice pick. The nude body of Veronica (who was known as Ronnie) had been found on her bed, while the body of her mother had been found under it. Byrnes, a boarder in the Gedeon flat at 316 East 50th Street, had been killed in his sleep.

The bodies had been discovered by Joseph Gedeon, father of Ronnie (and a second daughter, Ethel) and estranged husband of Mary Gedeon. He was an upholsterer who lived alone in a furnished room, and he had decided to have Easter Sunday dinner with his family. He told the police that he had arrived at the apartment (actually it was a cheap, rather dreary, badly furnished, four-room flat) shortly before noon, and when no one had answered his knock he had walked in to find that the place had been transformed into a ghastly abattoir. Gedeon was a thin nervous man with a scrubby, untidy mustache, sparse untidy hair, and the wrinkled, leathery neck of a senile tortoise. He stood in the bedroom completely dazed, and then daughter Ethel had walked in with her husband, Joe Kudner. She too came there to have Easter dinner with her mother and sister. She notified the police, and within minutes the Homicide Squad was in control and the three bodies were hurried to the morgue to be examined by Dr. Thomas Gonzales, acting chief medical examiner of the city of New York.

The investigation was put into the able hands of Inspector John A. Lyons, who had done a brilliant job only a year previous in finding the bathtub murderer of Nancy Evans Titterton, slain just two blocks from the Gedeon flat. There was one witness to the triple slaying, but this was a witness who could not speak. The name of the witness was Tonchi, and Tonchi was Ronnie Gedeon's pet Pekinese.

The police estimated that Ronnie and Mrs. Gedeon had been killed about eleven o'clock on Easter Sunday eve, while Byrnes had died some four hours later. No one had heard Tonchi bark during the night, and police proceeded on the theory that the murderer had been someone known to Tonchi. Lyons knew something which most dog lovers don't know; he knew that the Pekinese is an intensely loyal, completely fearless dog who would resent the entrance

108

of any stranger into his home and would try to do something about it. A stranger might easily make friends with an English bulldog, a boxer, or a French poodle, but not with a Pekinese. The only thing that is small about a Peke is his size. Lyons was sure the murderer was an intimate of the family and known to Tonchi.

The newspapers presented an affecting picture of the beauteous model and sweet-faced mother who had been slain so brutally. They told of the grief-stricken husband and father, and they wept printed tears over sister Ethel, whose grief was so great that she had collapsed. Ethel too had been a model. It was a touching picture of a devoted, closely knit family that was presented to the public. The fact that Joseph Gedeon had left his wife and daughters some time previously was given only a once-over-lightly treatment, and the fact that he had come home humbly to break bread with his family on Easter Sunday was played up. The beauty of Ronnie and Ethel, both highly photogenic, was displayed lavishly by the papers and their devotion to their mother emphasized.

The police were a bit more realistic in their appraisal of the Gedeon family. With commendable restraint they refrained from issuing their appraisal to the press. But when their careful investigation failed to turn up any more obvious suspect, they were forced to the conclusion that Father Gedeon might have had something to do with the crime.

He was questioned for thirty-three hours, and afterwards claimed that he had been severely beaten by the police. (This was vehemently denied by Police Commissioner Lewis Valentine.) The walls of the furnished room in which he lived reflected his personality. They were covered with mirrors and pictures of nudes. He told detectives quite bluntly that he despised his wife and had nothing but contempt for his daughter Ronnie, who he said was "wild and undisciplined."

When neighbors repeated rumors that Mary Gedeon and roomer Frank Byrnes had a relationship that transcended the conventional one of landlady and boarder, the case against Gedeon as painted by the newspapers seemed even stronger. Had he killed his wife and Byrnes in a fit of jealousy and had he added Ronnie because his disapproval of her way of life amounted to a fixation? The newspapers more than hinted that this was the case, but Inspector Lyons became convinced that Gedeon was innocent, and he was finally released.

Ronnie earned her living by posing (with or without clothes) for illustrators, sculptors and artists. The newspapers, which had at first pictured Ronnie as an innocent twenty-year-old girl, soon had to revise their estimate slightly as Ronnie's own diary told its revealing story. Ronnie was a girl who liked a life of careless gaiety, who embraced quick, casual pleasures. She had been married once at fifteen, but the marriage had been annulled a few months later. (Ethel had been married at sixteen, but her first husband had committed suicide.) Ronnie confided many of her romances to her diary, and Lyons sent his detectives to interview every man whose name appeared on its pages. Police were not sure whether or not Ronnie had been raped before being killed. There was medical evidence that she had had intercourse, and there was further evidence that she had just recovered from the result of an abortion. However, the man she had been out with on Easter Sunday eve soon resolved the problem of criminal assault. He had taken Ronnie to a party and then they had gone to bed together. It was that simple. He had brought her home about 3:00 A.M. and he said that she had been a little the worse for whiskey. His evidence was so straightforward and verifiable that he was never considered as a suspect.

Although Joseph Gedeon had been released, the police still kept an eye on him. So did the staff of the *New York Daily Mirror*, which wanted "by-line" stories of those close to the case. They rented a nice room for Mr. Gedeon at the Murray Hill Hotel. They also brought daughter Ethel and her husband Joe Kudner to the hotel. For three days David Charnay of the *Mirror* staff entertained them. Ethel (seconded eagerly by her young husband) told Charnay he was silly to bother with a story by Joseph Gedeon; she herself would furnish the story and how much would the *Daily Mirror* pay?

By now Charnay, a capable, experienced reporter, began to wonder if there wasn't something in the idea that Gedeon was the villain in the case. Perhaps Joseph Gedeon was the murderer. If he could only get Gedeon to talk and eventually to confess, he'd have one of the finest exclusives any reporter had ever obtained. Charnay's boss was Managing Editor Jack Lait, who had once made a habit of tearing exclusive stories out of the Chicago underworld, and Charnay was in the Lait tradition. So Charnay went to work. He flattered Joe Gedeon; he ordered the best food and drink that the hotel could supply. Gedeon accepted the good food and drink eagerly, but he did very little talking. "Get him a girl," Joe Kudner said, and Ethel eagerly broke in, "He may talk to a girl."

Charnay made a few phone calls and soon a girl appeared. Charnay explained the situation to the girl. He wasn't asking the girl to go to bed with Joe Gedeon; he was asking her to talk to him, have a few drinks with him and try to make him open up. The girl, intrigued perhaps by the thought of being a female Dick Tracy, went into the room with Gedeon. She came out an hour later, white-faced and shaking. Gedeon had chased her out of the room.

Charnay persevered. He went to bed in the same room with Gedeon and feigned sleep, hoping that Gedeon might have nightmares or talk in his slumber. Charnay and Dick Sarno, his photographer who was always within call, were certainly giving their all for the *Daily Mirror*. Gedeon didn't confess, but he did sell the rights to his story to Charnay, and the reporter who hadn't slept for two days and two nights hurriedly wrote a piece, "By Joseph Gedeon," and sent it to the *Mirror* office. Ethel was furious at this and she insisted that she could give Charnay a better story.

Ethel liked to talk, and on one occasion she came up with a new suspect whom she vaguely identified as an Army officer. Ethel in fact talked about everything under the sun—except Robert Irwin. She never once mentioned his name to Charnay. Previously, when Inspector Lyons had questioned Ethel about men who had boarded with the Gedeon family, she had shrugged off mention of Robert Irwin. He hadn't stayed with the family very long, she had said.

3

On Sunday evening, April 4, seven days after the murder, Charnay, still at the suite at the Murray Hill, received a phone call from his office. The city desk told Charnay to hurry to the East Fifty-first Street police precinct, a break had come in the case. "But keep Joseph Gedeon on ice," the desk warned, "he may be the guy." Charnay by now had two extra men to help him. They amused Gedeon while he and Sarno went to the station house.

Then for the first time Charnay heard the name of Robert Irwin. The police announced that the bloodsoaked glove found in the room with the bodies belonged to him. They had found a piece of soap in the room and said it might be modeling soap. Witnesses had seen him in the neighborhood just before the crime. A diary of his had been found in which he had told of his love for Ethel and of his hatred for Ronnie and her mother. The diary was discovered in a rooming house at Canton, New York, where Irwin had lived while attending the theological school at Saint Lawrence University.

Irwin's diary revealed that his relationship with Ethel had not been as casual as Ethel had said. Of course the romance might well have been all one-sided, especially after Ethel's marriage to Joe Kudner.

Irwin wrote:

God, how I adore Ethel. Perfection. That's what she is. Absolute perfection. I could go out of my head when I realize that she is married to someone else.

If only Ronnie and her mother hadn't interfered. It has made a shipwreck out of me. . . . Girl of my dreams. Can't you hear the still small voice in the night. Can't you hear me calling to you with words of adoration on my lips and a song in my heart. Sex? It means nothing now. How I hate Ronnie and her mother for what they have done to me.

Inspector Lyons said that Irwin had been nominated as the killer by a process of elimination plus a few tangible clues. He had investigated every man who had ever boarded with the Gedeons and all had been cleared except Irwin. But it was the dead Ronnie who had really directed attention toward him through two entries in her diary.

In June, 1934, she had written, "Bobby [Irwin] is certainly making a play for my sister Ethel. I think he is out of his head. He will never marry her if I have anything to do with it. I am going to take the matter up with Mother. She will help put the kibosh on it."

A month later she wrote, "I am afraid of B. He has been hanging around the house since Ethel handed him a large dose of ozone."

Ethel, when questioned by Inspector Lyons, had dismissed the importance of Ronnie's remarks about "Bobby." She hadn't known him very well, she said casually. The police didn't dismiss Ronnie's gossip as lightly as perhaps Ethel might have wished. Thoroughly, painstakingly, ploddingly, they investigated the name "Robert Irwin," and gradually the name assumed substance and became a man.

Charnay rushed to the phone, gave the story to George McGuirk, the rewrite man on duty, and then hurried back to the hotel.

"A crackpot sculptor named Robert Irwin did it," he said to Ethel. "Why didn't you tell me about him?"

"Bob Irwin? I didn't think he had anything to do with it," she said thoughtfully. "He might have killed me but he had no reason to kill Ronnie or my mother. But I knew him all right and," she added brightly, "I can give you a swell story on him."

"Let's all go to the office and talk it over with the boss." By now Dave Charnay was beginning to wish he'd never been put on the story. At the office, Ethel, for five hundred dollars, agreed to do a series of articles. Dave Charnay and Jimmy Whitaker would "help" her write them. Thousands hung on every word that appeared under the by-lines of Ethel and her father Joseph. It was good writing. It was Charnay at his best and experienced Jimmy Whitaker at his best, and both were masters of their trade. Even husband Joe Kudner got into the act. He walked three blocks downtown to the *Daily News* office and sold his story there. His prose was shepherded through the typewriter by veteran news writer Terry Donoghue, and under Terry's deft touch it came out a lot better than it went in.

Now that the police had declared themselves and a nationwide hunt was on for Robert Irwin, everyone concerned agreed that Irwin had always been odd. And he had always been in love with Ethel. The entries about Irwin and Ethel in Ronnie's diary now took on added significance. Ethel coyly admitted that Irwin had been fascinated by her, but that their relationship had been intellectual rather than physical. Ethel not only "wrote" thousands of words about Irwin for the *Mirror*, but she did an equally lengthy series for a magazine called *Love and Romance*, which billed the series under the title, "What Robert Irwin Meant to My Slain Sister Ronnie and Me—by Ethel Kudner."

The hunt and the literature continued (even the lad who had been out with Ronnie on the fatal Saturday night sold his story to a tabloid at twenty-five dollars an installment), and now the figure of Robert Irwin began to emerge a bit more clearly. The police had backtracked his life and had questioned witnesses considerably more reliable than Ethel or Joseph Gedeon. They were doctors, teachers, hospital and asylum attendants and psychiatrists.

4

He was born Fenelon Arroyo Seco Irwin, a burden almost enough to wreck any mind. His father deserted the family when Fenelon was eight. Poverty became a permanent guest in the Irwin household after that, but although his two brothers were always in hot water, Fenelon had no record of juvenile delinquency. There was no money for toys, but the youngster found amusement in molding the bathroom soap into recognizable shapes. It wasn't long before he found that he could actually shape the soap into a head. This was about his only diversion.

His mother encouraged him to read and gave him stiff doses of the Bible. Later he began to read Robert Ingersoll, and his admira-

tion was such that he dropped his first three names and was thereafter known as Robert Irwin. His mother, horrified at his worship of
the infidel Ingersoll, increased her Bible dosage. She encouraged
Robert to carry a Bible with him at all times. (Howard Unruh,
who ran amok in Camden in September, 1949, and shot to death
thirteen people, always carried a Bible with him, and psychiatrists
who examined him said that he reminded them a great deal of
Irwin).

Economic necessity prompted Irwin to apply for admission into a
juvenile home when he was a youngster. He was happy there. He
was given clothes, three meals a day, and a kindly attendant obtained some clay for him. Now he could really practice sculpture. It
became the dominating passion of his life, with something he called
"visualization" running a fair second. When he left the institution
he became a wanderer. His obvious talent for sculpture prompted
the eminent Lorado Taft to take him on as a pupil for a time.

Irwin had arrived in New York in 1930. He was twenty-three
then. He took odd jobs which usually terminated with Irwin and
some fellow employee in a fight. He went to Bellevue Hospital in
1931 where he was treated for congenital syphilis (he displayed a
4-plus average). He was working at the Ettel Studios then as an
"assistant sculptor," but when he discontinued the Bellevue treatment his employer. Alexander Ettel, discharged him because "I
didn't want any of the young people working for me to catch it." He
then went to work for Elmer Rowland, a taxidermist, and "I liked
him. He was quiet and well behaved. I let him go only because of
the depression." He moved to Brooklyn, and some months later
went voluntarily to the Kings County psychiatric ward. He told Dr.
Samuel Feigin that he was afraid that he would either murder
someone or kill himself. He was kept there for three weeks and then
sent to the Burke Foundation (a convalescent institution) in
White Plains. When his time was up, he remained on as a waiter.
He met another waiter, Charles (Chuck) Smith, and became casually friendly with him. Later on Chuck Smith, all unknowing, would
act as the catalytic agent that would bring death to Mrs. Gedeon,
to Ronnie and to the obscure Frank Byrnes.

Irwin hungered for any association at all with art, so he quit his waiter's job and returned to New York, and to itinerant job hunting. In the fall of 1932, he found himself washing dishes at MacFadden's restaurant, and there he met Chuck Smith again. Irwin didn't have a room, so Chuck suggested that he come to his place and share his room. He went to the rooming house owned by the Gedeons and which they shared with their boarder. That night he met Ronnie, Ethel and Mrs. Gedeon, but there is no evidence to show that either Ronnie or Ethel made any impression on Irwin at all.

A day or two later, in the Gedeon bathroom, he tried to emasculate himself (with a razor blade). He went to the surgical emergency room at Bellevue Hospital and the intern on duty was shocked to see that Irwin's penis was deeply lacerated and bleeding profusely, despite a tight rubber band he had put around it to ease the pain and stop the flow of blood. Irwin pleaded with the doctor to finish the job of emasculation, but instead the medico sewed up the wound with seven stitches and sent Irwin to the psychiatric clinic.

It was there that Dr. Frederic Wertham, psychiatrist on duty, first met Irwin. Dr. Wertham has told of his study of Irwin in his magnificent book, *The Show of Violence*. Because Dr. Wertham recognized Irwin as a potential menace not only to himself but to society, he saw to it that Irwin was detained in the Bellevue mental ward for five months. Irwin improved but did not recover, and Dr. Wertham persuaded him to commit himself voluntarily to the Rockland State Hospital, an institution for the insane. After a month at the hospital he escaped, but was caught and put in Building 37, the violent ward. Doctors at Rockland diagnosed his case as dementia praecox, hebephrenic type. A year later he was paroled and went back to working at odd jobs in New York. He met his friend Chuck Smith again, and in retrospect it seems as though this third meeting had been arranged by some persistent and malignant fate. Once again he had no place to stay and once again Chuck suggested the Gedeon rooming house.

He moved into the Gedeon establishment late in June, 1934, and for the first time felt an almost overpowering urge for Ethel. There was no doubt that he had become obsessed with the landlady's daughter. In August, he went to Bellevue to see Dr. Wertham. He seemed to feel that the psychiatrist was the one man who understood him and who sympathized with him. He just wanted to talk about Ethel. Dr. Wertham did his best to calm Irwin down, but the sculptor went back to the rooming house, still troubled in mind.

In January of 1935, he again went to lean on the crutch of the sympathetic and understanding doctor. Dr. Wertham was seriously concerned with Irwin's condition now. Ethel had wearied of him and of his theory of "visualization," which he felt would eventually give him the secret of life and immortality. Irwin had for a long time been a devoted student of Schopenhauer and he had buried himself in the pessimistic, materialistic philosophy of the gloomy German. Wertham, more and more convinced that Irwin should be in an institution where he could be treated (he felt there was a possibility of a cure), persuaded Irwin to recommit himself to Rockland, and the confused, unhappy sculptor returned to the state hospital. There he remained for nearly two years.

Jeremiah Last had just graduated from the medical school of N.Y.U. He and several other young doctors, in the course of postgraduate work, visited Rockland. Irwin was working on a piece of sculpture and Last complimented him on it. Irwin, without the slightest provocation, immediately flew into a rage and leapt at the surprised doctor. "I backed away," Last remembered, "and it took several of my fellow students and an attendant to restrain Irwin. He kept roaring and shouting. He seemed to have unbelievable strength for a man of his build."

He was discharged from Rockland on September 25, 1936, as "improved," and on the advice of Kenneth Iles, a sympathetic attendant at the hospital, he applied for admission to the St. Lawrence Theological School at Canton, New York. Irwin had an amazing capacity for inspiring sympathy. More than one professor and student tried to help Irwin out during the six months he spent at St. Lawrence. They all knew that he had been in an insane asylum, but instead of repelling them this only made them more anxious to help the ob-

117

viously unstable twenty-nine-year-old student. Dr. Angus MacLean, professor of religious history, saw that his interest in sculpture was intense and sincere, and he allowed Irwin to use his own home as a studio. "He talked about starting a new religious movement," Dr. MacLean recalled, "but this seemed to me to be an emotional bubble arising out of acute personal needs. We arranged for Irwin to teach sculpture to a class of children. He fought with another student, Roy Congdon, over some fancied wrong and then, because of his irrational behavior, I made Irwin give up his class. His anger at the time, his language and his complete lack of control made it apparent that he had disqualified himself for work with children." Albert Niles, a student, said, "I liked Bob. Outside of sculpture his chief interest was in what he called 'visualization.' He had a theory that if he knew enough history he could project his mind back into the past and understand the conduct of historical figures. He was also greatly interested in Yogism. He was emotionally and mentally unstable."

Anders Lund was another student who befriended Irwin. "He had an idea he called 'communistic religion,' " Lund remembered. "It was a confused theory. He talked in chapel once, but after his first few sentences his rationality left him and with tears streaming down his face he walked from one side of the platform to the other in the grip of uncontrolled emotion. Dr. MacLean did everything he could to help Bob, but finally he could do no more. He said to me one day, 'That boy is crazy.' I knew that the ministry was not for Bob, and my fiancée, Eleanor Sheldon, thought she might get him a job at a New York art museum. Bob had worked for a taxidermist and might be useful in assisting with animal sculpture."

Dr. MacLean was now deeply concerned with Irwin's behavior and mental condition, and he brought him to see Dean John M. Atwood. This was Palm Sunday, 1937, just seven days before the triple murder. Irwin made wild charges against Roy Congdon and accused Dr. MacLean of being "against him." Dean Atwood tried to soothe him and suggested the he apologize to Congdon (who was completely blameless) and forget the incident. "Irwin jumped from his chair," Dean Atwood said, "his eyes gleaming. He revealed his antipathy for Congdon in uncontrolled, violent fashion. Then he left. I was worried. I wrote to Dr. Blaisdell, superintendent of the Rockland Hospital, stating that we were alarmed and raising the question as to whether or not a man liable to such irrational and violent antipathy was not dangerous."

Irwin hurried to New York, arriving on the morning of Good Friday. He went to the Gedeon home, but was told by Mrs. Gedeon that there was no vacancy. Then he found a furnished room at 218 East 53rd Street, and paid the landlady, Mrs. Phlug, a dollar for the night. With him he had two bags, and a package. The package contained a bust he had done of Marlene Dietrich. He went to Astoria to see William Lamkie, whom he had known when Lamkie was a patient at Rockland State Hospital. He told Lamkie of his trouble at St. Lawrence. "He was shaking," Lamkie said. "He was irrational. I could see everything was coming to a climax."

Then Irwin went to see Clarence H. Low, chairman of the Rockland State Board of Directors, who had been kind to him when he was an inmate. "He was intensely excited," Low recalled. "Very upset. He gesticulated wildly and talked incoherently."

On Saturday morning he changed boarding houses, getting a room at 248 East 52nd Street. That afternoon he met the kindly Eleanor Sheldon, who introduced him to her brother in the hope of getting Irwin a job, but nothing materialized. "He acted strangely and talked incoherently," she remembered.

That night he went to the Gedeon home. He went looking for Ethel but she never came. And so Ronnie, Mrs. Gedeon and the harmless boarder Frank Byrnes had to die. That is how the police figured it—and weeks later they were proven to be correct.

Inspector Lyons said to reporters, "This is no longer a criminal matter. It is simply a medical case. The man is stark mad. In my opinion he should be placed in an institution. It makes no difference whether he committed three hundred murders, so far as the State is concerned. His psychopathic background shows that he is insane. He must be picked up because he is a danger to the citizens of the community wherever he may be."

The weeks passed and there was no sign of Irwin. Meanwhile the police kept gathering concrete evidence against him. They found that the glove left in the room with the bodies was one of a pair that Irwin had bought. They found his two bags in the checkroom at Grand Central Station. Irwin had left the St. Lawrence campus wearing a dark suit, black coat and yellow scarf. Witnesses identified pictures of Irwin as a man they saw dressed similarly on the fatal Saturday in a small restaurant a block from the Gedeon home. The police found plenty of evidence—but they couldn't find Irwin.

And then on Friday, June 25, three months after the murders, Robert Irwin walked into the office of the Chicago *Herald and Examiner*, gave himself up and made a complete confession. Every newspaper in the country screamed triumphant headlines when the story was released.

And if the attitude of the press reflected the emotions of the public, it was apparent that everyone wanted the lovely model, the sweet-faced mother and the innocent boarder to be avenged. Everyone wanted Robert Irwin to die—including Irwin himself, who said grandiloquently that he was ready for the electric chair.

Leibowitz? Leibowitz didn't care much either way. This was June 25, 1937, and the Dodgers were trying desperately to get out of the second division. Manager Burleigh Grimes was storming at umpires and at big Van Mungo, his fast but unpredictable right-hander. Luke Hamlin was tossing a nice game now and then, and Freddie Fitzsimmons was fooling them occasionally with his deceptive knuckle-ball, but Leibowitz, like any devout Brooklyn fan, was worried. This was an old team and the hot weather had come and the hard-baked diamond was bothering the ancient feet of outfielders like Heinie Manush.

Irwin? If he could hit left-handers and play the balls that caromed off the right-field wall of Ebbets Field, Leibowitz would surely have been interested. But this was just another murder case. Leibowitz had already been counsel for the defense in more than a hundred murder trials, and had kept every one of the accused from going to the chair. He wasn't a bit interested in another killer named Robert Irwin.

Not until two days later—that was June 27, 1937.

6. . . . AND THE LAW

"There is pleasure sure,
In being mad which none
but madmen know."

JOHN DRYDEN

Robert Irwin walked into the news room of the *Herald and Examiner*, asked for a cigarette, and said, "My name is Robert Irwin." Within two minutes he was sitting in the office of Managing Editor John Dienhart. An hour later he had signed a contract which began:

> Universal Service agrees that if the undersigned Robert Irwin proves to its complete satisfaction and to the satisfaction of the police authorities that he is the Robert Irwin now wanted by the New York police in the Gedeon case and upon fulfillment of the terms of this agreement, a sum of $5,000 will be paid to the undersigned.

Front Page had come to life. In New York, Ben Hecht, co-author of the play, said with mock solemnity, "We ought to sue Irwin for plagiarism." In that play a criminal had turned himself over to Hildy Johnson, a reporter for the same *Herald and Examiner*, and the paper had tried unsuccessfully to keep the knowledge away from opposition papers. In real life this newspaper had better luck.

The terms of the contract provided that Irwin refrain from giving interviews to any newspapers other than the Hearst press for a term of two weeks. It called for a complete confession from Irwin. Irwin was happy to comply. He dictated and signed a full confession. Then smart John Dienhart rushed Irwin to a hotel and kept him incommunicado for twenty-four hours. When the story of Irwin's confession broke in the *Herald and Examiner*, opposition papers (and the police) were furious. A squad of detectives stormed into the newspaper offices looking for the sculptor, but found that their bird had flown. Finally the newspaper turned him over to Sheriff John Toman of Cook County. Police and opposition papers continued to lambaste the *Herald and Examiner* for its high-handed tactics. They lost sight of the fact that had Irwin not given himself up to the newspaper, he would still be at large, a menace to any community in which he found himself. They lost sight of the fact that keeping Irwin on ice for twenty-four hours in no way prejudiced justice or the eventual disposition of the case.

Everyone on the *Herald and Examiner* was kind to Irwin. Irwin still had the uncanny knack of inspiring sympathy in others. He said that he wanted the five thousand dollars to help his two brothers; one was in jail and the other Irwin thought to be a dope addict. Austin O'Malley, who was writing the lead story for the paper and for Universal Service (the Hearst syndicate) told Irwin that he could better spend the money for his defense.

"Maybe you can get Samuel Leibowitz," O'Malley suggested. "He's the best in America. I'll send him a wire if you wish."

Irwin agreed that would be a wise move, and O'Malley sent a wire to New York. As soon as the story broke the New York Police Department hurried Detectives Marty Owen and Frank Crimmins by plane to Chicago. The *Herald and Examiner* chartered an American Air Lines plane, and when it took off, New York-bound, it carried Irwin, the two detectives, Ray Doyle of the *New York Daily Mirror* staff, Austin O'Malley and Roy Howard, *New York Journal-American* photographer. It was a pleasant trip and Irwin chatted amiably enough with the detectives and reporters and Stewardess Bernadotte Andrel.

"He's a young boy," she said afterwards. "Nothing like his pictures. He was very courteous and nice to me." But Pilot Charles Allen said succinctly when queried by reporters, "He looked nuts to me." The plane landed at Floyd Bennett Field in Brooklyn. While driving to Police Headquarters in Manhattan they let Irwin read the New York papers. He read his Chicago confession and nodded with satisfaction. They had everything correct.

He must have been a little bit startled when he saw some of the other stories. The spotlight was right back on the Gedeon family. Under the heading:

BEREAVED GEDEON GLAD HE'S CAPTURED

the *Mirror* wrote:

Pain stabbed the blue eyes behind the old fashioned pince-nez. For a tortured moment the brows above them knit themselves and the lean lips set themselves to combat the shock. Then came a mist on the glasses, the face relaxed, and for a moment it looked as though Joseph Gedeon was going to weep.

"I'm free," he cried, and exaltation crept into his voice. "The cloud is gone. Now there will be no more staring, no more fingerpointing."

Ethel had resumed her literary labors and her ghosted story was headed:

HAUNTED SHADOW OF DREAD
LIFTED FROM ETHEL GEDEON

"Many a night," Ethel wrote, "Joe and I have dozed side by side, only to wake up and start at some little noise. Sleep would be gone and we would sit up in bed with the lights turned on looking at each other."

The Gedeons, father and daughter, with husband Joe Kudner, gathered at the home of their attorney, Peter Sabbatino, that afternoon to receive the press. Everything was fine until the photographers wanted to take a picture of father and daughter. Ethel gave the old gentleman a look of contempt and refused to pose with him. Then she left for the *Mirror* office to help Jimmy Whitaker write a brand-new series.

Irwin was hustled to Police Headquarters and brought to a room where Police Commissioner Lewis Valentine, District Attorney William C. Dodge and Inspector John Lyons awaited him. Detectives Owen and Crimmins brought Irwin into the room about midnight. At first Irwin refused to answer any questions. He looked at Dodge and said, "You can beat the Jesus out of me, you won't make me talk."

123

"We don't do things like that here," Dodge smiled. It was Detective Owen who explained Irwin's reluctance to talk. "Irwin thinks that his contract with the *Herald and Examiner* is so binding on him that he can't make a statement to anybody or the contract will be null and void and he will lose the five thousand dollars. This contract provides that he is not to give his story to any other newspapers (turning to Irwin). It doesn't mean that you can't talk to the District Attorney or to the police."

Dodge explained that all the police wished to know was whether the confession he signed in Chicago was a true confession. For two hours Irwin continued to evade direct questions. Finally Irwin started to speak of Dr. Frederic Wertham. He would like to see the doctor before he did any talking, he said. The police phoned Dr. Wertham and sent a car for him. He soothed the excited Irwin and advised him to answer all questions freely. To Wertham the sculptor was an unfortunate sick man—not a criminal—and by advising him to talk freely he unwittingly almost sat Irwin in the electric chair. At five-twenty in the morning, just as the first light of dawn was slanting into the shabby detective offices of Police Headquarters, Irwin let go and talked.

It was obvious that the confession he had made in Chicago was complete and truthful. As Irwin talked, Inspector Lyons must have had a feeling of satisfaction. Based on only a few clues and two diaries, his department had reconstructed a story of Irwin and the Gedeons which varied only in unimportant detail from the one Irwin was telling now. In his confession (repeated now under questioning) he told of his early life and of his hopes to gain immortality as a sculptor. He talked of his theory of "visualization" and of how he was beginning to master it.

In 1932 when I went to Bellevue and asked the doctors to emasculate me I had one thing in mind. The one driving impulse of a man's life was sex. I figured that if I could remove sexual impulse and put myself under pressure that I could solve that problem and get that thing done. All the time I knew there was one way out of it, that is by murdering somebody. If I were to do something like that I would put myself on a spiritual plane and make everything even.

124

I have nothing against anybody. First I was going to kill myself. Then I said to myself I was going to kill someone else.

He discussed his mental state on the Saturday of the slaying. He was penniless, out of a job and brooding over the unsatisfactory ending to his collegiate career. He walked down Fifty-third Street to the East River. He looked into the dark oily water and considered suicide. (This was the spot on which Sidney Kingsley based his play *Dead End.*) Then he began to brood about Ethel.

That night I said to myself, I am going up there and kill Ethel. I never intended to get anybody but her. I thought that after killing Ethel, then they will emasculate me.

He turned from the river and started to walk toward First Avenue. He saw an ice pick lying in the gutter and he picked it up and put it into his pocket.

I went to the Gedeon apartment. No one was home. Finally Mrs. Gedeon came home. She was very tired. She asked me if I would take her dog out for a walk. I took him for a walk around the block and brought him back.

I drew Mrs. Gedeon's picture to kill as much time as possible. Then in comes this little Englishman (Frank Byrnes). She introduced him to me. He went to his room. I took just as long as I could on that picture, and all of the time I was feeling her out about Ethel. She didn't tell me anything, though. She was holding out on me about Ethel and whether she was going to be there. She was holding out on me about Kudner and whether they had broken up.

Then I said that I wanted to see Ethel. She said, "Bob, Ethel isn't here, and it is very late." I said, "I am going to stay here until I see Ethel." All of a sudden she flew at me and yelled, "Get out of here or I'll call the Englishman."

Well, I hit her with everything I had. I choked her. I strangled her. All the time this damn Englishman was in the next room just ten feet away. She died right in the front of that room just ten feet away. She put up a hell of a fight. I can't understand why she didn't bring down the whole town on us. [Irwin didn't know that Byrnes was quite deaf.]

I had Mrs. Gedeon by the throat and I never let loose of that throat for twenty minutes.

She fell back on the floor with her legs back over her head and her

125

dress over her head. She was all bare. She scratched my face like nobody's business. When she was on the floor I knew what the damned dog's place was in that family.

My face was scratched. My hands were full of blood. I smeared it on her, on her face, and on her breast. I threw her in the bedroom under the bed.

Finally Ronnie came in. I was outside in the other room. She went into the bathroom and stayed there the longest time. I thought she was never coming out. I was in the first bedroom.

I went in the kitchen and got some ordinary soap and made myself a blackjack out of it with a cloth. Suddenly Ronnie came through the bathroom door, and I let her have it. The soap went all over the floor. It didn't have the slightest effect. I can very well believe that she was drunk because she didn't put any fight at all. (The autopsy on Ronnie showed a high concentration of alcohol.) I grabbed her by the throat and took her in the room. I did not attack Ronnie. I held her the longest time just tight enough so that she could breathe. I didn't know what to do. The Englishman could identify me, but I didn't have anything against Ronnie.

I kept Ronnie there until early morning holding her just so that she could breathe. She asked me not to attack her, that she had just had an operation. I didn't know what to do. I could wait to see if Ethel would come in. I disguised my voice as well as I could, but it wasn't enough. Finally she said, "Bob, I know you. You are going to get in trouble if you do this."

Then I strangled her. I ripped her clothes off. She didn't have much on, only a thin chemise. That wasn't the first time I had ever seen Ronnie stripped. I never had sexual intercourse with Ronnie. She went with a class of people who were way above me. She went with millionaires' sons and she didn't have any reason to be interested in me, except that I was interested in Ethel, but Ronnie occasionally messed around with me.

Ronnie asked me to sleep with her in July because she was very lonely. I never touched her any time. She stripped for me on another occasion. I gave her a bath once. I stayed with Ronnie for three nights when Ethel and her mother were away and she went around the house half naked. But it was no job for me to control myself with anyone except Ethel. She fooled around with me a lot though. She was a nice little brainless, blue-eyed blond, a beautiful fluffy thing.

I only used my hands, nothing but the pressure of my hands. I asked her where Ethel was. She said she was married to that kid Kudner. I held her a long time, at least an hour. I was holding her on the bed and

126

strangling her. Afterwards I went right out because she imme...
came the most repulsive thing I had ever seen in my life when ...
dead. It was like blue death just oozing out, a spiritual emanation
oozing out.

Then I went in and fixed the Englishman. I just went in and gave
it to him in the temple with the ice pick. I hit him once and he just
kept on twitching. I didn't want to kill him. My original intention
was to kill Ethel. When you get in a mix-up like that you don't think
what you are doing and time means nothing. The whole night seemed
just like a half hour to me.

After I put the Englishman out of his misery, I went in and took
a little clock and pictures that belonged to Ethel.

When I did that thing I never took any precautions. I knew I
left my glove there.

Whatever is coming to me I will take. When I went out of the
apartment, the last thing I did was to look around. The last thing
I said to myself then was, "Buddy, you did it."

If I don't get the chair and I go to an institution, I want a dollar
a week because with that money I can make someone work for me
to drill me on visualizing. I want to develop myself.

I killed Mrs. Gedeon because she caught me in a rage. I did it
before I knew it.

I killed Ronnie out of necessity.

I never wanted to get any one of them except Ethel.

I wanted to kill Ethel because I loved her and hated her. Even
when I knew her before when I made the bust of her I was going
to model her on a straight block, beheaded with her hair hanging
down and her eyes closed.

If Ethel had come in first I would have killed her and nobody
else, if she had come in while I was drawing her mother's picture.

I don't know whether it was hate or love that made me want to
kill Ethel. My choice was to either die or put myself under pressure.
If I did that won't be the end of it. That cycle comes back. These
people I killed aren't lost. Theirs are borrowed lives, and if I live I
will repay them. I only meant to borrow one life. I will repay these
lives by developing that power of visualization which is the next step
in the evolution of the human race.

My contribution to civilization will be along this visualizing line.
Ethel affected my life more than anyone else I had ever met.

Ethel worked for me a while in visualizing. She would say, "Can
you visualize an eye, an ear, a nose?" and I would. When she worked

as when anyone else worked with me. ...ork, and she got tired of it.

...sion. Questioning by Dodge and Lyons ...ded little in the way of new factual ... why he had gone to the theological ...rwin answered, "To lose myself in reli- ...mehow or other, with God's help, solve

When Dodge questioned Irwin about the clock he had taken from the Gedeon flat Irwin seemed to be embarrassed, ashamed. He was furtive in answering queries about the inexpensive clock. Dodge, his curiosity aroused, persisted.

Dodge. What was there about the clock that attracted you?
Irwin. Because I looked at the clock and saw the green lights.
Dodge. The luminous hands? Something about the clock that attracted you and you wanted it?
Irwin. It was not the clock. I had a clock. It was the green light . . . not the numbers . . . I don't know.

Neither the District Attorney nor the police attached any significance to the phrase, "It was the green light." That didn't mean anything to them at the time. Later that one sentence would mean a great deal. They let Irwin sleep for a few hours and then woke him to arraign him formally in Homicide Court. As he emerged from Police Headquarters a huge crowd booed and jeered. Women in the crowd shouted curses at the handcuffed prisoner. "Thou shalt not suffer a witch to live," society was saying.

Leibowitz met him at Homicide Court and conferred with him for ten minutes. Two days later Irwin was indicted for first-degree murder by the Grand Jury, which heard only seven witnesses.

"I expect to prove," Dodge said, "that Irwin was not insane at the time of the murder, and I will prove that he knew the nature and quality of his acts. I don't care a whoop what some of these psychiatrists say," Dodge added darkly.

Detective Frank Crimmins was one of the witnesses. He had sat with Irwin on the plane ride from Chicago, and he was asked what

128

Irwin had talked about. Crimmins told of the various conversations they had held while speeding toward New York. One of the questions Crimmins asked Irwin concerned the clock.

"The clock was in front of me as I strangled Ronnie," Irwin said (according to Crimmins). "Its dial shone. It looked like two green eyes. It fascinated me."

When the Grand Jury handed down the indictment Leibowitz, who by now had several opportunities to confer with his client, said simply, "Irwin is as crazy as a bedbug." The legal jockeying had begun. Henceforth this would be a battle royal between Leibowitz and Dodge. Dodge of course anticipated the insanity defense which Leibowitz would depend on, and he immediately took steps to puncture it before the actual trial was to begin. Somewhere in New York City there were twelve citizens, reading their morning papers, hurrying to work, returning home, reading their evening papers and discussing—as everyone was—the case of the Mad Sculptor (as the *Mirror* had tagged him). Dodge wanted these twelve men, whoever they were, to know about Section 1120 of the Penal Law, about "legal insanity," before the case came to trial. Dr. Russell E. Blaisdell, superintendent of the Rockland State Hospital issued a statement about Irwin. Blaisdell said that the defendant "suffered from a psychosis, but was legally sane." Dr. Wertham was called to the District Attorney's office. He told of his long association with the "patient" Irwin. He explained that he had been thrice instrumental in having Irwin committed to state institutions, and emphasized that Irwin had co-operated each time. Only a few months before the murders Wertham had delivered a lecture at Johns Hopkins Medical School. Its subject was "Catathymic Crisis." He had used Irwin as an example of a case of violence turned against itself in the form of Irwin's attempted emasculation. He emphasized that Irwin was typical of an unrecovered (uncured) case in which the pattern of violence (either against himself or against others) could be predicted. The lecture was published in the *Archives of Neurology and Psychiatry* (April, 1937). It said with certainty that a man like Irwin must inevitably indulge in violence. It seemed almost as though Dr. Wertham had been reading Irwin's confused mind, which of course is just what he had done.

"This man is not cured," Wertham had written. "He will break out again either in some act of violence against himself or others."

Had he been kept under supervision then, Veronica Gedeon, her mother and her boarder would have still been alive, Wertham said. This is what Wertham also told those who questioned him at the District Attorney's office. The following day Wertham was horrified to see the following in a New York newspaper:

ALIENIST BLASTS IRWIN'S INSANITY PLEA!

An alienist familiar with every intricacy of his warped mind dealt a crushing blow yesterday to Robert Irwin's insanity defense. A confidant of the mad sculptor during the turbulent period preceding the murder of the artist's model, the psychiatrist certified officially to the district attorney that Irwin was legally sane when he "borrowed" three lives on Easter Sunday. This was learned despite the secrecy of the district attorney's consultation with the psychiatrist. From Dr. Frederic Wertham, chief of the psychiatric division of the hospital's mental hygiene clinic, came this first official pronouncement of Irwin's legal sanity.

Dr. Wertham, in a rage, hurried to Leibowitz' office to deny the story. He and the lawyer had a long discussion about Irwin. Wertham explained his theory of catathymic crisis and told Leibowitz that Irwin's violence was inevitable. As he talked, Leibowitz had a mental picture of a jury listening to the erudite doctor, and he knew that a jury would be bewildered by the technical phraseology of the psychiatrist. "Catathymic crisis" would be nothing but psychiatric double talk to twelve ordinary men. Dr. Wertham had testified in the celebrated case of Albert Fish, the mentally diseased man who had killed and dismembered children. Leibowitz had felt that in the Fish case, Dr. Wertham had tried to stretch the law to fit the medical facts. But the law as a rule refuses to be stretched, and Fish had died in the electric chair.

When Wertham emphasized the inevitability of Irwin's committing violence, he was making out an iron-clad case for Irwin's insanity, but he was making out a medical, not a legal, case. The fact that Irwin had a propensity for violence so great that he could not control it excused him in the doctor's eyes. But Leibowitz, thinking in legal terms, saw only Section 34 of the Penal Law. By now he could recite verbatim every statute dealing with the legal responsibility of the insane. Section 34, which was headed "Morbid Criminal Propensity No Defense," read, "A morbid propensity to commit prohibited acts, existing in the mind of a person who is not shown to have been incapable of knowing the wrongfulness of such acts, forms no defense to a prosecution therefor."

Granted that everything Wertham said was correct, you still couldn't stretch the statute to excuse Irwin legally. Reluctantly, Leibowitz decided not to use the sincere and capable doctor as a defense witness. They parted with mutual respect but with little understanding. To Wertham, Irwin was a desperately ill patient; to Leibowitz, Irwin was a client in danger of getting the electric chair. He needed a legal, not a purely medical defense if he was to be saved.

Each day the papers carried interviews with psychiatrists and "experts" of all kinds to the effect that Irwin was legally sane and responsible for his acts. True, these pundits added solemnly, Irwin might be medically insane, but he was certainly legally sane. A layman might have asked, "Insanity is a disease—yet you say there are two kinds of insanity, medical insanity and legal insanity. Suppose I have pneumonia, which is also a disease. Are there then two kinds of pneumonia, medical pneumonia and legal pneumonia?" But at this stage of the game the opinion of a layman didn't count.

2

A brisk young man named Thomas E. Dewey had replaced Dodge as District Attorney now, and Dewey assigned Jack Rosenblum to handle the Irwin case. Rosenblum was a good lawyer, careful, painstaking. He was not, Leibowitz told himself ruefully, a man to make mistakes. Rosenblum wasted no time in launching his attack. He asked the court to appoint a lunacy commission to study Irwin and to make a report on his sanity. Two years later lunacy commissions were abolished in New York. But such commissions were part of the legal system in 1938.

The court, over the strenuous objections of Leibowitz, appointed a

131

lunacy commission to study Irwin and to make a report on his sanity. In New York, the conclusions of a lunacy commission were not binding on the court. Such a commission was in the position of an investigator, and it could be called into being by either prosecution or defense. Usually defense counsel asked for the appointment of such a commission, but in this case Rosenblum, positive that such a board would find Irwin legally sane, made the motion that the court appoint such a commission.

Leibowitz, in his argument against it, made a good point (which he knew would be read by the twelve men who would eventually sit on the jury).

"Why not send Irwin to Bellevue Hospital for examination," Leibowitz said. "The city has capable psychiatrists at Bellevue. I feel that their findings would be impartial and unbiased."

Rosenblum insisted that if Irwin went to trial it would cost the, State eight hundred dollars a day. The whole situation might be resolved by the findings of a lunacy commission.

"The District Attorney has claimed right along that Irwin is sane," Leibowitz said dryly. "Now he insists that he be examined by a lunacy commission. Why is he so cocksure that the commission will find that Irwin is sane? Why does he hesitate to trust the city's psychiatrists at Bellevue Hospital?"

The court, however, agreed with the district attorney and appointed a commission consisting of an editor, a neurologist and a psychiatrist. According to the law, such a commission has no power to force a defendant to appear before it, and Leibowitz promptly announced that he would not allow Irwin to testify in front of the board. Nothing daunted, the board went right ahead holding frequent meetings (twenty-six open hearings and ten executive sessions) which stretched over six months. To a layman, the whole proceeding must seem rather absurd. The commission was to determine Irwin's mental state—but it could not examine him. Without examining the patient, it would make a diagnosis. This seemed to make little sense. It made no sense at all to Leibowitz, who said that it was like asking a doctor to diagnose a stomach ailment merely on the testimony of the patient's family. No doctor would attempt such a diagnosis, he said, without seeing the patient. Leibowitz was preparing against the possibility that the lunacy commission would find Irwin legally sane. He went ahead on that assumption. While the three-man commission is listening to twenty-eight witnesses (all of whom we have met before), let's see what Leibowitz is doing.

To begin with, he had read every leading case in which criminal responsibility of the mentally ill was in issue. He studied them all and derived comfort, especially from the case of Hans Schmidt, and the door which Judge Cardozo had opened when he said, "If there is an insane delusion that God has appeared to the defendant and ordained the commission of a crime, we think it cannot be said of an offender that he knows the act to be wrong. . . . It is not enough that he has views of right and wrong at variance with those that find expression in the law. The variation must have its origin in some disease of the mind."

That is the line he would take, Leibowitz decided. He was convinced that Irwin had a God complex and that he felt himself to be above the puny man-made laws (Leibowitz had heard Irwin's theory a dozen times from his talkative client). Leibowitz believed that Irwin's views of right and wrong, which were completely at variance with those of society, or of the ordinary decent citizen, did indeed have their origin in a disease which had infected his mind. What disease? Leibowitz was no doctor, but he knew that Irwin had been born with syphilis inherited from his mother, and he could find plenty of medical authority to the effect that congenital syphilis might affect the mind. But Leibowitz would not be a witness on the trial—he would merely be counsel for the defense. He would need witnesses who would testify as to Irwin's mental condition over a period of years.

The more Leibowitz learned about Irwin, the more he believed that his client was "as crazy as a bedbug" and had been since the age of sixteen or seventeen. But again, such witnesses could only testify as to acts and statements by Irwin. They could not say on the stand, "I have known Irwin ten years and always knew he was crazy." Only competent, expert witnesses would be allowed to form such conclusions.

Leibowitz asked two psychiatrists, Dr. Leland E. Hinsie, assistant director of New York Psychiatric Institute, and Dr. Bernard Glueck, to examine Irwin and make an exhaustive report on his mental condition and responsibility. He was careful in his selection of the psychiatrists. There is a small group of medical men in New York who spend more time on the witness stand than they do in office or hospital. Such men are apt to be vulnerable on cross-examination. They can often be tripped up by being confronted with expert testimony they had given in a case they had probably forgotten—testimony at variance with their present views. Knowing that juries look upon professional medical witnesses with some suspicion, Leibowitz picked two men who were practicing psychiatrists, and neither of whom was known as a professional witness. A jury would have to give considerable weight to any testimony they might give.

Each of the doctors spent hour upon hour with Irwin at the Tombs. Irwin was usually an easy subject to study. He liked to talk and explain his theory of "visualization." The questioning of Irwin on at least a dozen occasions brought out considerably more than his two confessions had shown. His "visualization," for instance, was revealed as being something that had fascinated him since childhood. At sixteen, he had thought of himself as "a molecule that had to be liberated from the barriers of mortality." He had felt for a long time that he was beginning to be omnipotent. Each year he believed he was getting closer to this goal. He was positive, for instance, that within a short time he would be able to develop every one of his senses to the ultimate; he said confidently that soon he would be able to smell any flower that was on the planet Mars, and that he would be able to see at least a million miles. (He remembered that he had actually seen a distance of a million miles when he was seventeen.) He said that eventually, when he had fully developed the possibilities of "visualization," he would be the supreme being in the universe. He added casually, in talking to Dr. Hinsie, that the three murders had brought him just about to the point of divinity.

Hinsie. How much responsibility do you take personally and how much responsibility do you give to God for the development of all these ideas?

Irwin. My dear sir, the two are one. God operates, but I say divinity operates through me—divinity is me. In no more sense than it is you potentially.

Hinsie. Actually, however, God is you?

Irwin. Not potentially—actually, too. Listen, in the same sense that you can say actually. This is why I wanted to study chemistry. I know a little chemistry so I can give you a very good illustration. If I knew more I could give you more. In the same sense that you can say—you ask me if God is me—oxygen and hydrogen are water. They are not water and yet they are water. I am not divine by virtue of my imprisonment in this mortal state.

Dr. Hinsie elaborated:

Q. Is divinity responsible for every movement that you make, for every thought you make?

A. Yes.

Q. Isn't that a crazy idea?

A. That is not crazy at all.

Q. Who was ultimately responsible for the murder of these three people?

A. Divinity. Absolutely!

Q. Divinity may be responsible but divinity is not in the Tombs; you are.

A. No, divinity is in the Tombs, and I am in the Tombs—the two are one.

Q. If someone is convicted of those three murders and sentenced to die in the electric chair, who is going to die?

A. I will die and that part of divinity will return and rise again and somebody—listen, if I do nothing else, I will get my ideas before the public and somewhere out of the millions of people there will be someone who will understand it.

Q. It isn't worth electrocution.

A. It is worth it if I can avoid the electrocution and finish it myself.

Q. In other words, by this last statement, you admit that you did the murdering and not divinity.

A. No, divinity did through me and by me.

Q. Did you have to obey the commands of divinity in murdering?

A. Exactly.

Q. Listen, I believe personally that Robert Irwin in and of himself by and with his own consent and knowledge murdered these three people.

A. Yes, but actually it is divinity that pushes it along.

Q. Therefore, you and divinity and God and the universal mind are all one.

A. So are you, of course.

Q. Then I can only conclude or reframe your statement to read as coming from you, "I am God."

A. Yes. Absolutely! Since you limit your whole statement to me, exactly.

Q. What does the statement read?

A. The statement reads that I am God.

Q. I consider that to be a very crazy idea.

A. I made such a statement only under your persistent questioning, but I will prefer to say the same thing in a different way. I am inherently divine.

Q. Do you wish to cancel anything that you said here?

A. No, I do not. If you leave it to me, I prefer to say that I am divinity, but you are too.

He told Dr. Glueck about the same thing. He explained to Dr. Glueck why he had asked Dr. Feigin to emasculate him (March, 1932) and why he had attempted the operation himself (October, 1932). It all came back to "visualization" and the eventual goal of divinity which he was sure he could reach. To reach it, however, he felt that he would need every bit of physical and mental energy possible. To reach it he would do as the Indian mystics did, mortify and subdue his flesh and his desires so that they wouldn't interfere with the one dominant impulse to gain spiritual ascendancy.

Glueck. Was it your idea that by removing the penis your temptation for sexual intercourse would be removed, and thereby you could conserve all of that sexual energy for mental energy?

136

Irwin. Yes, but it went beyond that. You can say sex is the corner-
stone. I wanted to make myself so that I would have an ever present bewareness of the fact that I didn't belong in this scheme of
things—so that would always be a goad after me to drive me to
what I was doing.

One day when Glueck went to the Tombs to see him, he found
Irwin in a towering rage against a young assistant in Leibowitz' office.
He had asked the law clerk to bring him copper wire, steel disks and
a magnet. Irwin screamed and cried because he hadn't been given
these articles. He needed them badly, he said, because he was "learning how to introduce electricity into my body. Now, that God-damn,
good-for-nothing bum has messed everything up."

Irwin explained that when other people stuck their fingers into a
light-bulb socket they jumped because of the shock. When he did the
same thing he merely felt a strong current of electricity flowing into
his body. He opened his shirt and showed Glueck several pieces of
steel wool stuck to his undershirt. He had gotten them from the men
who cleaned the jail. "This attracts electricity," he said. He needed
more steel wool and copper wire and then he would be able to induce
a continuous flow of electricity through his body.

"I have billions of particles in my body," he explained. "If I
could straighten them out so that there would be a continuous flow of
electricity through them, it would transform my body so that I could
fly if I wished. The electric chair wouldn't mean a thing then. The
electricity in the chair will have no power over me," he added
contemptuously. "I can walk through matter; I can walk through a
stone wall; bullets can go through me without affecting me, I am absolutely eternal. Certainly I'm God."

Any time the doctors brought the conversation around to those moments he was strangling Ronnie and he saw the "green eyes" of the
clock staring at him, Irwin became tremendously disturbed.

"While I was strangling Ronnie," he would repeat, "I saw two eyes
staring at me. They grew larger and larger. I had to obey them. I
would have killed forty people if they had been in the room
then. . . . Later I saw that the eyes came from the clock."

That was enough for Dr. Hinsie (and his colleague). Hinsie was convinced that at the time of the killings, Irwin was laboring under such a defect of reasoning as not to know the nature and quality of his act. The delusions under which he labored (his omnipotence, the eyes of the clock which told him to go on, the belief that his role was to be supreme master of the universe) were greater in their strength than his sheer intelligence. This defective reasoning caused him "not to know that the act was wrong," to use the words of the statute. Irwin always protested when any of the doctors referred to his "insanity." He denied that he was insane, although he knew that proof of saneness would mean the electric chair. Actually, he didn't care much about the consequences of his act. He had remained in the Gedeon apartment for more than an hour after the final killing (Byrnes) and he never bothered to lock the door. After he had gone from the flat he realized that he had left a glove there, but he didn't bother to go back for it. His delusions were so great by then, that he had virtually abandoned all contact with reality. His "flight" (Philadelphia, Washington, Cleveland, Chicago) was a haphazard affair and he had made no attempt to disguise himself or his movements. The instinct of self-preservation was, of course, as dominant as ever, but it lay dormant until real danger threatened. That happened in Cleveland when a waitress (Henrietta Koscianski) spotted him and asked him, "Do you know Robert Irwin?" He hurried to Chicago after that.

Dr. Glueck said bluntly, "Irwin is both medically and legally insane. He was diagnosed as a case of 'dementia praecox, paranoid trend' at Rockland, and this is a chronic and progressive type of mental disorder. His history of syphilis, which nearly always affects the central nervous system, means that Irwin is suffering from both organic and functional diseases."

Leibowitz studied the reports (each was a lengthy and exhaustive one) of the two doctors. There was absolutely no doubt in his mind now that Irwin was both medically and legally insane. He studied Karl Menninger's The Human Mind, with especial attention to the table listing the symptoms of abnormal psychology (page 166). It puzzled Leibowitz that any right-minded person could think of Irwin

138

as other than insane, whether you applied a medical or legal connota
tion to the word.

2

Then the lunacy commission made its report in 756 pages, which
added up to three words, "Irwin is sane." The commission admitted
that Irwin had been occasionally treated for mental disorders but said
primly that such disorders were caused by "poorly digested reading in
philosophy and psychology." The commission had listened to a full report given by Dr. Wertham, but it dismissed with utter contempt the
evidence of this brilliant doctor who knew Irwin's history so well.
The commission commented upon "Irwin's carefully planned and cleverly consummated escape," and ended by saying, "No evidence has
been presented to show the existence of a compelling delusion which
caused the crimes. Nor has any evidence been produced to show any
organic disease of the brain."

The commissioners chided Irwin for not submitting himself for
questioning, but added that the chairman of the commission had gone
to the Tombs and had watched Irwin "through the bars of the door
to his cell." "The commission entertained no prejudice against Irwin,"
the report said in a revealing bit of attempted self-justification. "It is
significant," the report said disapprovingly, "that the attitude of Irwin
toward the lunacy commission reflects precisely that of his counsel,
who opposed the appointment of the commission." It was very apparent that the three members of the commission were piqued at
counsel for the defense. "Irwin," the commission concluded, "is an expert actor, capable of feigning insanity," on a moment's notice.

Psychiatrists could only laugh at the absurdity of the report, but the
newspapers hailed the decision with joy. The *New York Journal-
American* headlined the story,

SCULPTOR INSANITY
FAKER, SAYS BOARD

and said that the "fiendish sculptor" was a "classic example of the insanity faker."

The *World-Telegram* gave the report its prim approval in an editorial which said:

Legally sane, in that he was mentally capable of knowing the nature of the acts for which he was indicted and that the acts were wrong is the upshot of the lunacy commission's long delayed report on Robert Irwin, who confessed to the triple Gedeon murders of last Easter.

The commission also finds him now sane in the sense that he is mentally able to understand trial proceedings and make his defense.

General Sessions Judge Freschi, with judicial authority to approve or disapprove the findings, has approved them. Irwin can be tried as soon as District Attorney Dewey is ready—which will doubtless be soon in view of the time already lost.

Here is one lunacy commission that seems to have done a thorough, albeit lengthy, job—perhaps made more difficult by the reported hostile tactics of the defendant. The full report should prove instructive for current efforts to make psychiatry a more efficient aid to criminal justice.

The crime was atrocious—one of the sort that calls for justice at its speediest and surest. Yet nearly a year has gone by. The more reason why the trial should now be as prompt and free from technical obstruction as judge, prosecutor and defense counsel can make it.

The charge by the commission that Irwin was merely feigning insanity was greeted with derision by members of the medical profession, but the papers took it quite seriously. Dr. Hinsie, who had visited Irwin ten times, scoffed at the thought of Irwin simulating insanity and wrote his views in a report in which he said:

A delusional system that modifies the entire course of an individual's career and one that has been developing to greater and greater heights over a period of at least twelve years cannot be regarded under the heading of simulation. There is no simulation as a means of avoiding punishment. Irwin's psychotic illness existed for at least twelve years before he murdered, and his delusional system did not change in essence during the murders, nor has it changed in its general purposes since the murders. His delusional system is all of the same fabric and it has a life history now of not less than twelve uninterrupted years. Moreover, Irwin has no hope of escaping punishment. By the time that the real act of punishment may be imposed upon him by the

State he knows that since he is immortal he cannot be punished. In fact, he is not interested in the State's case. He is not interested in his defense. He is solely interested in the further progress of his delusional system. This is borne out first by the indifference with which he discusses his fate from the standpoint of realities of life. Second by the fact that though he has been and is in police custody awaiting trial for the murder of three people, he will spend hours with intense interest on his delusions. He discusses his fate as a citizen only when he is forced to do so by those who examine him. The question of simulation is easily ruled out.

The Robert Irwin case, in the best tradition of American jurisprudence, was being tried in the newspapers, and Leibowitz realized this. It was not of his making. He demanded that Irwin be transferred from the Tombs to the Raymond Street Jail in Brooklyn. He said that Irwin had been brutally beaten by the guards in the Tombs. At the request of the press, he permitted Irwin to be interviewed. This took place in the counsel room of Raymond Street Jail.

The *World-Telegram* gave a graphic description of the interview. The story said in part:

Irwin was unshaven and haggard. He wore a dirty white shirt and wrinkled white trousers. His eyes were blood-flecked and staring. He was trembling.

As he entered the room, he clutched his throat, and backed into a corner. He began to scream.

"What is this?" he cried. "What are you doing to me? Who are these people?"

He ran to Mr. Leibowitz and grabbed him.

"Sit down," Mr. Leibowitz snapped. "Cut this out at once."

A reporter said:

"We're not going to harm you. Please sit down."

Irwin grasped a chair, held it a moment, then slumped to a bench, still holding the chair.

"Have you been mistreated?" someone asked.

"This has been going on for two weeks," Irwin said. "That doctor keeps staring at me. Leering at me with his eyes. I can't stand his eyes."

Then he broke down completely. He began to sob. He jumped from the bench and began to mutter incoherently.

Broken sentences were distinguishable: They beat me up from behind

141

. . . they beat me with blackjacks. Six men beat me up with blackjacks
. . . I can't stand up to six men with blackjacks."

Silent for a few instants, his eyes glazed above sunken cheeks, he
rushed wildly about the room. His shoulders were trembling and his
knees wobbled.

"I haven't had anything to eat for forty-eight hours," he cried.
"Only a bowl of soup and one slice . . ."

The two guards got hold of him. They pulled him to the door.

After he had gone, Mr. Leibowitz said:

"The law, district attorney, and that lunacy commission say that
this man is sane."

All of the papers carried similar stories. Leibowitz was well satisfied
with the result of the "interview." He had taken a rather desperate
chance. He knew that Irwin had occasional lucid periods when he
gave every outward evidence of normality. Had he chosen this particular time to relapse into apparent sanity, the reporters present would
have emphasized his behavior, and the public (and those twelve anonymous but so important men) would have been justified in thinking
that the lunacy commission's report had some merit. But Irwin was at
his worst (from Leibowitz' point of view—at his best). Not one of
the reporters present felt that Irwin was acting. Every one of them
left the jail convinced that Leibowitz had been right when he said
that his client was "as crazy as a bedbug."

Now Leibowitz was ready for trial. He had prepared not only his
defense but he had anticipated the case which the District Attorney
would present. The confession which Irwin had made gave the prosecution a mighty weapon. Irwin had gone out of his way to show that
he had strong motives for killing Ronnie and Byrnes. When he admitted that Ronnie had recognized him and had said, "Bob, I know
you. You are going to get into trouble if you do this," he was providing the prosecutor with a strong motive, with deliberation and with
intent. When Irwin said, "The Englishman could identify me," he
was virtually accusing himself of first-degree murder.

Leibowitz knew Dewey for a shrewd prosecutor, and he knew that
Jack Rosenblum, who would actually try the case, knew his way
around a courtroom. The forty-year-old Rosenblum had in a short
period of time tried ten first-degree murder cases and had sent ten

men to the electric chair. Leibowitz felt that Rosenblum would try Irwin only for the third killing, the murder of Frank Byrnes. It would be easy to prove premeditation, and of course there was motive. He had to kill Byrnes to silence him. Leibowitz knew that bright Jack Rosenblum would ignore the murders of Ronnie and her mother. If he could isolate the murder of Byrnes, he had a good chance of obtaining a first-degree conviction. Leibowitz would have to show that the killing of Byrnes was merely part of one general pattern of slaughter; that it could not be isolated and considered apart from the others.

The trial opened on Monday, November 7, 1938, in the Court of General Sessions before Judge James Garrett Wallace. Leibowitz strode into court, exuding smiling confidence. He wore a blue suit and a red tie. You will remember that more than twenty years before, when he had defended Patterson, he had worn a blue suit and a red tie. Ever since that time he had worn the same type of outfit on the opening day of a trial in which he appeared as counsel. When he had discarded the frock coat, he quickly discovered the costume that suited him.

He crossed to the table reserved for the prosecution, said, "How are you, Jack," to Rosenblum and shook his hand warmly. Rosenblum grinned, said, "Hello, Sam," and then, like two boxers who have shaken hands in mid-ring just before the gong, they withdrew to their respective corners. Judge Wallace, grizzled veteran of the criminal courts, entered the courtroom, banged his gavel and the trial opened.

Rosenblum arose and announced to the court that he was trying Irwin for the crime of killing Frank Byrnes, as Leibowitz had anticipated. Leibowitz said that he would prove that his client was legally insane, and then, almost as though to show his contempt for the statute, he added, "but insane or not, we will show that he is not guilty of first-degree murder." The selection of the jury proceeded slowly, with Rosenblum and Leibowitz clashing frequently, especially when Leibowitz asked talesmen if they had been affiliated with any group which had backed Thomas E. Dewey in his campaign for District Attorney.

143

Before the day was over, Leibowitz had aroused the ire of Rosenblum. He asked one prospective juror, "Do you feel that just because the District Attorney produces a witness, this witness is therefore shrouded in purity and truthfulness?" Rosenblum objected to that, and Judge Wallace sustained him, but every talesman in the court had heard the question and it gave them something to think about. Did Leibowitz mean to imply that the prosecutor was going to ride to a verdict on the fame Dewey had won by crushing the gangs of New York? Leibowitz, the master of courtroom psychology, was already spraying the jury box with the antidote. Rosenblum finally lost his temper and began to shout objections. Leibowitz, icily calm, objected to "the District Attorney's dramatics."

The papers had announced that Dewey would take an "active interest in the case," and Leibowitz expected that the young prosecutor, with his finely developed sense of the theatrical, would eventually march into the courtroom to take over the job begun by Rosenblum. Back in 1938, Thomas Dewey was a Galahad in shining armor with strong public appeal. Leibowitz wanted to blunt that appeal immediately. "Suppose Mr. Dewey comes into court, would you regard anything he said as holy and a symbol of purity and virtue?" Rosenblum objected furiously to these barbs aimed at his boss, but Leibowitz persisted in asking every juror the same question in different ways. One juror, about to be accepted by both sides, reacted to the question by saying that he had been one of a group which had tendered a testimonial dinner to Dewey after he had convicted Lucky Luciano. He was promptly disqualified. When the first eight men had been picked, Leibowitz felt that he had eight men who were not blinded by Dewey's reputation. One juror (Robert Brill) was excused when he said emphatically that Leibowitz had already convinced him that Irwin was insane.

Rosenblum seemed to lose confidence as talesman after talesman was examined by the lawyer for the defense. Leibowitz, on the other hand, seemed to be enjoying the whole proceeding. When Leibowitz is confident, there is a kind of combination of a chuckle and a purr in the deep voice, which is almost always, on such occasions, soft. Irwin, too, seemed pleased. He noticed a newspaper cartoonist sketching his picture. He leaned over to the press table and asked if he could see it. He studied it a moment, whispered, "Lousy," and passed it back.

Just after the eighth juror had been picked, Judge Wallace called Leibowitz and Rosenblum to the bench. He bent over and said to Leibowitz, "I've been puzzled by your questioning of the talesmen. What are you after?"

"Nothing," defense counsel said blandly. "I just want twelve fair-minded men in that jury box who can look at an insane man and have the intelligence to see that he's insane."

"You think you can prove Irwin insane after the lunacy commission report?" Wallace asked.

"Easily," Leibowitz said, smiling confidently. "The prosecution is after a first-degree verdict basing its case on the assumption that Irwin is sane. If I prove him insane, the whole first-degree case collapses. They'll believe that he is insane in the terms of the statute when I put my witnesses on the stand. Think of those two green eyes commanding Irwin to go on with the strangling of Ronnie. Judge, this man has been in insane asylums half a dozen times. He's as crazy as a March hare."

"Well, what is it you're after?" Wallace repeated.

"I merely say that he doesn't belong in the electric chair," Leibowitz said. "But I certainly don't want him running around loose, either."

"How does your office feel about that?" the Judge leaned over toward Rosenblum.

"I'll have to call the boss," the assistant District Attorney said. He left the courtroom, phoned his office and returned to the bench.

"The office is willing to accept a plea to murder in the second degree if you will impose a sentence that will assure us that Irwin will be confined for the rest of his natural life," he said. "What we're worried about is this, Judge; if the jury says that Irwin is not guilty by reason of insanity, he might be committed to Matteawan State Hospital. Eventually, he might sue out a writ of habeas corpus, saying that he had regained his sanity. We want to avoid that contingency."

145

(In back of Rosenblum's mind was the report of the lunacy commission which had said Irwin was sane. It was a decision which might backfire if Irwin were committed to an insane asylum. When he made the anticipated request for release, he could use that as evidence to support his plea of sanity. And he could not again be tried for murder because of the safeguard known as "double jeopardy.")

"Would you consider pleading guilty of second-degree murder?" Judge Wallace asked. "If you did that, it would keep Irwin from the chair but would insure that he would spend the rest of his life in confinement."

"I might," Leibowitz said, trying to keep the exultation out of his voice. "That is, if my client agreed to it."

Leibowitz felt now that his legal position was unassailable. He was convinced that he had won this case before the jury had been picked. He had won it by the months of sweat and toil on the part of himself and his whole office force. Let it come to trial. Let the jury hear Inspector Lyons repeat the testimony he had given before the lunacy commission. No district attorney could make him recant his publicly expressed opinion that Irwin was insane. Let the jury hear Hinsie and Glueck and Professor Angus MacLean and Dean John M. Atwood. Leibowitz had never been better prepared with a defense.

Leibowitz, who had maintained right along that Irwin was in no mental condition to take his place in society and that he should spend the rest of his life in confinement, was satisfied with the bargain. All of his work had been devoted to proving Irwin insane, and his contention was that an insane man belonged in a mental institution, not in an electric chair.

Leibowitz had quite a time persuading Irwin to plead guilty of second-degree murder. Irwin felt cheated. He wanted to appear on the stand and expound his theory of divinity to the public. It took all of Leibowitz' persuasive powers to convince him to plead guilty of second-degree murder. Irwin made one condition. He would allow Leibowitz to have his way if Leibowitz would give him five hundred dollars.

"What do you need the money for?" Leibowitz asked.

"I need it to continue my work on visualization," Irwin said. "But I need a helper. When they send me away they will have guards around all the time. I can train one of those guards to help me visualize. I am sure I can hire one for twenty-five cents a day. That is why I need the money."

Leibowitz agreed. He sent out for a five-hundred dollar bill and a safety pin. Irwin put the bill into the watch pocket of his trousers, then Leibowitz pinned the pocket with the safety pin. Now Irwin was ready for anything. The five hundred dollars assured his future experiments.

They came out of the conference and into the courtroom. Such a plea must be entered in open court. Leibowitz asked that the eight men picked for the jury be excused from the courtroom. Then he addressed the court and said that he would plead Irwin guilty of second-degree murder. He said bluntly that Irwin was insane and had been since he was twelve years old. He traced Irwin's career and told of his various commitments to institutions. He told of Irwin's infatuation with Ethel and he discussed Irwin's theory of "visualization." He recounted the events of the fatal Saturday night. In closing, Leibowitz attacked the frailty and inadequacy of the laws relating to insanity, and urged that they be brought up to date by the state legislature.

Rosenblum then stated the case against Irwin. It became obvious that Rosenblum, although willing to permit the second-degree plea, wanted a prison sentence, not an institutional commitment. He was probably thinking of Harry Thaw, recently released from an insane asylum.

The Judge interrupted to ask if Rosenblum was asking the court to deny the plea.

Rosenblum said he was not, and that for the best interests of the people he recommended the acceptance.

Judge Wallace then said, "All right, I'll accept it."

Rosenblum continued with his address. He said, "We have in Irwin's writing this statement, 'We can learn to be crazy to get what we want!' "

147

"That's a lie," Irwin shouted from his seat at the defense table.

When Rosenblum concluded, Judge Wallace called on Irwin to ask if he had anything to say.

Irwin arose and said, "Your Honor, the District Attorney has not only made misstatements but has deliberately lied."

"Do you realize," the Judge asked, "that you are pleading guilty of murder?"

"I do not," Irwin said. "Your Honor, I have looked up the word murder in the dictionary, and I find that it defines murder as the 'malicious killing of one individual by another.' There was nothing malicious in my killing."

"But you did kill them, didn't you?" the Judge asked.

"I did," Irwin answered.

"And you plead guilty to the killings?"

Irwin suddenly turned around and spoke to the reporters who were at the press table.

"I have nothing but contempt for you. You have lied about me continually. You have told untruths. You are dirty dogs."

"Technically," Irwin was again addressing the court, "because everything around here seems to be technical, I know that I am pleading guilty to a murder, but I didn't murder three people, I didn't murder even one."

"But you killed three people?" Judge Wallace asked again.

"Yes, I killed them, but I didn't murder them."

"Do you believe that you were justified in killing them?"

"I do."

Then Irwin spoke to everyone, summing up the frustrations that had plagued him all his life.

"Nobody understands me. Nobody wants to understand me," he wailed, and this was his judgment on a society which had failed to help him adjust himself to its standards.

He was finally quieted. Judge Wallace, as interested in the outburst and affected by it as anyone else in the court, was quiet for a moment. Then he set the date of sentence.

The jury was called back into the room and informed that the trial of Robert Irwin for murder was at an end.

Irwin was sentenced to be confined for life in a state prison. The newspapers did not take the decision kindly. Society seemed to feel cheated because Irwin was allowed to live. The ancient Greek gods were far kinder to the insane. Hercules ran amok several times, killing indiscriminately, but the gods excused him because he said that he only killed when he heard "children's voices in his head." Irwin had been hearing voices "in his head" ever since childhood, but society scoffed at that.

Irwin was sent to Sing Sing. It is routine at the big gray prison to give incoming prisoners a thorough physical and mental examination. Now medical science, released of the strangling limitations of criminal statutes designed to be used against the sane criminal, had the last word. Psychiatrists examined Irwin for ten days and then unhesitatingly pronounced him insane. He was immediately transferred to Dannemora State Hospital, institution for the criminal insane.

The prison psychiatrists had justified Leibowitz' contention that Irwin was "crazy as a bedbug." Leibowitz was satisfied. The first time he had talked to Irwin he had said that the man was obviously insane and should be put away for life. It had taken about six months of intensive effort and all of his legal skill to convince society of something which he felt should have been obvious to any fair-minded man.

A month after Irwin's arrival at Dannemora, he wrote to his counsel:

Dear Mr. Leibowitz:

First let me get the main thing off my chest. Will you please get my belongings and send them up here collect, especially the books and a big chunk of green wax like clay and my modeling tools.

All or nearly all of the belongings of any patient coming in here are held in the storeroom for censorship until the patient gets off the reception ward and I am still on this ward. There are many restrictions here for a new comer tho I can understand the necessity for it. Later on I think things will pan out pretty well. I haven't had one bit of trouble with anybody so far. My only real complaint is that I am not permitted to write more letters. I could write 20 letters right now to different people but I guess it would be a little hard on the Doctor to read them.

If you see Mr. Rosenblum give him my regards. He's one of the enemy and all that but he does have a good head to model in spite of all those lies he told about me.

What do you think? A beautiful senorita from Cuba has been writing me in Spanish and "I'm in love all over again!" I've nearly learned the Spanish language since I came here. I will make you those heads of yourself and your wife and daughter. Especially the little girl, I'll make you something to cherish all your life, something beautiful you wait and see. For this I will need those photographs and some goods ones as I told you. Please don't forget my brothers.

I got your Christmas cards and hope you got mine. I would have written you sooner but I do all my writing to the little senorita. I'm going to tell her to learn English so she can write to people for me. *Please* send me *at least a good book on astrology*. Will you also give Dr. Wertham and Mrs. Wertham my regards and tell Dr. Wertham I got his Christmas package and I can't write for the present—because of the Senorita and Dr. Hinsie etc. and last but not least tell the charming Miss Schiffer [Leibowitz' secretary] that if she will send me a photograph I will make a good picture but it must be a *profile* because it is *very* difficult to draw from photographs for me at least.

Sincerely,

Bob Irwin

Irwin still had the knack of inspiring sympathy. Leibowitz did collect Irwin's belongings and sent them to the asylum. His belongings consisted of thirteen books, one pair of shoes, one bottle of eye wash and one large envelope filled with letters—and Leibowitz also included the book on astrology.

7. COMPASSION

"The law of nature, as a set of uncodified commands implicitly accepted by the mind and conscience of every reasonable person, is merely the concept of Divine Law under another name. Time and time again it has operated to overthrow entire systems of positive law."

FELIX MORLEY, *The Power in the People*

The human mind is a complex mass of motives and mechanisms quite capable of going awry. The man with perception enough to know that something has gone wrong with his own mental processes and wise enough to go to a psychiatrist for treatment, may be able to emerge from the treatment if not cured, at least saved from permanent harm. Those who are unconscious of the fact that they are afflicted, or who mistake their mental confusions as something caused by digestive disorder not serious enough to consult a doctor about, often end up by needing the services of a good criminal lawyer.

The wise men of antiquity realized without benefit of Freud the potential danger of mental maladjustment. Horace wrote:

Quae Laedunt Oculum Festinas Demere; Si Quid Est Animum, Differs Curandi Tempus In Annum (If anything affects your eye, you hasten to have it removed; if anything affects your mind, you postpone the cure for a year.)

Murder, to the average well-adjusted man, is a repugnant, unnatural act. And yet each year hundreds of average men whose minds have

151

temporarily veered from the norm find themselves accused of first-degree murder.

There are many reasons why an ordinarily law-abiding, decent citizen will suddenly commit an act of violence; an act which has no relationship to his normal intent and which is a negation of every decent impulse and instinct in his character. Sometimes it is an overwhelming pressure of anguish, again it is what the laymen call "insane" jealousy. Occasionally the stimulus which causes the mental mechanism to become scrambled is physical. Samuel Leibowitz defended many clients who came under the category of the temporarily insane. Each presented a different problem. Basically, of course, his defense was always that there was no intent to commit a crime, for an insane man, like a sleepwalker, has no free will to act; forces over which he has no control compel him to violent acts which would ordinarily be impossible for him to perform.

An example of how a physical ailment can warp and twist a man's mental processes to the point, where killing seemed to him to be a reasonable and only solution, is the case of Ernest Wente, who, at sixty-two killed his forty-seven-year-old wife, Clara. A moment after he had pumped three bullets into his spouse, Wente turned to eyewitnesses and said, "Okay, I killed her. I'm not sorry for it, either." Wente was quickly indicted for first-degree murder.

Wente, Leibowitz found, had married his pretty wife, fifteen years younger than he, after a swift courtship. Soon she left him for another man and taunted her husband by thumbing her nose whenever she saw him, and saying she preferred younger men.

Wente, according to medical testimony Leibowitz introduced, was suffering from arteriosclerosis, and the resultant constriction of the arteries and veins so impeded and diminished the flow of blood to the brain as to induce, during moments of mental stress, a semicomatose condition.

On the day of the killing, Leibowitz contended, Wente was in a dream state, laboring under such "a defect of reason as not to know the nature and quality of the act he was performing, or that it was wrong."

This might have seemed rather a glib, far-fetched claim by the defense counsel, but he had spent weeks studying arteriosclerosis and had consulted the best medical men in the field as to its effects on the brain. From them he had gone to the psychiatrists. He found that he was on firm ground. Dr. Karl Menninger, in his monumental book, *The Human Mind*, had discussed the subject and had presented the history of a man who had lapses of memory as a result of the disease. "This case," he wrote, "was probably caused by hardening of the arteries of the brain so that the supply of blood nourishing the cells of the brain became diminished and the cells dried up and ceased functioning." The testimony of the medical men Leibowitz produced was irrefutable, and the jury quickly brought in a not guilty verdict.

2

When physical illness was absent or merely a contributing cause to the mental breakdown which resulted in homicide, it was much more difficult to map a defense. It would be easy enough to convince a jury of psychiatrists that a defendant should not be held legally responsible for acts committed while laboring under some overwhelming mental strain that precluded rational meditation, but juries are not composed of doctors.

A thousand years ago some communities believed that insanity (temporary or permanent) was the result of specific divine intervention. Leibowitz found that some remnant of that belief still exists in the minds of men. They cannot understand the medical reason for a temporary mental breakdown but they have an instinctive feeling that such tragedies are caused by forces outside the comprehension of man. Leibowitz convinced not one but a dozen juries that those who killed while in the grip of some mental disorder were not guilty because the blow was struck, the knife was plunged, the gun was fired, by "the hand of God." It is a strange anomaly that jurors who never go to church, to whom the Almighty is nothing but a legend for children, who sin casually against all of His precepts, should in the jury box become acutely conscious that there is a divinity who occasionally interferes with the actions of man. Leibowitz made good use of this attitude. It helped him to free many men who had not consciously sinned against society but who, nevertheless, sat in the defendant's chair on trial for murder.

3

There was tall, hollow-cheeked Duncan Ladd, for instance. Duncan Ladd lived with his wife Lydia and two children in Wallingford, Connecticut. He was a quiet man, liked and respected by his neighbors. Ladd worked at night in the boiler room of the Masonic Home outside Wallingford. He was a happy young man, devoted to his wife and children. Ladd was the average small-town citizen, well satisfied with his life, proud of the fact that he was making enough money to take care of his family. He was even able to buy a car for them.

His best friend was Michael A. Di Leo, who owned a barber shop in nearby Meriden. Di Leo was a good-looking, curly-haired man who could woo enticing strains from his guitar. He often dropped into the Ladd home with his guitar, and his music delighted vivacious Lydia Ladd, her twelve-year-old son and her fourteen-year-old daughter.

Di Leo was married and had two children, but he seldom brought his wife to visit the Ladds. Once he called with another woman, but Ladd, who had strong ideas about the sanctity of marriage, rebuked him and told him never to bring her again. Ladd liked his friend a lot, but he didn't approve of his careless acceptance of the married state. Di Leo would laugh jokingly at Ladd's puritanism, and explain that there was a difference between a Latin and a Yankee.

"You only live once," he'd smile. "Have some fun."

Ladd, in his quiet way, was a supremely contented man. His demands upon fortune were modest, and they had all been satisfied. He had never gotten over the wonder of winning the love of his Lydia. Shyly, he used to call her his goddess, and Di Leo would purse his lips, slap him on the shoulder, and say, "You are right. She is a wonderful girl." These two men of completely opposite char-

154

acter were great friends. Any time Di Leo wanted to borrow Duncan's car he only had to ask.

Then on September 18, 1937, Ladd walked into Di Leo's barber shop, raised an eight-gauge shotgun to his shoulder and blasted the curly-haired guitar player out of existence. Ladd had finally realized something which everyone in Wallingford had known for some time. It had finally dawned upon him that his friend and his wife had been carrying on a torrid love affair for three years. Everyone, even his young daughter, had known about it. And so he killed Di Leo and was indicted for first-degree murder.

The trial was scheduled for the New Haven Superior Court with Samuel Hoyt (then president of the U. S. Amateur Athletic Union) prosecuting and Judge John Rufus Booth presiding.

It was the prominence of defense counsel and prosecutor, rather than the killing itself, which aroused intense interest in the case. In the preliminary stages the Connecticut newspapers treated the proceedings much as they would have treated a circus or an opening of a new play. "Leibowitz Draws Full Courtroom," the *Hartford Courant* headed one story, while the *Bridgeport Sunday Post* printed an eight-column banner line, "Sam Leibowitz, Suave, Dynamic, Witty, Faces First Yankee Jury."

The fact that Leibowitz was trying the case on foreign territory didn't bother him a bit, although some editorials speculated on how the New England jury would react to the lawyer from New York. It seemed apparent that if the jury had any bias at all it would be in favor of popular Sam Hoyt, one of the state's leading citizens. Leibowitz was conscious of this. The public expected a flamboyant, imperial, patronizing, cocky Leibowitz who would try to dominate the courtroom from the opening gun, and spectators (and presumably jury) were quite prepared to resist anything of the kind. But Leibowitz fooled them. As always, the scenery of the trial and the cast of characters built themselves up in his mind so that he played his part within the frame. He never imposed himself on it. He was deferential toward scholarly Judge Booth; he was amiable in the preliminary stages of the trial with his opponent Sam Hoyt; outside the courtroom he answered questions by local reporters fully, and in fact asked their advice on some things. He asked them about real estate values and told of how he and Belle yearned for a home in the country—somewhere, say, outside New Haven or Bridgeport. Within three days everyone had forgotten that he was a "foreigner."

Harry Neigher, who did a brilliant job covering the trial for the *Bridgeport Herald*, wrote, "Leibowitz is the daring young man on the courtroom trapeze. He dared to invade a section of the north strange to him and pit himself against a Yankee judge, a Yankee prosecutor, a Yankee jury. Leibowitz is a 'showman' but not a 'show-off'. He is no exhibitionist. A round, mobile face, calm, poised, solemn, never a 'smarty', a relentless eye, a fighting jaw. His soft-spoken, mild manner is superb and effective in his worming his way into the hearts of jurors."

The prosecution wasted no time in establishing the facts of the killing. In cross-examining Patrolman Joseph Becker, who had taken Ladd into custody after the shooting, Leibowitz hinted what his defense would be. Leibowitz asked Becker particularly about Ladd's facial expressions and mannerisms during his questioning at Police Headquarters, apparently seeking to establish that Ladd was in a daze and mentally incapable of harboring criminal intent at the time of the shooting. Becker and other police officers testified that Ladd seemed bewildered, and several times placed his hands to his head and cried, "Oh! my head; oh! my head." Ladd's face was flushed and he fainted twice in the station, it was admitted.

Then Leibowitz, in a surprise move, put Duncan Ladd on the stand to tell his story. It is seldom that counsel leads off with his client. Such a move is usually analogous to a bridge player leading a trump to the team which made the bid. But Leibowitz wanted the jury to get the full impact of Ladd's story immediately; later he would buttress it with additional defense witnesses. Ladd said that his suspicions had been aroused by the remark of a neighbor, but that he just couldn't believe his wife had been unfaithful. He would confirm his suspicions or dismiss the horrible thought from his mind. He partly confirmed them with a piece of chalk.

"Did Di Leo call the house to obtain the loan of your automobile?" Leibowitz asked.

"Yes," Ladd replied in the earnest, level voice that marked his testimony.

"After you had granted him permission to use it, did you do anything?"

"Yes. I put a chalk cross on the seat next to the driver after it grew dark and before he came for the car."

"Did you later find the cross from the seat on clothing in your house?"

"Yes, on the back of my wife's coat."

Ladd then told of talking with both his wife and Di Leo about his suspicions.

"They finally convinced me my suspicions were unfounded," Ladd explained.

"Did you believe them?" Leibowitz asked.

"Yes," replied Ladd.

Leibowitz had Ladd describe his attitude toward his wife from the date of their marriage. Ladd said, "I'd say I idealized my wife—and that continued right through. "The next time I spoke to Di Leo was when a friend told me he had seen my wife and Di Leo in a tavern," Ladd continued.

Now all of the cruel doubts returned. Florence Hubert had once lived with the Ladd family and he rushed to her, hoping that she could clear away the ugly clouds of suspicion. But she told him frankly that often Di Leo would give the children money to go to the movies so that he and Lydia Ladd could be alone. And once she had come in unexpectedly and had surprised Di Leo emerging from Lydia's bedroom. Yes, Lydia was in bed at the time.

Frantic now, Ladd went to his daughter Virginia. Virginia told him that she had come home one afternoon to find her mother and Di Leo lying on the couch together.

"My God, baby, you didn't see that?" Ladd testified that he had cried and then he broke into sobs.

"And after that, Duncan?" Leibowitz asked gently.

"Everything after that was a blur," Ladd cried hysterically. "I don't want to know what happened. I don't want to know . . ."

Ladd leaned over, held his head in his hands and wept convulsively.

It was exactly noon. There was a hush among the spectators, and the sobs of the grief-stricken defendant echoed through the crowded courtroom for fully a minute. Then the lawyer said softly, "May we have a recess now, Your Honor."

The Judge wiped his glasses, cleared his throat, nodded wordlessly and left the bench. The jury filed out, their faces reflecting their sympathy. They would have one full hour for that sympathy to grow and strengthen into a conviction that Ladd was a decent, family-loving man, horrified beyond words to hear from the lips of his daughter of the infidelity of his wife. Leibowitz, of course, had timed this with careful calculation. Looking at the faces of the jurymen, Leibowitz was confident then that he would win an acquittal, although he hadn't as yet produced his real defense. He knew now that his timing had been effective.

When Ladd resumed the stand he told of how he had confronted his wife with her faithlessness. She had finally admitted everything, but she pleaded in extenuation that Di Leo had a hold over her which made it imperative that she do anything he asked. The hold? Four years previously she had been driving the Ladd car, and near Yalesville, Connecticut, her car had struck a man who was crossing the road. Panic-stricken, she had fled. The pedestrian had died and now she was being looked for as a hit-and-run driver. Somehow Di Leo found out about it and, Lydia told her husband, "he held this over my head like a club."

"That was a Sunday morning," Ladd testified. "I left the house and went out into the woods. I brooded all day—brooded on my broken faith in humanity—I could only think of my wife and my best friend. They had turned my home into a house of prostitution. I came home. I packed a bag and put my gun into it. I told Lydia I was going to commit suicide. She became hysterical and pleaded with me not to. I got into the car and went to work."

On Monday he drove about aimlessly and again walked in the woods. Tuesday he consulted an attorney; he had to confide in someone or go mad, he felt. On Wednesday he took his daughter and his son to his mother's house. Thursday? "I don't remember;

everything was muddled," Ladd testified. He just didn't remember Friday at all. Twice during the week he had driven to Meriden and had passed Di Leo's barber shop. Did he sleep well during that week of mental torture? "I didn't sleep at all . . . not at all," Ladd cried. And on Saturday he had taken his gun, gone to the barber shop and killed the man who was responsible for breaking up his home and smashing his life.

After he left the stand, the defense, in an effort to build up its contention that he was so distraught mentally he was incapable of forming criminal intent when he shot Di Leo, offered the testimony of a young woman who said Ladd's appearance a few hours before the slaying was so frightening it caused her to weep after he had left her presence.

Mrs. Betty Dombrowski said she saw Ladd early in the morning of the shooting. He had gone to her home about 1:30 A.M. to tell her that her stepfather had taken his, Ladd's, shift in the boiler room at the Masonic Home and would not be home.

She testified, "His eyes scared me. They were popping out and glassy—he didn't seem normal to me—he was looking into space—like in a fog. He was standing with his legs wide apart and his hands down at his side—he walked away very slowly."

"Was his condition such that you spoke of it to someone else?" Leibowitz asked.

"Yes."

"Did you do something?"

"Yes. When he left I began to cry."

Lyman A. Tyler, the fireman who worked with Ladd, testified that Ladd, who "always had been happy-go-lucky, began acting irrationally and often mumbled incoherently," during the week preceding the shooting. He said Ladd's condition grew worse as each day of that week passed.

Ladd, he testified, came in to work two hours ahead of time on the Wednesday and Thursday nights preceding the slaying, and sat in the boiler room brooding with his head in his hands.

Tyler saw Ladd Saturday morning, a few hours before the shooting.

Something Ladd said to him at that time made him think Ladd had lost his memory, he testified, although previous to that Ladd's memory had always been good.

"Ladd's eyes were staring, and his face was tired and drawn," Tyler said. "His eyes bulged and he dragged his feet."

Leibowitz put Ladd's daughter Virginia on the stand and she verified everything that her father had said. She had seen her mother and Di Leo in each other's arms and Di Leo had given her money and told her to "forget it." Hoyt did not cross-examine the girl.

The defense rested.

Leibowitz turned on the full force of his dramatic talent in his closing. Legal colleagues had warned him that a Yankee jury composed chiefly of farmers would not be moved by a dramatic or emotional approach. He didn't believe this for a moment. This was a case caused by emotions; love, hatred, humiliation, were the motivating forces. Leibowitz began by flaying the coolly analytical argument made by the prosecutor. "In this case we are not dealing with a bale of hay—but with human emotions," he cried.

"You see, this woman could do anything to this poor soul . . . you can't put the head of an experienced man on a Duncan Ladd. If it was merely anger, why didn't he take the gun Sunday, when he was stronger mentally and physically; if murder was in his heart—why didn't he shoot Di Leo then?" the chief defense counsel demanded to know. "He knew of the adultery then," he observed.

"It was the hand of God that killed Di Leo!" Leibowitz thundered at the jury. "The hand of the Almighty guiding the hand of this man bereft of reason killed him! If he weren't killed then, someone else would have killed him after he had wiped his passionate lips over the faces of the wives of other men!"

In arguing against the State's claim that Ladd was not out of his mind, because he had operated a car and done other things that only conscious men would have done, Leibowitz maintained that these things were done by instinct. "He was like a punch-drunk fighter getting off the floor. The fighter doesn't know what he is doing, but he strikes out by instinct and does hit his mark," Leibowitz contended.

"Take sleepwalking—a man will get up and walk around without hitting a table or a chair and do other things. A man can drive a car like that. When something is on your mind, you can drive like that, without remembering it. Drunken men can drive. Insane people drive cars."

Again and again Leibowitz reverted to the term "mental sleep," emphasizing that Ladd, during the days preceding the killing, was exactly like a sleepwalker; and a sleepwalker could not be held legally guilty of murder, for he is not moved by conscious intent.

"Sleepless for five days! Good heavens, what kind of a mind are we dealing with here? If it was a premeditated act, why did he wait until Saturday?"

"Why did he make two trips to Meriden on Saturday? Isn't that proof he had no intention to kill? Did he plan murder? If a man is going to kill, he is going to plan his escape! Would he do it at high noon—and before witnesses? Here is the reasonable doubt I promised to give you, gentlemen!

"A man must know what he is doing, and the consequences of his act. You must find beyond a reasonable doubt that Ladd really appreciated what he was doing, and the consequences of his act, before you may convict him. On all of the evidence before you this man is not guilty, not guilty!"

Hoyt then summed up for the prosecution. Hoyt said, "We are trying to find if a man in Connecticut with a grievance can take the law into his own hands." He banged away at defense arguments continually during his summation.

"The question is not if adultery was committed, but if the knowledge of it affected his [Ladd's] mind," he said. He argued that Ladd had not tried to run away because he thought that with the story his wife told him, it would make him a hero.

"Of course, he was naturally nervous and agitated. He was no hardened criminal—naturally he reacted according to his emotions," Hoyt declared. "I don't think God has taken Duncan Ladd into partnership with him to go out and take someone else's life. You are told you must let him go, because his wife didn't treat him right. A man can't

161

take the law in his own hands. I ask you to decide this case on the evidence and the law, and if you do, you can only reach one decision," Hoyt said.

In spite of Hoyt's masterful effort, this Yankee jury needed but four hours to reach a not guilty verdict. It was a great victory for Leibowitz; it was a greater one for Sigmund Freud, who first told us that in addition to a conscious mind we also have an unconscious mind which occassionally takes over and, acting independently of the conscious, impels us to do things ordinarily repugnant to us.

4

Harry L. Barck was a faithful, almost devout member of the Democratic party of the city of Hoboken, New Jersey. To be anything else was to invite disaster. As far back as 1896, his party regularity was rewarded by an appointment as Poormaster of Hoboken. For many years the job was a sinecure. Hoboken, until the crash in 1929, was a busy, bustling, prosperous seaport. There was almost no poverty and what little there was became the concern of private charities. The Poormaster had little or nothing to do.

The picture changed with the onset of the depression. Hoboken went downhill fast. The docks saw no ships and the factories were idle. Poverty came to Hoboken, and by 1938 the city was in deplorable shape. There was squalor everywhere. The population decreased more than 25 per cent. There were hundreds of empty houses and stores, and hundreds of other houses still occupied that wouldn't make fit rabbit warrens.

The Poormaster's job quickly became an important one as the depression became more bitter. There were seven thousand on the Hoboken relief rolls. Barck thought it time to do some slashing. He got the list down to a mere two hundred. His methods were harsh and his tongue was harsher. He felt, honestly no doubt, that most of the applicants for aid were chiselers and entitled to no public money. To those who faced the cutting off of electric light, he suggested that they

162

"burn candles"; to a man who showed him a dispossess notice, he snapped, "Go home and frame it."

His policy always was tough and hard-fisted; lacking in charity and sympathy, full of contempt for the poor. In 1938, Hoboken, with a population of sixty thousand, spent less than three thousand dollars a month on its needy. But though Barck was not suspected of lining his own pockets, Hoboken citizens were free in declaring that the money which should have been spent for relief—as well as plenty of other public funds—must have gone somewhere.

The McFeeley family represented the Hague machine in Hoboken. The McFeeley family? Well, there was Mayor Bernard J. McFeeley; his brother, Police Chief Edward J. McFeeley; Police Captain Bernard McFeeley, Jr.; Police Lieutenant Dennis McFeeley; James McFeeley, contractor; and David and Joseph McFeeley of the Hoboken Law Department. Harry Barck was a man who sang the right political songs. He'd been singing them for forty-two years under different mayors. The McFeeleys liked Barck. He knew how to run his department at almost no expense at all—he was not one to coddle the poor or the unemployed. He wasn't filled with the ideas of that crazy Roosevelt, who thought the country owed a responsibility to the poor. Not old Harry Barck.

Joseph Scutellaro, a small, dark, intense-eyed man, also lived in the city of Hoboken. He and his father operated a small building concern. They were prosperous in a modest way and their future seemed assured. Then father and son made a grave mistake. Frank Barletta, a member of the City Commission, broke with the McFeeley machine and ran as a Republican. Both Joseph and his father campaigned for Barletta. But Barletta lost and so did everyone who had been active in his campaign. Suddenly the Scutellaros found that they couldn't get any contracts. If they did manage to pick up a small job here and there, the people engaging their services found they couldn't obtain the necessary building permits at City Hall. Finally not a single vestige of a once prosperous business remained. No other contractor would hire either one of them. "You can't beat City Hall," they'd say, shrugging their shoulders. Joseph was married now and he had two

163

small children. He walked the streets occasionally, picking up a day's work at carpentry, but soon these jobs ran out and he was completely destitute. City Hall had beaten him. And then this thirty-six-year-old man of pride and quiet dignity had to apply for relief or his wife and children would starve.

Barck thought it presumptuous for a man who had supported Frank Barletta to apply for municipal relief. Mind you, that had been four years previously, but party irregularity was a sin never forgiven by the political bigwigs of Hoboken. There was no statute of limitations on such a crime. However, Barck did give Joseph a form to fill out. He could at least *apply* for relief. He applied ten times before Barck grudgingly sent him a check for eight dollars. The months went by and Scutellaro watched the rounded faces of his children grow thin and drawn. He couldn't sleep and half a dozen times he contemplated suicide. He felt that his mind was going but, determined to fight this horrible situation out somehow, he went to the Hoboken Medical Center for treatment. Dr. John J. Mackin examined him and heard his story. The doctor diagnosed his ailment as sleeping sickness and prescribed tincture of stramonium. It helped a little for a time, but nothing could soften the horrible reality of watching his wife and children actually hungry. Another relief check came for $5.70, but then the checks stopped. Again and again Scutellaro applied to Barck; again and again the surly Poormaster refused him. Finally Barck promised he'd mail him a check. The two children waited for each visit from the postman but there was no check in the mail. Scutellaro was frantic now. He would have to make another appeal to Barck. He waited in the outer office. A great many applicants for relief were there that morning and Scutellaro had to wait for hours in line. Finally the woman ahead of him went into Barck's office. She was Mrs. Lena Fusco, twenty-seven, and her voice pleading for help could be heard through the closed door. Barck's loud, angry tones ordering the woman out of his office could be heard, too, and then the door opened and Mrs. Fusco raged at Barck; her hatred and contempt for the man made her lose all restraint and she spat in his face and called down imprecations upon his head. A week

164

before, a desperate applicant had struck Barck and he had asked that a policeman be on duty in his anteroom at all times.

In a violent rage Barck called loudly for a cop, and Patrolman Thomas Carmody came hurrying to arrest Mrs. Fusco. Now it was Scutellaro's turn. He went into the office. Those in the anteroom heard loud, angry voices, a thump as though someone had fallen, and then they opened the door and found Barck slumped over his dozen ungranted applications.

This happened at 11:30 A.M. on February 25, 1938. At exactly that hour a check for eight dollars had arrived at the Scutellaro home on Munroe Street, and the family was rejoicing. But soon the cops came and took the check from the shaking hands of Mrs. Scutellaro. It would be needed for evidence in the trial of her husband.

Joseph Scutellaro was quickly arraigned for first-degree murder, and his desperate wife asked Leibowitz to defend him. The papers had been full of the case, and Leibowitz felt an overwhelming sympathy for Scutellaro. He took the case knowing that he would not only have to fight the evidence but that he'd have to fight City Hall.

Not only the obscure defendant was on trial; the whole civic administration of Hoboken was on trial. The *New York Post*, in an editorial headed, "Hoboken Committed a Murder," said:

For this homicide the entire community of Hoboken—not one pitiful, desperate, jobless man—stands indicted. The pillars of society in the city across the Hudson are guilty of a crime. The smug, the sleek, the self-satisfied who cheered Barck on from the sidelines as he pinched every penny, as he rolled up an appalling record of inhumanity, killed Barck.

The trial was held before Judge Robert V. Kinkead, with Assistant District Attorney William George as prosecutor. Leibowitz ran into trouble right at the start while questioning the first talesman. He wanted to know whether or not the prospective juror knew any of the McFeeleys, whether or not he knew any members of the prosecution staff, whether or not he knew Harry Barck. George protested to this line of questioning and he was sustained by Judge Kinkead. Leibowitz asked the first talesman one hundred questions. George objected to and had excluded seventy-five of them. It finally developed that defense counsel would only be permitted to ask the talesmen if they bore "malice or ill will" toward the defendant.

Prosecutor George, after establishing the facts of the killing, introduced a statement made by Scutellaro immediately after his arrest. In this statement, which Leibowitz said had been obtained by threats of a beating, the defendant purportedly admitted brandishing the sharp spindle in an effort to threaten the Poormaster. Then when Barck came at him he lunged at him, thinking to wound him slightly, but his aim was off and the instrument pierced the man's chest.

Police Lieutenant J. Romeo Scott described how the confession had been obtained. Leibowitz was not allowed to show that J. Romeo was the son-in-law of Mayor McFeeley.

"You didn't shove your fist under Scutellaro's nose?" Leibowitz demanded of the 220-pound cop. "You didn't threaten to knock his teeth down his throat?"

"No," Scott barked angrily, and the frail Scutellaro leaped from his seat at the defense table and cried out, "He did . . . he did."

Leibowitz's cross-examination of Scott, designed to show that the confession had been obtained by the usual police methods of intimidation, planted considerable doubt as to its authenticity.

Leibowitz decided to do just two things in the trial. He would establish the vicious, brutal nature of Barck's character—and he would let Scutellaro tell his story and allow the jury to decide whether Scutellaro or the police confession reflected the truth. He led frail, emaciated Joseph Scutellaro through his tragic tale and brought him to the visit to Barck's office.

"What did you say to the Poormaster when you went into his office?" Leibowitz asked.

"I said, 'My children are sick and starving,'" Scutellaro testified. "'I want my relief check; it's long overdue—I have only nine cents in my pocket.'"

"What did Barck say then?"

"He said, 'Why doesn't your wife go out and swing a bag on Washington Street? She's a good-looking girl.'"

"What did that mean?"

"It meant that she should become a prostitute," Scutellaro said, shaking with emotion.

"What did you say then?"

"I screamed, 'You can't talk about my wife that way,' " the witness sobbed. He said that Barck, still furious because of the woman who had spat in his face a few moments before, reached out and yelled, "Get out of my office," and grabbed his coat lapels. Scutellaro tried to twist away from the grip of the Poormaster. They struggled and Barck fell heavily across the desk. The sharp spindle pierced his chest. Barck raised his heavy body from the desk and then Scutellaro, filled with horror, yanked the spindle from the man's chest. It dropped to the floor, Barck's blood dripping from the ungranted relief applications that remained attached to it. That was Scutellaro's story, and Prosecutor George couldn't do much with it.

Dr. Lawrence J. Kelly went to the stand and his evidence just about discredited the "confession" the prosecution had counted on so heavily. Dr. Kelly, an intern at St. Mary's Hospital when the killing took place, had arrived in response to an emergency call. Police Chief McFeely was in the room when he arrived. While he examined Barck and tried to sustain life in his huge body, he heard McFeeley question Scutellaro. He heard Scutellaro deny that he had plunged the spindle into Barck; Scutellaro insisted, in fact, that he had pulled the weapon from his chest in an effort to help the dying Poormaster. Scutellaro, dazed, almost hysterical, nevertheless remained firm in his insistence that he had not stabbed Barck, Dr. Kelly said. He heard the questioning and never once, Dr. Kelly repeated emphatically, did Scutellaro admit that he had stabbed the Poormaster. Yet according to the police, only three hours later Scutellaro had made a voluntary confession admitting the killing. The newspapers of the following day reflected the general impression that the "confession" had been completely false.

Never once during his questioning had Leibowitz used the word insanity. Employees in the Poormaster's office who had seen Scutellaro just after Barck collapsed did testify as to his general condition. One said that his face was "like that of a dummy—without expression," and another said that "he sat there staring ahead of him out of empty eyes." If the jury believed the police confession, it would also remember the mental state Scutellaro was in; it would remember the final obscene insult hurled at him by Barck and it could reason that this was enough to bring a temporary madness to his mind.

When Dr. John Mackin testified that he had treated Scutellaro only a few weeks before the killing, he brought out the medical history of the defendant. He said that Scutellaro had previously suffered from an infection of the brain and that subsequently he had been treated for a cerebral concussion. "When I treated him," Dr. Mackin said, "I was impressed by his odd singsong voice, his vacant, blank expression and his inability to answer questions without being confused." That would give the jury plenty to think about when the time came for discussion. Could you convict a man with such a medical history of murder in the first degree?

Had Leibowitz staked everything on a defense of "temporary insanity," the result might have been a long confinement in a state asylum. Leibowitz wanted his client to walk out of the court a free man. And so he declared one defense (that the death of Barck had in effect been an accident) and inferred another (that Scutellaro had for a moment broken under the long strain and was in no mental condition to really entertain any criminal intent). His act was that of an automaton. In short, defense counsel was having his cake and eating it too, a phenomenon that occurs as rarely in the courtroom as it does anywhere else.

In his summing up, Leibowitz avoided the use of the word "insanity," but when he was finished the jury had been given the impression that Scutellaro was a tortured, confused soul who had finally reached the breaking point.

"He went to a Poormaster," Leibowitz declared, "who, because of his background, had lost touch with humanity. He had become a machine. Law or no law, statute or no statute, if I had gone there, with my kids without bread and starvation facing us, I wonder what I would have done if there was a drop of red blood in my body. What would any man do if a public official told him to tell his wife to go out in the streets and become a prostitute if he wants relief?

"All the prison terms in the world—whether they be of short duration or of long duration—all the severity of the law in man's world, will not prevent trouble of this kind where you have tortured souls, when men who are decent citizens hit the rocks of despondency and have to go to a Poormaster's office only to be told to send their wives to go out and peddle their bodies if they wish to keep starvation from their doorsteps.

"We are not dealing with a man physically fit here," he cried. "We are dealing with a bag of skin and bones. Today he weighs 110 pounds. Years ago he weighed 150."

Declaring that the little family had been living on bread and coffee for days—the $5.70 relief check given to Scutellaro on January 20, limiting their expenditures to a penny a day per person—Leibowitz asked, "If he had gone to Barck's office seeking vengeance, he would have armed himself, he would have had a knife or some weapon.

"It is my belief that the culprit responsible for Barck's death is not Joseph Scutellaro; it is not even Barck. The responsibility rests with a system which expects a man to live in this great democracy under such shameful circumstances. If Barck had not pushed this man aside and had been mindful of his misery and suffering, this would not have happened.

"It was the hand of God that struck down Harry L. Barck for all the misery he had brought to the poor and unfortunate. It was the hand of God that struck down Harry Barck." Once again in a courtroom the Almighty had been charged with homicide (excusable), and the jury apparently agreed that God was at least partially guilty, for instead of a first-degree murder verdict it brought in a "guilty of manslaughter" decision. Eleven of the jurors looked scathingly at the twelfth as their foreman announced the verdict. Eleven had been for acquittal from the beginning—one had held out for conviction. The eleven had not been able to persuade the twelfth to alter his views. Talking to reporters after the verdict was in, jurors said that they believed that Scutellaro had temporarily lost his sanity when Barck made the insulting suggestion that his wife walk the streets. Therefore, whether Scutellaro had actually plunged the spindle into the Poormaster's chest, or whether the scuffle had caused Barck to fall upon it, was entirely immaterial. In either case murder was not premeditated. It was as Leibowitz said, "an act of God," and if Scutellaro's hand held the spindle it was not his conscious mind that directed it.

Scutellaro was sentenced to two years by Judge Kinkead, who said in addressing the defendant, "I can't send you home today, but because Mayor Bernard McFeeley of Hoboken has asked me to be lenient with you I will be as lenient as I can." And so finally the name of McFeeley was brought into the trial and placed on the record.

Scutellaro served a year and eight months.

5

In 1939, Hollywood made a picture, *Murder by the Clock*. It was not a film that was considered for an Academy Award. It was the kind of picture you see in neighborhood houses as the second half of a double feature. It told of how a criminal gang used a feeble-minded boy to perpetrate a string of robberies. The dim-witted lad, of course, thought he was playing a game; he never realized that he was being used by criminals. It wasn't a very good picture, and when it was shown at a theatre on Sedgwick Avenue in the Bronx section of New York, the audience, with the exception of one man, was bored. This man sat in his seat, tense, and had the lights gone up in the theatre his face would have shown strain and his eyes horror.

This was not just another movie to middle-aged Louis Greenfield. He had a seventeen-year-old son, Jerome. Jerome was big for his age; he weighed 180 pounds. But Jerome had been an imbecile from birth, and at seventeen he had the mentality of a two-year-old child. Louis Greenfield didn't sleep much that night. Louis lay awake thinking of the seventeen long years that had passed since his son, Jerome, had been born.

Jerome was like any other baby (they thought). But Louis and his wife Anna were disturbed because at two they couldn't get him to say

"Mommy." Nor could he take even halting, unsteady steps as a normal two-year-old child does. Their uneasiness deepened into worry when Jerome was three. He couldn't say a word, he couldn't walk, he didn't seem to recognize either of them; he couldn't even grasp the handle of his milk jug. They took him to a doctor who sent the parents to a specialist. Then they were told the awful truth. They had parented one of nature's most grotesque mistakes, a hopeless, epileptic imbecile.

They refused to believe the verdict. They took him from specialist to specialist. Not one of them held out any hope. Physically, the child grew; mentally, he would never grow. They sent him to the ungraded classes in the public schools. Normal children cried "Looney" or "Dopey" when they saw him, and the parents took him home again. Twice they sent him to corrective institutions, but each time the boy was discharged as a hopeless case. Greenfield, a milliner, spent every cent he made trying to find a cure for the boy.

Louis and Anna Greenfield gave up all social life. The boy couldn't be left alone for a moment. He was big now, but his father had to do all the things for him that one does for a year-old baby. A doctor tried to persuade them to commit the boy to an institution for the hopelessly insane. They agreed tentatively, but visited the asylum first. What they saw there so horrified them that they refused to allow the boy to be committed. They felt the same love for this hopeless, shambling creature that they would have felt for a normal child; actually they felt a greater, protective love; for without them this boy couldn't live. Once Anna, to shield him from the cruel taunts which always greeted him on a city street, took him to a farm in the country. There she secluded herself with the boy for ten months. Louis worked with fanatic vigor trying to make enough money for further treatments.

At seventeen, the boy's right side was completely paralyzed. He couldn't walk upstairs, but he had strong hands. He didn't know they were strong; he only knew that if he held a cup or a plate, or the dolls he played with, they would immediately be crushed as his strong hands unsteadily closed on them. He slept in a bed in his

171

father's room. He was subject to horrible convulsions in which, quite unknowingly, he smashed things. It was his strength that worried the doctors. They told Greenfield that although the boy was still two years old mentally, nature had been cruel enough to develop fully the sex urge within him, and that having no mind to control this urge, it was possible that it would lead him to assault, rape, or kill; his strength, unfortunately, was great enough to make such possibilities far from remote.

Seventeen years of constant watching, guarding, nursing, had also left their marks on small, quiet Anna Greenfield. Her husband sent her for a physical checkup. The doctor called Louis and told him bluntly that he wasn't worried so much about her physical condition, but that he felt sure she would either go insane herself or commit suicide unless the boy was removed from the home. But neither he nor his wife would allow him to be committed. No one else understood him. No one else would bear with this creature, so immature that he had no conception of the function of a bathroom, and yet so strong that he could commit murder if the impulse came. Now Louis Greenfield became ill himself. The doctors told him that he had a serious gall bladder condition that would mean an operation. He was horrified at this. How could he leave Anna alone with the boy? All unknowing, the boy might harm her . . . might even kill her.

Weeks went by and Greenfield brooded over a problem that seemingly had no solution. One afternoon he was so distraught that his kindly partner, Edward Rothenstein, said, "Louis, take the afternoon off. Go to a movie; it might take your mind off your troubles." Louis left the shop and walked the streets. He passed the movie on Sedgwick Avenue and noticed *Murder by the Clock* on the marquee. Perhaps a good murder mystery would made him forget for a time the tragedy which, for seventeen years, had lived in his home. He felt peculiar, almost guilty, as he bought his ticket. He had never been to a movie in the afternoon before. But he went into the theatre and was soon watching with horror the story of an idiot lad being used by a master criminal. No, Louis Greenfield didn't sleep much that night. And when he did doze off, he heard blurred, indistinct voices telling him the only solution. It wasn't the first time he had heard these voices. Once, nearly three years before, he had gone to Trenton, New Jersey, where he had bought a bottle of chloroform for fifty cents. But when he returned home he couldn't use the chloroform as the voices ordered; he buried the bottle under his clothes in a bureau drawer. For years he had tried to thrust the voices out of his conscious mind, but they remained in his unconscious, returning to plague him when he slept. They were loud and insistent this night, and when he awoke in the morning he had decided what to do.

He told Anna he wasn't feeling well, and he asked her to go and open the millinery shop for him. Shortly after she departed, Jerome was seized with one of his fits and his father held him down on the bed to keep him from harming himself. The fit passed, leaving Jerome so completely exhausted that he lapsed into deep sleep. Greenfield took the chloroform from its hiding place, saturated a handkerchief with the drug and laid it gently on his son's face. He pressed the handkerchief close to the boy's nose and soon his breathing grew weaker and then stopped. For one hour Louis Greenfield sat there on the bed where his dead son lay. Then he walked downstairs to tell the apartment house superintendent what he had done. He asked him to call the police.

He was taken to the office of the District Attorney where he told the whole story calmly, unemotionally. Anna had reached home by now and police told her what had happened. She grew hysterical and moaned, "He did it because he loved Jerome so much."

The case was brought before a Grand Jury. Most district attorneys would have asked for a first-degree murder indictment. District Attorney Foley secured a manslaughter indictment instead. And so Louis Greenfield was arraigned on the lesser charge. He showed little interest in the proceedings; it was as though inner peace had finally come to him. He didn't speak, nor is it likely that he thought of the trial and of the possible sentence; he thought and spoke only of his dead son and his living wife. He asked if he might attend his son's funeral. Foley arranged that. And when Leibowitz, who had been retained by Anna Greenfield to defend her husband, petitioned that his client be admitted to bail, District Attorney Foley asked the

173

judge to make the bail as low as possible. It was set at three thousand dollars.

The unpleasant task of prosecuting Greenfield fell to Assistant District Attorney George Tilzer, and the case was tried before the late Judge Lester Patterson, a big and kindly man. Both of them showed sympathy for the tragic, middle-aged defendant; but both had sworn to uphold the law and the law was very clear in this case.

Sometimes nature makes a horrible and grotesque mistake, but the law is adamant in declaring that man has no right to correct that mistake. If nature throws a congenitally insane monstrosity into the world, the law, with savage insistence, forces it to live. Paradoxically the law is more merciful in the case of animals. The law, in fact, will punish a man who does not put an incurably ill and suffering animal out of his misery. But Jerome Greenfield was not technically an animal.

No one recalled any case of euthanasia that had ever been tried in a New York City court, and this one aroused intense interest. A great many doctors rushed into print to condemn Greenfield for taking his son's life. A great many more admitted, privately, that euthanasia was commonly practiced by the physicians of the country and that it was cruel and inhuman to allow a caricature of a living creature to live as Jerome had lived. An enterprising London correspondent managed to reach George Bernard Shaw, and he was glad to give his opinion. He was heartily in favor of legal euthanasia after a board composed of qualified doctors decided that a case was in fact incurable. The *New York Daily News* said in an editorial:

Of course, sane murderers are given a kind of euthanasia, in the electric chair, or at the end of a rope, or in a gas chamber; except that they have the agony of anticipation. We cannot see why criminally insane persons should be permitted to live on at the expense of the State after they have murdered somebody; why euthanasia should not be practiced on them.

We may come some day to a point where merciful deaths, without forewarning, will be administered officially, on their own or their relatives' application, to incurable invalids or defectives—after a rigid investigation of each case by disinterested physicians and police officials, to make sure that the relatives are not simply trying to get rid of something they consider a burden to them.

But neither Shaw, a group of doctors or the newspapers would decide Greenfield's fate. It would be decided by twelve citizens, and Leibowitz would have to persuade these citizens that Greenfield should be acquitted. Prosecutor Tilzer presented the State's case dispassionately. All of the facts of the mercy killing were admitted by Leibowitz. There was no conflict at all between Leibowitz and the District Attorney; the conflict was between Leibowitz and the law.

Leibowitz introduced medical witnesses who had treated Jerome, and they now confirmed what Greenfield had said—the boy was incurable. And he was strong enough to do grave injury to his mother. Leibowitz put Louis Greenfield on the stand. If the jury believed him they must free him. It was that simple to Leibowitz. In his summation he would give them legal excuses to justify an acquittal; all he wanted now was to let the jury hear the whole tragic story from Greenfield's own lips.

He brought him gently through the early years when both parents still hoped that a cure could be found.

"We were prisoners of fate. We could not mingle with our friends. My boy was tortured, abused and ridiculed," he said.

"You love your wife? You hate to see her suffer? Is that why you killed your boy?" asked Leibowitz.

"No," said Greenfield. "I killed him because I loved him more than anything in the world. Dr. Newton Kugelmass had told us Jerry was a hopeless imbecile and that my wife was in danger in the house with him. He advised us to have Jerry sterilized. I started coming home more often. I'd come home in the afternoons."

Greenfield told of going to the motion picture show.

"Jerry looked something like the character in the picture. The story was about a master mind who preyed on a boy like Jerry. I was afraid that after I was gone something like that would happen to him. I couldn't sleep thinking about him. I walked the floor. I couldn't get the urge to use the chloroform out of my mind."

Under the questioning of his counsel, he told of his troubled

175

sleep; of his dreams and of the voices. Then he told of the last morning of his son's life.

"I sat with Jerry for a while and then he started getting a fit. He began crying. He bent over, as if in pain. I put him in bed and made him comfortable; then he seemed to be sleeping. An unseen hand led me to the closet."

At this point Greenfield sobbed aloud. Then he continued. "I got the chloroform. I placed a handkerchief over his nose."

"You knew that to use the chloroform was against the law?" Leibowitz asked.

"Yes, it's against the law of man but not against the law of God. I loved my boy more than anything in the world. God urged me to kill my son. It was the will of God," Greenfield sobbed.

"Are you sorry he's dead?"

"For myself, yes. I loved him. I loved his company. I still miss him. But for Jerry, no."

Assistant District Attorney Tilzer cross-examined Greenfield only briefly.

In his summation, Leibowitz made a frankly emotional appeal, and when, overcome by his own emotion, he stopped, "the sobbing of women spectators was the only sound in the courtroom," said the *New York Post*.

"You talk about tragedy. You talk about purgatory. If that child had only been born blind or crippled or deaf and dumb—or even an invalid confined to a life in a wheel chair—the blow would not have been so terrible. But this child was just a lump of flesh.

"This mother would have taken her eyes out," Leibowitz declared. "She would have cut her arms off. This man would have cut his heart out—if that child could have taken just one step, could have said one word. This man's mind was worn down bit by bit. It was like a drop of water," he said. "Drop by drop, wearing down the stone. Hour after hour, week after week, and year after year, every moment—awake or asleep. Human flesh could not stand it! His mind could not stand it!"

Before reviewing the actual killing, when Greenfield chloroformed his son, Leibowitz said, "Suppose you were walking along the street

176

and saw a dog lying helpless in the gutter, his body torn by pain, after being run over by the wheel of an automobile—just a poor, yellow mongrel dog, lying there in agony?

"You would say, 'I wish some policeman would come along and put that poor thing out of its misery.'

"So, Greenfield saw his boy in agony that day, as he had seen him so many times before. The boy couldn't tell him where he was being hurt. Then something dragged him to the closet, where he had kept the chloroform hidden for two months. He took it out. He put it on a handkerchief and placed it on his son's face. And life went out of that lump of flesh. No more torture at the hands of doctors. No more suffering for this poor woman." Here he pointed out Mrs. Greenfield.

"If what he did was the moral thing to do, you can't find him guilty. How much more suffering does Louis Greenfield deserve?"

The jury was out only two hours. It came back with a not guilty verdict. Several of the jurors walked over to shake Greenfield's hand. They had believed him implicitly, they said. They believed (one of them told reporters) that something stronger than himself had forced Greenfield to do what society long ago should have done.

Leibowitz led Louis and Anna Greenfield out of the courtroom. He told reporters that he had arranged for them to spend some time in the country to recover from the ordeal which had taken so much out of them both.

"While you're in the country will you fish?" a reporter asked Greenfield.

"Fish? Fish?" The still dazed Greenfield repeated softly. "I don't know how. I've never had time to learn."

·

8. THAT'S THE MAN!

"A liar must have a good memory."
QUINTILIAN

1

Had Vincent Coll ever walked into the lobby of the University Club on Fifth Avenue and Fifty-fourth Street, the doorman probably would have thought him to be a recent graduate of the University of Pennsylvania. Coll always wore a blue serge suit and a tie striped with the red and blue of Pennsylvania. He had the freshly washed look of a recent college graduate and his large blue eyes were soft. He smiled easily, and he had fine white teeth. He had wavy auburn hair. Girls called him "Baby Face."

Vincent Coll's appearance was a complete negation of his character, for actually Vincent was a psychopath to whom killing was merely an incident in a busy life of crime. Coll was the only man in New York actually feared by rival mobsters. Coll in a temper was absolutely unpredictable. He might turn his own home into an abattoir or slay a group of his associates because of a fancied insult. They called him "Mad Dog" Coll.

The police had been trying to get Coll for some time. They knew that he was responsible for at least a dozen killings, all the result of his ambition to control the numbers racket, and they knew that as long as he walked the streets it was inevitable that he would be the center of violence. But they had no evidence against him that would stand up in court. At twenty-two, Coll had pulled off the most daring underworld coup of his time. He had kidnapped Big Frenchy de Mange, chief of staff to Owney Madden, the kingpin of all New York mobsterdom. Coll hotfooted Big Frenchy with lighted matches

178

until he sent to Owney for ransom money. Madden paid off and Frenchy was freed. This was something that just wasn't done among the elite underworld aristocracy. You just don't go around snatching important characters like Big Frenchy. Coll had offended Dutch Schulz and others of the underworld. It was common knowledge that it was only a matter of time when he'd be "rubbed out" by the vice lords of New York.

Coll's province was Harlem, and any time a crime was committed in that part of New York, the police, usually with good reason, nominated Coll as either the instigator or the perpetrator. One day, a car roared through East 107th Street. It slowed momentarily as it reached the middle of the block and the barrels of two sub-machine guns poked their ugly noses out of the windows of the sedan. And then both guns began to bark. Their target was one Anthony Trobino, a character with a long police record and many enemies. He dropped to the pavement unharmed, but when the car disappeared down the street five children lay writhing on the pavement with bullets in their small bodies. One of them, five-year-old Michael Vengalli, was dead.

As a rule the New York public is apathetic when it comes to homicide by and upon professional gangsters. But the murder of an innocent child and the wounding of four others aroused a wave of indignation and horror not often felt in New York. The gunmen who had fired so indiscriminately and so irresponsibly were immediately termed the "Baby Killers." Police Commissioner Mulrooney turned loose his whole army of human beagles to hunt the killers. Rewards totaling thirty thousand dollars were posted.

Two months later Vincent Coll was captured, taken into custody and charged with the shooting. When they asked Baby Face his profession, he said solemnly, "Bricklayer." Leibowitz was retained to defend Coll.

Coll claimed that he was far, far away on the day of the slaughter. He was in the Adirondacks, proverbial hideout for New York criminals looking for privacy and relaxation. A few days before the shooting in Harlem, police had picked up eight of Coll's mob in the Adirondacks, which gave some credence to his statement. But nothing that Coll said meant anything to the police, because like

179

manna from heaven, a witness had dropped into their laps. He was George Brecht, and the *New York Post* referred to him as a "naive hillbilly from Missouri." On the day of the killing he happened to be walking along 107th Street. He heard the roar of the car; he heard the bark of the guns and he stood transfixed and watched the whole tragic scene. There were two gunmen in the car, Brecht said, one in the front, the other in the back; both leaned out as they discharged their guns and he was able to see them clearly.

He told his story on the witness stand, and when asked if he saw either of the killers in court he stepped down from the witness chair, walked to the defendant's table, tapped Coll lightly on the shoulder and said confidently, "That is the man."

At that time Bob Burns and his hillbilly humor were popular on the radio, and Brecht reminded spectators of the droll Arkansan. Brecht was calm and composed under Leibowitz' cross-examination.

"By the way, where do you live?" Leibowitz asked.

Brecht turned to Judge Joseph E. Corrigan. "Do I have to answer that question, Judge?" he asked diffidently. "I have a wife and family, and although I can take care of myself, I am afraid that gangsters might harm them if I reveal my home town."

"I quite understand," Judge Corrigan said. "No, you don't have to answer that question."

Leibowitz bowed to the Judge, but he was very happy about the ruling. A very recent Court of Appeals decision had stated that a witness must reveal his background and his residence, so that his character could be investigated by defense counsel. This quite clearly was reversible error.

"You read in the papers that a reward of thirty thousand dollars had been offered for information resulting in the conviction of the murderers, didn't you?" Leibowitz asked.

"Me, I only read the funny papers," Brecht answered in his Bob Burns drawl, and the courtroom tittered. Even Judge Corrigan flashed an appreciative smile at this fine witness. Leibowitz hammered away at Brecht all morning, but the witness never lost his air of composure; he was either telling the truth or he had been beautifully rehearsed for the occasion. Leibowitz sensed that there was something wrong with Brecht. The ordinary witness would have shown some signs of nervousness or resentment at some of the questions. Brecht maintained a calm demeanor. Leibowitz asked what Brecht did for a living. The witness hesitated for a split second and then said that he sold Eskimo Pies. Leibowitz tucked that answer away in the back of his mind, and with it he retained the memory of that split-second hesitation before the witness had answered. During the luncheon recess Leibowitz sent out for an Eskimo Pie. When court resumed he asked Brecht to describe the wrapper on an Eskimo Pie. He didn't even recall the rising sun on the wrapper. Brecht for the first time appeared nervous. Did he use dry ice to keep the Eskimo Pies from melting? The witness hesitated and said that no dry ice was necessary. He said that he carried the delicacies around in a cardboard box and that their own frozen condition kept them from melting. Leibowitz stalked him relentlessly, and it soon developed that the witness knew no more about Eskimo Pies than he did about the nebular hypothesis. Leibowitz had branded him as a liar, but neither the jury nor Judge Corrigan seemed impressed. Brecht had told a small lie about how he earned his living, but his identification still stood.

Leibowitz asked Brecht what had brought him to the Harlem section, and Brecht said that he was looking for a job in a belt factory at First Avenue and 107th Street. With typical thoroughness, Leibo- witz had familiarized himself with every building in the neighborhood. "Suppose I told you that there is no belt factory there?"

"I can't help that," Brecht said with mock resignation.

"Were you looking for a crap game?"

"I don't shoot craps," the witness said a bit disdainfully.

"Were you looking for a place to buy a drink?"

"I don't drink," Brecht said.

Leibowitz brought out the fact that Brecht had been the guest of the Police Department for four months. They had installed him in a midtown hotel and had put him on the police payroll. They had taken him to night clubs, to fights at Madison Square Garden and ball games at the Polo Grounds. It had certainly been a charming four months' holiday for Brecht, marred only by the fact that the police never let him out of their sight. They wanted nothing to happen to this precious package through whom they would write finis to the murderous career of Mad Dog Vincent Coll. Now, as Brecht sat on the stand in this packed courtroom, he was paying off for the hospitality shown him, and when he was through and Coll had been convicted, the jackpot of thirty thousand dollars in reward money was waiting for him, and Christmas was only two days away. It would be a very happy Christmas indeed for Mr. George Brecht.

Leibowitz pounded away at Brecht all afternoon, but he couldn't shake the witness. And yet he felt that Brecht was lying. Two children who had escaped the bullets had testified that both gunmen had worn their hats down over their foreheads, nearly covering their faces; and Leibowitz was positive that the two thirteen-year-olds were telling the truth. But Brecht calmly swore that neither gunman had bothered to hide his face. With Brecht still on the stand, Judge Corrigan adjourned the court until the next day.

Leibowitz went back to his office to take stock. District Attorney James T. Neary had a pretty good case against Coll. When Coll had been captured, police found that his auburn hair had been dyed black, he had grown a mustache and was wearing glasses. The D.A. would claim that Coll had fled right after the killing and had disguised himself. This, coupled with the identification by Brecht, put Coll just a step from the electric chair. Leibowitz felt he could throw doubt on Brecht's identification in his summary. Brecht was just too certain, too emphatic in his statement that he had seen Coll. Leibowitz knew that men like Coll seldom did their killings in broad daylight unless they hid their faces behind handkerchiefs or masks. But it would be difficult to convince a jury of that. No, somehow he would have to destroy Brecht. But how? If he knew where Brecht had come from he could have him investigated. But he didn't know, and besides, there was no time for that now.

Leibowitz kept thinking of Brecht on the witness stand; how he talked out of the side of his mouth with his lips pressed tightly together. That might be a Midwestern mannerism or it might be . . . A sudden thought struck Leibowitz. Men who had spent time in jail where the silence rule still prevails often fell into the habit of talking that way to escape the vigilance of guards. Could it be that Brecht was an ex-con? Leibowitz had a hunch that he was. Brecht had denied on the stand that he had ever been in jail. He had gone further and said that he had never been a witness in a courtroom before. But he could be lying. That was Leibowitz' hunch.

While he was debating how best to make his hunch take on some substance, Joseph Gavin, a probation officer in the Children's Court of Brooklyn, walked into his office with an amazing Christmas present for Leibowitz.

"I saw this fellow Brecht's picture in this afternoon's paper," Gavin said. "I used to know him in Saint Louis. I was a probation officer there for seventeen years and he was one of my charges. Let me tell you about Brecht . . ."

Leibowitz listened. The next morning he went to court in a happy mood. Within a few minutes he had completely demolished Brecht's credibility and had branded him as a jailbird, perjurer and "professional witness" who made a specialty of helping police to "identify" suspected criminals. He had begun his rather unique career at the age of nineteen, when he had testified for the State of Missouri at the trial of two defendants he identified as the gunmen who had murdered Dr. August H. Sante. But the jury didn't believe him and turned the prisoners loose. Leibowitz forced him to admit that he had been paid not only by the State but by the family of Dr. Sante for that testimony. Later he was convicted of stealing diamonds in Saint Louis and served two years in prison.

Coldly, methodically, Leibowitz destroyed George Brecht. The hapless witness squirmed, he threw helpless glances toward Neary, he appealed to Judge Corrigan, but relentlessly Leibowitz kept after him and finally even the jurors looked at the sweating, red-faced witness with contempt in their eyes.

Finally Judge Corrigan banged his gavel on the bench. "In view of this development," he said angrily, "I direct the jury to return a verdict of not guilty."

Leibowitz could not resist one final barb. He arose, addressed the court and said, "I move that George Brecht be committed for perjury."

"That is a matter for the court to decide," Judge Corrigan said testily. "The court will mind its own business and prefers that you mind yours, Mr. Leibowitz."

And so Coll walked out of the courtroom a free man. The trial was over. As far as the public was concerned, Leibowitz had freed another criminal who should have been behind bars. But this time the newspapers were indignant not because another gangster had "beaten the rap." They were indignant because of the use of a jailbird and perjurer by the District Attorney's office and the police. The *New York World-Telegram* editorialized under the caption, "Why Didn't the Police Know?"

George Brecht, after his positive and dramatic identification of the two defendants in the courtroom, was shown to be a perjured witness who had concealed a police record of his own. The prosecution admitted the perjury of its witness and the breakdown of its case.

There was but one thing to do, and Judge Corrigan did it. He instructed the jury to bring in a verdict of "Not Guilty".

Nevertheless, a question remains—a grave question:

If police and prosecutor were ignorant of Brecht's record WHY were they ignorant?

That Brecht's address was not made public at the trial in order to protect his wife and children from possible gang vengeance seemed reasonable enough.

But that police and prosecutor themselves did not know where Brecht came from, that they could have accepted him as a witness without insisting upon knowing more about him, would have appeared incredible. Is such indifference customary—as to State witnesses—provided they have something to tell?

"It is hardly likely that we should have let him go on the witness stand if we had known. That would have been suicidal." So Police Commissioner Mulrooney was quoted last week.

But if the New York police failed to make the simplest routine effort to find out about Brecht's antecedents, if the District Attorney's office accepted him as a witness without making sure the police had used reasonable diligence to check his record, then the case is still an ugly blot on prosecution methods hereabout.

That Coll is a notorious gangster makes no difference. He was not being tried for his record but for a particular crime, and that

184

a capital one. The prosecution had but one key witness. It might have been expected to use extra care and scruple about that witness. The same applies to the police, who kept the witness on salary for months.

Suppose, on Brecht's testimony, Coll had been convicted, electrocuted—and then Brecht's record had come to light. Would that have been a high mark for justice in this Commonwealth? Would Coll's bad name have made the procedural injustice any less?

Commissioner Mulrooney should probe to the bottom the police element in this extraordinary case. The District Attorney's office should make full explanation of its part therein.

The *Daily Mirror* and the *Sun* accused the police of nothing more sinister than ignorance. Not once did anyone protest that the police, in taking direct action, had usurped the prerogative of the jury. The police had judged Coll, had in their own minds found him guilty and had then bolstered their case by the use of a disreputable witness. There was no cry of indignation from the public which undoubtedly felt, along with the police, that legal safeguards and constitutional guarantees were only for the benefit of the pure in heart and had not been written for the benefit of men like Coll.

And so Brecht was sent to Bellevue Hospital presumably for mental examination, but after a few pleasant days there he left, perhaps to resume his unique business as a professional witness and, incidentally, a professional brazen liar.

2

I once asked Judge Leibowitz, "After all these years as lawyer and judge, how expert have you become in spotting a liar in the courtroom?"

The Judge smiled. "I can smell a liar a mile away. My favorite piece on this subject is the one written by former Chief Magistrate William McAdoo, a brilliant wit and great jurist. It was published in the *New York Herald Tribune*.

The article said, in part:

I must confess I have a secret admiration for certain types of liars, and find amusement in other less clever, less tactful and less masters of mendacity. It is interesting to sit in court day after day and hear two, ten or even twenty statements with radical variations as to a single and comparatively simple occurrence. It is difficult not to admire the imperturbable falsifier who, with liberty and property at stake, withstands avalanches of direct and circumstantial evidence with the innocent look of an infant and the courage of a soldier and insists he is the victim of circumstances and the center of a conspiracy of prejudicial policemen and disinterested citizens.

It has a soothing effect to marshal liars mentally into companies and brigades and divide them according to their rank—clever liars, stupid liars, ignorant liars, intelligent liars, able liars, weak liars, picturesque liars, amusing liars, irritating liars, comical liars, tragic liars, unintentional liars, intentional liars, phlegmatic liars, nervous liars, composed liars, bold liars, timid liars, liars for love, liars for hate, liars for pleasure, liars for profit, liars to put you in jail, liars to take you out, professional liars for pay, amateur liars for friendship, liars who shorten the truth, liars who lengthen it, liars who suppress, liars who exaggerate, cowardly liars from threats and fears, cold-blooded liars, bribed liars, whom the defendant and crooks have more than requited for their losses, gangster liars shielding the gang on peril of their lives.

No two persons will give the same account of an incident they both witnessed or even agree upon the words used by a third person on a certain occasion. They will paint a door black, blue and green, and give more varieties of weather for the same day than the weather bureau does for all the days in the year. They vary the time of the day or night by minutes or hours; they differ in their measurement of space by inches, feet and miles; they will describe the clothing and the appearance of an individual that would apply to fifty persons and paint more varieties of faces than could be found in a photograph gallery.

These are the honest and well-intentioned people who, when they go on the witness stand, unconsciously distort the truth—exaggerating one circumstance and minimizing another. Under cross-examination by lawyers of a certain type they become antagonistic, throw truth to the winds and stick to any mistaken statement they have made without regard to its obvious falsehood. These are the witnesses, honest, im-

186

partial and disinterested who, if the court permits it, are badgered mercilessly in criminal trials by counsel for defense.

Of course, the magistrate or the presiding judge who permits an honest witness to be heckled and confused is derelict in his duty, and yet a good deal of this goes on in courts all over the country. Generally speaking, it is confined to certain types of lawyers, who are entirely conscienceless in adopting any means to win a case.

In court the constitutional and chronic liar, if such there be, is a standpatter. Having asserted a certain statement to be a true fact, he puts his back to the wall and rigidly and stubbornly stands to it. And no amount of cross-examination will shake him a bit.

Professional criminals may belong to this class of constitutional liars, but too often when they are on trial they avail themselves of the laws in most states that forbid the judge or the district attorney to comment to the jury on their failure to take the witness stand. And so they give no personal evidence in their own behalf.

There is another class of liars the witness stand knows very well—the liars who forget. Just when the public interest is widespread in some famous case they are amazed by the total lack of memory some of the witnesses suffer when the opposing lawyers begin their cross-examination. Here is a man who ranks high in the financial and business world, or is even a conspicuously able lawyer himself; a woman who has moved all her life in polished and intellectual circles, a careful, accurate and reliable banker, or the head of some great industrial enterprise. Under pressure their memory fades out entirely and a great cloud of vagueness, of forgetfulness, envelops them.

This loss of memory on the part of a criminal defendant is not infrequently the open lane of acquittal—at least it presents an ironclad defense to subsequent charges of perjury. Why recall anything on the witness stand which makes against your side of the case? Ignorance in such a case is more than bliss; it is liberty. But is the lying witness ever exposed and trapped in actual trials in court? Yes, I am glad to say, quite frequently. Much, of course, depends upon the lawyer who does the examining. The traps which catch the witnesses with bad memories or those who are willing to take desperate chances arise from direct and convincing contradictions. In most cases they are the compromising letter he wrote, the document he signed, the telegram he sent, the telephone conversation he had with another person or the betraying dictaphone. A crooked man or woman necessarily leaves

187

a crooked trail. Such persons twist and turn in their lying lives. They deceive and double on themselves until under severe examination they forget themselves—they forget where they have been and what they have done. They have deceived so many people they get intoxicated with a sense of their own infallibility and exceeding cleverness. They have turned so many corners adroitly that they get careless in turning the next one.

3

Vincent Coll? Two weeks after he had walked so blithely out of the courtroom he dropped into a drugstore on the corner of Eighth Avenue and Twenty-third Street. He went into the phone booth and then proceeded to violate one of gangsterdom's most inviolable rules. A man who lives in a climate of violence and to whom murder is a business, invariably observes a few fundamental precautions. No self-respecting mobster would ever take a seat in a restaurant so that his back would be to the door. No experienced practitioner would ever enter a cruising cab unless he knew the driver. No seasoned veteran of gang warfare would ever answer his own doorbell; and no killer worthy of the name would ever talk in a phone booth for more than three minutes. A man is very vulnerable in a phone booth. If you remain in a booth longer than three minutes you can be spotted, and someone can be summoned to take care of you. But Vincent Coll momentarily forgot this. Vincent was talking to a very influential mob leader, and the mob leader was making a very interesting proposition to Coll, so interesting that Coll forgot his usual caution.

While he was talking a small, thin man with a black felt hat pulled down over his eyes entered the drugstore carrying a violin case. Calmly, unhurriedly, he laid the case on a stool by the soda fountain. He opened the case, took out a machine gun, walked two steps to the phone booth and let Coll have it. Coll's right hand was holding the receiver to his ear. Fifteen slugs smashed through his right arm and entered his head and chest. The small, thin man, still unhurried, put the machine gun back in the violin case, tucked it under his arm and then walked casually out of the drugstore.

Coll, of course, was dead when the medical examiner arrived. Chief Medical Examiner Gonzales, after performing an autopsy, said, "There wasn't enough bone left in his right arm to make a toothpick out of."

Had Leibowitz been less zealous in exposing Brecht as a lying witness and had Coll been convicted, he would have enjoyed a few months of additional life. True, he would have been living in the death house, a hostelry not distinguished for either service or cuisine. Vincent Coll was a worthless savage, an avowed enemy of society, and no one shed any tears when he was "rubbed out." This does not excuse the police who had tried to convict him by lawless means.

In this country the police are bound by the same legal limitations as are the English police, but, unlike them, they do not always accept these rules or work smoothly within the legal limitations which centuries of experience have insisted are necessary. The American policeman often believes that "constitutionality" shelters the criminal.

4

The almost forgotten Wickersham Report issued in the early 1930's was a severe and frightening indictment of American police methods. It showed how "voluntary" confessions were obtained by brutality, drugs and other illegal methods of persuasion. The carefully documented report revealed that many American cities (Detroit was among the chief offenders) had suspended the writ of habeas corpus by declaring that it should no longer be immediately operative, but that a twenty-four-hour period of time should be allowed the police before habeas corpus could be used. It was apparent that some of the police felt that, given twenty-four hours, they could beat or cajole confessions from citizens held incommunicado for that time. The Wickersham Report also showed that where such "witnesses" were held for twenty-four hours, three out of five of them were then released. In short, 60 per cent of those held and completely deprived of their constitutional rights were absolutely innocent.

The lawless enforcement of law by the police had become custom so well established that public indignation aroused by the publication of the Wickersham Report resulted in nothing but minor (and soon forgotten) reforms.

The numerous rights guaranteed all citizens by the Constitution are considered by the police to be safeguards only for the innocent. Some of the police reject the fact that these rights were established for the protection of the guilty and the apparently guilty as well. In the first criminal case ever to be tried in an American court, the police offered a confession by a stable boy that he had burned several stables. The confession had been obtained by illegal means, and the court threw it out. There was no question of the lad's guilt, but the court ruled that he was entitled to the same protection of the Constitution given an innocent man.

The police and some district attorneys salve their consciences with the belief that man's traditional rights can be safely disregarded in the case of known criminals, and yet continue in full force for the protection of innocent persons. This was the legal philosophy of Nazi Germany, but it is one that is hardly compatible with democratic principles.

The best safeguard society has against police who insist upon enforcing the law through illegal means is an alert, capable defense lawyer who is equally zealous in defending the rights of both criminal and exemplary citizen. The Constitution was written for "all citizens." It is absurd to say that George Brecht was a typical witness and that the police make a habit of producing perjurers to obtain convictions. But it has happened often enough to justify a defense lawyer in looking with skepticism upon a "surprise" witness who is the only one to identify the defendant as a killer.

5

"Careless" identification is, of course, more frequent than dishonest identification. In July, 1945, the New York public was shocked to read the story of Bertram Campbell, who had just been released from

190

Sing Sing after serving more than three years for a crime he never committed. Campbell was a customer's man in Wall Street, and in 1938 he had been charged with forging two checks amounting to seventy-five hundred dollars. He protested his innocence in vain. Two men identified him as the man who had cashed the checks, and he was sentenced to a term of five to ten years. Three years later a dope addict, named Alexander Thiel, was picked up. He was in a talkative mood and while he was about it he told of having forged the two checks for which Campbell was in jail. He bore a superficial resemblance to Bertram Campbell. The two witnesses had been honest enough, but they had been careless, and their sworn identification had sent an entirely innocent man to jail. Thomas E. Dewey was the District Attorney when Campbell had been prosecuted. Now as Governor, he made what amends he could for the error society had made. At his behest the legislature passed a special bill remunerating Campbell for "shame, humiliation, and loss of liberty." Campbell received $115,000 from the State of New York. But he didn't live to enjoy it. A year later, his health completely broken by his long confinement, he died.

Mark Twain once said, "When I was a young man I could remember anything, whether it had happened or not." Youngsters often imagine things, and, if they try hard enough, the image assumes reality. Grown-ups, too, often mistakenly, think that their powers of observation are too great to be questioned. A witness who says with conviction, "That's the man," can, of course, be quite honestly mistaken. The eyes of man are useful but not infallible organs. It is not only possible for one man to make an honest but completely erroneous identification; it is possible for twenty men to mistakenly identify a defendant. Perhaps the classic case which illustrates the unreliability of the eyesight is that of John Barry Coughlin.

John Barry Coughlin lived in Brooklyn. He was employed by the Personal Finance Company, and his job was to investigate applicants for loans and decide whether or not they would be good credit risks. The company for which he worked thought highly of him. A veteran of World War I, he was active in American Legion affairs and

191

greatly respected by his neighbors. He was happily married to a schoolteacher. Coughlin was a tall man—six foot three—with rather sharp features.

He was in the Bronx one day investigating a few applicants. His search for one of them brought him to Fox Street. It was January, a cold, blustery day, and as he hurried along the street Coughlin had his coat collar up. He was startled when a small, well set-up man rushed at him and said angrily, "Hello, Miller, I hoped I'd see you again."

"Miller? You've got the wrong man, neighbor," Coughlin smiled. "My name is John Coughlin."

"Your name is Miller and you swindled me out of fifteen dollars," the man shouted, and then he cried, "Police . . . police!"

By chance there was a patrolman halfway down the block who heard the cry and came running. "Arrest this crook," the little man demanded, while Coughlin stood there apparently dumbfounded by the outburst.

"What's it all about?" the cop asked.

The excited complainant said that he was Landis Atkinson, superintendent of an apartment building at 712 Fox Street. He told the cop that Miller had called on him a few days previously and had offered him a job as superintendent of an apartment building in Astoria, Queens. The pay was almost double what he was getting, and he said he'd take the job. Miller said the owner of the Astoria building insisted that all of his employees be bonded. The bond cost only fifteen dollars, he added. That was all right with Atkinson. Miller said that he was licensed to handle such matters and he'd take care of the bond. Atkinson had handed over fifteen dollars and Miller wrote out a receipt and handed it to Atkinson. Then Miller said he'd be around the next morning with the bond and with instructions as to when Atkinson could move to his new job. But Miller never showed up.

"You've got me mixed up with someone else," Coughlin said.

"Oh, no." Atkinson turned to the cop. "I live right across the street. My wife is home. She was there when this swindler took my money."

"Well, let's go along and see if she can identify him," the cop said.

They walked over to the building which Atkinson "superintended." His was the basement apartment. As soon as they entered the living room Mrs. Atkinson shrieked, "That's the man! That's Miller!"

There was nothing for the cop to do but to take them all to the nearest precinct.

"I tell you, this is all crazy talk; these people have mistaken me for someone else," Coughlin said frantically.

The sergeant on desk duty looked at Coughlin's six foot three, at his striking features and said coldly, "Nobody in God's world could ever mistake you for someone else."

Each station house has a teletype, and the details of every arrest are immediately flashed to Police Headquarters. When the report of Coughlin's arrest came through, there was considerable satisfaction at Headquarters. During the past few weeks nineteen apartment house superintendents (the word "janitor" had become obsolete) had complained of being victimized in the same way. The description each gave fitted that of John Barry Coughlin. This information, with the names of the nineteen complainants, was forwarded to the office of District Attorney Samuel J. Foley in the Bronx.

The trial was held in the Court of Special Sessions with three judges presiding. One after another the complainants looked carefully at Coughlin and each one said, "That's the man." Each one of them said that he had been defrauded of fifteen dollars. Coughlin took the stand and swore that he was innocent. The Personal Finance Company records showed that Coughlin had been investigating credit risks on the days the complainants swore he had defrauded them, but the identification by the irate superintendents was so positive that the three judges found the defendant guilty in short order. Coughlin was sent to jail to await sentence.

The day after the trial ended, a frantic, despairing woman was ushered into Samuel Leibowitz' office. She was Coughlin's wife, an attractive and intelligent, if temporarily distraught, woman. She told Leibowitz the story. He listened impassively. On the face of it there seemed to be no doubt that the court had acted wisely in finding the

193

defendant guilty. But the woman protested that he was completely innocent.

"We both work," she said, close to hysteria. "We have saved up forty thousand dollars. Why should my husband stoop to steal fifteen dollars from a poor janitor? I tell you, Mr. Leibowitz, he was framed."

"Just a minute," Leibowitz protested. "Sam Foley is the District Attorney in the Bronx. No man has a greater regard for justice than he has. No, Mrs. Coughlin, neither your husband nor anyone else was ever framed by the office of the Bronx District Attorney."

"But he's innocent, I tell you," the desperate woman cried. Her sincerity and faith in her husband impressed the lawyer. She had a copy of the trial record with her and he took it up and read it. It was short, and it was obvious that the identification by the witnesses had been fair and not influenced by either police or representatives of the District Attorney's office. There on the third page of the record he read the testimony of the oddly named Landis Atkinson.

". . . then I asked him for a receipt," Atkinson had testified. "And on the back of a card he wrote, 'Received from Landis Atkinson, fifteen dollars.'"

Leibowitz finished reading the record. What about that card? If Coughlin was an innocent man, why hadn't his defense counsel introduced it into evidence? Did he feel that Coughlin was guilty and that the handwriting on the card would prove to be his?

"I can't find any reason to believe your husband is innocent," he said bluntly. "He had a perfectly fair trial. Had he been innocent, he would have insisted upon comparing his handwriting with that on the receipt."

"The receipt?" Mrs. Coughlin looked at him blankly.

"Yes, the receipt Miller gave to Atkinson."

"I never thought that was important," she said breathlessly. "Why, that card would prove his innocence."

"It could prove his guilt too," Leibowitz said dryly.

"But he never wrote on that card," she said excitedly. "He was nowhere near Fox Street on the day Atkinson claims he was swindled. Please, Mr. Leibowitz, get hold of that card."

194

Despite himself, Leibowitz was beginning to sympathize with the unhappy Mrs. Coughlin. He said he'd investigate. He went to the Bronx and saw District Attorney Foley.

"I'm not saying that this man is innocent," he said to Foley. "I do say that the handwriting on the receipt should have been examined by a reliable expert. That handwriting is more reliable evidence than all of the say-sos of these twenty witnesses that 'that is the man.' "

"I agree with you," the fair-minded Foley said. "John Stanton handled the case. Perhaps he has the card."

He lifted a phone and asked that Stanton bring him the file of the Coughlin case. Within a few moments Stanton had arrived. "Sam Leibowitz is disturbed about the Coughlin case," Foley said.

Stanton looked puzzled. "It seemed an open-and-shut case. Coughlin was a nice chap, I thought, but when twenty witnesses identified him there didn't seem to be room for any doubt as to his guilt. I've heard of one or two witnesses making mistaken identifications, but I've never heard of twenty men making such a mistake."

"Neither have I," Leibowitz admitted, "but the evidence of the handwriting should be conclusive."

"I agree with you," Stanton said. "The card was there if the defense wanted it. It was not part of the prosecution case. The chance of Coughlin being innocent is about a hundred to one, but he deserves that chance. Suppose we get samples of his handwriting and compare them with the writing on the card."

"Good idea," Leibowitz nodded.

Stanton phoned the jail. He talked to the warden and then hung up. "Coughlin writes to his wife every day," he said. "Suppose I intercept one of those letters. Then we'll have a good honest example of his handwriting."

Stanton did that and handed the letter over to the defense counsel. Leibowitz took the letter and the card to the late Albert S. Osborn, acknowledged to be the greatest handwriting expert in America. It was Osborn's testimony that had doomed Bruno Richard Hauptmann. Osborn and his brilliant son, who was his associate, returned their report within a few days. The Osborns declared that there was no similarity at all between the two examples of writing. They went

195

further. They said that it was virtually impossible for the man who wrote the letter to have written the receipt. Stanton looked at the communication from the Osborns and wiped his brow.

"It looks as though we almost made a bad mistake," he said. "Let's get moving fast."

Stanton and Foley, who had been apprised of the new development, were convinced now that Coughlin had been the victim of a horrible set of circumstances. The law in its wisdom does not authorize a district attorney to free a man already convicted. If it did, there might be grave danger of collusion between an unscrupulous district attorney and a guilty criminal, and the colonial lawmakers took steps to guard against such a contingency. In such cases the defense attorney may make a motion that the conviction be set aside on the ground that new evidence has come to light, and if the district attorney concurs, a new trial is ordered. Leibowitz made the motion and Foley agreed. A new trial was ordered. Coughlin was released in three-thousand-dollar bail.

The day before the new trial was to take place, the giant dirigible *Hindenberg* burst into flames as it was being attached to its mooring mast at Lakehurst, New Jersey. The next morning the newspapers were filled with stories of the tragedy. Leibowitz read the newspaper accounts on his way to the Bronx County Courthouse where the new trial was to be held. The *Daily News* carried pictures of some of the survivors of the disaster. Leibowitz was startled as he looked at one of the pictures. He put the *Daily News* into his pocket.

Atkinson was ordered to the stand and he repeated his story. Leibowitz cross-examined him. He folded the *Daily News* in such a way that only the picture was revealed. He handed the paper to Atkinson.

"Do you recognize the man in that picture?" he asked.

"Sure," the witness said, confidently. "That's Miller. That's this defendant who calls himself Coughlin."

"Open the newspaper and tell us what it says under the picture," Leibowitz ordered.

Atkinson opened the paper, read the caption identifying the man in the picture as a survivor of the Hindenberg disaster, a resident of

Berlin who had never been in this country before. He raised bewildered eyes to Leibowitz. "You gotta admit he looks just like him," Atkinson said defensively.

Leibowitz nodded. "You're right. And this defendant looks just like the man who swindled you and nineteen others. But he's not the same man."

Then the younger Osborn took the stand to testify that Coughlin could not have written the receipt that the swindler had given to Atkinson.

"I move," Stanton said, "that the charge against Coughlin be dismissed. This man is obviously innocent."

The court promptly discharged John Barry Coughlin. He not only had one double; he had two doubles. His resemblance to the first one, the swindler, had almost sent him to jail. His resemblance to the second one, the *Hindenberg* survivor, had helped establish his innocence.

6

Now, years later, as Judge Leibowitz, presiding over major trials in Brooklyn's highest criminal court, he carries with him a deep-rooted caution when witnesses make positive identifications. Many times when a witness points confidently at a defendant and says, "That's the man," he remembers the lying Brecht, the mistaken Atkinson and his nineteen fellow apartment superintendents. Time and time again, to make certain that an innocent man is not packed off to jail or to the chair, Judge Leibowitz takes over the questioning, and young lawyers who, at law school, had heard of Leibowitz the cross-examiner, watch such thorough interrogations with delight. More than once from the bench he has exposed lying witnesses, and more than once his judicial questioning has revealed positive witnesses to have been mistaken. No judge was ever more meticulous in probing every nook and cranny of the mind of the witness who says, "That is the man."

This caution is well known to lawyers and district attorneys who come before him. One night he was to speak at a lawyers' club dinner, and the toastmaster who introduced him dwelt humorously upon the guest's obsession and concern with witnesses who confidently (and, of course, usually correctly) make identifications.

"Our guest tonight," the toastmaster said, "may believe his own eyes, but he seldom believes the eyes of a witness. He looks upon eyewitnesses who appear before him with the suspicious eye of a physician peering at the label on a bottle containing a panacea which purports to cure all ills. In his court there has been established a new judicial presumption. It is, 'The eyewitness may well be mistaken.' But one thing is certain; no defendant in his court was ever convicted on false or mistaken testimony of eyewitnesses."

Judge Leibowitz winced at this. When he arose to speak he ruefully repudiated the aura of infallibility with which the toastmaster had surrounded him, and he told the gathering of lawyers the story of a trial which had just terminated in his court. The story was of a run-of-the-mill stick-up in the Negro section of Brooklyn. It was so unimportant that the newspapers hardly mentioned it. But it had given Judge Leibowitz many sleepless nights before the issues had been resolved.

Frances Jones was one of three defendants charged with robbery and assault. Her co-defendants were Steve Williams and Genevieve Brooks, and the evidence against them seemed to be overwhelming. The complainant in this case was a respectable citizen, Oscar Wheeler, who owned a small restaurant. At 3:00 A.M. Wheeler closed his restaurant and started to walk home. He had only nine dollars in his pocket. It had been raining. Wheeler was wearing a raincoat and carrying an umbrella. He had walked only three or four blocks when he was attacked by a man and two women. The art of "mugging" had been developed to a rather high degree in Brooklyn, and the male assailant was a workmanlike practitioner of the art. He hooked his left arm across Wheeler's throat, grabbed his left wrist with his right hand and began to apply pressure on his throat. Wheeler, a strong and determined man, resisted, and then two girls came to the aid of the assailant. One of them grabbed the umbrella which had fallen to the pavement and gave Wheeler a few unladylike pokes with it. An umbrella is an unwieldy weapon to use at close range. The male mugger realized this and called out to the second girl sharply, "Stab him! stab him!" A sharp instrument appeared in her right hand and she lunged at Wheeler's chest. The intrepid Wheeler grabbed the girl's arm, and then the mugger pulled a gun and ordered him to stop resisting. Wheeler, a Brooklyn version of Superman, reached for the gun. The mugger pulled the trigger and a bullet went through Wheeler's left hand. Wheeler finally realized that they were too many for him and ceased his struggling. They searched him, took what they could find and hurried away from the scene.

Wheeler went home, phoned the police, and within a few minutes a prowl car drew up in front of his house. He told his story and the officers suggested he accompany them while they cruised around the neighborhood, on the remote chance that he might see and identify the three robbers. They visited half a dozen all-night diners and then drew up in front of a well-lighted cafeteria. They looked through the plate-glass window and Wheeler pointed excitedly to a front table. A man and two women were sitting there. Wheeler's identification of them as his attackers was emphatic.

The man's name was Steve Williams and his two companions were Frances Jones and Genevieve Brooks. In the right-hand pocket of Frances' coat there was an ice pick which Wheeler said was the weapon she had used in her attempt to stab him. Williams had a .32-caliber gun in his pocket.

Steve Williams said that he had bought the gun the day before from a stranger he met in a bar, and that he had never fired it (although it held one discharged cartridge). Frances Jones explained the possession of the ice pick by saying she carried it for protection. Her story was that she and her friend Genevieve were merely out for a stroll, and getting hungry, they had dropped into the cafeteria. They met Steve Williams there and sat down with him.

Under constant questioning, Steve Williams finally changed his story and admitted that he had been at the scene of the crime. He had been out strolling (3:00 A.M. seemed to be a popular hour for promenading with his girl, Naomi Dukes). They had been walking along minding their own business when Mr. Wheeler happened along. Williams asked Wheeler for a match and then (accord-

199

ing to Steve) Wheeler had whipped out a gun. They struggled for the gun and it went off. Loyal Naomi Dukes came to the aid of her man by producing a knife and brandishing it at Wheeler. Finally Williams secured possession of the gun and Wheeler ran. That was Steve's story, and it seemed to be an absurd fabrication. A perfunctory investigation failed to locate anyone named "Naomi Dukes," and Williams with his two co-defendants was tried and a jury found all three guilty.

The jury didn't believe the tearful protestations of innocence made by either of the girls. Oscar Wheeler was unshakable in his identification of all three defendants. It was brought out that there was a lamp post not far from the stop where the mugging took place, and there was every reason to believe that Wheeler had been able to get a good look at his three assailants. Nothing remained now except for Judge Leibowitz to sentence the three.

A small, quite irrational doubt kept gnawing at the consciousness of the Judge. Not a single bit of evidence worthy of the name had been brought out in favor of either of the girl defendants, but Judge Leibowitz had an uneasy feeling that they might conceivably be telling the truth.

The Judge called in Chief Probation Officer Fitzgerald and confided his doubts. Fitzgerald went to work. Within a week he had returned to say that part of Williams' story might be true. There was in fact a girl named Naomi Dukes and she was considered to be Williams' "girl." She had disappeared but he was trying to trace her. She had a police record and was currently being sought as a parole skipper.

"Wheeler, the complainant, is a man of integrity who is sincerely convinced that these three defendants attacked him," Fitzgerald said. "He is of course absolutely right in the case of Steve Williams. He is guilty beyond any reasonable doubt. I'm not sure now about the two girls, Judge. They seem to be telling the truth but we've got to check further. If they weren't in this thing, we can prove it only by finding the women who were."

On November 21, 1945, Judge Leibowitz gave Steve Williams (a man with a long criminal record) fifteen to thirty years in Sing Sing, but held the two co-defendants pending further investigation. The search for Naomi Dukes went on.

And then Naomi Dukes was picked up. Questioned by Fitzgerald and an assistant district attorney, she readily told the truth. She had helped Steve Williams mug and rob Wheeler. Wheeler's story was true in every detail—his only mistake was his identification of the two girls. Naomi said that the third member of the hold-up trio was a girl she knew only as "Helen." She had met her for the first time the night before, and "Helen" had been glad to join Steve and herself in the nocturnal adventure. It was "Helen" who had wielded the knife. Naomi made a full confession which exonerated Genevieve Brooks and Frances Jones, and the next day both walked out of jail, free women.

Once again a witness had been honestly wrong in his identification. If Judge Leibowitz' instinct hadn't told him that there was a possibility that the two girls were telling the truth, and if the patient, careful Fitzgerald hadn't done such a thorough job (a job that should have been done by defense counsel), the two girls would still be in jail, victims of an honest mistake of identification and victims of twelve good men and true who had been unable to recognize the truth when they heard it. Later she gave the full name of her female accomplice.

"And that," Judge Leibowitz concluded, "is why I do not always believe the eyes of a witness. Witnesses can look at something without seeing it. The Edgar Allan Poe story of "The Purloined Letter" illustrates what I mean. Now you men, of course, being lawyers, are presumably good observers. Let me ask, 'How many of you smoke Camel cigarettes?' "

About one-quarter of the audience raised hands. The Judge who had introduced the speaker was one of them. Leibowitz asked him and four others who smoked Camels to stand up. He asked the toastmaster how much he smoked.

"I smoke two packs of Camels a day and I've been smoking them for twenty years," he smiled.

"Then you smoke about seven hundred packs a year," Judge Leibowitz said. "In twenty years you've smoked about fourteen thousand packages of Camels. Each time you take your cigarettes out of your pocket you see that package; it is a familiar sight to you. Why, you've taken a package of Camels in your hand at least half a million times in the past twenty years.

"I'm going to ask five of you a question about that camel," he said, picking up a menu and tearing it into five pieces. "Each of you take one of these pieces and write down your answer to my question. Ready? In the picture, is the man leading the camel, or sitting on its back?"

The men wrote, and the Judge read from their slips. "Two men say that the man is leading the camel; two say that he is on the camel's back, and one writes that there is no man there at all. Gentlemen, take out your packages of Camels and see who is correct."

There was a look of sheepish bewilderment on the faces of four of the men.

"You will find that four of you have answered incorrectly, and only one man is correct. There is no man in the picture." Judge Leibowitz laughed. "Four men, mind you, trained in the law, sitting here without any tension or pressure, were in error as to what is on a package of cigarettes they handle every day. Yet in courtrooms, we accept identifications made by poorly trained, perhaps prejudiced, perhaps confused witnesses."

"You don't believe in the old adage, 'Seeing is believing,' apparently," the toastmaster asked.

"The old adage is true," the Judge replied, "but gentlemen, you must not confuse 'seeing' with 'perceiving,' that is, seeing so that a definite, clear image is impressed on the sensitive film of the mind. This morning I got behind the wheel of my car, backed out of my garage and started for the courthouse downtown. The distance is about thirteen miles. I am sure that I kept a careful lookout ahead. I must have observed all of the traffic regulations, passed not a single red light and arrived safely at the courthouse. If any man here asked me to describe any particular object I recall seeing during that trip, I would have to confess that I can't mention one. Why? I 'saw' every car pass, but I didn't 'perceive' a single one, because my attention was not fixed upon any object or occurrence during my trip.

My mind was at work, it is true, but it was immersed in some problem involved in a case that was to come before me this morning. My driving was merely that of an automaton.

"How then can we determine the reliabiliy of an identification?" the Judge continued. "How certain are we that the identification of the witness is good? Ordinarily, the witness's capacity to see is rarely questioned. We accept his own estimate in that respect. Yet, a man's life may be destroyed on that witness's evaluation of his own power of perception. No lawyer, who is worth his salt, will ever fail to put an identification witness through a series of tests in the courtroom to determine that witness's ability to see what he has undertaken to describe to the jury. The eye is the lens through which the picture on the brain is impressed. If the eye doesn't see clearly, it follows that the mental picture must be blurred or distorted and the identification, therefore, worthless. Elementary, but how vital.

"Consider also the things that may distort the view of a witness. Consider the predilections and the bias of the individual. Is it not true that the man who drives an automobile will unconsciously favor the case of the fellow automobilist who is defending a suit by a pedestrian in an accident case? How many times have you men who drive cars called out to your fellow passengers, 'Oh, those damn fool jaywalkers; you'd almost think that they dare you to hit them.'

"Assuming, gentlemen, that the witness's eyesight is good and that his opportunity to see was ample, we have still another problem to consider, namely, the memory. Is his memory trustworthy? He tells the court and jury that he remembers the face of a robber. But how certain are we that his memory is reliable?"

"Judge," a man from the audience queried, "if the witness is an educated and intelligent man, does that not add weight to his identification?"

"Not necessarily," Judge Leibowitz replied. "The mind of the educated man may play tricks to a greater extent than the mind of the ignorant man. The educated man's mind is more susceptible to imagination. It is an acknowledged fact that the tribesman has much keener perception than does the civilized man."

"But, Judge," the questioner persisted, "isn't it true that when a per-

203

son is under a terrific mental stress, such as when the victim has a gun thrust into his face, his mental faculties are more acute and his identification of the robber, therefore, more reliable?"

"Again, I say, not necessarily so. Some people are so frozen with fear that they cannot honestly tell whether it was a white man or a black man who pointed the gun. Others, however, react in the opposite extreme. Their sense of perception is sharpened to a razor's edge when confronted with a smashing emotional impact. But how can we in the courtroom tell with any degree of certainty into which class the witness falls? We are bound to rely upon the witness's own appraisal of his capacity to see and to remember what he has seen.

"Then again, there is the element of suggestion. Suggestion may wield a powerful influence upon the mind of the prospective witness. You noted gentlemen, that only a few moments ago I put the question to this audience, 'Is the man leading a camel, or is he sitting on its back?' I did not ask, 'Is there a man on the cover of the package?' Four men, trained lawyers, succumbed to the suggestion contained in my question, namely, that there was a man in the picture. How much more amenable to suggestion is the 'run-of-the-mill witness' who clambers on and off the stands in our courtrooms?"

"Just think for a moment of a case that may not be at all unusual. Smith was held up by a gunman. Two months later his phone rings. The detective handling the case is on the other end. 'I'm coming over to take you to the station house. We have a suspect we'd like you to look at.' The detective arrives and Mr. Smith hurries down to the police car. On the way Mr. Smith asks, 'Who is this fellow?' 'Oh, a mug with a long criminal record, an ex-convict, a gunman who has been committing the very same kind of robberies as yours.' Soon they are at the precinct. If the suspect has already confessed and Smith has been told of his confession, his mind has thus been favorably conditioned to make an identification, especially if the suspect approximates the guilty person in appearance. In other words, what would have been a hesitating Smith is now a Smith who is positive 'that's the man.'

"I see several district attorneys here in the audience. They are probably swearing at me under their breaths for giving out 'shop

204

secrets'; but have no fear, gentlemen. There are few cases, indeed, which are barren of other evidence to support an identification. In the vast majority of cases there are facts and circumstances that cry aloud that the identification is an accurate one.

"The cases are rare where the lawyers cannot find corroborating circumstances. In cases where the guilt or innocence of an accused must stand or fall on an identification, you had better watch out, or you may be doing a horrible injustice."

"In your experience, who make the best witnesses—men or women?" the question came from an assistant district attorney.

"Men," the Judge said promptly. "Women are usually awfully sure of themselves, so sure that the possibility that they may be mistaken never enters their minds. They often tell what they call 'little white lies' even on the witness stand. To them a 'white lie' is an unimportant untruth that gives pleasure to someone.

"But both men and women can go completely away from the truth on the stand," he continued. "Even well-intentioned, honest witnesses. Remember the courtroom is a strange place to them. It is not their natural metier. A prosecutor starts shouting at them in cross-examination; a defense counsel objects; the judge bangs his gavel. All this is apt to confuse a normally intelligent, calm person. Confusion is not an ally of truth. It's up to the judge to see that a witness is given a minimum of heckling; that he or she gets a chance to reflect before answering.

"One of the most uncertain qualities of the human mind is the ability to remember. As time goes by, the image of the face of the robber fades more and more on the mental film of the victim. Yet, in our courts of justice, we behold, for example, the spectacle of an eighty-year-old, nearsighted, Amandus Hockmuth, sitting on the witness stand in the Lindbergh kidnapping case and swearing upon everything that's holy that Bruno Richard Hauptmann rode by in a car two years before on the day that the crime was committed. He swore that he was positive that Hauptmann was that man. Granted that he was sincere, it was only a belief, an opinion at best. Yes, gentlemen, when a witness says, 'That is the man,' he is merely expressing an opinion that the accused is the culprit.

205

"Then again, the hardest thing in the world," he continued, "is for the ordinary person to tell an accurate story of something that happened to him or her. Words are the most difficult of all paints to use, and if the person using them is untrained in their use, he will have trouble painting an accurate picture. If you have a witness on the stand, let the witness *show* how it happened. Supplement his story with demonstrative evidence. Even medical witnesses confuse juries. They tell of a shot that entered the body 'two inches left of the median line'—the jury nods but doesn't understand what is being said. Call a court attendant. Tell your witness to mark with a piece of chalk where the bullet entered. Have him mark where it emerged. Let the court attendant be your exhibit. That's the way to *show* the story to the jury. It's more effective than telling it.

"Last week in my court," he went on, "a defendant said he had killed a man in self-defense. He had been knocked down and had then shot his assailant as the latter straddled him. The jury was obviously uncertain as to whether or not the defendant was telling the truth; there were no eyewitnesses. I took a hand in the questioning, as I believe a judge should do whenever he can enlighten a jury. I asked the defendant to lie down in the position from which he claimed to have fired the gun. I asked him to place a court attendant over him in the position he said his assailant had been. I asked the defendant to take the gun in his hand and show us just how he had fired the shot. He lay on the floor, raised his arm and clicked the gun. Had he been telling the truth, the bullet would have entered the man's abdomen and traveled upward, emerging from somewhere between his shoulder blades. But medical testimony proved that the bullet had not been fired upward; the position it entered and left the body made it apparent that the dead man had been crouching down and that the defendant had been standing over him. The defendant, who might have been freed, was found guilty in short order because of the demonstrative evidence.

"The Germans have an old saying you once heard frequently in their courts," he added. "They say, 'as unreliable as an eyewitness.' You'll find the truth of that demonstrated in our courts every day."

9. MURDER AT BEEKMAN TOWER

"There is something about a roused woman, especially if she add to all her other strong passions, the fierce impulses of recklessness and despair, which few men like to provoke."

CHARLES DICKENS

1

Violent, unnatural death is not a rare phenomenon in modern society; three out of every hundred thousand citizens are victims of homicide in this country. Ladies and gentlemen, husbands and wives, lovers and mistresses are constantly disposing of each other with pistols, knives, poisons, or conventional dull, blunt instruments. A routine murder for profit seldom gets more attention from the public than does a routine burglary or forgery. If, however, there is a sex angle connected with the murder, the United Nations might as well meet in secret and the President might as well postpone his press conference for neither will get the usual newspaper notice.

There are those who deprecate the emphasis placed by the newspapers on crimes motivated by sex, but the city editors, backed by the managing editors, backed by circulation figures, say simply, "Sex crimes sell newspapers." Newspaper corporations are not eleemosynary organizations. They are in business to make money, and to make money they must sell a great many papers. You can only do that by giving the public stories it likes to read, and the public has shown, unmistakably, that most of all it likes to read about murders which are motivated by sex in one form or another. The *Christian Science Monitor* is the only daily newspaper in America which does not headline murder cases involving sex, but the *Monitor* is a taxfree enterprise subsidized by the

First Church of Christ and therefore is not dependent upon its daily circulation for its bread and butter.

It fell to the lot of Samuel Leibowitz to defend blondes, brunettes and even gray-haired old ladies whose homicidal impulses had gotten the best of them. Because the circumstances surrounding these cases were such as to be eagerly devoured by newspaper readers, the cases attracted wide attention.

In the movies, women defendants are invariably pathetic-looking lassies whose tears melt the collective heart of any jury. In real life, however, the woman killer is more likely to be an unkempt slattern, with no appeal at all to the ordinary male in the jury box. In many cases Leibowitz, prevented by the physical handicaps of his client from exciting the sympathy which invariably goes to a good-looking, wistful-eyed defendant, deliberately took advantage of her poor looks and hangdog demeanor to evoke a different kind of sympathy from the jury; the sympathy one feels for the ill-favored or the grotesque.

Mary Colucci was the mother of seventeen children. Mary shot her husband Joe, choosing a Ninth Avenue El train as the scene of her operations. Mrs. Colucci was not a figure to stir the pulses or flutter the heart of any juryman. She was plump, her teeth were jagged and irregular and her nose was considerably off center.

"How many times did your husband break your nose?" Leibowitz asked the defendant when he put her on the stand.

"Fifteen times," Mrs. Colucci answered.

"Step down and let the jury look at your nose," Leibowitz ordered. Later in his concluding address to the jury he said, "After viewing that nose, can there be any doubt as to what kind of beast her husband was? Can there be any doubt that she had a right to protect herself?"

Mrs. Colucci was, of course, acquitted very quickly.

2

Mrs. Angeline Mecili was sixty-seven when she shot her son-in-law, Anthony Colantuono. Mrs. Mecili was plain, with sunken cheeks and brooding eyes. Her son-in-law contemptuously called her "old crooked mouth." He had threatened to kill her, she said, and then her fear grew so great that "everything went black" and she shot him in the back as he sat at breakfast. Mrs. Mecili was not a very good witness in her own defense, chiefly because she wanted the electric chair. Relatives of her dead son-in-law had sworn vengeance and she feared their clumsy butchery more than she did the painless, scientifically applied high voltage administered so skillfully by the state executioner. But Leibowitz was determined to save her.

"Nobody wants her," he cried to the jury. "Nobody loves her. She herself prays for death. It is up to you, gentlemen, to give her freedom and life." They did. Mrs. Mecili was the oldest woman ever tried for first-degree murder in New York State.

3

Then there was Amy Donley, hardly the type to attract the eye of a man of any jury. Amy was a lean, angular woman looking more than her thirty-five years, with a defiant, aggressive manner. Amy had been married to John T. Donley, and husband John often used her as a punching bag. To forget the bruises of flesh and spirit which he had inflicted, Amy found solace in the arms of a handsome youth with the incredible name of James Pembroke De Pew. Amy decided to divorce her quick-punching husband and marry good-looking James Pembroke De Pew, who agreed amiably with the plan. But money would be needed to finance the trip to Reno. The State charged that they had conspired to rob John Donley. One night Donley was accosted in the vestibule of his home by a masked robber who held a gun. Donley handed over his money, but somehow the gun went off. Donley had the poor taste to linger long enough to identify De Pew as his assailant. Then he died.

Questioned separately, Amy Donley and De Pew confessed the conspiracy. De Pew was represented by two lawyers. He went to jail for thirty years, escaping the chair only because he was obviously mentally deficient. Amy Donley retained Leibowitz. He certainly couldn't make Amy a very appealing figure. So he did the reverse.

"Mrs. Donley is a victim of circumstances and a brutal husband," Leibowitz pleaded. "Look at her, gentlemen—nothing but a bag of skin and bones. Her husband beat her into this condition. . . ."

Amy Donley was acquitted.

4

No one had much sympathy for Mollie Quintz, who had stabbed Charles J. Wolfert, a middle-aged jeweler, nineteen times with a penknife. He died instantly. Mollie Quintz was married and she said that Wolfert had been pursuing her for five years. Prosecution witnesses (including Wolfert's eighteen-year-old son) testified that she had been pursuing him during those five years. There were a great many facts in dispute during the trial and Judge Thomas Downs, who presided, showed unmistakably that he disbelieved much of the testimony given by Mollie Quintz. At one point he himself took over the questioning.

"Did you stab Wolfert because you hated and loathed him?" Judge Downs asked.

"Yes, I did," the witness answered defiantly.

Leibowitz leaped to his feet and cried, "But you hated and loathed him because he tried to rape you. Isn't that correct?"

"Yes, it is," Millie said demurely.

In his summation Leibowitz referred to the dead Wolfert as "a slimy cur, a human sewer rat." When he was finished, Assistant District Attorney James Conroy began his closing speech by paying tribute to his adversary. "Mr. Leibowitz' summary was one of the greatest orations I have ever heard." The jury apparently agreed, because two hours after it had retired, a verdict of not guilty was brought in.

Judge Downs dismissed Mollie Quintz, but he couldn't resist adding caustically, "You are a fortunate woman—more fortunate than you deserve." All the same, Mollie Quintz went out of the courtroom a free woman. So did Two Gun Tillie Sachs and Anna Banbara and Bessie Lensky, who had liquidated her husband Sam with a bread knife. These were all sensational cases, every detail of which was devoured by the newspaper-reading public.

5

Then came the case of Laura Parr, accused of first-degree murder. This was not a killing resulting from such conventional motives as jealousy or hatred or the desire to enhance one's bank account. Before the trial began, the newspapers had already tried Laura Parr and had found her guilty. Lawyers, who have studied the hundreds of cases in which Leibowitz was the defense counsel, say that he reached his absolute peak in the case of *The People vs. Laura Parr*. And his defense, in addition to being legally ingenious and tenable, was completely honest. He called upon two key "witnesses" to prove his defense, and one of them had been dead for thirty-six years. The case is worth considering not only as a fascinating legal document but as a human tragedy told almost in terms of Greek drama. Laura Parr was not a Two Gun Tillie, an Amy Donley or a Mollie Quintz. Laura Parr was a girl of charm and culture to whom the thought of law breaking or physical violence was abhorrent. In her thirty-one years she had never even received a parking ticket. She was probably the most decent, certainly the most attractive girl, ever to be charged with first-degree murder in the state of New York. Her story begins with a handbag.

At 2:45 A.M. on November 25, 1935, Patrolman John Holden of the New York police force came upon a young woman sitting on the stairway just below the third floor of the Beekman Towers, a residential hotel at 3 Mitchell Place, Manhattan. She was sobbing and clutching her ample handbag to her side. Officer Holden asked her what she had in the bag. The woman raised tear-dimmed, rather bewildered eyes and said mechanically, "Lipstick and my keys and a passport and my engagement ring, a compact and a handkerchief." By now Officer Holden had been joined by Patrolman Walter A. Mitchell. They took the bag from the hands of the protesting girl and opened it. In addition to the articles she had described there were several other things not usually carried by girls in the City of New York. There was a .32-caliber double action revolver which was warm to the palm of Patrolman Mitchell. There was a box containing forty-six .32-caliber bullets. At the bottom of the bag, nestling among the handkerchief, the compact and the lipstick, there were two discharged shells. There was a passport made out in the name of Dr. Fritz Gebhardt (of the same 3 Mitchell Place address), seven shares of Baltimore and Ohio stock made out to him and a crumpled, thin, rose silk nightgown on which there were wet bloodstains.

Patrolman Mitchell knew that Dr. Fritz Gebhardt would never use the passport again nor would he ever benefit from the dividends of the Baltimore and Ohio stock. Patrolman Mitchell knew that Dr. Gebhardt, clad in an old-fashioned nightgown, was lying sprawled on the floor of his twentieth-floor apartment with four bullets in his body. Dr. Gebhardt was as dead as a stone.

"Did you shoot the man upstairs?" Patrolman Mitchell asked.

"Yes, I did," she sobbed. "But please don't ask me why I did it."

They took her up to Dr. Gebhardt's apartment and made her look at the body which lay there grotesquely contorted by death. She numbly nodded when they asked if this was the man she had shot. Then they rushed her to the East Fifty-first Street Precinct. Inspector Francis Kear of Homicide, who had hurried to the station house to question her, blinked when he saw her for the first time. Laura Parr did not look like a girl capable of murder. She had either recovered her composure or was suffering from delayed shock. She was attractive —not in the flashy, brazen sense, but quietly attractive. She had a nice face, a pleasant face. She had blue-gray eyes and soft, honey-colored hair and the kind of complexion (even at 4:00 A.M.) that went with blondness. She was wearing a gray coat with a caracul collar and a soft blue felt hat. Her voice was low and cultured as she answered preliminary questions put to her by Kear.

Her name was Laura Parr, she said. She was thirty-one. She had met Dr. Fritz Gebhardt when both were taking a winter cruise on the S. S. *Vulcania*. That was in December, 1934. Their acquaintance had ripened into friendship and finally blossomed into love. They had become engaged. Yes, this platinum ring with the karat-and-a-half diamond (found in her bag) was her engagement ring. Yes, she too lived at 3 Mitchell Place. Her apartment was on the nineteenth floor. Her early life? Well, she was a graduate of New York University; while there she had specialized in German. She had taught for a while, but she had an income sufficient to keep her going. Her mother had died and left her thirty-five thousand dollars, and she and her brother shared the rentals of some flats their grandfather had bequeathed them. Then she worked (part time) in the office of Frank Von Knoop and Co., an import and export firm headed by Dr. Gebhardt.

"Now, Miss Parr, why did you kill this man?" Inspector Kear asked.

"Please don't ask me that," she said calmly. "I . . . I think I should talk to a lawyer first."

Kear could get nothing further from her. He had sent for her seventy-year-old father and he arrived. Frank Parr was a musician who had once played with Victor Herbert. Now he was a band leader, well known in musical circles. He was a great favorite at the New York Athletic Club and he had composed a number, "The Winged Foot March," which was popular at club functions. He also played at Luchow's, the wonderful German restaurant on Fourteenth Street. He was a gentle, soft-spoken, and now completely bewildered man. Kear brought him into the room where he had been questioning Laura.

"Laura, what's happened to you?" he cried brokenly, and Laura's reserve broke too as she sobbed on his shoulder. But when he left her an hour later he was shaking his head and saying, "Laura wouldn't tell me anything . . . I don't believe she could shoot anyone, not little Laura."

By now police had combed both her own and Gebhardt's apartment and they brought the significant findings to the precinct. There were dozens of letters from Laura to Fritz and dozens from Fritz to Laura. They were filled with tenderness and protestations of eternal

213

love. They had found a will which Laura had made out. Actually it read like a combination will-suicide note. In it she named two girls as her beneficiaries and she added, "I am tired of it all. I am leaving this world in good sound mind." She would not tell the police when she wrote the will. There was also a receipted bill from the Hotel Lincoln found in Gebhardt's room. It was evident that he had spent the night of November 23 there. Although they questioned her all night and part of the next day, she refused to conform to standard procedure by collapsing and telling all. Calmly, unemotionally (or perhaps numbly), she kept repeating, "I think I should talk to a lawyer first."

Finally, they allowed her to talk to Attorney Arthur M. Moritz, a friend of her father's, but he emerged after an hour shaking his head sadly. He told Laura's father that he practiced only civil law. Laura, he said, was in a bad spot and the only thing to do was to get the best criminal lawyer in the country. Frank Parr said, "I will see if I can get Samuel Leibowitz."

Leibowitz took the case. Because Laura had refused to talk, the newspapers filled their columns with speculative articles. Why had she killed Gebhardt? Most of the papers thought it was because of jealousy. The *Daily Mirror* cried out, "Killed Him For Honor!" The *Daily News*, with the will-suicide note in mind, presented to its readers the headline, "Jealous Blonde Planned to End Life After Killing." Interest in the case was so intense that the *New York Times* reluctantly had to give four columns to it. The *Mirror* editorial page presented a picture of Laura and over it a caption which read, "With Such a Lady—Be Careful."

Quite definitely this was no one-day story. A new development as announced by police (and embroidered by the papers) was this. Forty-eight hours before the murder, Dr. Fritz Gebhardt had registered at the Lincoln Hotel, Forty-fifth Street and Eighth Avenue. His name was on the hotel register, "Dr. F. Gebhardt, Long Hill, Chatham, N. J." Police said that a blonde had accompanied him but that she had registered separately as "Miss L. Thompson, Pelham, N.Y." Each had been given a single room. That was all the police knew, but the *Daily News* purported to know a great deal more. The *News*, under the heading, "Laura Shadowed Lover to Tryst with 2nd Blonde," declared that Laura had trailed the doctor and had seen him meet the "slim, chic mystery blonde." The *News* went on to say that Laura had followed them to the hotel and that she then returned to the Beekman Towers to wait the return of her faithless lover.

There were several women living in Pelham named "Thompson," and each one of them spent an unhappy twenty-four hours. Those who could not account for their time during the hours which Gebhardt and "Miss L. Thompson" spent at the Lincoln Hotel were embarrassed no end. However, embarrassment and suspense only lasted one day. Then it was revealed that the newspapers had made a curious and very rare mistake in printing the name as "L. Thompson." The girl who had come into the hotel lobby with Gebhardt had registered as "Miss L. Templeton." The Thompsons in Pelham breathed a collective sigh of relief. Miss "L. Templeton" was finally located by the police. She was a trained nurse, she insisted that her visit to the hotel was strictly professional and she was allowed to bow out of the case and out of the headlines. One might wonder why her name was ever revealed by the police at all. Admittedly she had nothing to do with the murder. However, there is usually more than one victim in a murder case and often the punishment given to the living is even worse than that given to either the slain victim or the murderer.

By now the papers had a full dossier on Dr. Gebhardt. He was a dark, handsome man. He had served with distinction in World War I and had been in the famous Richtofen Squadron. He had become very friendly at that time with a pilot named Hermann Goering. He was a graduate of the University of Frankfurt and held two doctorates (philosophy and political economy) from his alma mater. He had taught at the university for a while and had then gone into business. He had been phenomenally successful and was purported by business associates to be worth half a million dollars.

He had made one slight early mistake. He had married a Jewish girl in Germany. But for this, his friendship with Goering and other Nazi officials might have resulted in high political office. He had even been mentioned as the possible ambassador to the United States. Gebhardt did his best to atone for his stupid *faux pas*. He left his wife and two children. He didn't divorce them—just moved out. And eventually his financial interests (fostered by another friend—Hjalmar Schacht) brought him to America. He was very successful during the early 1930's in exchanging raw German material for American commodities. This was a rewarding business, because he not only received a commission from the German firms which exported raw material, but from American firms which exchanged their finished products for the raw material. Gebhardt (reports were unanimous on this) was an attractive, fascinating, cultured man who spoke French and English in addition to his native tongue.

Laura Parr remained silent in her cell at the women's jail, which in New York is politely known as the Women's House of Detention, and the papers, understandably annoyed at her reluctance to keep the story alive by talking, now began to refer to her as the Icy Blonde. The *News* tagged her with that and the other papers followed suit. She was not getting a good press at all. It seems surprising that Gebhardt, the friend of high Nazi officials and a representative of German industry, should receive the sympathy of the public, but this was 1935 and it had not as yet become fashionable to hate Naziism. Hitler was regimenting for efficiency, he had stopped strikes and put labor in its place, and he had thrown a few thousand Jews into concentration camps and there were plenty of people saying, "By God, that's what we ought to do over here."

Dorothy Dunbar Bromley wrote a story for the *World-Telegram* headed, "Can True Love Yield to Murderous Hatred," in which she said, "This is the kind of tragedy that makes my heart ache. Not with exculpatory sentimentality but with sorrow that a young woman who had the advantages of education should adopt the underworld's methods of revenge. Like many other misguided people, she seems to have thought that she had a divine right to happiness." Other writers took the same view. Laura's continued silence was interpreted as something sinister; it was treated as the snarling "I won't talk" of the wounded professional gunman.

But Laura finally did talk. She talked to Leibowitz. Not at first, though. Even he had trouble breaking down that reserve. What had

216

happened in Gebhardt's room during the few minutes preceding the shooting? Why in Heaven's name had she shot the man? Had she been in a blind, uncontrollable jealous rage? It didn't seem likely. There were no powder burns on Gebhardt's body, which meant that the gun had not been held against his body. Now a .32-caliber double action Colt is not an easy weapon for an amateur to handle. The trigger pull not only cocks the hammer, it fires the gun. The .32-caliber Colt is a jumpy little thing. The trigger jerk and the kick throw it out of line when it is fired. Laura had hit him twice in the breast, once in the back and once in the arm. It seemed obvious that the first two shots entered the breast, then he had spun around like a dancing doll and she had fired again; this time into his back. He began to fall, swerving to the side as he did so, and the final bullet hit his arm. Laura did not fire four rapid shots in one flaming moment of madness. The fact that Gebhardt had had time to turn fully around showed that there was a distinct interval between the first two and the final shots. The District Attorney would know all this, and he would picture Laura as a cold-blooded, calculating killer with a steady hand and a keen eye.

During his first visit with Laura, Leibowitz did little more than to get details of her meeting and subsequent romance with Gebhardt. As soon as he began to question her about the immediate events which led to the shooting, she became nervous and evasive. Leibowitz kept wondering why. She was quite willing to discuss her intimacies with Gebhardt up to the night of the murder. What was she keeping back and why was she keeping it back? The possible truth suddenly struck Leibowitz. Something happened in that room of which Laura was ashamed. It was embarrassment that sealed her lips; something had happened which in her own mind was so awful that she felt ashamed to repeat it.

When Leibowitz suggested this to Laura, she looked startled for a moment and then dissolved into tears. Then she sobbed out the story to her lawyer. She told him everything, and he knew that the girl was telling the truth. When he emerged from this long session with Laura, he was stopped by reporters. Would Mr. Leibowitz say something?

"You bet I'll say something," Leibowitz said angrily. "I have heard Laura Parr's story and I can say that legally, morally and from every other human standpoint, Dr. Gebhardt got what was coming to him. She'll tell her story in court," he added.

It was the first time anyone had said a good word for the girl. The following day another spokesman gave the press something worth printing. Laura had asked Leibowitz to send the Reverend Albert Ribourg of Saint Andrew's Episcopal Church to visit her. She had attended his church for fifteen years. She told Dr. Ribourg the full story, and when he came out of the jail he said to reporters, "I would come to the defense of Laura Parr as strongly as I would if she were my own sister. I know her to be a decent girl of good character."

A few days before the trial Leibowitz allowed the press to interview Laura. He did not, however, allow her to say very much. She was calm now, and when asked why she had killed Dr. Gebhardt she said evenly, "Any decent person would have done the same thing." The reporters found her warm, genial, and anything but "icy." Henceforth they put away such phrases as "ice blonde," "iron-nerved tiger woman" and "cold killer," all of which had been used repetitiously by the less sedate newspapers.

6

The trial opened on March 20, 1936 (four months after the shooting), before Judge Cornelius F. Collins, a plump and rather stern jurist. Assistant District Attorney Miles O'Brien was the prosecutor. During the first three days it looked as though Friedrich Wilhelm Nietzsche (dead these thirty-six years) would be the defendant. Leibowitz asked prospective jurors if they had studied the philosophy of Nietzsche, and if they approved of it. It was evident that few of the puzzled talesmen had ever heard of the gloomy German. Leibowitz was glad to enlighten them as to some of the basic Nietzschian philosophy. And always by inference he was implying that Fritz Gebhardt was a devout follower of Nietzsche. The newspapers were quick to pick up this lead, and all carried stories of the philosophy of the superman. The *New York Journal-American* wrote:

The Parr defense will be that Laura squeezed the trigger in self-protection against the brutalities of a man who had sopped up a Superman complex from Nietzsche's writing; a man who could kick her in the stomach and say, "Thus spake Zarathustra."

Obligingly S. S. Van Dine, creator of Philo Vance, foremost of fiction detectives, proved to be a foremost authority on Nietzschean Kultur.

"His was a philosophy of aristocracy, a system of ethics designed for the masters of the race," Mr. Van Dine said.

He extracted from Nietzsche's prolific writings such pertinent comments on women as Leibowitz contends supplied the late Dr. Gebhardt with his he-man notions.

"Man," wrote Nietzsche, "shall be trained for war and woman for the recreation of the warrior; all else is folly."

And again—

"The happiness of man is 'I will.' The happiness of woman is 'He will.' "

"A man who has the depth of spirit as well as desires, and has also the depth of benevolence which is capable of severity and harshness, must conceive of woman as a possession, as confinable property, as being predestined for service.

"Egoism belongs to the essence of a noble soul."

But the pay-off line—the line which H. L. Mencken once said has helped to make Nietzsche "a stench in the nostrils of the orthodox"— is this one from "Thus Spake Zarathustra" which Leibowitz expects to read to a chivalrous and attentive jury:

"Thou goest to woman? Do not forget thy whip!"

Laura Parr will tell her jurors that Dr. Fritz Gebhardt obeyed that admonition—to the letter.

It was obvious that Leibowitz wanted no professional reformers on the jury. He dismissed a Y.M.C.A. secretary. He wanted no one who had ever had any serious domestic trouble and he threw out four men who had been divorced. The court-wise reporters at the press table gradually began to see a possible pattern of defense emerge from Leibowitz' questioning.

"If a woman has reason to fear for her safety—to fear that a felony is about to be committed upon her—do you believe that she has

219

a right to defend herself even if it means she must kill?" Leibowitz asked the talesmen.

If a man forces a woman to engage in what the law calls an "unnatural sexual act," that is considered to be a felony under the penal law. It seemed possible now that Leibowitz was going to claim that Laura killed Gebhardt to protect herself from a felonious assault.

"Do you believe a person has a right to kill to prevent herself from being forced to participate in a felony?" was another question he asked, and this one caused experienced legal minds in the courtroom (there were always a great many lawyers present when Leibowitz was in action) to speculate on the possibility of still another line of defense. Any sexual act which deviates from what the law says is the norm can under some circumstances be classed as felony. Under the laws of New York, if two people engage in such acts they are guilty of a felony. Now Leibowitz seemed to be implying that Gebhardt had tried to force Laura to join him in committing a felony, and that rather than comply she had killed him. Judge Collins made copious notes as Leibowitz threw searching questions at the talesmen. The Judge himself was undoubtedly trying to anticipate which defense Leibowitz would use. He too was curious as to what Laura's story would be.

It also seemed clear that the lawyer would not only call the ghost of Nietzsche but those of Marquis de Sade and Krafft-Ebing to testify as to the character of Fritz Gebhardt. Leibowitz indicated that he would prove that there is a philosophy and a philosophical way of living which could produce justifiable homicide. This had seldom been attempted in an American courtroom. Clarence Darrow had tried it when pleading for the lives of Leopold and Loeb, but he was arguing that case before a judge alone and not before a jury. Leibowitz was taking quite a gamble in staking everything on his ability to make twelve ordinary men understand the character of Gebhardt as shaped by his philosophical studies.

Leibowitz was finally satisfied with the jury, and the actual trial began with Assistant District Attorney Miles O'Brien making a quiet and brief opening. He contented himself with a lucid description of the known incidents of the tragedy and with a dispassionate demand for the death penalty, perhaps the more forceful and deadly because of the lack of dramatics or even emphasis.

The prosecutor told how policemen found Miss Parr on the third floor of 3 Mitchell Place after shots had echoed through the building. "She was fully clothed," he said, "still with her hat on and still with her bag in her possession. In the bag they found numerous articles which women use, but in addition to the articles which women use, we find a revolver in the bag. In addition to the revolver we find a box of cartridges and we find the empty shells in the bag, too. And, in addition, gentlemen, we have from the defendant's own lips the statement that she shot Dr. Gebhardt."

When the prosecutor stressed the point that Dr. Gebhardt was a married man, the defendant bit her lips and her head drooped. Color suffused her pale face.

"The police went to her room," said Mr. O'Brien, "and they went to Dr. Gebhardt's room, and in those rooms they found letters from Gebhardt to the defendant and from the defendant to Gebhardt. Gebhardt, gentlemen, was a married man; Gebhardt had children. We will show you that the defendant knew that."

The jury listened thoughtfully to this tall, soft-voiced, dead-pan Irishman with the tanned face, the well-cut brown suit and brown tie. O'Brien's manner was confident and contemptuous. It was obvious that he felt he had an airtight case against Laura Parr.

A significant and startling omission in O'Brien's opening was his failure to mention a motive for the killing. He did little but establish the killing and the fact that it had been done by Laura Parr. When he finished, Leibowitz arose and said, "The defendant waives the opening." It is rather rare in a criminal case to see a defense attorney waive his opening speech, which usually is an outline of the proposed defense. The advantage of waiving such an opening in this case is, of course, obvious. O'Brien had no clue (beyond questions asked by Leibowitz of the talesmen) to the defense. It could be insanity. It could be self-defense, or it could be the defense his questioning had hinted at.

This was not only good legal tactics; it was good theatre. "Why did she kill him?" was the question in everyone's mind. The jury was as anxious as anyone else to know the answer to that question. But Leibowitz, like a good T formation quarterback, was calling the plays and making the prosecution play his game. Miles O'Brien was in the position of a football coach whose team is playing an opponent that has never been scouted. He had no idea of what had happened during those moments preceding the firing of the fatal shots. The letters the police had found established little beyond the fact that Laura and Gebhardt had been in love. There was no indication in the letters that Gebhardt had discarded his mistress. There was no convincing evidence that Laura was suffering from jealousy. Only Leibowitz knew the real motive for the shooting, and he was playing his cards close to his chest.

O'Brien put Leslie Tate, assistant manager of the Beekman Towers, on the stand to tell of phone calls from tenants who heard the shots. Tate had investigated the upper floors but had found no signs of a shooting. He had finally gone to Gebhardt's room, opened the door with his passkey and found the body. On cross-examination Leibowitz brought out the fact that Tate had come across Laura on the nineteenth floor and it was she who had told him to go to Gebhardt's room, two flights above, that there was a man there who might need help.

"In other words," Leibowitz asked, "it was this defendant who directed you to the scene of the tragedy?"

"Yes sir," Tate answered, and now the jury received the impression that only a few minutes after the killing Laura was anxious to get help for the man she had shot. Leibowitz was beginning to make the jury think of a girl named Laura Parr in terms of a human being.

Patrolman Holden told of finding Laura on the stairway and of the contents of her handbag. He also said that she had admitted the shooting. Leibowitz didn't do much cross-examining. He was freely admitting the facts of the killing. He was amused to notice Dr. P. M. Lichtenstein, chief alienist for the District Attorney's office, sitting at the prosecutor's table studying Laura intently. Obviously O'Brien was preparing himself in the eventuality that Leibowitz should interpose a defense of insanity. This was the kind of situation Leibowitz enjoyed creating. He had O'Brien guessing. He had Judge Collins guessing. He had everybody guessing.

O'Brien, unsmiling and dour, continued to establish the picture of a cold-blooded, brutal killing on the part of Laura Parr. Through medical witnesses O'Brien tried to show that Gebhardt had been killed while he lay in bed. His body had been found beside the bed, his feet entangled in a blood-flecked sheet. O'Brien also brought out the fact that no furniture had been knocked over or was out of place, in an effort to prove that no struggle had taken place. Dr. Milton Halpern, the medical examiner, had been O'Brien's witness on these damaging circumstances, but Leibowitz was well prepared to throw doubt—not on the facts—but on the interpretation. There were certain marks on the body of the slain man not completely explained by Dr. Halpern.

"Could they not have been made by a woman's fingernails?" Leibowitz asked.

"They could have," Dr. Halpern admitted calmly.

Leibowitz also caused the witness to admit that it was quite possible that the impact of the first two bullets could have wheeled Gebhardt around and that this would explain the location of the other two bullets. He also caused the witness to state that the furniture was normally placed against the walls of the small bedroom and that a struggle quite conceivably could have taken place without the furniture being disturbed.

O'Brien didn't seem much concerned as Leibowitz cast extreme doubt on his theory that Gebhardt had been shot in bed without having a chance to fight back. O'Brien, in effect, was saying to the jury, "This woman and Gebhardt were having an affair. Something went wrong with it and she killed him. It's that simple. Why cloud the issue with irrelevant nonsense about Nietzsche or about possible unnatural acts? She was in her right mind and she deliberately killed him. That's all that counts and that constitutes first-degree murder."

When O'Brien closed for the People he had succeeded (through the testimony of twenty-three witnesses) in planting some provocative questions in the minds of the jury (and the public). What was Laura doing in Gebhardt's room at 2:00 A.M.? Why was she fully clothed right after the murder. Had she brought the gun to his room? What right did she have to own a gun anyway? The nightgown in her handbag was spotted with blood. Had she killed him while wearing the nightgown and then hurriedly changed to street clothes so she could flee? And finally why had she killed him? There was only one person who could answer these questions—Laura Parr.

Laura was considerably shaken by the long days in court. Several times she had broken down, and court attendants kept a bottle of smelling salts handy. No one could call her the icy blonde now. Her face was tear-stained and she kept clutching her handkerchief with her small hands. She was nervous, distraught. O'Brien, looking at her coldly, speculatively, felt that she would be a poor witness in her own defense. Laura herself would have to tell the story and she would have to be convincing enough to make the jury believe her. Leibowitz felt that he had a good defense. But it could only be presented by Laura Parr.

After Judge Collins had denied Leibowitz' routine motion to dismiss the indictment of first-degree murder, Leibowitz put Laura Parr on the stand. She was a pathetically pale and unhappy figure, and there was a rustle among the spectators and whispered comment on her appearance as she took the oath. Leibowitz' direct examination was unconventional in that he almost immediately took up the question of the fatal gun. He knew what questions were foremost in the minds of the jury, and before he did anything else, he wanted to answer some of them. Laura said she had bought the gun in 1930, after applying to the Police Department for a permit. She then lived with her father and brother on East 128th Street, a neighborhood which had recently changed its character to such an extent that her father worried when she was home alone. So she had bought the gun for her own protection and her brother had shown her how to use it. She had kept the gun when she moved to various downtown addresses. She still had the permit for it.

Next Leibowitz had her tell of her first meeting with Gebhardt. This was in December, 1934, on a winter cruise made by the *Vulcania*. They had met casually, but it developed that Gebhardt was a good friend of the Parr family doctor. Both Laura and Gebhardt had a great admiration for the physician, and as their casual shipboard acquaintance continued they found even stronger common interests. His English was poor then and he enjoyed talking German to her. The ship anchored off Havana, so the passengers could enjoy New Year's Eve in Cuba's gay capital, and Laura and Dr. Gebhardt joined another couple to tour the night spots. He kissed her that night. But there was no significance to the kiss, Laura said; it was New Year's Eve and at midnight everyone kissed everyone else.

Their relationship remained casual and uncomplicated through the rest of the cruise. It was a month before she saw him again, and now he began sending her flowers, candy and books.

"By the way, you shot Dr. Gebhardt, didn't you?" Leibowitz asked casually, and the crowded courtroom came to sharp attention.

Laura shut her eyes and said quietly, "Yes."

It was an unusual way of bringing out a vital fact but it was a coolly calculated Leibowitz maneuver. His casual question raised the heads of the jurymen sharply. They had begun to be bored with Laura's story of the mild courtship and the gifts of flowers. This renewed their lagging interest. They knew now they couldn't afford to doze. Leibowitz, in a subtle way, was reminding them that he was running this trial. If they wanted to doze while O'Brien was questioning witnesses, that was all right. While he held the center of the stage he wanted the full attention of the jurymen —and he got it.

Leibowitz had her discuss the development of the friendship. Dr. Gebhardt was a brilliant man, she said, charming, gallant and witty. He made a quick business trip to Europe, and when he returned he told her that he loved her. He confided that he had a wife and two children in Germany.

"But he never referred to her as his wife," Laura said. "He called her Thea. He said that he had not lived with her for ten years, that there was no love on either side, and he said that with conditions as they now were in Germany the marriage could only be a marriage in name. It was legally prohibited for them to be married in any other way."

Leibowitz broke in, "To make that plain, Gebhardt was . . ."

"No, don't make it plain," Judge Collins thundered. Leibowitz, of course, wanted to establish that Gebhardt, with typical Nazi brutality, had cast off his Jewish wife (which was the truth). Judge Collins was determined that Nazi policies should not be discussed in the courtroom. He felt that they were not germane to the issue. Leibowitz tried unsuccessfully to so word his questions that the fact of Gebhardt's Nazi beliefs would be brought out, but even before O'Brien could object, Judge Collins was banging his gavel angrily. However, by now the jury, listening intently, knew exactly why Gebhardt had thought of his German marriage as merely a marriage in name only. Leibowitz led Laura to a discussion of Gebhardt.

"He told me he loved me," Laura said. "And then he said that he was different from other men; that he was an unusual person. Ordinary laws applied to ordinary people, but for an unusual person there must be different standards. I . . . I was fascinated by him."

She reached back into memory and brought forth an age-old story of a girl's fascination for a man of extraordinary physical and intellectual charm. He would talk—she would listen. He called her Lauralein (little Laura) and he would say gently, "Lauralein, you are marvelous—you have so many wonderful qualities. I want to develop them." And in May (six months after they had met on the *Vulcania*), her love became so great that she agreed to go away with him. They went to Lake George as Dr. and Mrs. Gebhardt.

"Why did you yield to him?" Leibowitz asked.

"Because I loved him," Laura said simply.

Gebhardt suggested that they get married in New York State and blandly ignore his German marriage.

"But that would be bigamous," Laura said she told Gebhardt.

The *Daily News* told the story of Laura's first day on the stand under the heading:

LAURA REVEALS ALL;
RISKS HER DOOM—

Jimmy Witaker, then (and now) one of New York's most brilliant crime reporters, wrote the story. It began:

226

Almost suicidally honest, the cultured well-to-do bachelor girl refused to help Samuel S. Leibowitz, her lawyer, show that she believed
that Gebhardt could easily divorce an old wife and give her place
to a new.

She spent a whole day on the stand facing a gruelling examination
by her attorney.

However, the general effect of reckless honesty and sincerity was
perhaps one which will tell in the end with Laura's jury of middle-
aged business men more powerfully than any well-edited narrative
falsely depicting her a trustful idiot.

She was trustful, but not an idiot. Intelligence and generosity were
her downfall. That is her story now, and by it she will live or die.

Leibowitz returned to the matter of the revolver the next day.
After Laura and Gebhardt had returned from Lake George, he spent
a lot of time at her Fifty-seventh Street one-room apartment. One
night she was measuring a large French window for curtains and he
was helping her. He noticed that the window (more a door than a
window) opened on a fire escape.

"You should never leave this unlocked," Laura quoted him as saying. "Someone could come up that fire escape and into this room and
run away with the little girl I love."

"What did you answer?" Leibowitz asked.

"I said," Laura went on, "that I had a gun that would frighten
any robbers away. He asked me to show it to him and I did. He
knew all about guns. He didn't want me to have it; thought it was
dangerous for me. And he took it and the cartridges and put them
in his coat pocket. He kept the gun from then on."

Now Leibowitz began a line of questioning which seemed to
O'Brien to be absolutely irrelevant, but after considerable argument
with the court the questions were permitted. They concerned the
apparently unimportant matter of the health of Fritz Gebhardt. Laura
testified that he suffered from an abdominal complaint which often
resulted in severe pain. The pain usually came at night, and Laura
had bought an electric pad hoping that the heat would mitigate the
pain. It proved successful.

"Did he phone you often to say he was in pain and to ask you
to come and help him?" Leibowitz asked casually.

"Yes, he did."

"At what hour usually?"

"All hours," Laura said. "Sometimes at five in the morning he would wake up in agony and phone me. I would soothe him and apply the electric pad."

"This happened constantly?"

"Yes, at least once a week, sometimes oftener."

Leibowitz switched then to their marriage plans.

By now Fritz Gebhardt had given her an engagement ring and had said that they could be married the next spring. By then he would have arranged his domestic affairs in Germany so that there would be no legal entanglement to their marriage. To establish the fact that Laura had good grounds for thinking that Gebhardt's love was sincere and that she had every right to believe that he wanted to marry her, Leibowitz introduced several letters they had exchanged while he was making his frequent trips to Europe and to Canada.

In cold, mechanical tones, he read them aloud, these love letters that had been written in hot emotion.

The first letter was dated May 28, 1935; she had written it to Gebhardt while he was abroad. It read in part:

You know how I dread being earnestly melodramatic. But at the risk of appearing so, let me write that our friendship has already disentangled the real me from the maze of camouflage I've worn in the past three years . . .

The following will be difficult to write. During last March, I still wore my self-styled protective masks. Gradually, during April, I shed them, until last week I came home with at least an understanding of my true self and a longing to be so again.

Oh, Fritz, how I must force myself now to write the confession that came from feeling our friendship was something sacred. Then how I doubly despised the me who sullied it in its various stages. Fritz, did you not pass through similar stages?

Again, shying at drama, I must write that I shall always be grateful to you for being so patient with me. I hope I am strong enough now to go on alone. If the conclusion I reached in my search for truth is true, this is it.

You, Fritz, have a family, whom I have learned to admire through

228

your stories about them. The family, as an European institution, is something I appreciate.

But, more important, to betray and deceive a wife who has been and is so much to a man—and he to her—cannot be right. (I am speaking not biblically or morally, but ethically.) Those were my thoughts last week.

I realize now that my other thought—that you were suggesting a secondary place for me, which hurt my pride—was false in this instance. I realize now that you were suggesting a great honor for me . . .

In struggling to organize my thoughts, I find this thought is a part of me which I shall never lose while I am true to myself. Despite all my reasoning to the contrary, I find it is now the basis for my supreme self-content during the last ten months. It is this—the good, old-fashioned theorem that sexual intercourse is sacred and lovely, a unity of everything finest.

When I was immature, I called that unity love and believed its expressions were companionship, children and a communal attempt to make the world a better place to live in. What makes me happy now is the discovery that I still believe that. This is as well as I can explain myself at present. Can you understand?

The letter was signed "Laura."

The next letter was one addressed by Gebhardt to Miss Parr from Buffalo, May 22, 1935, while he was traveling. He wrote in German that all his thoughts had been "only with you." He was reading F. Scott Fitzgerald's *The Great Gatsby,*—"a good novel but without importance"—and Oscar Wilde's *De Profundis*. In English he wrote a few halting phrases, such as "Tell me, dear teacher, what is difference between stay and stood." He asked her to correct his mistakes.

He concluded, "I wish, dear Fräulein, you could feel my kiss."

As Leibowitz started to read from a letter written by Laura to Fritz dated July 2, Laura interrupted to say to Judge Collins in a low voice, "At first I wrote short letters. He complained, lover-like, about that, so I wrote longer letters."

The letter, written on a Sunday, read:

The new apartment is ready for you. The red roses, your photo, etc.

It was bad for you to leave me for so long. Perhaps after fifty years of married life it will be different.

The view from the window is exotic at sunrise—the massive silver chimneys, many lights in the windows, the bridge, ships.

A note, on August 2, from Fritz to "Little Laura," was read:

From the steamer quiet before departure, a hearty greeting. I have only an ardent desire to have you with me.

One dear, dear kiss again and again, as my adieu, farewell.

FRITZ

A letter she wrote July 30, to reach him as he sailed from Canada to Germany, August 2, read:

We are not separated, dearest. We create and our creation is mutual.

If you had given me only a child I would have been lost in the charming but selfish details of bearing and rearing it.

While you are busy, I too will be busy here.

Dearest, you feel with me this is a fervent love letter.

There is no reason to say *auf wiedersehen*, because we are together.

Could we not set a limit beyond which you would not need to scramble to make money, which is only a means to an end?

The thought that our life will always be so makes me content that we are living usefully and actively.

Next was a letter from Montreal, postmarked August 3, 1935, in which Fritz wrote from the boat train:

I am sad. For the first time in my life I am not in a traveling mood. I take comfort in leaving the best I have, my dearest Laura.

While he was away she studied, and it was apparent in her letters that she was straining to keep mental stride with her brilliant, erudite lover, trying to impress him that she too was more than a mere *Hausfrau*. She wrote of art and asked naively, "What degree of education is necessary to appreciate Rembrandt's paintings? His self-portraits are such a remarkable autobiography. Michelangelo's only painting has always been a favorite of mine, especially after your adorable modernization of it. Sweet, do you think we'll have time this autumn to see pictures?"

She wanted to tell him of her love for him and of how much

230

it meant to her, but she found she just didn't have the words. Instead she said, "May I quote from a book you don't like? What I want to say is expressed delicately and beautifully there."

She then quoted in its unexpurgated version the famous letter from John Thomas to Lady Jane, which has resulted in the banning of D. H. Lawrence's *Lady Chatterly's Lover* in many communities. Leibowitz read it in its entirety to the jury. It was certainly the most unconventional prose ever read in the dingy courtroom technically known as Part Five, Court of General Sessions.

Twice Judge Collins interrupted to ask Leibowitz to raise his voice. Leibowitz, obviously embarrassed, looked pleadingly at the Judge.

"May I read this so that only the jury will hear it?" he asked. "There are a great many women in the courtroom and the words used in this passage from the book are not fit for them to hear."

"If there is any woman spectator here," Judge Collins said, raising his eyes to the spectators, "who feels offended at the language being used, she may leave now. The attendant will open the door."

The door was opened and Collins waited for the sensitive-minded to leave. Not one woman arose from her seat—but three women slipped through the open door into the courtroom. Then Collins told Leibowitz to continue his reading of D. H. Lawrence. "But louder!" he ordered. The women in the courtroom listened avidly to the old Anglo-Saxon words Lawrence used in his dissertation on love. Finally Leibowitz finished, wiped his perspiring brow and his face still crimson with embarrassment he turned his attention to other letters less stark in their language.

In these letters to Gebhardt she wrote of Hemingway and O'Neill but always she discussed his views on them.

Among the many letters Gebhardt wrote there was one which Leibowitz emphasized. It was written from Germany and it read:

Koln, Germany

My Laura:

On the train from Berlin to Heidelberg, I could not write, it was so shaky.

My dear girlie, if you only know how I am longing for you, how I need you. You will have me soon to yourself, then all yours . . .

Yours, FRITZ

231

This last sentence, the love-blind Laura took to be a proposal of marriage. Apparently all obstacles had been removed.

And finally Fritz Gebhardt had returned to New York. It was Friday, November 8, 1935. By now Laura had rented a room at the Beekman Towers. He came directly from the *Europa* to her room. He kissed her and talked about how horrible the separation had been and then he added. "I am going away again in December and you are going with me."

"What did you say to him?" Leibowitz asked Laura.

"I said I'd better hurry with the wedding invitations," Laura answered. "And then he told me that although he loved me and couldn't bear to be without me, he had discovered in his travels that he was not the type of man to get married. He wanted to go on as we had before."

Q. What did you say to that, Miss Parr?
A. I told him I couldn't have that kind of life any more. I could not bear it; I didn't want it. I wanted a home and a husband.
Q. Anything else said that day?
A. He took me in his arms and said, "You love me." I pushed him away when he tried to kiss me again. I said I'd have to think about it. I left him. I walked and walked and that night went out to dinner alone. When I returned home there were chrysanthemums he had sent.
Q. When did you see him?
A. The next morning. He phoned me at seven to have breakfast. We did have breakfast in the hotel dining room. He said, "You will never find anyone like me. You cannot love anyone but me. What difference does it make if we are married or not?

But this was a new Laura. She remained adamant, but said that she would finish some work she had been doing on the firm's books. While she was about it, he asked smilingly would she do an errand or two for him? He had some English money. Would she change it at the bank? And the cover of his passbook had become torn, would she have it repaired? It was probably sheer habit that made her agree to run the errands.

She met him late that afternoon and he asked her to accompany him to the North River. The *Europa* was sailing and he wanted to see some people off. She went with him in a cab and he renewed his efforts to get her back on the old footing. She still refused. He got out of the cab and she went uptown to visit her father. She spent the night at her father's house and in the morning (Sunday) returned to Beekman Towers; Sunday night they had dinner together and again he tried to persuade her that they belonged together. She told him that it was all over and that she had decided to go to Paris for a while. Then they returned to the hotel. He tried to accompany her into her room but she refused to allow him in.

Q. What did he say, Miss Parr?
A. He tossed a key to me. He said, "You have my key. If you change your mind come up; the door will always be open to you."

She had shut her door firmly. She knew now that there could be no compromise. She wanted to make a clean, decent break; Gebhardt was too egotistical to believe her. He phoned her the next day and again they had dinner together. He read her extracts from letters she had written to him; he reminded her of things she had done and said during the idyllic days at Lake George. "No one has ever left me before," he told her arrogantly. "And you are not going to leave me."

She was seeing Gebhardt now through eyes that were not clouded with the astigmatism of intense love. Again they returned to the Beekman Towers and again she went to her room alone. It was about eleven o'clock. She put on her nightgown and slept. It was the phone ringing which was the signal for the curtain to rise on the last act of the tragedy. She had to get out of bed to answer the call. Leibowitz asked her whose voice she heard when she picked it up.

A. It was Fritz's voice.
Q. What did he say?
A. He said, "Lauralein, were you asleep? I'm in great pain. If it keeps up, I won't be able to go to the office tomorrow. I can't find my electric pad." I said to him, "Mine isn't working. I'll come

233

up to find yours and if I can't, I'll try using hot compresses." I put on my coat.

This seemed believable, only because Leibowitz had previously established the fact of Gebhardt's poor health and his frequent calls to Laura for help.

Q. Did the coat you put on over your nightgown have any pocket in which one might carry an object such as a gun?

A. No.

Q. Did you carry your bag?

A. No.

Q. Did you pause to think of the fact that you had in your keeping a key to Gebhardt's room?

A. Oh, no. I just went up. I pulled on my coat over my nightgown, put on my shoes and hurried. When I got up there by the back stairs, he opened the door and said "Lauralein!"

Q. What did you say?

A. I said, "You shouldn't be up like this. Go lie down." I sort of pushed him ahead of me to make him go back to bed. He did, and I felt his forehead. He looked all red, and I thought if he had fever it might not be right to try heat treatments. But I went to the bureau where he kept odds and ends and looked for the pad.

Q. Did you see various other things there?

A. Yes. A collar box. Some ties. The—the gun. Other things.

Q. Were you aware of Fritz rising from bed—any movement behind you?

A. Not until he seized me from behind. He grabbed my elbows and pulled them back.

Q. What did you say?

A. I said, "If you don't need me, I'm going." But he said, "No, you're not going. You're staying here as long as I want you." I said, "You won't keep me against my will." He picked me up and threw me on the bed. He flung himself on me. He had my arms over my head."

Q. Did you ask Fritz to let you go?

MURDER AT BEEKMAN TOWER

A. I begged, "Please let me go. I hate you. I hate you. Do you hear me? I'll scream and let the hotel people know." He said, "Oh, no you won't. You're a coward. Don't forget you're in my room. I'm not in yours."

Q. Were your shoes on?

The question elicited a series of replies outlining small moves in the drama rapidly mounting to its deadly finale. The shoes became dreadfully important. They had been wrenched off in the struggles on the bed, flying off like missiles as they worked loose and one lodging on the bureau.

Q. And Gebhardt did overpower you and have intercourse with you?
A. Yes.
Q. Against your will?
A. Yes, it was excruciatingly painful. I lay there moaning. Then he reached for me again and I sprang out of bed. I looked for my shoes. I saw one of them on the bureau. I found one mixed with the bedclothes. I put them on and said, "I hate you. I never want to see you again, you beast."
Q. Where were you standing then?
A. By the bureau, putting on my shoes. When I said that he got out of bed.
Q. All right, Miss Parr, what happened when the doctor got up out of bed?
A. He was swearing, he was cursing at me and used words that I never heard in German before. I don't remember many of them. He used one word, which means, "Oh, you damned whore." Then he said, "You are not like my others, but you will be before you leave this room, I will make you."
Q. Did he do anything?
A. "I will make you do everything I want you to," he said.
Q. Then what happened?
A. I just said, "Let me go, let me go," and he lifted—(weeping) he lifted up his nightgown—he took—he lifted up his nightgown and he took his penis—

235

By the Court:

Q. Go ahead. "He lifted up his nightgown and he took his penis . . ."

A. I screamed.

Q. Go on—go on.

A. And he said . . .

At this point Laura broke down completely. Now her sobs were uncontrollable. There wasn't another sound in the courtroom.

Judge Collins broke in, "You'll have to control yourself young lady. Stop that crying. Tell your story to the jury."

Laura made an obvious effort to regain her composure. She was close to complete hysteria. Then she clamped her teeth tightly on her handkerchief and nodded that she was all right. The trial record reveals the following dialogue:

By the Court:

Q. Go on now.

A. He said "You will do everything I want you to." I was horrified. I said, "No, no, never." I remembered the gun and I took it in my hand.

Q. You will have to take your handkerchief away if you are going to close your mouth up with your handkerchief.

A. He jumped at me and he said [Witness speaks German.]

Q. You will have to put your hand down, young woman, and tell that.

A. He said, "You damned whore, I will kill you," and he grabbed my hand.

By Mr. Leibowitz:

Q. What happened?

A. He grabbed my hand and he pulled me towards him and I pulled away from him and that is when the gun went off.

Q. And what happened?

A. He fell on the bed and he staggered up.

By the Court:

Q. He fell on the bed and staggered up?

236

A. And he sprang up again with his hands.
Q. He sprang up again?
A. Yes. And I shot again.
By Mr. Leibowitz:
Q. How many times did you shoot?
A. I don't know.
Q. Were you afraid of serious bodily harm at the time you shot him?
A. Yes.
Q. Were you afraid that he was going to commit an act of sodomy? [Section 690 of the Penal Law defines sodomy as a crime against nature and specifies that a person violates the statute "who carnally knows any male or female person by the anus or by the mouth."]
Mr. O'Brien. Wait!
The Court. Objection sustained. Strike it out. It is entirely uncalled for from any of this evidence.
Mr. Leibowitz. Exception.

Everyone in the courtroom (except members of the jury, court attendants and the spectators) seemed to be shouting. Judge Collins banged his gavel. O'Brien was infuriated because he thought Leibowitz was trying to lead the witness. Leibowitz knew that Laura Parr had not as yet told the jury what it was that had horrified her to the point of homicide. He knew that the witness, by her refusal to use the ugly words that would clarify the picture, was saying nothing to justify her shooting Gebhardt. The act of rape which Gebhardt had committed might not be excuse enough in the eyes of the jury for the homicide. What had he ordered her to do after the rape was over and he stood in front of her with his penis exposed? Laura Parr swayed from side to side as though evading the cruel thrusts of her inquisitors. At this horrible moment she had no fear of the electric chair; she had room for only one emotion—shame. It was this which caused the blood to rush to her neck and then to redden her cheeks. It was not ordinary reluctance—it was deep, soul-shattering shame, and Leibowitz, frantic because he knew

237

that her silence might be construed otherwise by the jury, tried desperately to make her tell just what it was that Gebhardt had ordered her to do.

Years of experience with all kinds of witnesses had made Leibowitz something of a practical psychologist. He knew that women often deliberately thrust unpleasant things out of their consciousness. Any psychologist knows that mothers deliberately "forget" the pain of childbirth. It is normal to remember only those things one wants to remember, and now it appeared as though Laura was trying desperately to "forget" the thing that Gebhardt had ordered her to do. If she could keep from actually uttering the words Gebhardt had said, it would help her bury the horrible episode in the misty recesses of the subconscious. Her hysteria was the result of the inner conflict between her sense of shame and a compulsion to tell the whole truth.

The *Daily News* reported:

The story was literally battered from the witness by an array of roaring inquisitors, among whom she seemed to find no friend.

Her defense counsel, himself, Samuel Leibowitz, was so maddened by the cultured young woman's suicidal reluctance to tell exactly what occurred in all its loathsome details that he joined the circle of harassers and finally resorted to questions that were as so many bludgeons in order to beat the truth out of her.

And finally Leibowitz made the sobbing, writhing witness repeat the words that Gebhardt had uttered as he stood there before her. Gebhardt was laughing at her now, sneering at her as a woman to be used, not as a woman to be loved.

"If you want to make it the last night, you will have to make it a good one," he had laughed, secure in the strength which Nietzsche and his Nazi colleagues had assured him was his. And then he had told her what to do. Medical men would say that Gebhardt ordered her to practice fellatio upon him. Dr. Kinsey; in his *Sexual Behavior of the Human Male*, referred to it as oral intercourse. The law calls it sodomy. But Leibowitz made Laura use the ugly words which Gebhardt had used, words which the jury would understand. And when she had used them once, Judge Collins made her repeat them louder, and when she had done that she collapsed.

238

The demand Gebhardt had made upon her was in keeping with the prevailing Nazi custom of "using," not "loving" a woman. His visit to Germany had given him a reindoctrination course in Nazi behavior and philosophy. He had been to Berlin on the trip and he had rubbed shoulders with many of the new young industrial leaders, all of whom were party members. He had gone to parties with them; the place of women in the new Germany was graphically shown to him. You didn't have to "woo" girls in the Germany of 1935. They were cheerfully acquiescent if you were important in political or industrial circles. And Gebhardt found that he quite definitely was important both industrially and politically.

Until recently homosexuality had been fashionable among Nazi leaders (especially in S.A. and S.S. circles). This fashion had changed, Gebhardt learned. Ernest Roehm and a large group of his friends had become so promiscuous that their sordid relations with each other had become common knowledge throughout Germany.

Roehm, leader of the S.A., was an important figure in Berlin and although neither the American nor British ambassadors would think of having him as a guest, less sensitive diplomats, hoping for favors, often received him. At one such party (which three other correspondents and I attended) the host, merely trying to make conversation with the now thoroughly intoxicated S.A. chieftain, said, "Sorry, I couldn't find any good-looking girls to invite tonight." Roehm tossed off the dark remnant of his Scotch and soda, laughed and roared, "*Es macht nichts; ein Fräulein or ein Junger.*" ("What's the difference—a girl or a little boy.") The ordinary rules of behavior did not apply to men like Roehm or to hundreds of other Nazi leaders. They were not all congenital sexual deviates. Few of them were tragic figures embracing perverse sexual habits because of hereditary or unfortunate constitutional defects or maladjustments. Many of them excused their behavior by pointing to the mighty leaders of ancient Greece. Perhaps in their own minds they identified themselves with some of those titans of the past and consciously aped their customs.

They turned to the philosophy of Nietzsche, which Hess and Rosenberg were always quoting. In the Germany of the 1930's, ten-

239

derness toward a woman was considered to be a weakness. In the Nazi philosophy, woman was an object to be used either for breeding or for pleasure, but never as an admitted partner in any enterprise. You had to show your mastery over women by degrading them, by ordering them to perform according to your rules. The ordinary act of sex implied an equality, a partnership which was distasteful to the ego of the superman of the master race.

On his last trip to Germany, Gebhardt had in effect received "booster" shots of this philosophy. For a time he had almost succumbed to the effete customs of the democratic world. There is no doubt that he had sincerely loved Laura Parr for a time, but his visit to Germany showed him that this was a weakness beneath the dignity of one of the Nazi party's most promising young industrial leaders. Henceforth he would use Laura—not love her. "Thou goest to a woman? Do not forget thy whip."

And so, figuratively, he had brought his whip. He had ordered her to do something which was to the sensitive, cultured girl a weird and repulsive thing. First he had raped her; that was horrible enough, but he was only taking something by force which she had given him gladly many times, and it is possible that somewhere in the clouded recesses of her mind there was a guilt complex, and she suffered the indignity and pain of rape as partial atonement for her sin of initially yielding to him. This was not an act that in her mind called for homicidal retaliation. It killed her love and disgusted her, but now all she wanted to do was to flee and be rid of him forever.

But this was not enough for him. The fight she had put up had apparently prevented him from the full completion of the act, and he was still unsatisfied. It was then that he came toward her, mouthing the vilest epithets (in German and English) and ordering her to participate in an act which she considered perversion. Shame, fear and anger all struggled for mastery, blunting her reason, and no one (including herself) will ever know which of these emotions prompted her to reach into the bureau drawer for the gun. And the gun in her hand kept blazing away as he wheeled, lurched against the bed and then fell beside it. Then she stepped over the body and left the room.

After a few minutes Laura revived to the point where Leibowitz could continue his questioning.

Q. What was the next thing you remember, Miss Parr?
A. I was ashamed. I wanted to throw myself out of the window. I wanted to go downstairs and shoot myself. I took the gun and cartridges down to my room.

Once again the harassed girl covered her face with her hands and broke down, sobbing hysterically. Judge Collins turned to her. "Put your hands down and sit in a proper position," he said coldly. Leibowitz requested that a glass of water be brought.

When Laura recovered, she testified that she had gone to her room, had taken off the nightgown (when she had stepped over the body a few drops of blood had stained it) and put on a sweater and skirt. She had only one desire now—to get away. Where? She had no idea. Actually, without knowing it, she wanted to run away from herself, from her shame. She rang for the elevator and it didn't come. She began to walk and had met Leslie Tate on the nineteenth floor. She rested at the third floor and it was there the police found her.

Q. You asked for a lawyer?
A. I was so ashamed I would die rather than tell the police what had happened; ashamed of what had happened between Fritz and me.

Leibowitz turned to O'Brien. "You may examine," he snapped.

There was a sigh of relief from the spectators. They had been watching a woman being stripped of all reticence; they had seen her tortured and bludgeoned with questions and they had seen her writhing with mental pain as she had been forced to utter words which she had never used before, the very utterance of which seemed to fill her with self-degradation. O'Brien would never be able to convice a jury that this woman had been playing a part. Her emotions had been too obviously real to admit of any acting. An expert on that whispered to her neighbor, "They can't possibly send that girl to the chair. She wasn't acting; she was completely sincere." The ex-

241

pert was Tallulah Bankhead, and her neighbor, Walter Winchell, nodded in agreement.

O'Brien cross-examined for four hours. Despite the verbal battering, nonetheless painful because it was polite, she emerged without having involved herself in a single damaging contradiction. Then finally it was over and Laura stepped down from the witness box to slump into a chair, completely exhausted. She had been on the stand exactly seventeen hours.

Leibowitz immediately made a motion to dismiss the indictment on the ground that the "people have failed as a matter of law to prove the crime of murder in the first degree."

The court excused the jury while he considered the motion. In a long peroration he discussed the facts in the case which O'Brien had claimed showed premeditation. "On the question of first degree, is there sufficient to predicate premeditation and deliberation beyond a reasonable doubt? Would a first-degree verdict stand up before the Court of Appeals," he asked O'Brien.

"I believe so," O'Brien said. "May not the jury infer that she took that gun from her room?"

Collins questioned O'Brien for nearly an hour while Leibowitz remained discreetly quiet. Leibowitz knew Judge Collins well. What Judge Collins was satisfying himself of now was that a conviction for first-degree murder would stand up on appeal. Premeditation and deliberation could only be inferred circumstantially in this case. No one had seen Laura carry the gun from her room to Gebhardt's room. On the other hand, there was nothing but her unsupported word that the gun had been lying so conveniently in the upper bureau drawer. Finally the Judge said he would reserve decision until the morning. When court adjourned, most of the press felt that Collins would throw out the first-degree charge and allow a lesser charge to stand.

COURT HINTS LAURA PARR

WILL NOT GO TO THE CHAIR

the *World-Telegram* bannered in its late editions, and the other papers took the same line. But they were all wrong. The next morn-

242

ing Judge Collins opened court by saying, "The court denies all motions made by the defendant." Leibowitz was ready for his summing up. He spoke for four and a half hours.

Leibowitz began his appeal to the jurors quietly and in hushed whispers, begging for a fair verdict "without spleen" for this poor girl. In a few moments, he plunged into a review of the case from the legal angle.

"This charge should be proven by evidence," Leibowitz asserted.

"You must prove that she premeditated, that she deliberated. You must prove the intent to kill. You've got to prove this woman didn't have the right to kill. You must prove it by evidence, not mere guesses; not by the fact that she wasn't chaste, or how she acted afterwards. You must prove the point that the shooting was wrongful. That is the law. Show me where the prosecution has proven that she had no right to shoot."

Early in the summation Leibowitz frankly told the jury he would be satisfied with no compromise verdict.

"I hope you won't compromise upon a lower degree of homicide," he said. "Don't let anyone talk you into a compromise, unless it is shown by the evidence that a compromise verdict is justified."

Gebhardt was a charmer from the continent, who knew how to sweep a girl off her feet, Leibowitz charged. He spoke of the tactics the doctor used to win the girl. Passionately, Leibowitz demanded to know why Mrs. Gebhardt wasn't here to defend the memory of her slain husband.

"If this poor girl were an enchantress or an adventuress," he said, "wouldn't the wife be here? If Gebhardt were a decent man, wouldn't Mrs. Gebhardt be here in widow's weeds?

"Well, what about it? Are you going to send this girl to the chair because she listened to this man's yarns? Gebhardt was a roamer, he had been all over the world for years before he met this poor girl and he never bothered about his wife. When he was in Germany with his wife he wrote passionate love letters to this poor girl."

Leibowitz disdainfully referred to the batch of love letters as "hash" but said, to Laura, they were life itself.

"Look at this poor girl," shouted Leibowitz. "Does she look like

243

a honky-tonker? Does she look like a gold digger? Did Gebhardt ever give her a penny in his life? Did he ever pay her rent? She had thirty-five thousand dollars in her own right. What kind of a chap was he? What did he offer her? What she wanted was respectability, a home. She wanted to be able to say to the lady next door, 'Meet my husband, Dr. Gebhardt,' that was all she wanted from Fritz."

Leibowitz did not spare his client. He smashed into the *Lady Chatterley's Lover* quotation she wrote to Fritz, and said it was the only point in the long correspondence that could be used against her.

"A thing like that is apt to prejudice you against the girl more than anything else in the world," Leibowitz said. "What a tragedy it would be to try this girl on a puritanical point like that. Miss Parr is an educated woman, a woman of the world, but a "sucker" for a man like that. What do we men know about love? What do we know anyhow about that complex bundle of nerves in the skull of the human species that we call woman? He whispers sweet nothings in her ears and she says in her heart, 'Why, this is love!'

The defense lawyer, insisting that premeditation and intent had not been established, shouted to the prosecution, "Prove, I dare you, that she did not have the right to kill that man as the law governing her case stipulates!"

To the jury he said, "Please put passion out of your hearts. Because a woman once submits to a man's importunings is no reason why she must do so again. Even if a man attacks a woman of the streets, he is just as much guilty of assault as if he forced himself on a vestal virgin. He is guilty of a felony. If she seeks to prevent that, she is not guilty of murder, manslaughter, or anything else."

As Leibowitz pounded point after point home, his voice grew hoarse—all week he'd been fighting against a severe cold.

Once when the courtroom tittered at a reference to the torrid love affair, he turned from the jurors to the crowd and shouted:

"I hope the ladies here are having a good time."

Impassioned reference to her broken love upset the calm of the girl who for three hours had sat quietly. Tears washed down her pale cheeks as Leibowitz loudly proclaimed Gebhardt was the type of man who cared more for himself than any woman. The lawyer called Miss

Parr a loving and tender girl who loved too sincerely and honestly. He claimed it was "an act of God" that the gun was in Gebhardt's room the night of the shooting.

"God knows what might have happened to this girl if the gun weren't there!" he thundered.

In a hushed whisper, Leibowitz repeated the unnatural acts the girl had mentioned on the stand.

"That girl went through her Calvary that night," he shouted. "She had every reason to fear him."

And then O'Brien came to argue for the People of the State of New York. He painted Laura as a "vine of poison ivy, not the shrinking violet that her counsel has painted her." He hammered away at the defense. Time and again he turned to point an accusing finger at the defendant.

And then in a loud voice, trembling with emotion, he shouted, "You men of the jury took your oath, not on a book of philosophy, but on a much greater volume, the Bible.

"And in this book there is no distinction between rich and poor, black and white, male or female. There is one law in this book that still holds for all classes—"THOU SHALT NOT KILL."

Laura shuddered and hid her eyes. O'Brien paused, the courtroom was silent in the early evening hours. Then the prosecutor turned and faced the defendant and shaking his finger at her again shouted in a booming voice:

"THOU SHALT NOT KILL!"

This was too much for Laura. She shook with her violent sobbing. And in a choked voice she begged of the prosecutor, "Oh, please don't shout any more."

O'Brien spoke for two hours. He went through the evidence carefully. He answered statements made by Leibowitz. He criticized and leveled the gun of his sarcasm at the defense. He called Leibowitz a "crafty, clever, shrewd counsel, who, if he had lived in the time of Napoleon, would have served on the staff as a general. Mr. Leibowitz' histrionic ability would do credit to Edwin Booth," he growled.

And of Laura's jealousy:

"They speak of fever in the deceased, but they won't tell you of

245

the fever in the mind of this woman because Gebhardt wouldn't give up his wife for her."

The prosecutor scoffed at the defendant's frequent tears. He called it a "display of human emotion very well staged."

"If you never saw a piece of acting before, you saw it when the defendant took the stand. She is an experienced woman, not a child. She is a tigress when provoked. What is the defense here? Simply, 'I am a woman.' She wanted Gebhardt at all costs."

The charge by Judge Collins lasted five hours and included lengthy definitions of first-degree murder, second-degree murder, first-degree manslaughter and detailed explanations of reasonable doubt, excusable homicide, justifiable homicide, and the credibility of witnesses. Judge Collins discussed the defense. "I can't see where we can blame poor old Nietzsche," he said commenting upon the love affair, and the crowd tittered appreciatively. "If you believe her story, acquit her," in a tone which showed unmistakably that he for one didn't believe a word of it.

The jury filed out. Three hours later the court attendant told Judge Collins that the jury had reached an agreement. Laura walked into the courtroom ahead of Sam Booth, the elderly court attendant who had been at her side during the eleven days of the trial. It was this sympathetic, kindly man who was always ready with a glass of water or smelling salts when she had faltered. She sat down, her face drained of color, and Booth smiled reassuringly and patted her shoulder. The jury filed in. The clerk of the court stood up and mumbled, "How say you? Guilty or not guilty."

Handsome, curly-headed, Curtis Lee, the youthful-looking Virginia-born foreman, a bank clerk in private life, fingered the Phi Beta Kappa key that hung from his watch chain and called loudly and emphatically, "Not guilty." Sam Booth grinned happily and said, "I told you. I told you to keep your chin up," and Laura looked at him numbly, not quite comprehending. A dozen women spectators at the back of the courtroom uttered shrill squeals and cries of delight, and Judge Collins, his face dark with rage, banged his gavel on the bench.

"The defendant is discharged," Judge Collins said grimly, and disappeared into his chambers. It was one of the few occasions in General Sessions when a jury went unthanked by the presiding judge for its efforts. Leibowitz, physically exhausted, took Laura's arm and led her out of the courtroom.

"What do you want, Laura?" he asked gently.

"An ice-cream soda," she gasped, "Oh, please, an ice-cream soda."

The reporters all wanted to speak to Laura, and the next morning she received them in Leibowitz' office. She only wanted to talk about two people . . . Sam Booth and Leibowitz.

"Sam Booth was so good, so kind," she said softly. "He was like a father to me. He said he had a daughter just my age. And Mr. Leibowitz—well, he was just wonderful. I wasn't afraid of dying; I was afraid of going to prison. And Mr. Leibowitz saved me from that."

"Well, he was well paid for that," a reporter cracked.

"Why . . . I didn't have anything." Laura flushed with embarrassment. "I wasn't able to pay him anything."

"But what about that thirty-five thousand dollars your mother left you?" another reporter asked.

"That all went a long time ago," she said. "I spent a lot on my studies, my books. I made several trips to Europe. I haven't a penny now. Neither has my father."

"Well, don't let this ruin your life," a woman reporter said sympathetically.

"My life is ruined already," Laura said bitterly. "It is ruined."

10. TWO SOUTHERN LADIES

"Prejudice is the spider of the mind. It is the womb of injustice."

ROBERT INGERSOLL

1

The case was an unimportant one involving a bastardy charge. The District Attorney was bored; defense counsel was bored, and even the defendant didn't seem to care much how things went. There was only one spectator in the courtroom, Judge Samuel S. Leibowitz of New York. He was in Florida on a two-week vacation. For Judge Leibowitz says he can't get away from courts. He has visited courtrooms all over Europe. He prefers courtrooms to monuments. He likes to see how the other fellow does it. So when he passed the Miami courthouse he hadn't been able to resist the impulse to drop in for a visit. There was nothing in the case to interest a jurist; but Judge Leibowitz' attention was focused on the jury box. Eleven white men and a Negro sat there. When court recessed for lunch, the defense counsel walked past the benches reserved for spectators. Judge Leibowitz attracted his attention.

"Counselor, I'd like to ask you a question," he said. "I'm from the North, and I never knew you allowed Negroes on your juries here in the South. Isn't that something new?"

"Yes, it is something new," the lawyer said bitterly. "This is the first time in our state we have had a nigger on a jury and it's all on account of a son-of-a-bitch named Leibowitz from New York. He came down to Alabama a few years ago to try a case and somehow he got to the Supreme Court in Washington, and damned if we haven't had to put niggers on our juries ever since."

Now Leibowitz felt that he had been well paid for the years he had spent defending the Scottsboro boys.

248

In 1933, practically every adult able to read was interested in the trial of nine Negro boys accused of rape and found guilty in a rapid trial at Scottsboro, Alabama. Leibowitz read the newspaper accounts of the trial and he shared the indignation felt by millions; his indignation was directed toward the shoddy, inept defense conducted in the courtroom. He read the story of the trial as a defense lawyer would read it, and he was horrified at the way the prosecutor had ridden roughshod over defense counsel. He was shocked not only at the way the human rights of the defendants had been violated, but at the way their legal rights had been brushed aside.

When he read how the nine boys in Scottsboro had been convicted on scanty and what might well have been perjured testimony, his sense of legal decorum was outraged. But this was an Alabama case, and he was busy in New York City. He had no expectation of ever being a participant in the defense of the nine hapless Negroes.

Then, early in January, 1933, he received a letter that catapulted him into the case of the Scottsboro boys, a letter that almost led to his death by lynching, a letter which made him the most hated man in the South and eventually made him an international figure who had effected a revolutionary change in methods of judicial procedure in the South. The letter, on the stationery of the International Labor Defense, read:

Dear Sir:

You no doubt have heard and are undoubtedly, if only from a legal point of view, interested in what has now become internationally known as the Scottsboro cases. Unquestionably it is the most important legal issue before the American courts.

Nine Negro youths, ranging from fourteen to twenty years of age, are in jail in Alabama, awaiting retrial on a charge of rape, which charge under Alabama law is punishable by death.

The circumstances surrounding the trial of these boys; the speed of the trials—four separate trials completed within a period of a few days; the lynch mobs surrounding the court where the trials took place in Scottsboro; terrorization by state militia with machine guns mounted on the courthouse and soldiers surrounding the same; mobs parading in the court square led by a band blaring out the significant tunes, "Hail, hail, the gang's all here" and "There'll be a hot time in the old town

249

tonight"; the evident terrorization of court, jury and prosecution; the denial of counsel to the defendant, all served to rouse world-wide resentment; the Supreme Court of the United States in its decision ordering a new trial stated:

"It is perfectly apparent that the proceedings, from beginning to end, took place in an atmosphere of tense, hostile and excited public sentiment."

The United States Supreme Court reversed on the ground that there was no effective appointment of counsel for the defendants and that this constituted a denial of the constitutional rights of the defendants.

Twelve million Negroes in the United States have come to look upon Scottsboro as symbolizing their struggle for the right to live as human beings and the right to enjoy those privileges guaranteed by our constitution which unfortunately up to the present have remained, so far as these Negroes are concerned, mere paper rights.

The new trials are tentatively set for March of this year. We are anxious to engage the most competent and able trial lawyer in this country for the purpose of insuring the best legal defense possible in order that the innocence of these boys may be established.

This is why we write this letter to you. After studying and combing the list of attorneys who we feel are competent to properly present this case, we have decided that you are eminently fit for this great task.

We have no money to offer you as a fee; if you undertake this task you will perhaps be compelled to spend considerable of your own funds in some of the necessary disbursements attendant upon a trial. We do have this to offer you: An opportunity to give your best in a cause which for its humanitarian appeal has never been equalled in the annals of American jurisprudence. You will not only be representing nine innocent boys, you will be representing a nation of twelve millions of oppressed people struggling against dehumanizing inequalities.

If you undertake these trials we offer you the assistance of our legal staff and our fullest cooperation.

We do not ask you as a condition of your acceptance as trial counsel to give up any of your social, economic or political views.

We are certain that you will give this matter your sincerest consideration and we hope you will favor us with a favorable reply at your earliest convenience.

Sincerely,
WILLIAM PATTERSON
National Secretary

Leibowitz had never heard of the International Labor Defense. He made some inquiries and discovered that although its officers denied that it was a creature of the Communist party, it was closely aligned with the party and was apparently affiliated with it. He also discovered that the organization had financed the appeal to the United States Supreme Court and was raising funds to be used for the defense in the retrial of the Scottsboro boys. Leibowitz knew little and cared less about the methods used by the Communist party. Leibowitz was a Democrat whose political and economic views coincided with those of any regular member of the Democratic party.

The world (including *Pravda* and *Izvestia* in Moscow) thought of the Scottsboro courtroom as a significant political battleground on which nine Negroes were fighting against southern ignorance, intolerance and a political system which granted only white defendants the protection of the Constitution. Leibowitz looked upon it primarily as a criminal trial in which the defendants were desperately in need of good legal representation. And he was horrified because the basic legal rights of the defendants seemed to have been ignored. It had developed into the greatest cause célèbre since the Sacco-Vanzetti case, and the legal aspects of it fascinated Leibowitz. He answered the letter three days after he received it. He wrote:

Dear Sir:

While, as you are quite aware, your organization and I are not in agreement in our political and economic views, your letter arouses my sympathetic interest, because it touches no controversial theory of economy of government, but the basic rights of man.

Let me say at the outset that if I serve this cause, as you suggest I should, I will not serve it for money; nor will I permit you to repay the expense I may incur.

You have given me to understand that the defense was not properly presented before the first trial court; and in that assertion you have the support of the appellate tribunal's reversal of the conviction. At the moment, when I stand on the threshold of the case, I think it improper to discuss any of its ramifications.

Some of my friends have advised me to take no part in this case. They fear that the defendants have been prejudged; that irrespective

251

of the action of the appellate court, they are doomed because their skins are black. I cannot partake of that opinion.

North and south, east and west, we Americans have a common tradition of justice. And if it is justice that these black men be adjudged innocent—if it is justice, I repeat—I cannot believe that the people of Alabama will be false to their great heritage of honor, and to those brave and chivalrous generations of the past, in whose blood the history of their State is written.

If the views I have expressed match yours, then I will accept the task of conducting the defense.

Very truly yours,
SAMUEL S. LEIBOWITZ

A week later Leibowitz received the following reply:

Dear Sir:

The views you have expressed do not match ours, and yet despite the wide gulf that lies between us ideologically we stand ready to accept your services as trial attorney in the cases of the nine innocent Negro boys in Scottsboro. We do not expect our political and economic views to harmonize. We repeat, we appeal to you on the basis of your proven ability as a legal practitioner and out of our intense desire to secure for these boys what we regarded as the best possible legal counsel. The terms you have specified are acceptable to us.

We, however, regard mass defense as an inseparable part of defense activity. We shall raise the political level of the struggle of the conscious and sympathetic Negro and white workers for the unconditional release of the Scottsboro boys. We recognize that it was their activities which effected a reversal of the decision in the Supreme Court. They alone have been responsible for keeping the Scottsboro boys from the electric chair.

The people of the South are not a homogeneous mass. The poor whites of the South are exploited almost to the same degree as that to which the Negroes are victims. Certainly it is undeniably true that someone benefits through the exploitation of both. Perhaps among those who benefit are some who unconsciously subscribe to this exploitation and oppression. Their "cultural" and material benefits determine their point of view and obscure their vision. Among these— those who are sincerely opposed to such bestial, dehumanizing treatment as is accorded the Negro masses of the South, we must carry on a

252

process of clarification. A mass defense protest movement can, we believe, best effect this change.

As an attorney you have probably not delved into these sociological trends—they are not of interest to you. You believe yourself unaffected by them. We believe that this is not so, but we shall not here attempt to debate this issue. We have full faith in your ability as an attorney—we have implicit faith that you will try this case as few other attorneys could, and upon these conclusions, in behalf of these boys and this mighty mass organization to which they have entrusted their defense, we accept your services.

Sincerely,
WILLIAM L. PATTERSON
National Secretary

Patterson was right—Leibowitz was not at that time at all interested in sociological trends. The born and bred New Yorker is apt to be the most provincial of men. If he has never experienced or seen the effects of racial prejudice, if he has never seen mob ignorance manifest itself in vicious violence, he is apt to disbelieve the existence of such American phenomena. As a Jew, Leibowitz had never personally suffered from anti-Semitism. As a lawyer he had seen the poorest Negroes receive the same protection given any white defendant in the New York courts. When colleagues told him that he had no chance of getting a fair trial for his nine clients in the Alabama courts, he just couldn't believe them. A New York Jew defending Negroes in the South would have the jury against him from the start, they told him, but Leibowitz scoffed at this. Juries, he said, were the same all over. He could handle a jury whether it was made up of citizens of Nassau County, New York, or Jackson County, Alabama. It seems incredible that anyone as intelligent as Leibowitz should have had such a lack of understanding of the dark prejudices of vicious hatreds, and, of course, abject fear of the Negro, that seemed to lurk in the hearts of most men born in communities like Scottsboro, Alabama.

By now he had read the record of the first trial. To a lawyer it was a shocking document. The testimony of the medical men who had examined the complainants alone seemed to establish strong doubt as to the guilt of the defendants. If he could show a jury that

253

these nine boys were innocent, as the record indicated, the jury would surely free them. To Leibowitz it was that simple.

He took the case and Patterson wrote to him again, ending his letter with the statement that there was an impression that the International Labor Defense "is a Communist organization when as a matter of fact it is nothing of the sort."

Mr. Patterson, in disavowing any connection between his organization and the Communist party, was indulging in a bit of double talk, which is a more polite way of saying that he was deliberately lying. But by now Leibowitz was so engrossed in preparing his defense that he had no time to consider Patterson or the I.L.D. It must be remembered that this was 1933, a decade before congressional committees were to teach us that a handful of American Communists were a threat to the lives and liberties of 140,000,000 of us.

The I.L.D. had retained a southern lawyer, George W. Chamlee, to help Joseph Brodsky (until now their chief counsel) with the defense. Chamlee, of Chattanooga, Tennessee, was the successful and courageous son of an illustrious father who had fought against the Union during the Civil War. A former district attorney of Chattanooga, Chamlee was the perfect southern associate in such a case.

From Brodsky, Chamlee, newspaper stories and the records of the first trial Leibowitz obtained the facts of the case. About noon on March 25, 1931, Victoria Price and Ruby Bates, two white millworkers, clambered aboard a freight train at Chattanooga, Tennessee, to hobo their way back to their home town, Huntsville, Alabama. They had spent the night before in a hobo jungle near the railroad tracks outside Chattanooga with Lester Carter, an ex-chain-gang convict, who was Ruby's boy friend, and a new acquaintance, Orville Gilley, who told them to call him Carolina Slim.

Carter and Gilley boarded the train with the girls. There were five other white lads on the train and several Negroes. The freight train, half a mile or so in length, sped along westward from Chattanooga toward Memphis. The two girls, dressed in men's overalls, and their seven white male companions occupied a gondola—a freight car with sides but no top—filled to two-thirds of its capacity with crushed gravel.

254

At Stevenson, just across the Alabama state line, the train stopped. Then it crawled out of the station and began laboring upgrade. At this point the human cargo of the half-mile long freight train was augmented by the addition of twenty or thirty Negroes. They climbed into the gondola where the white youths and their two girl companions had settled. A quarrel arose. The actual cause of it was never established, but some of the Negro lads gave what appeared to be a reasonable explanation.

According to them, one of the white men angrily shouted, "You niggers get out of here!" So thoroughly is the principle and practice of "Jim Crow" embedded in the southern consciousness, that the white hoboes felt there ought even to be "Jim Crow" freight cars as well as passenger ones. The whites, including Lester Carter, alleged they were overpowered by the larger number of Negros and thrown from the train. One of the white men (Orville Gilley) in his haste to get off fell between two cars and, about to be injured or killed, was pulled back to safety by one of the Negro boys. One of the whites who had been tossed off the train hurried back to Stevenson and telephoned the sheriff at Paint Rock, Jackson County, Alabama. He told the sheriff what had happened and asked that he stop the train and arrest the Negroes. Paint Rock was a scheduled stop for the freight.

The sheriff and an armed posse halted the train at Paint Rock. Only nine of the Negroes who had originally boarded the train remained on it. These nine were scattered along the length of the train. The two girls wore overalls and at first they were thought to be white boys. They were put to one side while the nine Negro boys were hurried to the jail at nearby Scottsboro. Scottsboro was the county seat. The station master began questioning the two girls and one of them, Victoria Price, suddenly fainted (or at least simulated a faint). When she "recovered" she told a story which the world would soon be debating. She said that she and her companion, Ruby Bates, had been raped by the nine Negroes on the freight car. Her story spread rapidly and the local populace was immediately swept by hysterical rage. The cry of "rape" in such a community is much like the cry of "fire" in a crowded theatre. No one bothered to investigate the

255

truth of the charge (any more than a panic-stricken theatre audience would wait to see if in fact there was a fire). Any time a white woman accuses a Negro of rape in Alabama, her mere accusation is enough to establish his guilt. No corroboration is needed. Even southern jurists accept this as legal dictum on the ground that no white woman would make such a charge unless it were justified. Jackson County seethed with indignation and hatred.

As a sort of gesture to the legal proprieties, the two girls were promptly sent to a county physician's office to be examined. The examination took place forty minutes after the alleged rape. It developed later that this was a bad mistake from the prosecution's viewpoint. Two physicians testified at the trial that neither girl showed physical evidences of rape, nor did either display the mental agitation that such a harrowing experience might well have produced. In their testimony, both doctors reported that they found the girls "in normal condition both mentally and physically." It is true that there was evidence that both girls had indulged in sexual relations prior to the examination, but the semen found was of the non-motile type that might well have been deposited twenty-four hours previously. There was a strong likelihood that these relations had occurred the night before at the hobo camp outside of Chattanooga. Victoria said that she and Ruby had put up a desperate fight to save their unblemished virtue, but neither showed the type of scratches, bruises, or cuts that one might have supposed would have been an inevitable result of a desperate fight.

But the inflamed mob neither knew nor cared about the result of the medical examination. A crowd feeding avidly on its own rage gathered about the tiny county jail while the nine terrified Negro youths huddled inside, wondering what crime they were supposed to have committed. The walls of the jail were thin and the roar of the blood-hungry mob outside was loud in the ears of the boys. So ominous was the behavior of the swelling crowd that deputy sheriffs took advantage of the early darkness to bundle the Negroes into cars and hurry them to a stronger jail at Gadsen.

A week later the defendants were returned to Scottsboro, speedily indicted for rape and put on trial. One hundred and three national guardsmen with drawn bayonets, tear-gas bombs, and machine guns surrounded the Jackson County courthouse to prevent lynchings. The courtroom and the space outside for a great distance around the courthouse were packed tight with ten thousand people, many of them armed. Scottsboro's merchants, who catered on ordinary days to the simple needs of fifteen hundred souls, did a thriving business with the augmented population.

Judge A. J. Hawkins assigned to the defense the entire Jackson County bar, consisting of seven lawyers. Six hastily made excuses, and were relieved by the court from the obligation of serving. One remained on the case—Milo Moody, getting along in years but true to his reputation of being a mild village iconoclast, willing to take hopeless cases.

The nine ragged defendants were Roy Wright, 13; Andy Wright, his brother, 17; Haywood Patterson, 17; Eugene Williams, 13; Clarence Norris, 19; Olin Montgomery, 17; Willie Roberson, 17; Ozzie Powell, 16; and Charles Weems, 21. One was crippled by venereal disease to such an extent that he couldn't stand upright. The disease had left chancres on his penis and it would have been medically impossible for him to have engaged in an act of sexual intercourse. One was almost totally blind. One had a facial twist that had contorted his features into an insane grin. Four of them were mental defectives of the lowest possible intelligence. Only three of them could read or write at all. All were undereducated, underfed and unhealthy.

The defense provided the nine boys fell considerably short of perfection. When Victoria Price jauntily told her story, reveling in the exciting spotlight so utterly different from the accustomed dreariness of her work in an antiquated cotton mill, out of the crowd came a roar which repeated banging of the Judge's gavel could not suppress. Outside, tightly packed thousands sent their message of venom and hatred through the windows, opened in the sultry heat of a prematurely warm spring day. The atmosphere was already appallingly hostile.

With sickening rapidity, one after another of the boys was found guilty and sentenced to death. Only one, Roy Wright, escaped the

257

death penalty. The prosecutor asked only for life imprisonment for him because the defendant had just then attained his thirteenth birthday. But seven jurors were adamant for the death penalty for him as well.

The prospect of early deaths for the other eight appeased the crowd. Taking advantage of the subsiding of the lynching atmosphere, the defense attorneys encountered no objection when they placed on the witness stand the officer in charge of the national guardsmen and a local court official. From these the admission was gained for the record that the roar of approbation which greeted announcement of the verdicts of guilty of the first two boys tried had unquestionably been sufficient to penetrate to the room where jurors deliberated over the cases of the others. Such admissions are of vital importance in appealing the cases to a higher court, for the United States Supreme Court ruled in 1915 in the famous Arkansas Riot Cases (*Moore vs. Dempsey*, 261 U.S. 86) that trial in a court dominated by a mob is not due process of law.

Steps were promptly taken by the I.L.D., the National Association for the Advancement of Colored People, aided by the Commission on Interracial Co-operation and other bodies, to appeal the case to the Alabama Supreme Court. When the boys were safely incarcerated in the stout Kilby State Prison, near Montgomery, two of them who had testified against several of their co-defendants now declared in affidavits that they had been induced to do so by beatings and by threats that they would be shot down in the courtroom if they varied in the slightest from the stories they were forced to tell.

Thirteen-year-old Roy Wright was threatened by a deputy sheriff in whose hands was a rifle complete with bayonet. The intrepid representative of law and order made what he probably intended as merely a threatening lunge at the boy, but his handling of the bayonet showed a certain lack of skill and the steel-edged bayonet cut a hunk out of the boy's cheek. It left the kind of scar that only a bayonet or a machete would make.

All nine of the boys vehemently protested their innocence, declaring that had they had the faintest notion that they were to be accused of

258

any crime, however trivial, they too would have fled the train between Stevenson and Paint Rock.

A highly competent newspaperwoman and investigator sent to the scene by the American Civil Liberties Union revealed that the reputation of the two girls was far from savory. Conversation with one, Victoria Price, according to this investigator, "convinced me that she was the type who welcomed attention and publicity at any price. The cost in this case means little to her. . . . Having been in direct contact from the cradle with the institution of prostitution as a sideline necessary to make the meager wages of a millworker pay the rent and buy the groceries, she has no feeling of revulsion against promiscuous sexual intercourse such as women of easier lives might suffer. . . . The younger girl (Ruby Bates) found herself from the beginning pushed into the background by the more bubbling, pert personality of the older girl, and resented the monopoly of the spotlight her companion had obtained." The decision was appealed to the Supreme Court of Alabama. By now the National Association for the Advancement of Colored People, and the International Labor Defense, found themselves at each other's throats in competition for control of the case, with the N.A.A.C.P. charging that the other group was using the case solely for the purposes of Communist propaganda.

The truth of this accusation is too apparent even to question. The case presented the Communists with a strong opportunity to put into effect the plan decided upon by the Third Internationale and upon which they had been working assiduously but with only small success. The plan was to capitalize Negro unrest in the United States against lynching, Jim Crowism, social degradation and refusal of official America to grant the Negroes the benefit of the Bill of Rights. As far back as 1925, a segregated wing of the party, "The American Negro Labor Congress" (later called "The League of Struggle for Negro Rights"), had held a convention and announced that its purpose would be to win Negroes to the cause of communism. In 1928, a lengthy plea was addressed to the Negroes of the United States by Moscow, urging them to "form organizations which, properly led, could play a considerable role in the class struggle against American

259

Imperialism," and in leading "the movement of the oppressed masses of the Negro populace."

These efforts at organization were based on the theory that the Negroes, being the most oppressed group in America, would be the most fertile field for revolutionary propaganda. The nine Negro lads offered a wonderfully dramatic opportunity which Communist policy makers were quick to grasp.

Mass meetings were held all over the world to raise funds for the defense of the Scottsboro boys. It will never be known how many millions of dollars were collected. They sent the mothers of the boys to Europe and they appeared at Communist-sponsored meetings. Feeling ran so high against American justice as represented by the conduct of the Scottsboro trial that the American Embassy in Paris was stoned. The Communist party was riding high, wide and handsome. Thousands who had no sympathy at all for the party willingly contributed funds on the theory that at least the Communists for once were on the right side, and were actually doing something about the boys.

The nine boys were very useful to the party, but it seems certain that the policy makers of the party were only looking forward to the inevitable execution of the lads. Nine young Negroes in jail made acceptable enough symbols of capitalistic justice and American imperialism, but nine young Negroes executed would be far more useful. They would be martyrs then, and the Communist party has always been able to get considerable mileage out of even a single martyr— let alone nine.

Now the N.A.A.C.P. washed its hands of the case and Chamlee presented affidavits to the Supreme Court to the effect that he and his co-counsel Brodsky were the sole representatives of the nine Negroes. Attorney-General Thomas E. Knight, Jr. argued the case for the State before a Supreme Court that included among its members his own father, Justice Thomas E. Knight. The Alabama Supreme Court affirmed the verdict of the lower court with the exception of one defendant (Eugene Williams) who was thirteen. He was given a new trial.

Chief Justice Anderson of the Alabama Court wrote a dissenting opinion in which he said that the boys did not "get a fair and impartial trial as required by the Constitution." Executions were set and then an appeal was made to the United States Supreme Court. The I.L.D. had been smart enough to retain Walter H. Pollak, an experienced and brilliant constitutional lawyer, to present the case, and to the surprise of the South, the appeal was successful.

Upholding the defense argument that denial of time for securing counsel constituted an infringement of the due process clause of the Fourteenth Amendment, the U. S. Supreme Court went even further "The casual fashion" in which the appointment of counsel was handled by the Scottsboro court was scored in the majority opinion. Judge Hawkins had "assigned the entire bar of Jackson County" to the defense, and this assignment the Supreme Court held was actually no assignment at all. Stressing the fact that the boys were "ignorant and illiterate," the court pointed out that they were residents of other states and far away from their families and friends. It read:

"However guilty the defendants upon due inquiry might prove to have been, they were, until convicted, presumed to be innocent. It was the duty of the court having their case in charge to see that they were denied no necessary incident of a fair trial."

2

That was the status of the case when Leibowitz took over. After Leibowitz had thoroughly digested everything that Chamlee, Brodsky and reporters who had covered the trials could tell him, his confidence in justice as practiced in Alabama was considerably shaken. This was not "just another criminal case" as he had at first believed. The Alabama jury was not a Nassau or New York County jury, objectively interested in the guilt or innocence of the defendant. He took a trip to Scottsboro and what he saw and heard there filled him with a great indignation. It was the first time that he had ever been in the South, and it was a soul-shattering experience. All were interested in giving "justice" to the defendants; everyone wanted them hung if for no other reason than "to teach them niggers a lesson." That constituted justice to the rank and file of the citizenry of Alabama.

He realized now that it would be impossible to find an Alabama jury that would view the facts dispassionately. Never in his legal career had he been confronted with anything like this. And suddenly —almost overnight—Samuel Leibowitz grew up. He had always fought for the life of a single defendant. This was his profession. Now he found himself filled with a zeal to fight for the human and legal rights of a minority people, as well as the freedom of the boys.

The second trial began March 28, 1933. The scene had shifted from Scottsboro to Decatur (pop: 22,000 whites, 2,500 colored) in neighboring Morgan County, and Judge Hawkins had been replaced by Judge James E. Horton; Attorney-General Thomas Knight headed the prosecution forces. Leibowitz decided that he would begin by attacking the prevailing jury system. The custom in Alabama, as everywhere else in the South, was to draw a jury from a venire of white citizens. No Negro had ever served on an Alabama jury. True, there was no specific legal directive that Negroes be barred from serving, but it was the inviolable, unwritten rule. Actually the Alabama code defining the qualifications of jurors read:

> The Jury Commission shall place on the jury roll and in the jury box the names of all male citizens of the county who are generally reputed to be honest and intelligent men and are esteemed in the community for their integrity, good character and sound judgment, but no person must be selected who is under 21 or over 65 years of age, who is an habitual drunkard, or who, being afflicted with a permanent disease or physical weakness, is unfit to discharge the duties of a juror, or who cannot read English, or who has ever been convicted of any offense involving moral turpitude.

Leibowitz decided to prove that this statute was merely a nice bit of legal verbiage that didn't mean a thing and that in fact Negroes were "systematically excluded" from consideration as possible jurors. This if proven would be a direct violation of the "due process" clause of the Fourteenth Amendment to the United States Constitution, for it would show that the defendants tried before a jury from which

262

qualified Negroes were barred, were not being tried by "due process of law," within the meaning of the Constitution.

Leibowitz by now had talked with a great many southern lawyers, and he was thoroughly familiar with the legal philosophy upon which the whole of southern jurisprudence was based. The United States Constitution had grown out of three periods in our national history. The original seven articles and first twelve amendments were enacted as a groundwork and were completed by 1804. The second period in history which had produced additional amendments was the Civil War period, and even in southern universities and law schools the conviction was prevalent (and was taught) that the Thirteenth, Fourteenth, and Fifteenth Amendments were devised by vindictive groups intent upon punishing the South as a rebellious and conquered province. These amendments, the legal pundits of the South believed, had been enacted as punitive measures set up in the heat of passion immediately after the war. Because of this the southern courts paid slight attention to these three amendments which granted civil rights to all individuals. (The later amendments enacted after 1913 did not concern civil rights.)

Leibowitz thought that it was about time the state of Alabama took cognizance of all of the United States Constitution. He began by making a motion that the indictments be quashed because no qualified Negro had ever been on the county jury rolls from which the grand jury that voted the indictments had been selected. To prove this he put a dozen Negroes on the stand. Each in every way was qualified to act as a juror. Each met the tests listed in the statute, but not one had ever been called upon to serve.

Here Leibowitz was doing some legal trail blazing. It was the first time in history that living exhibits were placed on a witness stand to challenge the southern custom of making Jim Crow the thirteenth man in the jury box. The question had been argued by lawyers before, but only in legal briefs. Leibowitz was trying the case by producing human exhibits, not legal arguments. The spectators who sat sullenly on the bare benches in the little courtroom with its two small windows and high bench, were hardly conscious of the fact that they were watching legal history being made.

263

Among the witnesses he called was a fifty-five-year-old Negro, John Sanford. When his questioning had brought out Sanford's obvious qualifications to serve on a jury, Attorney-General Knight took the witness.

He shook a long bony finger at him and began, "Now, John . . ."

"Please move away from the witness," Leibowitz snapped. "Take your finger out of his eye and call him *Mister* Sanford."

Knight blinked as if he had just received a sharp blow on his head. There was a sudden stunned silence in the courtroom. "I am not in the habit of doing that, Mr. Leibowitz," Knight said angrily, and Judge Horton leaned over and said, "This has nothing to do with the case."

Actually it had a great deal to do with the case. It was an open declaration of war by Leibowitz against Knight, and everything that Knight stood for. It was Leibowitz at his belligerent best beginning to bait Knight, beginning to harass and torment him. By his one statement Leibowitz had (quite knowingly) incurred the hatred of every spectator in the courtroom (except the grinning reporters who had been sent from New York to cover the trial). For two days Negro witnesses paraded to and from the witness chair. Each one was intelligent. Not one had ever been convicted of a crime. Each showed that he was qualified to serve as a juror, but each one insisted that he had never been called for service.

Now Leibowitz was satisfied that he had demonstrated in open court the fact that qualified Negroes were systematically excluded from serving on juries. But that was not enough. It was imperative that he show that the names of no Negroes appeared on the jury rolls. He asked that they be produced, and Judge Horton shocked the prosecution by ordering them brought into court. Sheriff Bud Davis carried in a huge red book containing the names of two thousand prospective Morgan County jurors.

Leibowitz challenged Knight and Jury Commissioner Arthur J. Tidwell to point out the name of one Negro among those two thousand names. Tidwell said angrily that he didn't know a Negro fit for jury duty. So did J. S. Benson, editor of the oddly named

Scottsboro *Progressive Age* and he added, "Only a white man has the sound judgment which is essential for a fair and impartial verdict." Other witnesses blandly denied that Negroes were barred from the jury rolls just because they were Negroes. Leibowitz challenged them to name one Negro ever listed in the big red book.

"If you put me to proof, I'll go through this book and prove no Negroes appear on the lists if it takes me fifteen years," Leibowitz said grimly.

Leibowitz then made a motion to quash the indictment. Judge Horton denied it and Leibowitz excepted. Then Horton ordered Knight to go on with his case.

That night feeling ran high against Leibowitz in Decatur. Groups of sullen citizens gathered on street corners ranting against the "New York Jew nigger lover" who had the temerity to insult southern custom by asking Knight to call a Negro "Mister." Captain Joseph Burleson, in charge of the National Guard platoon that surrounded the courthouse, heard the angry whispers and immediately stationed five armed Guardsmen outside the Cornellian Arms where Leibowitz and his wife were living.

Attorney-General Knight, who was also staying at the Cornellian Arms, was himself apprehensive. In the courtroom young Tom Knight was a stern defender of southern custom and tradition. Outside the courtroom he was a charming, genial man who made no secret of his admiration for the courage and legal acumen of his distinguished adversary. He was charmed by the lovely wife of his opponent and he pleaded with her to go back north.

"Sam has to stay, I suppose," he said, his voice tinged with worry. "But you should go home. We can protect Sam, I think, if I have to get the Governor to call out the whole militia, but mobs are unpredictable; you never know what they'll do. Why, some lunatic is as liable as not to toss a bomb at this apartment house while you're here and we're in court."

But Belle Leibowitz smilingly refused to leave, and Tom Knight shook his head sadly and went to look up some of the New York reporters. The New York reporters had brought typewriters and bourbon with them, and Tom Knight was a sociable soul who liked to sit around, swap yarns and hoist a bourbon "and a little branch water." Knight was neither vicious nor stupid. He was merely a complete product of his environment. He had been brought up on the doctrine of white supremacy and he believed this as fervently as he believed in God. Negroes to him were inferior beings and he couldn't understand how an intelligent, cultured man like Leibowitz could get so excited about a little rape case that should have been cleared up in a few hours. His bewilderment was honest.

Judge Horton opened court the next morning with an amazing plea for tolerance. Speaking with sincerity and obvious feeling, he concluded by saying:

> It would be a blot on the men and women of this country, a blot on all of you, if you were to let any act of yours mar the course of justice in this or any other case. I trust you will not show by discourtesy or violence anything but a proper regard for law and order. Your fellow-citizens would bow their heads in shame if any act of yours were to interrupt the course of justice.
>
> If any among you are tempted, remember that they would consider it a disgrace and a shame upon the fair name of this and the other counties of our State to have anything happen here to reflect upon the administration of justice in our courts. I expect from you proper restraint and a fair decision according to the law and the evidence. We must be true to ourselves, and if we be true to ourselves we can't be false to any man.

While Leibowitz was questioning a prospective juror, another waiting his turn suddenly arose, walked to the bench and cried out, "Us jurors in Morgan County are not accustomed to taking the charge from the defendant's lawyer and we don't like it. I never heard the like of the way this man is questioning us white talesmen." This was Fred Morgan, a leader of the All Day Singers, a fanatical religious sect which believed it could croon its way to heaven. Judge Horton stopped the man's tirade by saying sharply, "In our laws we know neither race nor color, Jew or gentile, nativeborn or foreigner. All are alike. Please take your seat."

266

That morning all spectators entering the courtroom were searched for weapons. During the questioning a member of the National Guard spotted a gun protruding from the overall pocket of a tall, grim-faced farmer. He grabbed the man and took him outside.

"Why did you bring that gun into the courtroom?" he was asked.

"Just in case," the farmer said sullenly.

The jury was finally selected and Knight began to present his case. He announced petulantly that one of his complaining witnesses, Ruby Bates, had disappeared. But Victoria Price was very much in evidence and she took the stand and, led by Knight, told her story. She identified Haywood Patterson as one of the Negroes who had raped her. (In this trial Patterson was the sole defendant.) It was Patterson, she said, who had hit her on the head, who had (with help from the others) ripped off her clothes and had thrown her down on the gravel that formed the floor of the gondola. Knight questioned her about this.

Q. You say the defendant helped take your clothes off?

A. Yes, sir.

Q. What clothes did you have on?

A. Overalls, shirt, three dresses, a pair of step-ins, girl's coat and girl's hat. He pulled off my overalls and tore my step-ins undone—tore my step-ins apart.

Q. What happened then, Miss Price?

A. Well, one of them held my legs and one held a knife on my throat while one of them raped me.

Q. Did Haywood Patterson on that occasion while one of those boys had a knife at your throat, and the other one holding you by the legs, did he have sexual intercourse with you?

A. Yes, sir, he was the third one, or the fourth one, I won't be positive.

Q. I will ask you whether or not his private parts penetrated your private parts?

A. Yes, sir.

Q. Miss Price, did you resist this defendant when he attempted to have intercourse with you?

A. Yes, sir, I resisted him, I fought at them as long as I could.

Q. After he had sexual intercourse with you what did he do then immediately thereafter?

A. He took my overalls and set down on them.

Q. What was happening to you then while he was sitting on your overalls?

A. There was another one raping me.

Q. Did they have hold of you then?

A. Yes, sir, one of them had hold of my legs and one had a knife at my throat.

Q. Where did you get off of that train?

A. Paint Rock, Alabama.

She finally finished her glibly told tale, and then Knight turned to Leibowitz and said smilingly, "Your witness." Leibowitz wasted no time in making Victoria uncomfortable.

Leibowitz had asked the Lionel Corporation to manufacture a replica of the train on which the alleged rape had taken place, and it was placed on the counsel table. It was a beautiful set of toy trains, and members of the jury looked at it enviously. Victoria was very hazy about the various cars; it was as though she had never seen the original of the Lionel-made duplicate.

Within ten minutes it seemed apparent that Leibowitz knew more about Victoria Price than she remembered about herself. She was sullen, indignant, evasive, as he dissected her life with the scalpel of his questioning. He had her police record showing that she had been convicted and served a prison sentence for adultery and again for vagrancy. He charged that she had consorted with many men, including Negroes. Hate and spite flared out of Victoria's eyes as Leibowitz recounted the wasted years of her horribly misspent life. A dozen times Knight interrupted savagely to object, but Judge Horton usually overruled his objections. Leibowitz continued to tear her character to shreds, and Knight once leaped to his feet and cried, "I don't care what her previous convictions and actions are—but she never lived with niggers."

In a previous trial Victoria had denied that she and Ruby Bates

268

had spent the night before the alleged rape in the hobo camp outside of Chattanooga. She had testified that she and Ruby had stayed at a Chattanooga boarding house on Seventh Street run by Mrs. Callie Brochie. It was two or three blocks from the railroad station, she had said. She had repeated this under Knight's direct examination. Leibowitz had investigated Seventh Street in Chattanooga. There wasn't anything resembling a boarding house the length of the street. He had assigned Chamlee to locate Callie Brochie. Chamlee, a lifelong resident of Chattanooga, searched birth and death notices and tax reports. He interviewed merchants in the neighborhood of the "boarding house," and after a thorough investigation he reported to Leibowitz that no woman named Callie Brochie lived or had ever lived in Chattanooga. The name Callie Brochie struck a familiar chord in Leibowitz' remarkable memory. He knew that he had heard or read the name before. Then one night in bed he suddenly remembered where he had seen the name. Callie Brochie was a character in the Octavus Roy Cohen short story series then running in the *Saturday Evening Post*. Now he made Victoria repeat her story of staying at Callie Brochie's house.

"Do you know that actually Seventh Street is two miles from the railroad station?" Leibowitz said.

"I don't know," Victoria said, looking toward Knight for help. "I haven't got good enough an education."

"Do you know Florian Slappey?" Leibowitz demanded.

"No."

"Do you know a lawyer Evans Chew?"

"No."

Knight came to the rescue of his witness in distress by saying that Leibowitz was bringing in irrelevant matters. This gave Leibowitz an opportunity to say that Florian Slappey and Evans Chew were, like Callie Brochie, characters out of the *Saturday Evening Post* stories. He charged that Victoria had lifted the name Callie Brochie from Octavus Roy Cohen. The reporters at the press table couldn't restrain their laughter; Victoria Price couldn't restrain her rage, but the jury looked balefully at Leibowitz. Why, he was actually calling this fine young southern girl a liar.

When Victoria Price stepped down she cast a venomous look at Leibowitz and then sent a grateful smile toward Knight.

Knight put on various witnesses to buttress the shaky story told by Victoria Price. One of them, Deputy Sheriff Arthur Woodall, testified than he had taken a pocket knife from one of the defendants at the time of the arrest. According to Woodall, the Negro said he had taken the knife from Victoria Price. When Woodall made this statement, apparently damaging to the defense, Prosecutor Knight, unable to retain his exuberance, clapped his hands loudly as if applauding the witness.

"I move for a mistrial," Leibowitz snapped. "Never in fifteen years of practice have I seen anything like this. The chief prosecuting officer for the State of Alabama told me that he intended to give these Negroes a fair trial, yet he jumps up, laughs and claps his hands at something a witness says."

Knight apologized profusely for his display; Judge Horton denied the motion and the trial continued. Dr. R. R. Bridges, one of the physicians who had examined the girls about an hour after they had made their charges, testified as to their physical condition. Neither had displayed any nervousness or hysteria. Both showed evidence of intercourse, but it was impossible for the physician to say whether that intercourse had taken place during the past two hours or during the past twenty-four hours. The doctor said he found no evidence that Victoria Price had suffered lacerations of the head, as she had claimed. Leibowitz led the doctor to tell of the condition he found in the vaginas of both girls. Neither showed signs of bleeding or laceration. There was in fact no physical indication that force had been used during the intercourse in which both had recently participated. The prosecution gained little satisfaction from the testimony of the doctor.

That night a Ku Klux Klan meeting was held outside of Decatur. Angry threats were made. There were those who suggested that the Klan march on the flimsy Decatur jail, take the boys and lynch them. Others suggested lynching Leibowitz. Judge Horton knew the people of this community, and he obviously had friends who kept reporting the temper of the crowd to him. He felt that the prejudices and hatred that were smoldering among the local citizenry were about to burst forth in the form of violence, and when court opened the next day he made a solemn address to the spectators, an address which sealed his political doom in Alabama. (Two years later, when he came up for election, he was reviled as a "nigger lover" and defeated, and five years later he died a heartbroken, disillusioned man.)

He said that he had heard reports of possible mob violence and he felt that he had to take cognizance of them. He said he would strengthen the guard in the courtroom and that anyone attempting to get at the prisoners would have to first kill the guards. The *Decatur Daily*, in reporting the unprecedented speech from the bench, said:

There was no mistaking Judge Horton as in vigorous tones he warned against any attempt at mobs forming.

The usual softness of his voice in ruling on points during the trial faded as he took up his warning.

"Anybody or any group of men that tries to take charge of these men, not only are being disobedient to the law, but they are unworthy to the protection of the State," the Judge said.

"Anyone who attempts it may expect to forfeit his life or the guardsman to forfeit his," he said. "I am speaking with feeling."

All persons connected with the trial he said would be protected.

"Now gentlemen, I've spoken straight words. I've spoken harsh words," he said in conclusion, raising his voice so it carried clearly throughout the packed courtroom.

Judge Horton's speech was received in sullen silence. The eyes of the spectators shifted to the National Guardsmen, who now had added bayonets to their rifles. They were southerners too, but Judge Horton had made them conscious that the uniforms they wore stood for something they had either forgotten or had never known. Then Judge Horton, his strong nose, his heavily lined cheeks and deep eye sockets giving him a Lincolnesque appearance, told Leibowitz to go on with his case. Knight had rested for the State.

Leibowitz put Lester Carter on the stand. The twenty-two-year-old confessed hobo said that he had met Victoria and Ruby when all three were in jail at Huntsville, Alabama, where he and Victoria were guests of the county. Ruby had come as a visitor. He said that

271

he had been with the girls in the Chattanooga jungle and had hopped the freight with them. He said that Victoria Price had concocted the story of the raping for two reasons. First, because it would save her from being charged with vagrancy, and secondly, because she would earn a witness fee if the case came to court. She had persuaded Ruby to go along with her story, Carter said.

Why had he come here to testify? Well, his conscience bothered him, he said. He had been up North the year before and he'd been reading the newspapers, and it looked as though the Negroes were being sent to their death for something they hadn't done. He didn't know anyone in New York so he decided to go to Albany and tell his story to Governor Franklin Roosevelt. He couldn't get to see Governor Roosevelt, but he had told his story to someone in the Governor's office. Finally he had reached Lawyer Brodsky and told him his story.

Then Leibowitz stunned the prosecution by announcing that his next witness would be Ruby Bates. Even Judge Horton stood up to scan the one door through which witnesses and spectators entered the courtroom. And Ruby Bates walked in.

Leibowitz was justifying his reputation as a magician who pulled legal rabbits out of a hat. There was a gasp from the courtroom, and consternation was evident on the faces of Knight and his assistant, Wade Wright. They had been searching for Ruby for two months. Leibowitz, anticipating that Knight would later insist that any testimony Ruby might give had been concocted by Leibowitz and that he had rehearsed her in her part, immediately asked, "Have you ever seen me before, Miss Bates?"

"Not to my knowledge," the girl answered calmly.

Ruby Bates then testified that everything she had said in the first trial at Scottsboro had been false. Victoria Price had persuaded her to support her story of having been raped to escape what would be jail sentences. Ruby admitted that she had sexual relations with Carter in the Chattanooga jungle; she didn't spare herself even when Leibowitz brought out the fact that she was little more than a female hobo. She said she had hitchhiked her way to New York, and having read that Dr. Harry Emerson Fosdick, pastor of the Riverside Memorial Church, was interested in the case, had gone to see him to confess her perjured testimony. He had persuaded her to tell her story on the stand. Knight wasn't able to do much with her. He did bring out the fact that she was suffering from both syphilis and gonorrhea, and he implied that she had contracted it from the Negroes who had raped her on the freight car.

That night the air in Decatur was charged with electricity. The Decatur reading public was given the opportunity of purchasing a bit of prose in pamphlet form which bore the provocative title *Kill the Jew from New York* (fifty cents a copy). There were whispers that a mob of two hundred was coming from Huntsville to take care of Ruby Bates, the defendants and Leibowitz. Mary Heaton Vorse, writing for the *New York World-Telegram*, gave a good word picture of the feeling of the local citizenry toward Leibowitz:

Samuel Leibowitz is showing himself to be more than a great trial lawyer; he is the supreme artist. His methods, his technique, are as far above those of the ordinary lawyer as a Paderewski is above an ordinary good pianist. The most routine question he asks in his beautifully modulated voice becomes eventful and living.

He plays upon his audience with an incredible mastery. His methods are quiet, simple, unhistrionic. Whenever he opens his mouth there is the excitement of drama. He has a clever face, a fresh color, grayish hair, and he is challenging the very essence of the Southern system. No wonder the men bend forward in their seats. Two well-dressed old men behind me are saying:

"It'll be a wonder if ever he leaves town alive."

A fine looking young fellow next to me confides: "I'll be surprised if they let him finish the trial. They ain't advertisin' or makin' speeches, but they'll know what to do when the time comes."

He has received many threatening letters. Friday night additional guardsmen were sent for to guard his apartment. This hostility is as yet restrained and under the surface, but a very real factor to be reckoned with.

He has laid the foundation for an appeal. He has done exactly and with precision what he set out to do. People in the courtroom whisper: "It'll be a wonder if Leibowitz gets out alive."

273

Finally all the evidence was in and Solicitor Wade Wright began to sum up for the prosecution. He sank to almost unbelievable depths in his attempt to work on the passions and prejudices of the jury. He roared, "Ruby Bates couldn't understand the things they told her in New York because it was in Jew language." In referring to Lester Carter, he said, "That's the prettiest Jew you ever saw— this Carterewsky who moved his hands this way and that way. That's the Brodsky in him."

Mr. Wright was a highly esteemed member of the All Day Singers, and it was easy now to see why. His voice rose and fell, and at times he seemed to be chanting invective. Occasionally a spectator would cry out a fervent "Ahhh-men" to punctuate Mr. Wright's tirade. He ended his summation by crying, "Show them that Alabama justice cannot be bought and sold with Jew money from New York." When he finished Leibowitz asked for a mistrial on the grounds of that last statement, but Judge Horton, although directing the jury to disregard it, denied the motion. Then Leibowitz summed up for the defense.

He began, "Now, I'm not going to assault your ears with any such ranting and raising of the roof as you have been forced to hear from the gentleman seated over there. I shall appeal to your reason as logical, intelligent human beings, determined to give even this poor scrap of colored humanity a fair, square deal.

"What is the argument of the learned solicitor? What is it but an appeal to prejudice, to sectionalism, to bigotry? What he is saying is, 'Come on, boys! We can lick this Jew from New York! Stick it into him! We're among our home folk.'

"It was the speech of a man taking an unfair advantage—a hangman's speech.

"Now, as for the 'Jew money from New York,' let me say this: I'm not getting any fee in this case and I'm not getting a penny toward expenses for myself and my wife, who was here with me.

"Mobs mean nothing to me. Let them hang me; I don't care. Life is only an incident in the Creator's scheme of things, but if I can contribute my little bit to see that justice is served, then my mission is fulfilled."

He talked for three hours to a stone-faced jury.

Judge Horton in his charge explained the law of rape, pleaded for tolerance and asked that the jury thrust prejudice and hatred from their hearts. Then he rapped his gavel and the twelve men filed out of the courtroom. They were back twenty-two hours later and they walked in laughing. It was Palm Sunday. The foreman handed a slip of paper to the court clerk who handed it to Judge Horton.

"We find the defendant guilty as charged and we fix the punishment at death in the electric chair," Judge Horton read gravely. The trial was over and the delighted spectators cast mocking eyes at Leibowitz. Raymond Daniell, who had covered the trial so brilliantly for the *New York Times* said, "God knows, Sam, you did your best."

"It's a pity the law didn't allow us to put the case into the hands of Judge Horton. He is one of the finest jurists I have ever met," Leibowitz said. "This verdict is the act of bigots spitting on the tomb of Abraham Lincoln," he added bitterly.

The next day he returned to New York. He was amazed to find an enthusiastic crowd of five thousand waiting for him at Pennsylvania Station. For the first time in his life Leibowitz found himself on the popular side. Suddenly he was a hero. Newspapermen grabbed him and he discussed his plans for an appeal. A reporter from the *New York Herald Tribune* asked him what he thought of the convicting jury that had entered the court laughing—the jury that had just condemned a boy to death—and Leibowitz exploded. "If you ever saw those lantern-jawed creatures—those bigots whose mouths are slits in their faces, whose eyes pop out at you like frogs, whose chins drip tobacco juice, bewhiskered and filthy—you wouldn't have to ask that question."

This was hardly the temperate kind of statement one might expect from a lawyer who still had eight clients to defend on the same charge of rape; clients who would have to be tried in the state of Alabama. But for the first time in his life Leibowitz had lost his calm, objective attitude. For the first time in his life Leibowitz realized that he was a Jew and that being a member of a minority race entailed a responsibility that hitherto he had ignored. Haywood

275

Patterson had been found guilty merely because he was a Negro. Another man might be found guilty merely because he was a Jew— or for that matter a Catholic or a Quaker.

He was burning with anger and disgust. There were a dozen important cases in his office waiting his attention. He told his assistants either to take care of them or throw them out of the office. Henceforth he would spend twenty-four hours a day if necessary to work on the Scottsboro case. Nothing else interested him. Leibowitz had reverted to the philosophy of the East Side again. Now he was the hard, tough fighter who realized that legal knowledge and tactics would not be enough to win this fight in Decatur. No holds were barred in the southern courtroom (even when you had an exceptionally fair and decent jurist like Judge Horton).

On April 17, Judge Horton sentenced Patterson to death (the verdict of the jury made this mandatory). Leibowitz' statement about the bigoted jury had been given wide circulation, and now Attorney-General Knight seized upon it. He made a protest to Judge Horton, and Horton said gravely that the statement made a fair trial for the remaining defendants impossible at the moment and that he would order "a continuance until in his judgment a fair and impartial trial could be held." Brodsky, the Communist, was representing the defense in the courtroom that day. He agreed with the Judge that no fair, impartial trial could be held at the moment, and then added:

"Leibowitz' view is that in Decatur and the South, the white ruling class is imbued with the idea of white supremacy and that only in union of the white and Negro workers warring against the ruling class can they gain their ends."

Mr. Knight, with pounding of his fist upon a table, entered an objection "to such orations in a courtroom in Alabama," and Judge Horton halted Brodsky.

When Leibowitz read Brodsky's statement the next day he was furious. He had the faith in democracy held by any ordinary American, and the idea of "white and Negro workers warring against the ruling class" was not only a disturbing but a dangerous, inflammatory thought. In addition, it seemed damned silly to Leibowitz. The office

276

boy brought in the latest copy of the *Daily Worker*. William Patterson of the I.L.D. had written an article for it.

The ranks of the Communists were split because the I.L.D. had retained Leibowitz. The *Militant*, a publication expressing the views of the Trotsky faction in the Party, had criticized the I.L.D. saying that in retaining Leibowitz it was guilty of "rotten, dangerous opportunism." Patterson in the *Worker* article defended the action of the I.L.D. in retaining the man it thought to be the best trial lawyer in the country. Next Patterson followed with a vicious blast at "capitalistic justice" and the "ruling classes." He referred to Haywood Patterson, the boy who had been convicted, and called him a "class war prisoner." He said that only "mass pressure" could free him. He quoted from Lenin to justify his argument, and he ended his article by crying, "Onward to mass mobilization of the American working class in defense of the Scottsboro boys, of Tom Mooney and all class war prisoners. An end to capitalistic justice."

It was inevitable that the contempt Leibowitz had for such sentiments would eventually cause him to disassociate himself from the I.L.D. He hesitated to break openly only because so far he had been given a completely free hand by the I.L.D. Then came an unexpected and amazing development in the case. Two months after the jury had found Patterson guilty, Judge Horton granted the motion Leibowitz had made to set aside the verdict. Judge Horton's decision was like a thunder bolt. It stunned the South. It was a carefully and beautifully written twenty-five-page document which showed how thoroughly Horton had studied and weighed the evidence.

He said:

The testimony of the prosecutrix (Victoria Price) in this case is not only uncorroborated but it also bears on its face indications of improbability and is contradicted by other evidence and in addition thereto the evidence greatly preponderates in favor of the defendant.

History, sacred and profane, and the common experience of mankind teaches that women of the character shown in this case are prone for selfish reasons to make false accusations both of rape and of insult upon the slightest provocation for ulterior purposes.

With seven boys present at the beginning of this trouble, with one seeing the entire affair, with some fifty or sixty persons meeting them at Paint Rock and taking the women, the white boy, Gilley, and the nine Negroes in charge, with two physicians examining the women within one and one-half hours, according to the tendence of all the evidence, after the alleged occurrence of the alleged rape, and with the actions charged committed in broad daylight, we should expect from all this cloud of witnesses or from the mute but telling physical condition of the women or their clothes, some one fact in corroboration of this story.

A considerable part of Judge Horton's opinion was devoted to a review of the testimony of Dr. R. R. Bridges, the Scottsboro physician who examined the girls after the alleged attack and who was called as a witness by the State.

The doctor's testimony that he found the girls' nervous reactions normal and that he saw no wounds such as Victoria Price said had been inflicted on her scalp with a pistol butt should be taken into consideration, Judge Horton said.

The Judge expressed the opinion that the condition in which the doctor found the girls could have resulted as easily from their conduct with white hoboes in Chattanooga as from any assaults by Negroes. Evidence had been offered by the defense, he pointed out, to show that the girls spent the night before the arrest of the Negroes with men in a "hobo dive."

Continuing, the opinion stated:

Doctor Bridges said when these two women were brought into his office neither was hysterical or nervous about it at all. He noticed nothing unusual about their respiration and their pulse was normal.

Such a normal physical condition is not the natural accompaniment or result of such a horrible experience, especially when the woman testified she fainted from the injuries she had received.

The fact that the women were unchaste might tend to mitigate the marked effect upon their sensibilities, but such hardness would also lessen the probability of either of them fainting. If her faint was feigned, then her credibility must suffer from such feigned actions.

And this witness's anger and protest when the doctors insisted upon an examination of her person was not compatible with the depression of spirit likely to be caused by the treatment she said she had received.

278

Declaring the crime of rape was usually one of secrecy, Judge Horton pointed out the Negroes were accused of having committed it in broad daylight in an open gondola car passing through half a dozen small towns. He went on to say:

Orville Gilley, a white boy, pulled back on the train by the Negroes, and sitting off, according to Victoria Price, in one end of the gondola, is a witness to the whole scene. Yet he stays on the train and he does not attempt to get off the car at any of the places where it slows down.

He does not go back to the caboose to report to the conductor or to the engineer on the engine, although no compulsion is being exercised upon him, and instead of there being any threat of danger to him from the Negroes, they themselves have pulled him back on the train to prevent him from being injured from jumping off the train after it had increased its speed.

And, in the end, by a fortuitous circumstance, just before the train pulls into Paint Rock, the attacks cease and just in the nick of time the clothing is restored and the women appear clothed as the posse sights them. The natural inclination of the mind is to doubt and to seek further.

Regarding the credibility of Victoria Price, the Judge said:

Her manner of testifying and demeanor on the stand militate against her. Her testimony was contradictory, often evasive and time and again she refused to answer pertinent questions. The gravity of the offense and the importance of her testimony demand candor and sincerity.

In considering any evidence for the defendant which would tend to show Mrs. Price swore falsely, the court will exclude the evidence of witnesses for the defendant, who themselves appear unworthy of credit, unless the facts and circumstances so strongly corroborate that evidence that it appears true.

Turning to Lester Carter, the hobo who testified that he and one Jack Tiller spent a night in the woods with Ruby Bates and Victoria Price before the Chattanooga journey, Judge Horton said:

Whether or not he is entitled to entire credit is certainly a question of doubt, but where facts and circumstances corroborate him, and where the failure of the State to disprove his testimony, with witnesses

279

at hand to disprove it, the court sees no reason to capriciously reject all he said.

Leibowitz was overjoyed. His oft-expressed confidence in the fairness and legal competence of Judge Horton had been vindicated. However, in setting aside the verdict Horton ordered a new trial for Patterson. As far as Patterson and the other defendants were concerned, their status was the same as it had been when they were first brought into the courtroom at Scottsboro in 1931. Judge Horton might have thrown the case out of court and thus established the innocence of the defendants. He set aside the verdict because the weight of evidence did not support it; he did not consider the various constitutional questions of law involved.

In short, Judge Horton made what must have been an agonizing compromise with his own principles. Had he upheld the defense contention and voided the conviction on constitutional grounds, he would have been striking a smashing blow at everything the South held sacrosanct. It would have been a negation of white supremacy and an admission that Negroes were entitled to the same rights and privileges granted to white citizens. Horton, inherently decent, honest, and judicially wise, just couldn't bring himself to do that although his conscience and legal judgment must have been urging him mightily. So he compromised. He would set aside the verdict because the evidence did not support it. He probably hoped that the prosecution would delay in bringing the case on for retrial, that public clamor would die down and that, eventually, the case would be nolle prossed and forgotten. In compromising, Judge Horton let greatness slip through his fingers. He had shown great courage throughout the trial. Now he showed a different and less laudable type of courage; the courage to overcome his own convictions.

However, Judge Horton showed unmistakably that he believed the defendant to be innocent, and Alabama promptly looked around for another jurist to conduct the third trial of Haywood Patterson. Alabama found one to its liking, Judge William Washington Callahan, and when the third trial opened on November 27, 1934, he was on the bench.

280

Once again Leibowitz knew that he would have to address not a jury but the record, and he began by demanding the list of jurors from which the original Grand Jury, which had indicted the boys in 1931, had been selected. To his surprise Callahan was glad to comply, nor did Knight make any objection. The alacrity with which the jury rolls were produced was explained when it developed that the names of six Negroes were inscribed thereon. Leibowitz noted that in each case the name of the Negro had been added to the end of an alphabetical list.

Leibowitz, who had done considerable research on the subject of Jackson County jury rolls, had discovered that late in 1931 a state law required completely new jury lists, and at that time a red line had been drawn horizontally across each page of the jury book one space below the last name of each alphabetical grouping. The name of each of the six Negroes was superimposed over a red line; it seemed obvious that the names had been added recently, and Leibowitz brought John V. Haring, nationally known handwriting expert, to testify to that effect. He did so, but Judge Callahan merely said that the handwriting expert "confused him."

Leibowitz, in accusing county officials of adding the names after the 1931 Grand Jury had been picked, was in effect charging the State of Alabama with forgery, the first time such an accusation had been made against a sovereign state in the history of American jurisprudence. But Callahan said he found it impossible to believe that "his neighbors in Jackson County would stoop to forgery," and summarily denied the motion.

Judge Callahan was a native of Decatur. He had never graduated from either college or law school, and his judicial conduct reflected his lack of legal knowledge. The trial was costing Morgan County twelve hundred dollars a day, and Callahan told Leibowitz that he wouldn't waste more than three days on it.

Ruby Bates, quite understandably, had refused to go again to Decatur to testify. She was afraid of violence. She was also a sick young woman, and a few days before the trial she had been operated on in New York. Her evidence was taken in affidavit form and read into the record by Leibowitz.

The townsmen's emotions were no longer suppressed, and the Judge accurately reflected the opinions of his neighbors. Gone were the tolerance and integrity of a Judge Horton; in their place were heard the wisecracks of a small-town politician on the bench catering to his constituents. It was impossible to escape the impression that Judge Callahan was following a carefully prearranged plan of procedure laid out by abler minds. A Birmingham paper charged that the Alabama Supreme Court was responsible for the removal of Judge Horton from the trial and the substitution of Judge Callahan.

From that time on, the defense suffered staggering blows from the jurist's rulings. In fact, Judge Callahan was often a more able prosecutor than the Attorney-General. Vital testimony which Judge Horton had admitted was barred by Callahan as "immaterial." At one point Callahan leaned over the bench and said angrily, "I don't care a snap what Judge Horton did or how he ruled. You're before me now and I'll do the ruling."

Leibowitz was prevented from showing that Victoria Price had several times been convicted of fornication and had served time in the Huntsville jail. He was barred from showing that Ruby Bates and Victoria had spent the night before the celebrated train ride in the hobo jungles of Chattanooga, together with Lester Carter and Orville Gilley. This was extremely important evidence for the defense, as it explained how the girls could have acquired the small amount of non-motile semen which Dr. Bridges of Scottsboro testified he found in examining them immediately after they were taken from the train at Paint Rock.

Callahan heckled, interrupted and glowered at Leibowitz throughout the trial, to the delight of the spectators. "Now we got a *real* judge," spectators whispered to each other. The defense wasn't putting anything over on him. No one expected a Judge Callahan to set aside a verdict of guilty. The State did its best to strengthen its case against the Negroes. It got hold of Orville Gilley, the only white hobo riding with the two girls who was not thrown off the train during the fight. Although he had been held in Scottsboro throughout the original trials, he had not been called upon to testify, presumably because the State could not rely on his testimony. This time he appeared after one of Tom Knight's men had brought him back from California. It was common knowledge that Knight was sending Gilley's mother money each week and giving him small amounts from time to time. His testimony now could be counted upon by the State.

Gilley was a thoroughly charming witness. Oh no, he was not a hobo, he said. He was a poet and entertainer. He had tremendous poise, and smiled a superior smile when asked questions that cast reflections upon him. Newspapermen covering the trial showed in their stories their belief that the tale he told was one falsehood after another, uttered with remarkable ingenuousness. In his summation Leibowitz referred to Gilley as a "dirty, filthy liar." He was quite mistaken; Orville was a slick, charming one.

Victoria Price appeared on the witness stand in finery that startled the spectators. Particularly intriguing was a spangled half-veil. Victoria was a Huntsville millhand now, and under the NRA was getting no less than fourteen dollars a week. She contradicted herself more than ever. Each time she was asked a question by Leibowitz, her eyes would turn to Tom Knight for assistance. Finally the defense counsel protested, and the Judge rebuked not Knight, but Leibowitz for "daring to insinuate such a thing."

Dr. Bridges repeated once more his testimony that he had examined Victoria about an hour after she was taken off the train, found her temperature and respiration normal, no sign of nervousness or fright and no marks of violence. On her clothing there were no seminal stains to indicate intercourse or rape by the defendants. He further testified that she was not bleeding and had suffered no blow from a pistol. In short, he again discredited a large portion of Victoria's tale.

Wade Wright summed up for the prosecution. He ranted for an hour on the purity of southern womanhood. He talked himself into a kind of trance, and his voice carried through the open windows for blocks outside the courtroom.

"If you let this here nigger go," he screamed, "it won't be safe for your mother, wife, or sweetheart to walk the streets of the South."

Leibowitz leaped to his feet. "Your Honor, must we continue to try this case in a welter of such inflammatory appeals?" Wright turned toward Leibowitz with a puzzled look on his face. "I ain't said nothin' wrong." Then he raised his eyes to Judge Callahan and added, "Your Honor knows I always make the same speech in every nigger rape case."

Judge Callahan ordered the orator to proceed.

3

The prosecution showed itself sensitive for the first time to the charge of "frame-up." "Can you gentlemen of the jury believe that men of Jackson County, your neighbors, would frame a case against anybody?" Wade cried.

The most dramatic moment in the trial came during Attorney-General Knight's summation. At the end, while Tom Knight was telling the jury that a conviction with the death penalty would mean staying the hand of future rapists, Leibowitz again stood up with an objection. "Your Honor, this is an appeal to passion and prejudice . . ." Tom Knight whirled around, still excited. "It certainly is . . ." He attempted to correct the blunder, but too late.

The Judge in his charge behaved as he had all along. He even forgot to tell the jury that they had the right to find the defendant not guilty, until reminded by Leibowitz after he had finished his charge.

Thanksgiving Day was a gala occasion in Decatur, with the big football game of the year between Decatur and its closest rival, Hartselle. The natives were out to see a smashing victory—but the referee was a Hartselle man. Time after time he penalized the Decatur team. The crowd became more and more furious. Finally it shouted at him, "Leibowitz, Leibowitz!"

The verdict, of course, was guilty. When the reporters now sought an interview, Leibowitz said, "I'll do my talking to the Supreme Court." A jury was immediately picked to try Clarence Norris, second of the defendants, and his trial lasted only three days. He too was found guilty. Both Haywood Patterson and Norris were then brought before the bench for sentence.

"Haywood," Callahan said, smacking his lips, "the jury has found you guilty of rape." He lingered over the word "rape," mouthing it as though reluctant to let it go, and it came out "raaaaaaaape." He continued, "It is now my duty to pronounce sentence upon you. You shall be taken to Kilby Prison and there the warden is to do execution upon you by applying a current of electricity to your body of sufficient voltage to cause your death, and he is to keep it applied until you are dead." He turned away, and then remembering that he had left something out, he again addressed Patterson, adding perfunctorily, "May God have mercy on your soul."

Brodsky finally exploded at what he (and reporters who were present) felt to be the sadistic attitude of Callahan, and before Leibowitz could stop him he half arose, looked straight at Callahan and said firmly and very audibly, "And may God have mercy on yours." There was a shocked silence for a moment. Leibowitz pulled the white-faced, shaking Brodsky down and Callahan turned to Norris. Apparently shaken by Brodsky's action, he hurried through the death sentence and this time completely omitted the "May God have mercy on your soul."

Leibowitz asked that the trials of the remaining five defendants be postponed until he had appealed the cases of Patterson and Norris to the higher courts. Judge Callahan agreed to the postponement and Leibowitz hurried back to New York. This was December 6, 1933. Leibowitz was confident that Judge Callahan's obvious bias had resulted in a dozen errors, any one of which would be enough to justify reversal by the United States Supreme Court. And he felt that the court would most certainly agree with his contention that the State had forged the jury rolls.

Physically Leibowitz was exhausted. He had been following his usual custom of mapping out defense tactics while the rest of the world slept. He and sleep had become absolute strangers, and when Belle Leibowitz insisted that he take a trip to Europe with her, he didn't have the energy to resist. He knew there was nothing he could do for the moment; Chamlee and Osmond K. Fraenkel would handle the appeal to the Alabama Supreme Court. Before he could change his mind Mrs. Leibowitz had herded him aboard the French liner *Champlain* for a ten-week vacation.

When he returned, completely refreshed, he plunged into preparing the appeal to the U. S. Supreme Court which he felt would be necessary. His trip to Europe had done more than refresh him physically. In France and in England he had learned a great deal about Hitler and the new German philosophy of totalitarianism. He had read the magnificent articles which the *Manchester Guardian* was running on the dangers of Fascism. This opened up a new trend of thought in Leibowitz' mind. As he studied the propaganda methods used by Dr. Goebbels, he couldn't help but feel that there was a great similarity between Fascist tactics and the Communist tactics he had observed at meetings held under the I.L.D. auspices. The Fascists used the Jew as a scapegoat, blaming him for the injustice suffered by the working class. The Communists merely substituted "capitalistic class" for "Jew." More and more Leibowitz was feeling a growing distaste for the methods used by the organization which had retained him to represent the Scottsboro boys.

On October 5, 1934, the highest court in Alabama affirmed the verdict of the Decatur court in both cases. The court said it found no evidence that the constitutional rights of the defendants had been violated. On that same day an incident occurred that forced Leibowitz finally to break with the I.L.D.

Two I.L.D. agents were arrested in Nashville. The charge was that they had attempted to bribe Victoria Price to change the story she had told on the stand. Leibowitz could take no more of the Communist maneuvers, and the next day New York headlines screamed:

LEIBOWITZ QUITS SCOTTSBORO
CASE UNTIL REDS GET OUT

I cannot continue as counsel in the Scottsboro Case until the Communists are removed from all connection with the defense [Leibowitz said]. In taking this position, I believe I am acting in the best interests of my clients of whose innocence I am as certain today as when I first took up their cause.

The events of the past week in Alabama have convinced me there is

286

no other course left open. My defense has been hampered by mysterious moves behind the scenes by the International Labor Defense. I knew nothing of the activities of the two men from the International Labor Defense, who were arrested in Nashville, charged with attempting to bribe Victoria Price. The defense needed no such help. If anything, the developments referred to have dealt a foul blow to the Scottsboro defendants.

The Communists have raised huge sums of money by the exploitation of this case through paid-admission mass meetings throughout the country and kindred forms of lucrative ballyhoo. I gave my services free.

I do not propose to have myself or my clients used any longer to provide funds for their parades to City Hall to disconcert the Mayor of our City or for similar expeditions to Washington to embarrass the President. Until all secret maneuverings, ballyhoo, mass pressure and Communist methods are removed from the case, I can no longer continue. I am not deserting the Scottsboro boys. I have given of my best and am prepared to continue to do so to the end that the Scottsboro boys shall not die.

11. . . . AND NINE SOUTHERN BOYS

"Our progress in degeneracy appears to me to be pretty rapid. As a nation we began by declaring that 'All men are created equal.' We now practically read it, 'All men are created equal, except Negroes.' "

A. LINCOLN

Nine ignorant, bewildered Negro lads for the first time in their lives found themselves in the unfamiliar position of being courted by white men. A group of Harlem clergymen had organized the American Scottsboro Committee and had begun collecting money to continue the defense. They backed Leibowitz' stand that the case should no longer be a springboard from which the Communist party could launch its propaganda. The I.L.D., however, refused to give up. Mr. Brodsky went to Alabama to persuade the boys to stay with his organization. The nine boys, completely unable to understand the conflict between their attorneys, were sadly bewildered and tortured by doubts. The I.L.D. too worked upon the mothers of the boys.

The mother of Haywood Patterson (obviously at the behest of I.L.D. representatives) wrote the following letter to Leibowitz:

Dear Sir:

I authorized the I.L.D. and the I.L.D. only to collect money to defend Haywood. Furthermore, I have given my boy's defense to the I.L.D., Mr. Brodsky, Mr. Fraenkel and Mr. Pollak. I want them to handle my boy's appeal and I don't want you or anybody connected with you.

You just stay away from Haywood. I want you to leave him alone. He's my son and you haven't got anything to do with him.

Signed,

Mrs. Janie Patterson

Haywood Patterson wrote a pathetic letter to Leibowitz:

My reason for sticking to the I.L.D. is because they are the cause of me living today. I want you to be pleased with me. I want you to live and like me as I do you. This is the God's truth out of my heart. Dear Mr. Leibowitz I want you to help me and I want the I.L.D. to help me too. You have did great things for me. Mr. Leibowitz the I.L.D. people came to me and all the boys in 1931 when we were helpless and hopeless. At that time I didn't have a friend in the world. I prayed for help and God sent someone to me.

Two of them came—we were in the old County Jail, not the new one—and they got cigarettes and gum and other little things for us. They have tried in every way to get us our freedom. When you were here I signed with you and then I signed with the I.L.D. Can you come down and talk to me.

İ am sincerely
HAYWOOD PATTERSON

Clarence Norris was not troubled by any sense of divided loyalty. The most articulate of the defendants, he wrote to Leibowitz. He said,

Montgomery, Alabama
Kilby Prison
11-27-34
Dear Sir:

Just a few lines to inform you of my spirit and courage, which is very good at this writing.

For the last few days I have been bothered a great deal by the I.L.D. lawyers. When they come to my cell I always find something interesting to look at out of my window. I don't have anything to say to them. Nothing they have to say will interest me. I am really through with that bunch.

I have made up my mind not to ever be their tool any more. They have used my name and misfortune too long now, and it all was for their own benefit. They can fish in this pond all they like to, but I am one sucker that will not bite their hook.

So you can rest assure that all of my faith and confidence are in you.

Hoping you are being served with the very best of health,
Accordially yours,
CLARENCE NORRIS

289

Olin Montgomery, nearly blind now, wrote:

B'ham, Ala.
Oct. 12th, 1934.

Dear Mr. Leibowitz it affords me the greatest of pleasure to address you these few remarks in regard of your most kind and welcome letter of which I received yesterday. It also found me feeling pretty well in health. Only a little worried. I have layed in jail almost four years. And it seems to me like I should have done been free from under this depression this is absolutely killing me I be frank.

I can't make it much longer do I be gone that's true. And I do hope that you will free me soon. I'm sick of jail. I have a poor mother that needs me. And I want to be with her. I have lost my health almost. Here in this jail house. And I hope you will get things straight real soon and free me. I don't like to be in jail this ain't no pleasure to me what ever.

Oh, well I am looking for you to come down real soon. I want to talk with you awful bad.

Yours very truly
OLIN MONTGOMERY

The *Daily Worker* had urged its readers to write to the defendants and persuade them to stick to the I.L.D. The nine boys were bombarded with mail, telegrams and Communist leaflets. Roy Wright wrote plaintively, "Mr. Leibowitz, they keep telling me all they are doing for somebody in Germany. All I ask is what is they doing to help Roy Wright in Alabama." The tug of war continued and the morale of the defendants was lowered by the fierce fight in which they appeared to be nothing but helpless pawns. By now the mentally tortured boys were getting suspicious of each other. Patterson sent a despairing telegram to Leibowitz. "I would like to see you. I am in bad shape," he cried, and Clarence Norris, fearing for Patterson's sanity, wired, "It is important you should come down here as Haywood Patterson is playing crazy and has been acting funny. He says if he goes to the chair he will take all of us with him."

Leibowitz was no longer the hero of the Communist publications. "Leibowitz," the *Daily Worker* thundered, "is a typical product of a corrupt capitalistic system. The official lynchers are using Leibowitz and this clique of Negro reformists (American Scottsboro Commit-

290

tee) to silence the growing upsurge of Negroes and whites." The I.L.D. held a mass meeting in Harlem for the avowed purpose of "driving Sam Leibowitz out of the Scottsboro case." Speakers, most of whom were candidates on the Communist party ticket, attacked Leibowitz and the organizers of the Scottsboro Committee. Despite the advance publicity, the "mass meeting" attracted only three hundred men and women, according to the *New York Times* of the next day. Ben Davis, Jr., later Communist member of the New York City Council and one of the defendants in the famous trial before Judge Medina in 1949, called for ten-dollar contributions to support the I.L.D. fight, but when none were forthcoming he lowered the ante to five dollars. "Who'll give five dollars to fight Sam Leibowitz?" he cried. The audience sat on its hands, and then he came down to two dollars. When with infinite sadness he came down to a dollar, there were a few scattered contributions. Harlem was beginning to be a bit suspicious of the political leadership of the I.L.D. The Baptist Ministers' Conference of Greater New York adopted a resolution pledging moral and financial support to Leibowitz and the Scottsboro Committee. Other organizations which had remained out of the battle because of the Communist affiliation of the defense now hurried to join the ranks of those supporting the fight to free the nine lads.

I.L.D. representatives said that no help could be expected from the United States Supreme Court, before which the Haywood Patterson and Clarence Norris appeals were pending. William Patterson, National Secretary of the I.L.D. (whose letter originally brought Leibowitz into the case) was emphatic in warning against any faith in the fairness of our highest court. "No illusions of fairness and justice must be permitted for a moment," he said. He charged that the Supreme Court was a servant of capitalism, that its record was one of biased opinions and injustice to the working class. He called it a court of "last illusions where the lynch verdict would be confirmed unless the protest of millions of workers and sympathizers was loud enough to affect the decision."

The controversy was at its height when Leibowitz received notice to appear before the United States Supreme Court to argue the case of

291

Clarence Norris (Patterson would be represented by Osmond Fraenkel and Walter H. Pollak). Leibowitz had never before appeared in the Supreme Court. For the first time in his career he was nervous. He knew that the impassioned oratory which had convinced a jury that Laura Parr was innocent would fall upon very deaf ears in the high tribunal. He knew that it would be useless to make an emotional appeal; the justices were not interested in anything but questions of constitutional law.

He looked at the eight justices (southern-born Justice McReynolds had absented himself) with curiosity as they walked into the paneled room and took their places at the bench. It is quite possible that they felt the same curiosity. It wasn't often that a trial lawyer out of the criminal courts appeared before them. Chief Justice Charles Evans Hughes nodded to Leibowitz to begin, and he immediately launched into his attack on the Alabama jury system. He said that the Alabama law did not specifically exclude Negroes from serving on juries, but that the administration of jury selection did in fact exclude them and that this was unconstitutional. Van Devanter, Stone, Hughes, all interrupted with questions. It was obvious that they were giving their entire attention to the argument. When Leibowitz told them that the names of six Negroes had been forged on the Jackson County jury rolls, Van Devanter wanted to know the motive behind the alleged forgery. Leibowitz, never at home reading a prepared written argument, was at his best in ad libbing answers to the justices' questions.

Experienced constitutional lawyers had warned him against becoming emotional in his arguments before the court. He had begun his appeal slowly and in a soft, controlled voice. But gradually he forgot that the eight black-robed justices were sitting on the highest bench in the country; gradually the enormity of the crime committed by the State of Alabama against his nine ignorant, wretched clients made him forget his vow to confine himself to strict legal arguments and to forego the dramatic approach. In talking of the forgery, Leibowitz pulled out all the stops. This was a fraud, he said passionately, not only against the defendants but against this very court itself.

"Can you prove this forgery?" Chief Justice Hughes snapped.

"I can, Your Honor," Leibowitz said. "I have the jury rolls here with me."

"Let's see them," Chief Justice Hughes said. There was complete silence in the room while a court attendant came to the counsel table and picked up the huge red book. He carried it to the bench. Leibowitz had marked the pages which purported to show the names of Negro talesmen.

The Chief Justice bent over the pages. Finally he raised his head and his whiskers were bristling. "It's as plain as daylight," he said, passing the book to Justice Van Devanter, who sat at his right. Van Devanter looked and nodded agreement. He passed the exhibit to Justice Brandeis, who scanned the pages and slid the book along to Justice Butler, who picked up a large magnifying glass, held it over the pages in question and nodded his head slowly. Justice Roberts, sitting at the end of the bench, took a quick look and handed the book to a page boy.

The courtroom was absolutely quiet as the boy carried the big book to the other end of the bench and placed it before Justice Cardozo. From him it went to Justice Stone. The next chair was empty. This belonged to Justice McReynolds. Stone passed the book across the vacant space to Justice Sutherland, who peered at it carefully, turned to Chief Justice Hughes and nodded emphatically. Leibowitz waited for word to continue. He caught the eye of Justice Brandeis on him and he was warmed by the benign, almost paternal smile on the face of the man whom he admired perhaps more than any living jurist. Justice Brandeis knew something which Leibowitz didn't learn until later. He knew that this was the first time during his career as a Supreme Court justice that an attorney had been allowed to introduce such an exhibit into this court. The function of the court was to decide questions of law—not to decide whether or not names had been forged on a document.

When Leibowitz finished, Thomas Knight, representing Alabama, presented his arguments. Alabama had honored Knight for his prosecution of the Scottsboro boys by electing him Lieutenant-Governor. Now he had been assigned as "special counsel" to represent the State. In discussing the names of the six Negroes which had somehow found their way onto the pages of the jury rolls, Knight said a bit helplessly (and quite honestly), "I cannot tell you whether or not those names were forged. I simply take the position that I do not know."

Three months later (April 1, 1935) the court handed down its opinion. Although couched in restrained, judicial language, the opinion thoroughly castigated the mode of trial in the Alabama courts and sustained every one of Leibowitz' contentions. The opinion ordering new trials for the defendants was unanimous.

Asserting that Negroes had been arbitrarily and systematically barred from jury duty, Justice Hughes held that court proceedings were invalid where citizens were excluded because of race and color from jury duty. He reviewed the evidence that Negroes had not been called for jury duty and the addition of Negroes' names to the jury rolls after the first trial.

The Chief Justice said, "We think that the definite testimony as to the actual qualifications of individual Negroes, which was not met by any testimony equally direct, showed that there were Negroes in Jackson County qualified for jury service.

"We think that the evidence that for a generation or longer no Negro had been called for service on any jury in Jackson County; that there were Negroes qualified for jury service; that according to the practice of the jury commission their names would normally appear on the preliminary list of male citizens of the requisite age, but that no names of Negroes were placed on the jury roll, and the testimony with respect to the lack of appropriate consideration of the qualifications of Negroes established the discrimination which the Constitution forbids," the opinion added.

Chief Justice Hughes condemned the "sweeping characterization of the qualification" of Negroes in Alabama as stated by the authorities of Morgan County. "Upon the proof contained in the record now before us, a conclusion that their continuous and total exclusion from juries was because there were none possessing the requisite qualifications cannot be sustained," he declared.

Leibowitz was overjoyed at the ruling. During the twenty-four hours following the announcement of the Supreme Court decision, he received more than two thousand congratulatory telegrams, some, to his gratified surprise, from Alabama.

In the first flush of delighted enthusiasm Leibowitz told reporters that he was sure that the cases against all the defendants would be nolle prossed and that the boys would be set free. He underestimated the tenacity of Thomas Knight and the vindictiveness of Alabama. Knight immediately announced that he would move for new indictments against the nine defendants. The whole South seemed indignant at the decision of the Supreme Court, though Governor Bibb Graves of Alabama did say that, as chief law enforcement officer of the state, he would order Negroes to be put on the jury rolls. He said that the Supreme Court made the law of the land and he would comply. A more typical southern reaction came from Tom Linder, Commissioner of Agriculture for Georgia. He said:

"The United States Supreme Court reversed all the courts of Alabama in a case where some Negroes had been convicted of an assault on two white women, on the grounds that no Negroes were on the jury or in the jury boxes.

"I notice where the Governor of Alabama has ordered the names of Negroes to be put in the jury boxes. It is extremely difficult for white men of Georgia to realize that this has happened in a sister state of Alabama. I ask you men and women of Georgia—do you intend to submit to this kind of proposition? Do you intend to submit to the proposition that no Negro can be convicted of assault on a white woman unless Negroes sit on the jury to try him?

"Remember, no question is ever settled until it is settled right. We still have the right to secede!"

The Montgomery (Alabama) *Advertiser* editorialized, "Mr. Hughes's pontifical deliverance of the opinion is a lot of baloney. The *Advertiser* may be dumb, but to save itself it cannot see what the political rights and privileges of Negroes in Alabama have to do with the guilt or innocence of the gorillas who are charged with criminal assault upon two women." It seemed obvious that the *Advertiser* had taken a dim view of Judge Horton's careful opinion, which in effect

295

exonerated the defendants from guilt. The *Daily Worker* said that the decision of the Supreme Court was the result of "mass pressure" generated by the Communist party.

Leibowitz immediately petitioned Governor Bibb Graves to appoint a fact-finding committee of men of the caliber of Bishop W. G. McDowell of Birmingham, and he added, "I for one would abide by any decision made by such a committee." The petition was refused, and it looked as though the whole monotonous business of a trial and subsequent appeal would have to be gone through again. But Leibowitz had to wait for Knight to act. This was April, 1935.

Knight indicated that he would take no action until the fall, and Leibowitz took advantage of the respite to augment his sadly depleted family finances. There were, happily, a great many characters accused of mayhem and murder clamoring for his services, and for a few months Leibowitz plunged back into the exciting give-and-take of the New York criminal courts. He found a great satisfaction in addressing juries which had no interest at all in the pigmentation of a defendant's skin.

Meanwhile the American Scottsboro Committee and a great many other organizations, including the American Civil Liberties Union, the N.A.A.C.P., the National Urban League and men like Morris L. Ernst, Walter A. White, Whitney North Seymour, Roger N. Baldwin and Norman Thomas banded together under the name Scottsboro Defense Committee. It was headed by the Reverend Dr. Allen Knight Chalmers of the Broadway Tabernacle Church. The treasurer was William J. Schiefflin, president of the Citizens' Union of New York. Nationally known church and civic leaders from all sections of the country were sponsors.

Alabama liberals had always insisted that the defendants could never get a fair trial until "outside radical interests" withdrew from the case. Now that the I.L.D. had decided to remain in the background, Leibowitz thought he'd give that theory a try. He would divorce the case from all radical sponsorship. He retained Attorney Clarence L. Watts of Huntsville, Alabama (home of Victoria Price), to assist him with the defense. He would call the plays but he would let the southern attorney carry the ball.

On January 19, 1936, Lieutenant-Governor Knight (who had himself appointed Deputy Attorney-General to conduct the prosecution) asked for the indictment of Haywood Patterson (now before a Grand Jury on which one Negro had been placed), and for the fourth time the gawky, sleepy-eyed Negro youth went on trial for his life. Watts asked for a change of venue, but that of course was denied. He also claimed that Knight could not hold two jobs; that of Lieutenant-Governor and that of prosecutor. It was unconstitutional for a man to draw two checks from the State payroll. It was the first intimation that Knight was receiving additional compensation for his work as prosecutor, but Callahan brushed the objection aside.

Judge Callahan summoned a venire of one hundred Morgan County farmers, textile workers and small merchants, and among them were twelve Negroes. It was the first time since Reconstruction days that Negroes had been called for jury duty in any southern state. Leibowitz could not refrain from a feeling of deep pride. No matter what happened in this trial, he had done something never before accomplished by a lawyer; he had brought the Fourteenth Amendment to life in the South.

Diffidently and uncertainly the twelve Negroes entered the courtroom, took their places before the bench and with right arms raised swore to weigh the evidence carefully and "a true verdict render" should they be chosen to sit in the jury box. The Negroes appeared frightened and regretful under the spotlight that had so mercilessly singled them out. The Negroes needn't have worried about the possible consequences of serving on a jury with white men—Knight had no intention of allowing any but white men to serve. He challenged them off peremptorily. By calling the twelve Negroes, the county officials had lived up to the letter of the law—but certainly not its spirit.

Leibowitz sat at the counsel table, occasionally prompting Attorney Watts, who conducted the examination of jurors. Finally a jury was completed. They were calling the Judge "Speed" Callahan now, and he was living up to his popular nickname. He said that there would be no taking of pictures in the courtroom, and to emphasize his point

297

he held aloft a confiscated camera and said sharply, "There ain't goin' to be no flashes around here."

Victoria Price, hard-faced and vindictive, told her story once again. Then the prosecution pulled a new rabbit out of the hat, a witness who had suddenly remembered that Haywood Patterson had confessed his guilt three years previously. The witness was Opie Golden, a guard at the Kilby Prison. Patterson had been in the death house there early in 1934 and Golden said he had told him, "Me and Clarence Norris messed around with them girls. So did the other boys." Leibowitz couldn't resist the impulse to cross-examine this witness himself. Golden had never bothered to get the "confession" in writing nor had he reported it to Mr. Knight until the preceding Saturday. When Leibowitz finished his cross-examination no one but a Decatur juror would have put any faith in the testimony of the former prison guard.

Judge Callahan assisted in the questioning of the prosecution witnesses. He did almost as much interrogation as did Knight and Knight's assistant, Melvin Hutson, Morgan County Solicitor. The Judge was also free with comment and with asides to the jury, and when Leibowitz felt that enough prejudicial remarks had been noted by the court stenographer, he had Watts move for a mistrial on the grounds that the court had "infected the jury with bias and prejudice."

"I must confess," Callahan said, apparently bewildered, "I don't see what I've done wrong."

Watts quite calmly told Judge Callahan that he had been "irritable and impatient" and that his repeated remarks that the defense "was wasting time" precluded any possibility of a fair trail. Callahan seemed more hurt than angry at the accusation made by a Huntsville neighbor, and he denied the motion for a mistrial. Capable New York reporters like Tom Cassidy of the *News* and Raymond Daniell of the *New York Times* seemed to feel that Callahan was ignorant as well as vindictive. A second-year law student would blink in amazement reading the record of Judge Callahan's judicial decisions and comments as reproduced in the court record. Matching Callahan against Leibowitz was like pitting the Bloomer Girls against the New

298

York Yankees, but law and courtroom technique didn't count very much with this jury.

The trial lasted only three days. Solicitor Hutson, who had replaced Wade Wright, told the jury that "the women of Alabama are looking to you for protection. Don't go out and quibble over the evidence," the solicitor roared. "Say to yourselves, 'We're tired of this job,' and put it behind you."

Leibowitz allowed Watts to sum up for the defense, and Watts made a restrained, well-tempered plea for the acquittal of the defendant. Judge Callahan delivered his charge and Watts immediately excepted. Callahan in his charge had accused Patterson of "conspiring to commit a rape." The indictment was for rape, not for conspiracy to commit a rape, a fine point perhaps, but one that defense counsel felt to be a reversible error. The jury remained out for seven and a half hours and brought in the expected verdict of guilty, but with a recommendation that the defendant be sentenced to seventy-five years' imprisonment. It was the first break in the succession of death sentences, a slight indication that the defense attorneys were getting somewhere.

"It ain't fair. They should of all got the chair," Victoria Price said angrily. "Justice wasn't done."

The foreman of the jury was John Burleson, whose brother was Captain Joseph Burleson of the National Guard. John Burleson was a cut above the average juror in Morgan County. He was the only non-tobacco-chewing member of the jury, and he subscribed to *Collier's*, the *Saturday Evening Post*, and *Time*. He was a farmer who augmented his income by refereeing basketball games. He had been to New York once and he never tired of telling of the home run he had seen Babe Ruth hit. It was Burleson who had held out in the jury room for the seventy-five-year sentence instead of the death penalty. By Morgan County standards, Burleson was practically a subversive radical. To hold out for anything less than the chair where a Negro was accused of raping a white woman, was to court the contempt of one's neighbors. He believed that Patterson was guilty all right, but as he explained to his fellow jurors (and later to news-

299

papermen), "You gotta realize that a nigger has more animal in him than white folks. The beast in them overpowers them and they go temporarily insane. That's what happened here." And so Burleson, on the theory that the Negro defendant was not entirely resposible for his act, had held out for what was considered in Alabama to be an unbelievable act of clemency.

Meanwhile, a disturbing incident had occurred to again fan the flames of hatred against the Negro defendants. While three of the boys were being transported by car to the Birmingham County Jail, one of them, Ozzie Powell, suddenly drew a knife and attacked Edgar Blalock, one of the deputy sheriffs, stabbing him in the neck. Sheriff J. Street Sandlin, who was sitting in the car, drew his gun and shot Powell in the head. Powell was rushed to Hillman Hospital in Birmingham and operated upon. When the twenty-one-year-old Negro came out of the ether he explained why he had stabbed Blalock. "I heard him and another white man say they was going to kill us." He said he had bought the knife in jail. The prosecution forces leaped upon the incident and said that it was obviously part of an escape conspiracy. Leibowitz scoffed at that, reminding the prosecution that Powell was manacled to both Roy Wright and Clarence Norris in the back of the speeding car.

Ozzie Powell had been sixteen in 1931 when he hopped the freight car. He was a quiet boy, more reflective than the other defendants. He had literally grown up in the shadow of the electric chair, and it seemed reasonable to suppose that the terror which constantly gripped him for five hopeless years had finally been too much for him; he had become temporarily maddened under the pressure and his act of violence was almost an inevitable reaction. After talking to Wright and Norris, Leibowitz said he was convinced that the guards had deliberately goaded Powell into the stabbing. They had tried to get Powell and the other boys to repudiate their attorneys and ask the court to appoint a southern lawyer to defend them, and when the boys refused they had threatened to kill Powell and the others.

Northern newspapers viewed the shooting as a savage and unnecessary attack on the part of Sheriff Sandlin, who had deliberately shot a manacled prisoner. Protests poured into Governor Bibb Graves, but his only answer was a statement praising the sheriff for his quick action. Ozzie Powell miraculously was on his way to recovery.

One day the *New York Times* carried a short story. It was buried on an inside page, but as far as Leibowitz was concerned (and fourteen million American Negroes) it was the most important news story of the year. The story read:

NEGRO JUROR FINDS NEGRO GUILTY

Wynne, Ark., Feb 6 (AP)—Arkansas' first "Scottsboro" jury sentenced a Negro to death in the electric chair today. Andrew Heffley, Negro, was convicted of first-degree murder for the slaying of his wife. With eleven white men, Joe Edwards, a Negro concrete mixer, sat on the jury —the first member of his race to occupy such a position in this State since reconstruction days. The jury deliberated only ten minutes. Selection of the Negro juror followed the raising of a Scottsboro plea at the outset of the trial by Heffley's attorneys.

A New York attorney trying a case in Alabama, later arguing it befor the United States Supreme Court, was the direct cause of placing a Negro in an Arkansas jury box. That one item in the *Times* gave Leibowitz more satisfaction than any not-guilty verdict he had ever demanded and received.

Meanwhile, thirty-one Alabamans organized the Alabama Scottsboro Committee. Dr. Henry Edmonds, pastor of the Independent Presbyterian Church of Birmingham, headed it. Most of them were clergymen, who were disgusted at the way the trials had been conducted. Mr. Knight, who apparently had friends on the new committee, announced that this committee would get Leibowitz to withdraw from the case and that it would ask the Alabama State Bar Association to name two lawyers to conduct the defense. This report received wide circulation until it was denied by Dr. Edmonds. The Alabama Committee, however, did think that the case of the defendants would be helped if Alabama attorneys played prominent parts in the conduct of the defense.

Leibowitz, after denying that he had any intention of leaving the case, wrote to Watts and told him that he thought the Alabama Com-

301

mittee would be doing the defense a great service if it could use its influence to have Knight taken off the case and have future trials conducted before someone other than Judge Callahan. Watts went to work on that. Four months passed without the Alabama Committee accomplishing anything of any consequence, and Leibowitz wrote to his associate Watts again. His letter read:

June 30, 1936

Dear Mr. Watts:

I thought it best to reduce to writing my present attitude towards the Scottsboro case.

Frankly, I am disappointed at what has been accomplished up to the present by the Alabama Scottsboro Committee. It was my impression that they represented so influential a section of the South that they could properly effect the withdrawal of Lieutenant-Governor Knight from the prosecution and likewise be influential in having another judge appointed as trial judge in the cases.

On the basis of performance, namely, the withdrawal of Knight from the cases, and the substitution of a judge who may come with a more open mind to the trials and the transfer of the cases to a different county, I am forced to the conclusion that the net result so far has been exactly zero. I do not mean this as an attack upon the good intentions of the gentlemen who constitute the Alabama Committee. Certainly, the efforts of any enlightened Alabaman to see justice done for the innocent Scottsboro boys is to be welcomed, and I have always exerted my best efforts to encourage this sentiment in Alabama, believing as I did that there was such a worthwhile sentiment existing, and that an avenue should have been found through which it could express this.

Under the circumstances I cannot help but feel that for me to step out of the picture would constitute a desertion of the Scottsboro boys, and such an act I never have and never will voluntarily commit. I do not intend this in any shape, manner or form to constitute reflection upon you or any of the other southern attorneys who have expressed their willingness to co-operate with me in this case; I have long been convinced of your high ideals in this case; I have taken to heart your assurances to me that it is your personal conviction that the Scottsboro boys are innocent and that this latter conviction was the impelling motive in inducing you to accept a retainer herein.

As I said to you in person, what we are both after is performance instead of finely expressed sentiment. I do trust that the Alabama

302

Committee will be in a position to report real definite progress. Until then the matter should remain in statu quo.

With kindest personal regards, I am

Sincerely yours,

SAMUEL S. LEIBOWITZ

It is true that the Alabama Committee had accomplished nothing tangible, but the very conservative respectability of the men who headed it was a jolt to the southern press, which in its way had been as active in the prosecution as Tom Knight had been. Alabama newspapers could no longer dismiss the defense forces as a group of "Communist nigger lovers headed by a Jew lawyer from New York." A small but obviously sincere and very very southern group had spontaneously aligned itself with the defense. Gradually the South (the trend is obvious in editorials of this period) was getting disgusted with the whole unsavory mess. The realization that most decent civil, fraternal, church and legal organizations in America were looking at Alabama justice with loathing and contempt was finally percolating into southern consciousness.

Leibowitz, whose sources of information were excellent (practically every newspaperman who had covered the trials had appointed himself an unofficial member of defense forces) heard of a new and damaging blow to the prestige of Alabama. The governor of Alabama had come to New York to obtain a state loan. In the past, the obtaining of such loans from banks had been a routine matter. Banks usually consider sovereign states to be pretty good financial risks. But the governor was shocked to be turned down by a bank which for years had been dealing financially with Alabama. A bank official told him bluntly that the depositors and directors would take a very dim view of any loan given to Alabama. The governor, humiliated and horrified, hurried back to Montgomery.

A few days later Leibowitz received a phone call from Tom Knight. The Lieutenant-Governor was in New York. He and Albert Carmichael, Alabama's new Attorney-General, had just arrived and were staying at the New Yorker Hotel.

"Would you mind coming over to discuss some things with us in the morning?" Knight said anxiously.

303

Leibowitz had never forgotten Knight's kindness to his wife during the dangerous days in Decatur. Outside the courtroom he liked Knight, and now that the Alabaman was in New York he hoped to repay Knight for his hospitality in Decatur. He suggested that he send a car to pick up Knight and his group the next day and bring them to his home for dinner.

"Belle and I would love to see you, Tom," he said. "We owe you a good dinner. And I promise not to mention the case at all."

"But I came up here to talk about the case," Knight said miserably. "And any publicity about my coming here to see you would be prejudicial to what I have in mind. Could you come to the hotel instead and keep it dark?"

"Of course," Leibowitz said, beginning to put two and two together. It seemed fairly obvious that Knight was waving a white flag. He went to the New Yorker the next morning. The Alabamans were waiting in a bedroom. It was still early and the bed hadn't been made. Knight greeted him warmly and then almost apologetically locked the door. Leibowitz sat on the bed and asked blandly, "What ever brought you to New York, Tom?"

After preliminary verbal sparring Knight said that he and the Attorney-General were "prepared to make a disposition of the case satisfactory to all elements concerned." Leibowitz noted that Knight had lost some of his former confidence. His attitude was, "This damn case is costing the taxpayers of Alabama a lot of money. It is proving itself a nuisance politically and every other way. We're sick and tired of the Scottsboro boys, let's sit down and find some solution to the case that will satisfy you and allow us to save face."

Leibowitz, a dead-pan poker player, remained non-committal. Finally Knight said that he was amenable to any proposition Leibowitz might make. As long as Leibowitz would allow three or four of the defendants to plead guilty of rape, they could make a deal on the others.

Leibowitz got up from the bed and walked to the window. "Come here, Tom, I want to show you something." Knight blinked, but went to the window. Leibowitz opened it, pushed aside the curtains and pointed down. "Just three blocks from here in that direction you'll find the 14th Precinct Police Station. The sergeant behind the desk there probably gets a dozen complaints a day. A lot of the complaints come from crackpots, publicity seekers, or liars who want to use the police to satisfy some personal grudge. Now the sergeant is no genius, but years of listening to such complaints has given him some ability to tell whether or not a complainant is lying. Had Victoria Price and Ruby Bates walked into that station house to complain to the sergeant on duty that nine Negro boys had raped them, that sergeant, after questioning them for five minutes, would have known them to be two liars. He would have tossed them out of the precinct and that would have been the end of the whole affair."

"What's the point?" Knight asked.

"Even the dumbest cop on the force would have spotted those two as tramps and liars," Leibowitz snapped. "You know damn well they lied that day at the Paint Rock station, and the Price girl has been lying ever since. Now you want me to plead three or four of the boys guilty of something they never did. The State of Alabama finally realizes that it has made a horrible mistake. You want me to pull your chestnuts out of the fire. You want a chance to save face. Tom, you ought to know me better than that."

"They fought with those white boys on the train and threw some of them off the train," Knight reminded Leibowitz. "That's assault."

"That's true," Leibowitz said gravely. "And it calls for a five-year sentence. But not all of the boys were involved in the fight on the train."

"Suppose," Knight said cautiously, "you were to plead four of the Negroes guilty of assault on the white boys? Say you entered guilty pleas in the cases of Haywood Patterson, Clarence Norris, Charles Weems and Andy Wright. We might discharge Montgomery, Roberson, Roy Wright and Williams. We'd discharge Ozzie Powell on the rape indictment if you'd plead him guilty to knifing the sheriff. Of course we'd have to see if Judge Callahan will go along."

"See Callahan," Leibowitz said, "and then if you can give us a concrete proposition, we'll talk it over."

They hurried back to Alabama and discussed the settlement with Callahan. The Judge was outraged. He told Knight that such a settlement would be equivalent "to fining each of the defendants a fifty-dollar bill." Knight phoned Leibowitz that the compromise was off. Actually Leibowitz hadn't decided whether or not he would accept the settlement at all. Playing his cards very close to his chest, he had agreed to nothing but had allowed Knight to discuss everything. He knew now that Knight was worrying and that the new Attorney-General was uneasy.

Leibowitz had once more appealed the Patterson case to the Alabama Supreme Court, and the trials of Norris and the others were postponed until the result of that appeal was known. It was not until June 14, 1937, that the court announced the decision. It affirmed the seventy-five-year sentence and Leibowitz immediately announced that he would appeal to the U.S. Supreme Court.

Death suddenly removed Thomas Knight from the case. The body of the young lawyer, whose role as prosecutor of the Scottsboro defendants had brought him to national notice, lay in state at Alabama's capital, with Governor Bibb Graves paying high tribute to the dead attorney. The *Montgomery Advertiser* said, "To us he was Tommy Knight, a lovable, impulsive boy, a gallant figure mantled in tragedy with which death invests those it takes in their youth." None of the nine defendants joined in the state-wide eulogies.

The trials were resumed on July 13, 1937, with Thomas S. Lawson, assistant to Attorney-General Carmichael, prosecuting, and Judge Callahan again presiding. In rapid succession Clarence Norris, Andy Wright and Charles Weems were tried and convicted. The three trials covered only nine days, and Callahan was proud of the way he had dispatched them. Norris was given the death sentence. Wright was given ninety-nine years in jail and Weems was given seventy-five years.

Leibowitz did something in the trial of Norris he hadn't been able to do before. He managed to show the character of Victoria Price by the testimony of white witnesses. Mrs. Emma Bates, the mother of Ruby, testified that in 1932 she had visited Victoria and Ruby in jail (where they were serving a sentence for vagrancy) and that she was horrified to discover two men sharing the cell with the girls. When she protested, Victoria told her the men were her "two

306

half brothers." Victoria added, "I wanted them here for company."
Then Richard S. Watson, a former Huntsville deputy sheriff, testified
that he knew Victoria Price and that she had a bad reputation. "I
wouldn't believe her under oath," he said contemptuously. Sol Wallace, another Huntsville law enforcement officer, said the same thing.
But the jury believed no one but Victoria and Judge Callahan, who
again showed unmistakably that he felt that the defendents were
guilty. He told the jury in his charge that where the complaining witness was a white woman and the defendant a Negro, the unsupported
word of the white woman was enough for conviction.

Leibowitz entered a plea of guilty to the stabbing on behalf of
Ozzie Powell. He said that six years of confinement had caused the
boy to become insane. Powell was sentenced to twenty years.

Then came the most sensational development in the whole six years
of the case. Just after Powell had been sentenced, Assistant Attorney-
General Lawson announced dramatically that charges of rape against
five of the defendants had been dropped. Olin Montgomery, Willie
Roberson, Eugene Williams and Roy Wright were freed and turned
over to Leibowitz. The charges of rape against Powell were dismissed,
but he would have to serve his sentence for assault on the sheriff.
Lawson said the defendants had been freed because the State "is convinced that they are not guilty." He issued a formal statement in
which he discussed each defendant. Willie Roberson, he said, was
suffering from a severe, apparently incurable venereal disease; Olin
Montgomery was almost completely blind; Eugene Williams and Roy
Wright were both under fourteen when the alleged rape had taken
place in 1931.

It was noon, and now Leibowitz was faced with the task of getting
the four boys safely out of Alabama. The streets were crowded with
ominously silent men. Allen Raymond of the *Herald Tribune* and
Tom Cassidy of the *News* mingled with the crowd and then told
Leibowitz that the good citizens, with the help of local corn whiskey,
were gradually working themselves into a rage. The newspapermen
had lined up a couple of cars. They suggested that this was the moment for a very precipitate retreat. The cars were parked in front of
the back entrance to the jail. Leibowitz hurried his bewildered charges

into the cars and accompanied by Raymond, Cassidy and Daniell of the *Times*, the two-car convoy hurried out of town. Neither Leibowitz nor the reporters breathed freely until the cars sped across the state line into Tennessee. They reached Nashville without incident and found that a train for Cincinnati was to leave in a few moments. Leibowitz was lucky enough to get a couple of drawing rooms, and finally the train drew out of the station.

Leibowitz had wired New York and Decatur asking that any important messages be forwarded to the train. When they reached Cincinnati there were dozens of messages of congratulations and a great many offering the four boys money if they would appear at county fairs, carnivals, vaudeville houses. He showed them to newspapermen, adding that there would be no exploitation of the boys if he could help it.

"No barnstorming, no theatricals of any kind. I'm going to put them in charge of some responsible and respectable agency with a view to giving them a chance to resurrect lives which were almost crushed out by the State of Alabama," he said.

Wright was asked by a reporter how it felt to be free.

"Feels like I always felt when I was free," he drawled.

"What do you want to do now?"

"Sleep, I guess."

Leibowitz said the youths had confided to him that they had ambitions. One wanted to be a musician, another a mechanic.

"They'll get every chance," he said.

"First of all, they've got to get some sleep. Then to a tailor. The boys have to have their teeth fixed. They need rest. After that, we'll see," Mr. Leibowitz said.

The startling development had been headlined in every newspaper in America. The following day an editorial in the *Washington Post* summed up the general sentiment:

THE SCOTTSBORO CASE

Dispatches describing Alabama's abrupt action in freeing four of the nine "Scottsboro boys" suggest that the books on the case may now be closed. It is predicted from Decatur that if no appeals are made in behalf of the other five Negroes, the Governor will commute at least the single death sentence now standing.

Undoubtedly most of Alabama hopes for just this. The six-and-a-half-year rape trial has done little to enhance the State's reputation. On the contrary, mention today of the name of Alabama raises all manner of unpleasant thoughts of injustice, blind prejudice and abject social failure. Ten times Alabama prosecutors rose in court with only the word of a female tramp to justify their demand for the lives of nine Negroes. Ten times Alabama juries acceded to the request, closing their eyes narrowly not only to competent medical testimony but—most important—to the oath of one of the women involved that the whole story of the attack on them was "framed."

A more evident miscarriage of justice the Nation has rarely witnessed. Yet Alabama persisted in it until last week when, apparently, even its stomach turned and it sought to find a way out of the disgrace by canceling the charges against the last four boys scheduled for retrial. Much as the whole country, too, would like to forget the unpleasant affair, the books should not be closed with only this. Partial justice is almost as bad as none.

Alabama has at last admitted that there is no case against four of the indicted Negroes; what about the other five whose retrials have already been finished? Are they not eligible for rehearings in the light of the State's sudden change of mind? The organizations and individuals who have been defending the Negroes have let it be known that they will fight the conviction of the five "to hell and back."

Alabama's shame is the Nation's shame. Some little redemption was achieved when, after the Federal Supreme Court had set aside the death verdicts because only white men had been called for jury duty, Alabama admitted its error and ordered Negroes listed as veniremen. But more than this is needed. Only a complete review of the cases of the five convicted Negroes, conducted in the fullest spirit of honesty and fair play, will restore the injuries done American justice by the long, sickening years of the Scottsboro trial.

New York took the four bewildered lads to its heart. A howling cheering mob of twenty thousand met them at the Pennsylvania Station, but it wasn't the kind of mob they had feared for six and a half years.

309

2

Nine boys had been accused of a crime in which they were charged with being joint participants. Now five were exonerated. By all rules of logic, if five were innocent—all were innocent, but the sovereign State of Alabama refused to see it that way. Alabama had made its magnanimous gesture, and its press seemed puzzled because the rest of the world didn't applaud it. The dictum that truth always triumphs over persecution is one of those pleasant falsehoods which experience constantly refutes. It is a piece of idle sentimentality that truth, merely as truth, has any inherent power denied to the forces of prejudice and evil. And in Alabama truth always lost out when confronted with the unholy doctrine of white supremacy. The remaining Negro lads stayed in jail.

The Scottsboro Committee fought valiantly to obtain paroles for the boys. The International Labor Defense continued to hold protest meetings, but Negro audiences were becoming increasingly reluctant to contribute funds. Actually the worker-versus-capital issue which the Communist party kept belaboring was quite remote from the case, and Negroes were beginning to realize this. To put it bluntly, the nine boys had been at the time of their arrest nine unemployed vagrants. They had been convicted under the pressure of race prejudice and mob excitement aroused by sex fears, not by economic antagonism. Leibowitz had always emphasized the point that no economic class struggle was involved. This was primarily a race issue.

The Communists were probably well satisfied that Alabama still kept five of the boys in jail. It enabled them to keep up their intensive drive to enlist Negro support, and there is no doubt that the constant attacks made by the Party speakers upon Negro leadership as exemplified by the Negro church, Negro publishers and the National Association for the Advancement of Colored People, did result in obtaining thousands of converts to the Party. There was no political device the Communists didn't use to gain Negro support. They even nominated a Negro for the vice-presidency on their national ticket.

They dismissed Walter White and the other sincere, intelligent Negro leaders as "bourgeois traitors to their race." They boasted that it was their efforts alone which had freed four of the Scottsboro boys.

Negroes had long since accepted capitalism, and they understood the deep-lying urge of democracy that uprooted chattel slavery and tardily gave the freedmen and their children a chance for education and advancement. Communist leaders argued with them that because of mob murder, Jim Crowism, and other evils that persisted, the slow step-by-step advancement advocated by their leaders held faint hope of ultimate freedom. They pointed to the years of Communist reorganization of class relationships in Russia. They argued that Marxian economic and social doctrines were sounder bases for economic salvation of American Negroes than the slowly trodden path of the past hundred years of abolition, emancipation and education.

And they always emphasized the fact that there was no economic or social restriction against the Negro in the Soviet Union. Theoretically, they may have been right on this point. I spent nine months in Moscow during the war and the only Negro I met in the city was the representative of the *Daily Worker* of London. But this made a powerful argument that made many Negroes turn away from the intelligent realism of men like Walter White to embrace a theoretical Utopia. And they used the still incarcerated Scottsboro boys to draw the crowds to whom they could sell their doctrines.

No one knows just how much money was raised by the Communist party for "the defense of the Scottsboro boys." Earl Browder once said that one million dollars was collected. Other estimates ran to twice that figure. When the New York *Daily Worker* installed magnificent new presses in its plant a few years ago, there were many who joked about the source which had supplied the money, and more than one Harlem Negro leader hinted broadly that the presses had been paid for by Negro donations intended to help the Scottsboro defense. The defense actually cost about sixty thousand dollars. Communist leaders assert that they made no misrepresentation when they appealed for funds. The funds were to be used for the "defense of the Scottsboro boys and for mass protest against the ruling capital class."

There was nothing that Leibowitz could do in a legal way to help

311

the five boys still imprisoned. Dr. Allen Knight Chalmers (now teaching at the Boston University Theological School) and the Scottsboro Defense Committee which he headed never stopped fighting for their release. And almost surreptitiously the State of Alabama began to give the boys belated "justice." One was paroled, then another. Finally over the years they were all paroled except Haywood Patterson. And he escaped from the Kilby Prison Farm and is still (if alive) at large. Andy Wright violated his parole by leaving the state without permission. He went back to prison and is still there. Roy Wright has a job with a furrier in New York. Eugene Williams is now somewhere in Tennessee. Olin Montgomery is employed in a restaurant in New York City, and Willie Roberson is a janitor in Brooklyn. Ozzie Powell is still paralyzed and unable to work. Charlie Weems works for a laundry in an Atlanta suburb. Clarence Norris is married and is living in Georgia.

The wonder of it is that any of the boys managed to grow into decent citizens. Beaten, jailed, flattered, idolized, by turn, it seems inconceivable that any of them was able to retain any mental balance or human dignity. But they survived in one way or another, and today they are pretty much forgotten; not even objects of curiosity in the shops where they work or neighborhoods in which they live. Patterson, of course, is nothing but a hunted, perhaps half-crazed creature. He didn't have much mentality to start with.

The Scottsboro trials did little to reform the thinking of the South. Lillian Smith, in her courageous book, *Killers of the Dream*, published in October, 1949, made it plain that the doctrine of white supremacy is as firmly implanted as ever in the minds of southerners. The uncorroborated testimony of a white woman (even a prostitute) can still be used with telling effect against any Negro defendant. The Judge Callahans, the Wade Wrights, the Tom Knights, still outnumber the Judge Hortons in Alabama and her sister states.

But Leibowitz' dramatization of the defense did reveal to the rest of the country the horrible conditions that prevailed in a section which for so long had blithely ignored some of the more important parts of the Constitution. It did force the South to give the Negro at least a few legal safeguards. And if it hadn't been "for that son-of-

312

a-bitch Leibowitz," no Negro would be sitting on any southern jury today.

3

During the closing stages of the 1949 pennant race I sat with Judge Leibowitz in Ebbets Field. Jackie Robinson, brilliant Dodger second baseman, singled, stole second, went to third on a passed ball and then stole home with the run that won the game for the Dodgers. As we left the ball park we talked about Jackie Robinson and compared him with Frank Frisch, Joe Gordon and other great second basemen we'd seen. And inevitably we talked about Branch Rickey, president of the Brooklyn baseball club, who had the courage to sign up the first Negro ever to play ball in the major leagues.

"Once," the Judge said thoughtfully, "you asked me what the Scottsboro case meant to me. At first I looked at the case merely through the eyes of a trial lawyer. I tried hard not to be gripped by the anger which the terrible injustice had caused so many to feel. It is difficult to see monstrous injustice being done before your very eyes and retain your sense of perspective. But there is no excuse for a lawyer to lose his temper, as I did once during the case," he said ruefully. "I mean the time when I returned to New York and lambasted the jury as a group of 'lantern-jawed men whose eyes pop out' that was the one time I blew my top. You must not lose your temper while trying a case, any more than you can lose it out on the pitching mound.

"What did the Scottsboro case mean to me? Well, I like to think that I helped a little in convincing the public that a Negro is a citizen, entitled to the full privileges of citizenship. Every time I see Jackie Robinson and Don Newcombe and Roy Campanella out there in Dodger uniforms, I get a kick out of it. Baseball wasn't worthy to be called our national game until it recognized that a Negro had every right to play in the big leagues. I like to watch Jackie out there playing alongside of Pee Wee Reese of Louisville, Kentucky; each giving the other harmonious support; each encouraging the other.

You get a feeling that the late Judge Horton was more representative of the real South than was a Callahan or a Wright. You get a feeling that Pee Wee and other southerners in baseball, who so casually accept Negro ball players, are molding a new and fine tradition.

"Yes," he smiled, "I had a little to do with that, and that's what the Scottsboro case means to me."

12. PUBLIC ENEMIES

"No guilty man is acquitted at the bar of his own
conscience."

JUVENAL

Al Capone was a man of simple tastes who only wanted the best.
He insisted upon the best of food, the best of wine, and when he
was in trouble, the best of lawyers. Early in the 1920's, when Capone was little more than a promising but quite prosperous hoodlum,
Leibowitz had represented him in a Brooklyn murder case and without much trouble had succeeded in establishing that there was a very
reasonable doubt as to Capone's guilt of the homicide in question.
Capone decided that both the climate and the acquiescence of law
enforcement officials in Cook County were more to his liking, and
he made Chicago his permanent headquarters.

His relationship with the police during the following decade was
such that Capone seldom needed a lawyer, and it was not until he
was indicted by the federal prosecutor for income tax evasion that he
felt the need of trial counsel. Then he sent a frantic S O S to Leibowitz. Leibowitz answered the call.

He checked into a Chicago hotel. Capone called for him and suggested that they "take a ride." The unconscious humor of the phrase
didn't register on the headman of probably the greatest crime syndicate the world has ever known. With Capone at the wheel of his big
Cadillac, they rode through the crowded streets of Chicago's Loop.
There was no one else in the car. The window alongside the driver's
seat was rolled down, and anyone who wanted to take a pot shot at
the high potentate of crime would have had a perfect target. Capone,

315

who had a sentimental streak in him that bordered on the maudlin, talked not about his case but about his dead brother.

"I was up at five this morning, Counselor," he said. "I drove out to the cemetery. I just finished building a beautiful mausoleum for my dead brother. It's the most wonderful thing you ever saw. I stood there beside his grave and blubbered like a baby. Yeah, I had a wonderful cry and now I feel better."

They drove on toward Cicero and Capone chatted about his family.

"Tell me," Leibowitz said suddenly, "why don't you quit? They say you're worth twenty million dollars. You've got a boy you love. You've got everything a man could want. Why don't you give up this business?"

"You know, Counselor," Capone said, directing the big car smoothly, "you just don't understand human nature. Why does the president of United States Steel keep working? Hasn't he got all the money he can ever spend? Then there is another thing. I just can't quit. Suppose I stepped down and let someone else take over. He'd always have the feeling that some day I'd want to come back and take over again. My life wouldn't be worth a plugged nickel. No, I couldn't quit," he added gloomily. "Beside there are an awful lot of people working for me who depend on me to see that everything runs smoothly. No one else would have their confidence. They trust me."

"I hear Johnny Torrio quit. He was your predecessor. Why can't you quit as he did?"

"You wouldn't understand, Counselor," Capone shook his head. Then he began to talk about the forthcoming trial. He was highly indignant at the federal indictment.

Why, for years he had been paying these government characters big salaries to take care of his interests; now they were double-crossing him. He'd paid them all, he told Leibowitz, with resentment in his voice. Had he bribed them? Hell no, Capone snapped, he was paying them for protection. You couldn't call that bribery. It was legitimate, he insisted. Everyone knew you had to pay for protection. Whom had he paid? Everyone in Chicago, and so many in Washington, he declared. Why, his payroll extended to all the points of the compass.

This came as no surprise. The public knew that no vast criminal empire such as Capone headed could have lasted a moment without the co-operation of grafting law enforcement figures. Capone insisted that he had made a bargain with the prosecution to plead guilty and take a two-year rap on the income tax charge. A Chicago newspaper learned of the "bargain," and had printed the story; now the prosecutor refused to go through with his part of the arrangement. This, Capone said heatedly, was a political persecution. Leibowitz felt that even a Capone was entitled to a fair deal from the authorities.

He also learned that the Treasury Department investigators had apparently furnished the Attorney-General with indisputable evidence of Capone's tax defalcations. The indefatigable Elmer Irey, head Treasury Department sleuth, had direct evidence in the form of bank accounts, canceled checks, and the statements of one or two former Capone henchmen, who to save their own necks had told the truth about the financial structure which Capone had built.

Capone was hurt and bewildered at what he, with his twisted code of ethics, considered to be a double cross. He was resentful and a bit puzzled at the attitude of the newspapers, which were calling for his scalp, and he kept insisting that he was being subjected to political persecution. What should he do?

"You've got to face the facts," Leibowitz said. "You say that this is political persecution. You say you've been bribing government officials for years. If this is true it wouldn't be a complete defense, of course, but it would help your cause. But you'd have to prove these statements in court. You'd have to name the men you've bribed."

"You know I couldn't sing, Counselor," Capone said in shocked tones.

"You're up against it," Leibowitz answered. "My advice to you is to go into court and tell the complete truth. You have evaded paying income taxes. Admit it and take whatever penalty the government imposes. If you would expose the men who have been accepting your bribes I'm sure the government would take that into consideration. I couldn't undertake your defense unless you agreed to follow my advice."

Capone said that he wouldn't name any of the officials on his payroll. That to Capone would have been treason. If a man double-crossed you, it was standard business practice to "rub him out." To complain to the law would have been a strong breach of ethics. As the acknowledged leader of America's underworld, Capone above anyone else had to set an example. The suggestion that he or his men "sing" was completely repugnant to him. In his mind the way to fight a lawsuit was to "fix" the right people. He'd been doing this successfully for years and he saw no reason to change his tactics now. In the back of his mind there was undoubtedly the hope that he would be able to arrange some fix before the trial opened. And so, he insisted stubbornly that Leibowitz go into court and fight the charges against him.

"You can name your own fee," he said. "What do you want . . . a hundred thousand? Two hundred thousand?"

"I can't do a thing for you," Leibowitz said. "You want to fight the government, but the government has all the ammunition. You want to go into court and tell the government to prove its case. Well, they will prove their case and you'll probably rot in jail."

Leibowitz took the next train back to New York. Not long after, Capone took a train to Alcatraz.

2

On the evening of March 1, 1932, the twenty-month-old son of Colonel Charles A. Lindbergh was kidnapped from the Hopewell, New Jersey, home of the Lindbergh family. Leibowitz did not become connected with the case until February 13, 1936. I became involved in it (only as a reporter) an hour after the crime took place. To understand the problems which confronted Leibowitz when at the request of Mrs. Richard Hauptmann (wife of the man who had been tried and sentenced to die for the crime) he visited the death house to interview Hauptmann, it is necessary to provide a brief summary

318

of what newspaper headlines so rightly called the Crime of the Century. For me the tragic drama opened with a phone call on the fateful night. I was then a reporter and rewrite man for *International News Service*, and the voice on the other end of the phone was that of Barry Faris, my editor.

"We got a flash one minute ago that Lindbergh's baby was kidnapped." His voice was perfectly calm. "Get to Hopewell, New Jersey, right away."

"Where is Hopewell, Barry?" There was nothing calm about my voice.

"Somewhere near Trenton," he snapped. "There's a train leaving Penn Station in forty minutes. Dorothy Ducas and George McGuirk will meet you on it. As soon as you get there, tie up a phone and keep it open. I'm arranging for a direct wire. Jim Kilgallen and Dave Sentner will be in the office to do the rewrite. Feed them everything you can get. All we have so far is the flash from the state police that the baby was taken from its crib. I'll have a messenger with money meet you at the train. Expense doesn't matter. Okay?"

"Okay, Barry," I said, and that precipitated me into the most famous criminal case of our age. The temptation to reminisce and to recall the way our little team worked when we arrived at Hopewell is strong. We were in Hopewell, but Barry Faris was in our office in the Mirror Building in New York doing our thinking for us, reminding us sharply of angles that we had missed, praising us when we occasionally managed to beat the opposition wire services. During that hectic week we three threw thousands of words into a telephone quick-witted Dorothy Ducas had "tied up," fed additional thousands of words into the telegraph wires that had been hurriedly set up in little Hopewell. Kilgallen and Sentner, calm, efficient, wrote eighteen hours a day, and the words they wrote were good words.

We who were at Hopewell soon grew to know the tangle of heavily wooded land that surrounded the white stone home of Colonel Lindbergh. We got to know Colonel Henry C. Breckinridge (spokesman for the Lindbergh family) and Colonel Norman Schwartzkopf, in charge of the New Jersey State Police; we met Anne Lindbergh and without exception gave our wholehearted admiration to this gallant, courageous woman who refused to break under the horrible strain. We met men like Millard Whited, a local woodsman who described a man he had twice seen loitering in the vicinity of the Lindbergh home; we met dozens of local citizens, each of whom was positive he had seen the kidnapper. All had their brief moment of glory as we threw their names into telephones and rewrite men spelled them out in their typewriters and headlines blazoned them for all to see. Names like Betty Gow and Red Johnson and Sebastian Ben Lupica and Elsie Whately became familiar to us as members of the cast of this great American tragedy.

Mysterious strangers, usually with coat collars turned up to hide their faces, were constantly arriving at the Lindbergh home to confer with the Colonel and the authorities. And then the burly figure of elderly John F. Condon, Bronx educator, emerged from anonymity. He had inserted a newspaper ad in the *Bronx Home News* offering his services as a "go-between", and, incredibly, he had received an answer. The symbol, drawn crudely on the note he received, was a replica of one drawn on the ransom note left at the Lindbergh home and not revealed to the press. There was little doubt that Condon had established contact with the actual kidnapper. Eventually Lindbergh authorized him to deal with the man who had taken his child from its crib and Condon paid the kidnapper fifty thousand dollars in small bills.

And then silence. Nothing but silence. Was the child alive or dead? No one knew for certain. Now the tips began to come into the newspaper offices. At *INS*, Jim Kilgallen and I were assigned to follow up every tip, no matter how absurd it appeared.

One day a man came into the *INS* office, introduced himself, and said quite calmly and rationally that he had met two men who claimed to be holding the child. He said he had known them years before when he himself had been a rum runner. He added that he had tried to get in touch with Colonel Lindbergh but had failed, and so he was enlisting our aid.

Barry Faris hustled him to the office of the late Joseph V. Connolly, head of King Features and other Hearst enterprises, and they both questioned him thoroughly. He had run into these men in a bar on Cape Cod the week before. They wanted fifty thousand dollars in small bills.

The only thing that impressed us about our informant was the fact that he wanted nothing for himself. He would lead us to the two men and we'd take it away from there. He emphasized the fact that the two men had said if we appeared with police the child would be killed. He told his story again and again under the adroit questioning of Connolly, Faris and the famed Walter Howey and they couldn't trip him up.

"It's another hundred-to-one shot," Connolly said to me wearily, "but even that's worth following up. Go along with this character. If the two men he talks about really exist, keep this in mind; the important thing is the safety of the child. Don't think of this as a story until after the child is safe."

Joe Connolly's attitude was typical of the feeling held even by editors during those months. For once we were all confronted with something bigger than a story. To say that the police and the F.B.I. were better equipped in every way to follow up such a lead as this one, is to state the obvious, but the authorities were swamped with similar "tips." Newspapers and wire services were being deluged by men and women who claimed to be in contact with the "actual kidnappers," and each story, no matter how absurd it looked, was investigated. It is easy for the cynical to sneer that newspapers and wire services were interested only in breaking what would have been the greatest story of our time, but the attitude of the editors I worked for completely contradicts this viewpoint.

Neither Connolly nor Faris was sold on the man's story, but every tip was worth following up. Within two hours I was on my way to Boston with the man, and in my pocket was a letter from William Randolph Hearst authorizing a Boston bank to give me fifty thousand dollars in small bills without "asking any questions." From Boston we went to Cape Cod. Our informant had said that the child was being held on a boat off shore, and Connolly and Faris had arranged for a fast boat and an airplane to be held in readiness just in case they were needed. My friend and I spent two blustery nights going from place to place on Cape Cod looking for men he claimed to represent. One night he said he had received a message to wait at a Boston hotel. We shared a room there; I wouldn't let him out of my sight. During the night I awoke to find him going through my clothes.

"If you're looking for my money, it's here under my pillow," I told him.

"I was looking for your gun," he said which was pretty fast thinking. "I thought I heard a noise outside. It might be a rival mob."

"The gun is under my pillow, too," I told him. There was, of course, no gun. The next morning my friend started to babble about a rival mob, and I phoned Barry Faris and said that this was just one more blind alley; one more eccentric had precipitated himself into the case.

I mention this incident to emphasize that the bizarre and the grotesque were the commonplace during the months after the kidnaping. Poor Jim Kilgallen (then as now one of America's really great reporters) was going all over the country following leads that took him to such intriguing spots as the lair of the Purple Gang in Detroit. He and I were known in our office as the Dippy Tip Editors, an accurate enough appraisal, for not a single tip either of us followed ever led anywhere except to frustration.

All this time the pitiful remains of the baby lay in a shallow, scooped-out grave only a few miles from the Lindbergh home. The awful truth burst upon a shocked nation seventy-two days after the child had been kidnapped. During the following months several bills of ransom money appeared in circulation, and eventually they led to the arrest of Bruno Richard Hauptmann of the Bronx. New York City police lost no time in weaving a net of evidence around Hauptmann. German authorities cabled his prison record there, and added, "he is an exceptionally sly and clever criminal." Hauptmann's handwriting tallied with that on the ransom notes, even to the same mis-spellings. Sincere and often misunderstood John F. Condon, without making a positive identification, said that Hauptmann resembled the man with whom he had negotiated and to whom he gave the ransom money. And $13,750 in gold certificates (all identified as the ransom bills) were found in Hauptmann's garage. Additional money was discovered later on the Hauptmann premises. Hauptmann's explanation of how the money had come into his possession was neither ingenious nor convincing. He said one Isadore Fisch had deposited a box with him just before he sailed for Germany in 1933. Hauptmann put the box into a closet for safekeeping. He had accidentally knocked it off the shelf one day and the bills had fallen out. He never swerved from this incredible story.

Tried in the Hunterdon County Courthouse in Flemington, New Jersey, Hauptmann was prosecuted by David Wilentz, Attorney-General of the State. Coldly, remorselessly and brilliantly, Wilentz presented a mass of evidence against Hauptmann that neither his denials nor the efforts of Edward J. Reilly, Egbert Rosecrans and C. Lloyd Fisher, defense staff, could contradict. The handwriting, the fact that the ladder was in part made of wood that experts proved came from Hauptmann's attic, a more positive identification by Condon, and less exact but equally damning evidence by witnesses to whom Hauptmann had passed ransom notes, all combined to convince the jury (and the public) that Hauptmann was guilty. There were many who found it difficult to believe that he had committed the crime alone, but Hauptmann, except stubbornly to plead his complete innocence, would not talk. And in due course, white-haired Judge Thomas Trenchard (a stern opponent of capital punishment) sentenced Hauptmann to die.

The sentence was automatically stayed when his attorneys appealed to the New Jersey Court of Errors and Appeals. Reilly now withdrew as Hauptmann's chief counsel, leaving Lloyd Fisher to represent the condemned man. The thirteen judges of the high court unanimously denied Hauptmann's appeal for a new trial, and when the United States Supreme Court turned down Hauptmann's petition for a writ of review, Judge Trenchard fixed the date of execution as the week of January 13, 1936.

Governor Harold G. Hoffman of New Jersey made an unprecendented midnight visit to the death house to interview Hauptmann, and then startled the world with an announcement that the case was not yet solved. And he granted a thirty-day reprieve to the prisoner. It was at this point that Leibowitz entered the case.

323

One day a man called to see Leibowitz. He said that he represented Mrs. Evalyn Walsh McLean, millionaire social leader of Washington, D.C., and that she wanted to see him to discuss the possibility of his representing Hauptmann. He went to the Washington home of Mrs. McLean to see her. He had followed the trial carefully, and he had several strong ideas on the case. He discovered that Mrs. McLean had a few convictions about it herself. She had come into the case at the behest of a crook named Gaston B. Means, a discredited member of the Department of Justice, who convinced her that he was in touch with the actual kidnappers and that she could deal with them through him for the return of the kidnapped Lindbergh baby. She told Leibowitz how she had pawned her Hope Diamond in a Madison Avenue shop for $104,000, and how she had given this to Means, who said that he in turn had handed it over to the actual kidnappers. By now, Means had been convicted and sent to a federal prison for a long term for swindling her out of this huge sum of money, but Mrs. McLean had a strong suspicion that the child was still alive and that there was a possibility that Means was part of a gang that had perpetrated the kidnapping. She firmly believed that Hauptmann was innocent.

"What makes you so certain that Hauptmann is innocent?" Leibowitz asked curiously.

"Several things," she said eagerly. "For one thing, I know that the Lindbergh child was examined by a pediatrician shortly before the kidnapping. At that time the doctor measured the child. I know that the measurements of the tiny body found varied by two inches from the measurements made by the doctor. I do not believe it was the body of the Lindbergh baby at all."

"Had that point been vigorously contested at the trial, it might have raised havoc with the prosecution's case," Leibowitz admitted. "It is quite possible that the doctor made an error in the measurements. At any rate, Hauptmann's defense attorneys conceded the corpus delicti. Personally, I think they made a mistake, but it's on the record and too late now to question."

"I'm not interested in technicalities," the Washington social leader said. "I still believe that Gaston Means is involved in this crime. I just think that there is a good chance the child is still alive and that Hauptmann is innocent. Thousands of people in the country feel as I do. These doubts will remain long after Hauptmann is executed. I'd just like to settle all doubts. I brought Governor Hoffman of New Jersey here, to this very room, and I told him flatly that Hauptmann is innocent and I asked him to get to the bottom of it."

"Disabuse your mind of one thing," Leibowitz told her. "Hauptmann is not innocent."

"Why are you so convinced of his guilt?"

"The handwriting experts proved at the trial, beyond the shadow of a doubt, that only Hauptmann could have written the ransom notes," he said. "The shading of the letters, the mistakes in spelling, all proved this. Dr. Condon's phone number was scrawled on the side of the broom closet in Hauptmann's kitchen. One of the uprights of the ladder was proven to have come from Hauptmann's attic. The ransom money was found in his home, and his story that it had been given to him for safekeeping by a man named Isadore Fisch is absolutely absurd. Mrs. McLean, I have studied the trial record from cover to cover. I have examined the photographs of each of the exhibits and I am convinced beyond doubt that he is guilty. If the case takes its normal course, he is bound to be executed and that would be a pity, not because he doesn't deserve the chair for the horrible crime he committed, but because he would take with him to the grave the names of those who undoubtedly helped him to commit the crime. I believe that if Hauptmann would only open up and tell the whole truth, those implicated with him could then be brought to justice."

"Didn't Attorney-General Wilentz say that Hauptmann alone committed the crime?"

"I cannot agree with the Attorney-General in this respect," the lawyer replied. "Never in a thousand years will I agree that this was a "one-man job"; that Hauptman did not have at least one accomplice. I'll tell you why. The flimsy ladder that was used in the kidnapping was built in three sections, and, when fitted together, the ladder just reached the sill of the window to the child's bedroom. To what bedroom, Mrs. McLean? To the bedroom of the child's nursery in the

Morrow home in Englewood. You will recall that the Lindberghs and their child lived with their in-laws in the Morrow mansion in Englewood. We may therefore ask some very logical questions: How did the individual who built the ladder and who planned the kidnapping know where the child's nursery room was located; how was he able to build a ladder, in sections, with such precise measurements? The answer is obvious. Someone supplied that information; someone who knew the facts. Then again, you will remember, the evidence disclosed that, without any warning, the Lindberghs moved into their newly constructed house at Hopewell in the Sourland Mountains of New Jersey. No one but members of the household knew that this was to happen. Another question: who informed the kidnapper of this move? The kidnapper, whoever he was, did go to Hopewell with the ladder and planted it against the wall right below the window to the child's room at Hopewell. How did the kidnapper know where the child's room was located, unless he had been tipped off by someone? Then again, the ladder in three sections was too long and would have obstructed the window at Hopewell. Therefore, only two of the sections were used. The ladder then was thirty inches too short."

"Why do you say that the kidnapper had to have the assistance of an accomplice when the child was kidnapped?" Mrs. McLean asked.

"Just recall the conditions that prevailed on that night. Here you had a flimsy ladder, all three sections of which could be carried in the hand of one man. The wind was howling, it was a blustery night; the kidnapper ascended the ladder, and with his powerful hands, (and Hauptmann did have great strength in his hands and arms) managed to lift himself over the window sill, and entered the child's room. No criminal, unless he were absolutely bereft of reason, would have permitted that ladder to remain there in that wind, without making certain that it would be there when he was leaving with the child, for that window was his only means of escape. The criminal would never have dared to walk down the main staircase, with the baby in his arms, and pass within view of Colonel Lindbergh who was sitting in the library. What probably happened is this: Hauptmann had someone on the ground holding the ladder fast because he knew that if his means of escape were cut off, he would be caught like a rat in a trap. He would have been cornered in the "hottest spot" in the world; he would have been done for if Lindbergh had laid eyes on him.

"He got into the room, took the child out of the crib, stifled a possible outcry by clamping his huge hand over its little mouth, and then made for the window. I don't think that he ever intended to descend the ladder with the child in his arms. To begin with, that would have been almost an impossible physical feat, even if he were an acrobat.

"When he got to the window, he tried to hand the child down to the person who stood on the ground one floor below. Either he misjudged the distance or the angle, or the child fell from his grasp. I believe that an occurrence like this explains the presence of one large footprint in the mud adjacent to the right rail of the ladder, for that individual must have stepped forward from off the gravel and on to the muddy strip in an endeavor to catch the child as it came hurtling down. The accident probably injured the child severely, and in the excitement of attempting to flee as quickly as possible, Hauptmann came through that window; instead of going down the ladder slowly and carefully, he came fast, and the extra pressure must have broken the ladder.

"You will remember that at the trial Colonel Lindbergh testified that he did hear a noise which sounded like an orange crate being smashed. I believe that the noise caused by the breaking of the ladder was what Colonel Lindbergh heard."

"Whose footprint do you think that was?" Mrs. McLean asked.

Leibowitz shrugged his shoulder. "If Hauptmann opens up, he can supply the answer."

"Well, perhaps you can get Hauptmann to talk," she said.

Leibowitz again shrugged his shoulders. "Don't forget I'm not his counsel. I can talk with him only if he sends for me."

"I'll attend to that," said Mrs. McLean. "If any red tape or any obstacles are thrown in your way, I am quite sure that I can handle such a situation without too much trouble with the authorities. But after you have had a talk with Hauptmann, will you come back and tell me what you have learned?"

327

"I'll come to see you," the lawyer assured her.

Leibowitz went back to New York. A few days after his visit to Mrs. McLean, he himself had a caller, Mrs. Bruno Richard Hauptmann. She asked that he see her husband in the Trenton death house. Permission was granted by the authorities and he found himself facing perhaps the most despised man in America. Only the cell bars were between them.

"You know about Mrs. McLean and how and why I came here?" Leibowitz asked. Hauptmann nodded and said in his guttural, heavily accented voice, "My wife has told me."

"I only want to get the truth," Leibowitz said. "I think you ought to know that whatever you tell me will be reported to Mrs. McLean and to Governor Hoffman, and to anybody else that I think ought to know."

"Sure, sure," Hauptmann said, "my wife told me. There is nothing that I say that I do not want the world to know. I am an innocent man and I shouldn't be in this place."

"We'll talk about that later," the lawyer said. Then Leibowitz opened by asking Hauptmann how he was being treated. His sympathetic air seemed to thaw the cold-eyed prisoner, and Hauptmann discussed in detail the prison routine.

"Let me see you jump up and grab that bar over the cell door," Leibowitz asked, smiling, and Hauptmann, surprised, sprung lightly to grab the iron bar. "Can you chin yourself?" Leibowitz asked. Without answering, Hauptmann drew himself up, let himself down, and then repeated the performance a dozen times. He had been in prison a full year, and yet, without any physical exercise whatever during that time, he retained the strength to accomplish a feat that only men in fine physical condition would even attempt. Leibowitz could well believe that drawing himself up to the sill and entering the bedroom window had been child's play to Hauptmann.

"You must think about the kidnapping a great deal," Leibowitz suggested.

"I never tink on dot at all," Hauptmann said with some contempt. "I didn't do it, so why should I be interested."

"But, man, you've been cooped up here in this cell a whole year, with no one but your thoughts to keep you company. Surely you must have turned it over in your mind a thousand times. You must have said to yourself, 'Here's how the crime must have been committed. It wasn't done the way Wilentz says.' " Hauptmann shrugged his shoulders indifferently.

Leibowitz over the years had learned a great deal about the psychology of the criminal. The impulse of the criminal is to lie. Almost invariably he will tell even his lawyer that black is white. Leibowitz was using this knowledge now. Ask Hauptmann how the crime was committed and he'd probably give you an answer diametrically opposed to the truth. The guilty criminal always has a compulsion to run away from the truth.

"Well, I'll come to see you again in a few days," Leibowitz said. "Think it.over. Let me know then, how you think the child was taken from the house."

Leibowitz went to report to Mrs. McLean. He and his wife arrived at "Friendship," the McLean house in Washington. When they entered the house, they were surprised by the sight of rain water leaking through the roof of the aging mansion. Two huge Great Danes lounged comfortably on the carpet, munching on enormous bones.

Around the dinner table they discussed Hauptmann's attitude. It was Leibowitz' belief that there was a chance that he might get the prisoner to crack. Then the talk turned to the Hope Diamond. Mrs. McLean had redeemed it from the pawnshop and now she insisted on getting it and showing it to her guests. Leibowitz blinked when he saw her remove it from an ordinary filing cabinet. A penny-ante burglar would have made short work of such a strong box. Mrs. Leibowitz held the necklace from which the glowing midnight blue stone hung, and then raised her arms to put it around her neck.

"No, no," Mrs. McLean protested. "Don't put it on. It brings bad luck to everyone who wears it."

As the Leibowitzes said goodbye, Mrs. McLean asked the lawyer, "Do you think he will 'break and open up'?"

"I'll see him again within a day or so," Leibowitz replied, "and if you will phone me, I'll tell you what I think the score is."

On the next visit, Hauptmann was more communicative. Leibowitz noticed that he had half a dozen pictures of his son Manfred on a shelf in his cell. Hauptmann talked feelingly and at great length about the boy. Tears welled in his eyes as he gazed at the pictures of his son. He didn't mind being in the death house, he told Leibowitz, but he hated the thought that his son would grow up with the stigma of his father's conviction upon him.

"Remember that you promised to tell me how you think the crime was committed," the lawyer said to the condemned man.

"I'll show you," Hauptmann said, eagerly now. He had constructed a cardboard replica of the east side of the Lindbergh home. Now he told Leibowitz how he thought the kidnapping had been accomplished. The kidnapper had used the ladder to enter the bedroom, had taken the child from its crib and had then gone down the stairs and out the front door.

"But Colonel Lindbergh was sitting in his study that opened just off the front hall," Leibowitz said. "He would have heard anyone coming down the stairs to open the front door; he would have heard the howl of the wind outside."

"That is how it was done," Hauptmann said stubbornly.

"No, Richard, you know better than that," Leibowitz said. "Tell the truth and there is a good chance that your death sentence will be commuted to life imprisonment."

"I tell only the truth," Hauptmann said sullenly.

"Now, you told the jury that you got the box containing all those thousands of dollars from a friend named Isadore Fisch when he left for Germany; that Fisch gave you the box to hold for him until he returned; and that you accidentally found out what was in the box when it fell from a shelf in a closet in your kitchen.

"Let's take your story of Isadore Fisch," the lawyer said in a conversational tone. "Suppose you were on that jury, would you have believed the story that you told? You say that Fisch was probably a criminal. You say that you are an honest man; that Fisch knew you to be an honest man. You say he left all that money with you in a shoebox. Does that sound like common sense? Wouldn't Fisch have asked himself, 'Suppose this honest man, Hauptmann, finds out that I have left all these thousands of dollars with him; suppose he finds out

330

that that is the "hottest" money in the world, the Lindbergh money; wouldn't that man Hauptmann go to the police with it? Wouldn't he tell that I, Isadore Fisch, gave it to him, and wouldn't I be arrested?' Hauptmann, you tell me that Fisch was a pretty smart fellow. He had a safe deposit box. Why wouldn't he put the money into that box, instead of taking all these chances by leaving it with you? And isn't that exactly how the jury felt?"

Hauptmann thought for a moment. "The story about Fisch don't sound so gut," he admitted.

"What was the most damaging point scored against you by the prosecution?"

"Dot handwriting," the prisoner exploded. "Dot was bad."

"You see, Richard, that's what the jury thought." Leibowitz shook his head. "Have you told the whole truth, Richard? If you haven't and want to tell it now, perhaps I can help you."

But Hauptmann continued to shrug his shoulders.

"Now, suppose you and I talk about that handwriting. Do you remember that all the ransom notes had certain words that the kidnapper did not spell correctly? Do you remember s-i-n-g-n-a-t-u-r-e? Do you remember l-i-h-g-t? Do you remember r-i-g-t-h? Do you remember b-o-a-d? When they asked you to write these words after your arrest, you misspelled them exactly as they were misspelled in the ransom notes. How do you account for that?"

"Well," Hauptmann smirked, "the police spelled them out for me in the station house."

"But, Hauptmann," the lawyer replied, "you must know now that that can't be so. If you had written these words while the cops were dictating the spelling, the handwriting expert could have detected that under the microscope in a moment. After each letter that was dictated, the microscope would show a break between one letter and the next. There were no such breaks in your handwriting."

The prisoner smiled quizzically and said, with a shrug of his shoulders, "Well, dot's why I say that the handwriting was the worst ting."

"Then again," Leibowitz continued, "tell me, Hauptmann, how much chance is there that a man would make the same mistakes not

331

once, but twenty times, as the kidnapper made in the ransom notes? Let's try it out and see how it works." Leibowitz went to the turn-key's desk and picked up some bits of blank paper. He tore them into a hundred small pieces. On one of the pieces he wrote the number one, on another the number two and on a third the number three. He then tossed all the pieces into a hat and mixed the contents with his finger. "Now, Hauptmann," he said to the prisoner, "let's try this little stunt. There are three pieces of paper in that hat among all of the others that contain three misspelled words. Now, you put your hand in that hat and see if you can draw out the three pieces of paper with the writing on them."

"I know how foolish it is this whole thing about making the same mistakes in the handwriting, Mr. Leibowitz, but that's how it was," Hauptmann observed. He then obligingly stuck his hand into the hat and withdrew three slips of paper, all of which were blank. "I know," he said with resignation.

"You see, Hauptmann, I'm not paying any attention to all of these so-called eyewitnesses who pointed you out as the man seen around the Lindbergh grounds shortly before the child was kidnapped. I don't believe that after two years their identifications are entitled to much consideration, but how can we get away from all of these other things that stand out like so many red lights in the dead of the night, and that cry out, 'Guilty, guilty, guilty!' "

3

Again and again, Leibowitz pointed out obvious absurdities in Hauptmann's defense. He wasn't either forceful or tough with him. More than once Hauptmann shrugged his shoulders and admitted, "That was bad." Again and again, Leibowitz went back to the subject of little Manfred, or "Bubi." Whenever Hauptmann talked of "Bubi," he was a different man. His dull eyes gleamed with interest and delight. If Hauptmann had any vulnerable spot, it was this child.

Finally, after more than three hours, the lawyer took his leave.

"There are at least twenty reporters waiting outside. What shall I tell them, Hauptmann?"

"Tell them anything you like. I am innocent and I am not going to the chair. Will you please come back, Mr. Leibowitz?" Hauptmann said as they shook hands through the bars.

"Yes, in a few days," the lawyer said as he walked from the death house.

The next day the telephone bell jangled in Leibowitz' office. It was Mrs. McLean calling.

"Well, what are the new developments?" she inquired eagerly.

"Nothing," the lawyer answered, "but I have a feeling, judging from my talk with this man and my observation of him, that he is like a player at a poker game sitting with a pat hand, with a pat royal flush. I am puzzled no end. For three solid hours he convicted himself out of his own mouth, and yet there must be something or someone that is either making or inducing him to stand pat. I don't believe that Hauptmann thinks that there is one chance in a million of his going to the chair. Perhaps the Governor's interest in him, as borne out by the Governor's personal visit to his death cell at midnight, has given him this overwhelming confidence. Perhaps it is something else, but I'm going to see Hauptmann once more and give it a final fling."

Two days later, at the Towers Hotel in Brooklyn, four men sat around a dinner table in a private room. They were the Governor of the State of New Jersey, Harold Hoffman; the chief counsel for Bruno Richard Hauptmann, Lloyd Fisher; Samuel Leibowitz; and his investigator, John Terry. The talk at times was heated and spirited.

"Governor," Leibowitz said with emphasis, "I've gone over every ramification in the case with Hauptmann. There is no doubt that both you and Fisher are entirely sincere in your conduct of this case, but there is no question in my mind that the man is guilty. Although the prisoner has made no direct admission of his guilt, only a child would be so credulous as to think that he himself doesn't realize that the word 'guilty' is plastered all over his person. Yet, he stands pat. I have been wondering why. Perhaps, you are partly to blame. If we consider

333

the matter soberly, we should all appreciate that we are dealing here with an extreme case of egocentricity.

"When Hauptmann wanted to commit a burglary in his home town in Germany, whom did he select as his victim? Not the ordinary citizen—he picked the Mayor. After he was released from prison, he held up a woman at the point of a gun in a most sensational fashion. Again he was put in a cell. He broke out. He wasn't content, however, with escaping. His egocentricity prompted him to leave a note for the warden sarcastically joshing the warden and thumbing his nose at the authorities because of the ease with which he made his escape.

"He stowed away on a ship to America. He was caught and sent back. He tried it again and met with failure. Finally, on the third occasion, he succeeded in making his way off the ship. He hung onto the rafters under the pier for hours until, under cover of darkness, he succeeded in smuggling himself into the country. That's the kind of a creature we are dealing with. When he decided to kidnap the child of a wealthy citizen, it had to be the child of Colonel Lindbergh, the most famous man in America. The child of an ordinary rich citizen would not satiate his demoniacal craving for the spotlight, even though he alone would be the audience looking upon Bruno Richard Hauptmann as the star in the performance.

"Now here we have additional obstacles, and you, Governor Hoffman, are bolstering his ego. He'll never confess just as long as you are in his corner, and while I am breaking my back to get him to talk, Lloyd Fisher is issuing statements to the newspapers that he believes Hauptmann is innocent. He has said if Hauptmann should change his story for Leibowitz, he, Fisher, would immediately withdraw from the case. If we are to get anywhere with this man, we must knock the crutches from under his ego. You, Governor, must make it known that you are through and Fisher must make this man understand that the jig is up, and that if he expects to beat the chair he must open up and talk."

The Governor and Fisher agreed to "co-operate."

"And suppose Hauptmann does not change his story, what then?" Fisher inquired.

"There is one more move which I believe will produce the goods. His one weak spot is that boy of his. If Hauptmann can be made to understand that he is going to the chair and that everyone has washed his hands clean of him, if an hour before he is to walk "the last mile" to the chair, you will take his child into the cell and let him feel that kid's arms around his neck, I tell you he'll break down and tell the truth; he'll name his accomplices."

"We've got something better than that," Governor Hoffman said grimly, and Attorney Fisher nodded with understanding. That ended the conference. Governor Hoffman never explained what he meant by "something better."

On the following day, Leibowitz again made the trip to the death house at Trenton Prison. This time Fisher came along. For hours Leibowitz went over and over all the details of the case with Hauptmann. Fisher did say that there was nothing more that could be done unless Hauptmann confessed and named his accomplices. But Hauptmann didn't put any stock in what Fisher now said. Hauptmann was standing pat. Never for a moment did Hauptmann concede that the Governor had retired from the prisoner's corner. The interview ended and the lawyers left the death house, one still firmly resolved that the prisoner was innocent, and the other equally as certain that he was guilty.

Why didn't Hauptmann confess and name his accomplices? What did Governor Hoffman mean when he told Leibowitz at the Towers Hotel that he had "something better than that"?

4

While the heated discussion was raging in that Towers Hotel room, a man named Paul H. Wendel, a one-time lawyer who had formerly practiced in New Jersey, sat bound and handcuffed in a chair, cemented to the floor in a cellar of a Brooklyn home. He was being "worked on" by three men who were trying to "coax" him into confessing that he was the real kidnapper of the Lindbergh child.

It was Ellis Parker, a legendary figure, whom the tabloids had built up into a modern Sherlock Holmes, whose brain child it was to "snatch" Wendel. Ellis Parker, a New Jersey detective, was an intimate friend of Governor Hoffman. Parker had protested right along that Hauptmann was innocent. Ellis Parker had apparently succeeded in planting in the mind of the Governor seeds of doubt as to Hauptmann's guilt. Hoffman had granted a thirty-day reprieve to the condemned prisoner, and it was the general opinion that he did it on the advice of Parker, who said that he was on the trail of the "real kidnapper."

Ellis Parker (acting entirely on his own) sent his son to New York to get in touch with the three men who were to "snatch" and torture the unfortunate Wendel. Young Parker had no difficulty in persuading the three men to grab the unsuspecting victim. Posing as police, they kidnapped him, brought him to the cellar of the Brooklyn house and held him there. For days they starved him, they applied conventional methods of torture, plus one or two variations. Rather effective, Wendel testified later, was the application of a lighted electric bulb to the back of his neck. Wendel found that the heat generated by the bulb was considerable. When Wendel, desperate, and wet with pain, cried out that the law would take care of them, one of them said confidently, "Even if we haven't got police credentials, we are protected by a high police authority in New Jersey." They persisted in their efforts to make Wendel admit that he had kidnapped the baby and brought it out of the front door of the Lindbergh home. It took them several days to break Wendel down completely. He had been handcuffed to a chair all of that time, with intermittent sessions of lighted cigarettes applied to vulnerable parts of his anatomy, varied by the old-fashioned method of spread-eagling and beating. Then he wrote out a confession. By now he would have confessed to the sinking of the *Maine*.

In the meantime, Ellis Parker was making nocturnal visits to Hauptmann's cell in the death house to acquaint the condemned man with the "latest developments." Bruno Richard Hauptmann was being informed that the "real kidnapper" was in custody, that he had confessed, and that Mr. Hauptmann would soon walk the streets as free as a bird. Leibowitz, all unknowing, was beating his head against a stone wall, in attempting to have this wily, cunning, egocentric criminal make a clean breast of his part in the kidnapping of the child. Once Wendel had made his "confession," he was hustled by his kidnappers to Mt. Holly, New Jersey, home of Ellis Parker. He was then taken to a house eighteen miles south of Mt. Holly and kept under guard for thirty-three days. Then he was handed over to Mercer County (New Jersey) authorities. Attorney-General David Wilentz, prosecutor of Hauptmann, was summoned. Wendel told Wilentz the story of how he was kidnapped and tortured in an effort to obtain a confession. He was then immediately released by the irate Wilentz.

When Governor Hoffman told Leibowitz, "We have something better than that," was he thinking of Paul Wendel who, of course, did not have the slightest connection with the kidnapping and death of Colonel Lindbergh's baby? The Governor, incidentally, had no knowledge of the methods used to obtain the "confession" from Wendel. Throughout he acted in entire good faith.

Parenthetically, it might be added that the three men who held and tortured Wendel were tried and found guilty in Brooklyn and were sentenced to prison terms. New York State then tried to extradite the two Parkers, but Governor Hoffman refused to sign the extradition order. However, the federal authorities were not hamstrung. They seized the two Parkers and brought them before the bar of justice in the federal court. There they were tried, convicted and given prison terms.

Suppose Governor Hoffman had displayed a little less confidence in Attorney Lloyd Fisher and Detective Ellis Parker, and a bit more in Leibowitz? Suppose he had accepted the Leibowitz suggestion to confront Hauptmann with his child just before he set out on that last long walk? Would Hauptmann have talked? Leibowitz is convinced he would have cracked.

Did Hauptmann have an accomplice or accomplices? Even today, in the minds of many, the doubts remain. The evidence against Hauptmann was such that only a fool could doubt his participation in the crime. But did he do it alone? Is there somewhere an equally guilty man? Leibowitz and many others who were closely connected with the

337

case are convinced that there is. And Leibowitz is convinced that this cunning, defiant, desperate criminal would have confessed if the Hoffman, Fisher and Parker crutches had been knocked from under him; that he would have named his partner or partners in the crime had he been confronted with his child on the night he was led to the chair. If Hauptmann had only talked. . . !

13. ONE FOR THE STATE

"No one who has seen himself the prey and sport and the plaything of the infinite forces that move men can tell what justice is for someone else or for himself."

CLARENCE DARROW

During the early 1930's, one of the finest assistant district attorneys to represent the People was the man who is now Judge James Garrett Wallace. Wallace was a stern man with a booming voice and an intense hatred of all lawbreakers. For many years he conducted what amounted to a personal vendetta against the underworld, and New York became a better city for his efforts. Wallace was a tough, relentless prosecutor who prepared his own cases. He took nothing for granted. In his passion for thorough preparation and his reluctance to allow assistants to do even the spadework necessary to the presentation of a case, he was much like Leibowitz. Every time they clashed there were fireworks aplenty. Their most significant legal fight (and one which both have reason to remember today) took place in 1931. The case is memorable for no important legal principle, nor for the personality of either defendant or complaining witness. The star witness in the case of *People vs. Brown* was a long, ugly surgical scar on the body of one Rita Antonina.

Assistant District Attorney Wallace was prosecuting members of the New York Vice Squad who had been charged with perjury and extortion. Charges against them had emerged from the investigation by the Seabury Committee into extortion and framing practiced upon prostitutes by police assigned to the Vice Squad. Several of the cops, defended by other lawyers, had been convicted and sentenced to prison in short order. Then Officer Robert E. Murray, defended by

339

Leibowitz, was acquitted. It was Wallace's first loss in the series of trials.

Now came the trial of Patrolman Peter Brown. Some months before, he had arrested Rita Antonina for soliciting. She had been sentenced to two days in jail, a humiliation that she never forgot. When former Judge Samuel Seabury, by order of Governor Herbert H. Lehman, began his investigation, he let it be known that he was interested in questioning all women who believed they had been unjustly arrested for soliciting. Rita Antonina, a buxom French Canadian housewife, was happy to co-operate. Patrolman Brown had framed her, she said stoutly. When she had refused to be shaken down, he had taken her to Magistrate's Court and had her arraigned. She was happily married, Rita said, and a good woman. Why, the members of her immediate family were prominent citizens and leaders in their various professions in this country and in Canada.

The newspapers put a journalistic halo around the head of Rita Antonina. And, of course, they made Patrolman Brown the villain of the piece. The *Journal American* caricatured him as "The Gorilla Cop," and the entire New York press attacked him so savagely that by the time the trial was to begin there were few newspaper readers who hadn't already convicted the vice cop.

He retained Leibowitz to defend him. His story, which the newspapers had already printed and rejected, was simple and uncomplicated. But was it the truth, and if it were true, would a jury believe it?

Brown had been investigating houses of prostitution on the East Side of Manhattan. One afternoon he had passed a tenement on Third Avenue, and looking up, had seen a woman leaning out of a window. Brown said that the woman had smiled and beckoned to him to come up to her room. He had done so. He told her that he had no time to do anything but make an appointment. He suggested that he return the following afternoon. That (according to Brown) was quite agreeable to Rita. They even discussed business terms and both agreed that five dollars would be a reasonable price for the exploitation of Rita's charms. This was a little above Third Avenue scale,

340

but then Rita was a little above Third Avenue personnel. The next afternoon Patrolman Brown kept his appointment. This was July and Rita quite sensibly was combating the heat by wearing nothing but a thin housedress. Brown handed her a five-dollar bill (marked) and Rita slipped it under the mattress, dropped off her garment and placed her nude body on the bed, all set to fulfill her part of the contract. It was then that Brown revealed who he was. He told her to get up, put some clothes on and take a walk to the nearest precinct with him. He then went to the window to signal his two partners to come upstairs. Rita (again according to the vice cop) quickly retrieved the five-dollar bill from under the mattress, tore it into small bits, and running to the bathroom had flushed it down the drain. When Brown's two colleagues walked in, she began to protest that she had been attacked by Brown.

The angry story that Rita told to the Seabury investigators was quite different from that told by the cop. Brown had burst into her room and with carnal intent had grabbed her arm, twisted it and tried to force her to the bed. She knew nothing of any five-dollar bill. No, she had not removed her clothing nor had she stretched herself invitingly on the bed. She had remained fully clothed and had managed to fight Brown off. The fact that she had appeared voluntarily at Seabury's headquarters, the fact that she was apparently happily married, the fact that she came from an undeniably respectable family, all appealed to the investigators, to Judge Samuel Seabury and to Prosecutor James Garrett Wallace. All firmly believed that "The Gorilla Cop" was guilty.

Leibowitz believed Brown's story. He had investigated the officer's financial standing and had found that he lived very modestly on his cop's salary, that he neither drank nor gambled and that his bank account was the kind one would expect of a cop. If the accusation against Brown were true, it seemed hardly likely that he had shaken down and framed merely one prostitute. If guilty of one misstep, it seemed reasonable to suppose that he had been extorting money from prostitutes for years and that he had received considerable money out of his activities. The temptation to spend such ill-gotten gains was one

341

which few could resist, and when Leibowitz found that as far as neighbors, friends and fellow cops were concerned, Brown had never been known to go on any spending spree, he felt that there was a very good chance that the accused cop was telling the truth. All of his colleagues on the force insisted that Brown was an honest cop, and that he was being made a sacrificial goat to appease the hysterical clamor of the newspapers and rabid reform organizations. He made Brown go over the story again and again. Always the cop insisted that the woman had slipped out of her single garment and had thrown herself, invitingly naked, upon the bed.

"The trouble is," Leibowitz said, "that it's your word against hers, and the newspapers have prepared a jury to believe her rather than you."

"I can't imagine anyone wanting to have an affair with that woman," Brown said miserably. "Honest, Mr. Leibowitz, that scar alone would be enough to scare anyone off."

"Scar?" Leibowitz looked puzzled. "There was a picture of her in the *News* this morning. I didn't notice any scar on her face."

"Not on her face," Brown said casually. "On her belly, like an appendicitis scar, but it must be seven inches long. I never saw such an ugly scar."

"When did you see this scar?" Leibowitz asked impatiently.

Brown was surprised at the urgency in his lawyer's voice. "I couldn't miss seeing it," he said. "I told you she lay there on the bed without a stitch on."

"Why didn't you mention this in the Magistrate's Court when you testified against her?" Leibowitz demanded.

"Nobody asked me to describe her," the cop said, puzzled at the interest the lawyer was manifesting. "Why, Mr. Leibowitz, what's so important about the scar?"

"Nothing . . . nothing," Leibowitz said sarcastically. "It's just an interesting little detail. Now listen to me, Brown. You're going on the witness stand tomorrow morning and Jim Wallace will try to beat your ears off. Wallace is completely honest and he is sold on this woman's story. When you get on that stand, don't be afraid. Answer

342

every question that he asks and answer it honestly. Don't try to evade anything. He'll try to get you mad but don't lose your temper when he starts after you, and don't mention the scar unless he asks you to describe how the woman looked."

"Suppose he doesn't ask me?" Brown was a little out of his depth.

"You let me worry about that," Leibowitz smiled.

The next morning Leibowitz put his client on the stand. His direct examination was brief, almost perfunctory. He merely led Brown through his story and turned him over to Wallace. Wallace was a masterful cross-examiner. Leibowitz sat at the counsel table, and reporters at the press table were puzzled at the look of smiling confidence on his face. It was not like Leibowitz to casually toss a client to a cross-examiner like Wallace. But Leibowitz had in his own mind anticipated Wallace's moves. He knew exactly what he would do if he were Wallace. He knew how painstakingly thorough the Assistant District Attorney was. Wallace must have known all about that ugly surgical scar, all right. Wallace would figure that Brown (had his story been true) would have seen the scar and would have mentioned it in the Magistrate's Court. If Brown had seen the woman naked, he would certainly have mentioned the scar to his lawyer and Leibowitz would have brought the question of the scar out in his direct examination of the defendant. It would be obvious to Wallace that Brown had never seen the naked body of Rita Antonina.

And the trial proceeded as though Leibowitz had written the scenario. On cross-examination, Wallace played with Brown like a cat with a mouse, saving his denouement for later. His booming voice filled the courtroom as he hurled question after question at the defendant. At one point Leibowitz protested sharply to Judge Charles C. Nott, who was presiding, at the tone of Wallace's voice.

"Ask him to lower his voice," Leibowitz snapped. Wallace glowered at him. Spectators and reporters sat there enthralled at the spectacle. It wasn't often you saw two champions in action. Wallace's questions came like trip hammers; they were quick, concise, and sitting there Leibowitz had to give ungrudging praise to his opponent. Wallace was

343

a master of what lawyers call "spotlighting testimony." This is a technique of cross-examination only used by the real artist, for in the hands of a tyro it can backfire.

"Spotlighting" is a device used to focus the attention of the jurors on one important point which, above everything else, will remain in their minds when they go into the jury room to deliberate. "Spotlighting" in the courtroom can be just as effective as it is in the theatre.

Leibowitz watched Wallace as he set the stage. Wallace did it by saying abruptly, with a contemptuous smile, "That will be all." Brown started to leave the witness stand. He had almost reached his seat at the defense table when Wallace broke in, "Just a moment, Brown. Please resume the stand. There was one other question I wanted to ask."

The hook was baited, the cast was made and now Wallace was prepared to pull in the line. Leibowitz muttered, "Here it comes." The jurymen raised expectant eyes to the stand.

"You testified that Rita Antonina lay there on the bed naked," Wallace boomed. "Now, Brown, is there anything about her that stands out in your memory?"

Brown paused a moment and then said thoughtfully, "Now that you mention it, Mr. Wallace, there is. She had a long, ugly scar on her belly that ran all the way from her navel right down to her . . . well . . . her privates. I could never forget that scar as long as I live."

Wallace had pulled in the line and there was nothing on the hook but an old shoe. Judge Nott, an expressionless, taciturn jurist, blinked in amazement. The jurors raised startled eyes. Wallace? His habitually ruddy face was purple. He wheeled quickly, looked at Leibowitz and sputtered, "You . . . you. . . ." Leibowitz merely smiled and looking benign and virtuous, and with one hand shielding his face from the jury, he gave Wallace just a little wink. Then Wallace turned back to Brown.

"Why didn't you mention this scar before?" Wallace thundered.

"No one ever asked me about it," Brown answered with complete truthfulness, and then Wallace dropped him. Leibowitz recalled the complaining witness to the stand to ask her just one question.

344

"Do you have such a scar as the defendant described?" he asked gently.

Her eyes searched the floor, and for a moment she hesitated. The crowded courtroom was tense with expectancy.

Then she choked out a mumbled, "Yes, I do."

"I can't hear the witness's answer," Leibowitz said. "May I have the court stenographer read it?"

"Yes, I do," the loud voice of the court stenographer rang through the courtroom. The jury spent little time in deliberation. The verdict, of course, was "not guilty." Peter Brown, happy tears streaming down his face, embraced his attorney. Incidentally, Murray and Brown, defended by Leibowitz, were the only two vice cops who were acquitted of the charges.

2

Exactly 18 years later, over the luncheon table, the Judge let his inevitable pipe go out and I asked, "Suppose Wallace had not fallen into the trap? Suppose he hadn't asked the witness the all-important question?"

"I was prepared for that contingency," the Judge smiled. "I would have recalled Brown and asked the question myself. Brown's answer would not, of course, have had the same impact upon the jury that it had in response to the same question by the prosecutor."

"There's so much talk about the all important art of cross-examination—"

The Judge broke in, "Not only talk but books and books on the art of cross-examination. I do hope that someone will do a good book on the art of no cross-examination. Cross-examination is like an atomic bomb in a courtroom. It rarely destroys a shrewd old warrior like Jim Wallace, but in the hands of a tyro it can smash a defendant into a cell, or blow a good prosecution case out of the courtroom window.

"In other words, more cases are lost by cross-examination than are won by it. When you have a hostile witness who, you are convinced, is lying, a George Brecht, a Victoria Price, your only weapon to combat these lies is a cross-examination. Cross-examination is your best weapon against an unwarranted indictment. If a witness has been intimidated by police or prosecution authorities, or if he has been promised immunity in return for favorable testimony, you can bring this out only by cross-examination. The object of cross-examination is twofold; first, to elicit more truth that will favor your side of the case; second, to impeach the witness. Cross-examination for the purpose of impeaching a witness can certainly backfire if you aren't careful."

"The way it did on Jim Wallace when he was cross-examining Peter Brown?"

"Exactly," he said, and then added ruefully, "it has backfired on me, too. Once, years ago, I was cross-examining a policeman. My client had said that this cop had beaten a confession out of him with a blackjack. I asked the witness what he carried in his back pocket, hoping he'd say it was a blackjack. He didn't. He said he carried a medal in his back pocket. "So you are a hero, eh,' I suggested, with what I intended to be sarcasm. The witness took a religious medal out of his pocket and held it aloft. 'No,' he said, 'not a hero—a Roman Catholic.' And with four Irishmen sitting there in the jury box! I could feel my face turning red. I'd trapped myself by going fishing in waters that held no fish. Yes, cross-examination can be a double-edged sword if you aren't careful how you handle it."

"How about some other examples?" I asked.

"Well, here are a couple. The charge was incest. The fourteen-year-old girl sat trembling on the witness chair. She was facing her father whom she was accusing of being the parent of her expected child. His lawyer was cross-examining.

" 'Do you hate your father?'

" 'Yes.'

" 'Do you want to see him go to prison?'

" 'I want to see him dead every time I feel the child kicking in my body!'

"It took the jury only five minutes to come in with a verdict of guilty.

"Here's another example," the Judge went on.

346

"The man on trial was charged with a holdup of a passenger on the mezzanine of a subway station. The counsel for the defense proceeded as follows in cross-examining the victim:

" 'What was the condition of the light on the mezzanine?'

" 'Very dim,' responded the witness.

"The lawyer rubbed his palms together and instead of letting well enough alone plunged ahead.

" 'Now, Mr. Witness' he thundered, 'inasmuch as it was so dim, where you say the holdup took place, how can you swear positively that my client is the robber?'

" 'Why, Counselor, the platform may have been dimly lighted but your client and I were right under an electric light when he stuck the gun into my face and told me that he would blow my head off if I didn't give him my wallet!' "

3

It was shortly after the Brown trial that Prosecutor Wallace became Judge James Garrett Wallace. Today he is regarded by lawyers and fellow judges to be one of the really top-flight jurists in New York State. He is still an implacable foe of the underworld; he still has a hatred of lawbreakers.

And that brings us to the case of Salvatore Gatti, a character important to this narrative only because he unwittingly brought Samuel Leibowitz, the lawyer, and James Garrett Wallace, the judge, together again in the old familiar courtroom in the Criminal Courts Building on Centre Street in Manhattan. It was some years later, but neither had forgotten the scar on the belly of Rita Antonina.

The case of Salvatore Gatti is one which Leibowitz discusses with the rueful regret of a pitcher who will retell again and again the story of the one mistake that spoiled an otherwise perfect no-hit game. Leibowitz will never forget Salvatore Gatti.

It all began with an American Legion parade on September 23, 1937. Now a parade in New York means different things to different people. To the Fifth Avenue merchants, it means a few

347

hours of lost trade and possible damage to store windows. To spectators, it means a free show, and wide-eyed New Yorkers love free shows with bands, uniforms, majorettes and floats, just as much as do their country cousins. A parade means something quite different to an imaginative criminal. A criminal knows that a parade not only draws spectators; it draws cops to keep those spectators in line. On the day of an American Legion parade, for instance, more than a thousand cops are taken from their regular posts to line up on Fifth Avenue. And to make the picture more attractive to the larcenous-minded, at least two thousand cops are members of the Legion themselves, and they too want to march in the parade. Everybody (well, nearly everybody) loves a parade.

Louis Rudisch quite frankly wasn't interested in the parade. He owned and operated the Rudisch Refining Company, with an office and workroom on the second floor of 65 Fulton Street, in the jewelry center of lower Manhattan. He usually had a stock of gold and platinum on hand. At ten thirty in the morning of September 23, just as the Legionnaires were starting their march up Fifth Avenue, three men walked into the front office of his concern. Rudisch was seated at a desk talking on the phone. One of the three men walked to his desk, pointed a gun at Rudisch's forehead and said quietly, "Drop that phone or I'll kill you." Rudisch carefully put the receiver back on its cradle.

The other two men, with drawn guns, rounded up four business associates of Rudisch, men who were on the premises. They missed one eyewitness, Max Statz, Rudisch's father-in-law. He had been in the workshop at the back, and he immediately scurried down a fire escape and went looking for a cop. It was a rather forlorn hope, for that morning every cop on patrol had a double beat to take care of, but luck was with Max Statz. He ran right into Patrolman John H. Wilson.

He blurted out the story and Wilson, with reckless disregard for the three-to-one odds against him, ran to the entrance of 65 Fulton Street and started up the stairs. Wilson apparently felt that if he took the time necessary to go to a call box and ask for help, the robbers might have finished their job and been on their way. His action,

348

in wading into an office where he knew there were three armed men, was in the best tradition of New York's great police force.

Meanwhile, the three gunmen had made Rudisch lie on the floor where they tied him with wire they had brought with them. Keever Abraham, a sub-tenant of Rudisch's; Myron Reich, a jeweler; Louis Wolk, who had dropped in to present a bill; and Haroux Wyatt, a utility man who kept the place clean and who ran errands for Louis Rudisch, had also been in the office when the bandits arrived, and now their hands had been wired behind their backs. All had been brought to the back workshop.

Patrolman Wilson burst into the room with drawn gun. He had taken only a step when one of the men (whom he hadn't seen) came up behind him, placed his gun against the base of his skull and fired. Wilson refused to drop. He lunged forward, and now it seemed to the terror-stricken witnesses that all three robbers were firing at the policeman. Wilson was whirled around by the impact of three additional slugs, and he slumped against a radiator and slouched to the floor. One of the intruders had been leaning across a work bench on which there was a lighted gas heater. It was heating and liquefying a panful of wax that was used to make molds for jewelry trinkets that the concern manufactured. In his haste to get a direct shot at Wilson the gunman knocked over the pan and the white hot wax spattered all over. Some of it poured over the left hand of the man who had knocked it over. This man leaned over to pick up Wilson's gun, which lay almost under the table. Some of the wax had fallen on that, too. The bandit picked up the gun with his left hand, but probably because of the pain caused by the burning wax, immediately dropped it. Then the three bandits fled. Wilson, with bullets in his head, heart and abdomen (any one of which would have proven fatal) somehow lurched to his feet and went toward the door after them. At the doorway he collapsed. He died that afternoon.

When a member of the force is killed in line of duty, every cop in New York feels a personal and sacred obligation to apprehend the killer. They went to work with grim determination to break this case. They had a fairly good description of the men and they had a

349

couple of tangible clews. One was a hat that one of the men had dropped in flight, and the other was a windbreaker which a second robber had thrown away. Oddly enough, the windbreaker had been dry-cleaned, and the mark of the cleaning and dyeing establishment was attached to it. That gave them something to start on.

Thirteen days after the killing of Patrolman Wilson, the police picked up Salvatore Gatti and Charles Sberna and charged them with the murder. Gatti had just finished serving a five-year stretch at Sing Sing for robbery. Sberna (whose name looks like a typographical error) had an unsavory criminal record which, in addition to the more conventional crimes of violence, included rape and sodomy. (The third robber was never caught.) Both were identified by the witnesses who had been trussed up in Rudisch's establishment.

Gatti's left hand was burned, and the police claimed it was he who had knocked over the panful of white-hot liquefying wax. The police also said that Dr. Achille Baretta of 209 East 126th Street had treated both Sberna and Gatti on September 24, the day after the killing. Sberna had an ear infection. Gatti had been treated for a second-degree burn. Both men vehemently asserted their innocence.

Gatti's mother and sister went to Leibowitz' office and asked him to defend Salvatore. They protested his innocence and insisted that he was being framed. They were all against him, just because he had a record, the sister said bitterly. The burn on his hand? He had been burned somewhere around September 12, they said, while making candy. (His mother had dressed the burn herself and had bandaged it.) A few days after this (and several days before the killing at 65 Fulton Street) another daughter had been married. Salvatore, of course, attended the wedding. His hand was bandaged then.

"I will get the priest who married my daughter to prove this," the mother said tearfully. "He must have seen the bandaged hand. And we took some wedding pictures that will show Salvatore and the bandage on his hand. I sent the pictures to my daughter, who is on her honeymoon. This all happened days before the killing of the policeman."

"Why didn't Salvatore have his burn treated by a doctor immediately?" Leibowitz asked.

"It was only a burn from the candy," she said. "It wasn't serious. I put Unguentine salve on it. It didn't bother Salvatore much until later. Then one day he ran into Charlie Sberna, and Charlie was on the way to the doctor's to get his ear treated. Salvatore thought he'd go along with him and have the hand looked at."

Leibowitz was deeply impressed with the story told by the sincere old lady and her equally sincere daughter. If a priest was ready to testify that he had seen a bandaged Salvatore several days before the killing of the policeman; if there were actual wedding pictures showing the bandaged Salvatore—why this might well be another one of those cases where the police had been over-zealous or identifying witnesses careless. Leibowitz decided to see Gatti. His story checked in every detail with that of the two women. Where was he, Gatti, on September 23? Oh, he had an alibi all right. He had been home all morning and his mother and sister would verify that. They did, and Leibowitz felt that these two tearful women were telling the truth.

Leibowitz took the case. It didn't seem to present any exceptional difficulties. There seemed a very good chance that Salvatore Gatti was the victim of circumstances and of mistaken identity. Gatti and Sberna were indicted for first-degree murder, and bright young Jacob J. Rosenblum (whom everyone still called Jack), now head of the Homicide Bureau in District Attorney Thomas E. Dewey's office, was the prosecutor. Caesar Barra, veteran lawyer at the criminal bar, had been retained by Charlie Sberna.

As the date for the trial approached, what had seemed to be a routine case began to take on unexpected complexity. The priest who had married Gatti's sister just didn't remember seeing a bandage on Salvatore's left hand. He couldn't say that Salvatore didn't carry a bandage; he just didn't remember seeing one. The wedding pictures? Gatti's mother brought them to his lawyer, but in each picture Salvatore's left hand was covered by someone else, or it was behind his back or in his pocket. Not one of the pictures revealed a bandage.

351

Friends close to the district attorney's office hurried to tell Leibowitz of what they "had heard."

"Jack Rosenblum isn't saying anything," they told him, "but we hear that he has Gatti right where he wants him. The boys in the D.A.'s office are chuckling over a fingerprint on Wilson's gun. That wax that spilled on the gun preserved a wonderful print. Whose print is it? The boys from the D.A.'s office aren't saying, but if you bet it was Gatti's print you couldn't lose."

Leibowitz went storming to the Tombs to see his client. What about that print? It couldn't be his, Gatti said calmly; he wasn't there at the time of the shooting. Leibowitz looked at Gatti speculatively. This man was charged with first-degree murder. He was facing the electric chair. It seemed inconceivable that he would lie to his own attorney at this stage of the game. Leibowitz had often said that a lawyer is the last person to whom a guilty client tells the truth. He had known dozens of defendants to lie to their attorneys. Later, as a judge, he had often seen defense attorneys taken completely by surprise during the course of a trial by evidence which showed their clients to be guilty; clients whom they honestly felt to be innocent.

"You've met my mother, Mr. Leibowitz," Gatti said suddenly. "Do you think she'd lie even to save me? Why, she couldn't tell a lie if she tried."

Leibowitz nodded. "That's the only reason I took your case," he said. "I believed your mother and your sister. They say and you say that those witnesses are mistaken in their identification of you. That could be. But a fingerprint doesn't lie and isn't mistaken. If your fingerprint is on that gun the D.A. has, then you have deliberately lied to me and I want no part of defending you."

Gatti was a big man with a placid, expressionless face. "That's fair enough," Gatti said calmly. "I'm telling you it can't be my print because I wasn't there. If you find it's my print, okay, withdraw from the case. My folks have already paid you a retainer. If you find it's my print, keep the money and bow out of the case. Is that fair enough?"

"That's fair enough," Leibowitz agreed.

"I'll tell you what I'll do," Gatti said. "I'll put it in writing.

I'll write that if they produce a gun with my print on it, I release you as my lawyer. Do you want it in writing?"

"Yes, I do," Leibowitz said, and then Gatti signed a statement to that effect. Leibowitz walked out of the Tombs a puzzled man. Gatti appeared to be telling the truth. His signed statement was evidence of that. But he was disturbed by the reports his friends had given him about that print. A sudden thought hit him. Could the print have been forged? He had never heard of a case in which a print had been forged, but could it be done? Might someone with a suspicion that Gatti had done the shooting, but with no real evidence, have forged the print on the gun and given it to the D.A.'s office?

Leibowitz went to see a fingerprint expert. Yes, a print could be forged, he was told. It was a complicated process but it could be done. First you'd need a photograph of the print. (They had Gatti's prints at Police Headquarters; it would be easy to photograph them.) Then you had to make a die of the print, put some wax on the gun, impress the die on the soft wax; then let it cool and harden. Yes, it could be done, all right. But who would go to all that trouble?

Leibowitz was in a quandary. Of course the gossip emanating from the D.A.'s office might be poorly founded. Then, too, he knew Jack Rosenblum. Rosenblum would have quit his office rather than connive at manufactured evidence. Nor did he believe that the Police Department would actually forge a print to insure a conviction. One or two cops, acting on their own and intent on avenging their friend Wilson, might do such a thing, however. He decided to see Rosenblum.

Leibowitz asked permission of the D.A.'s office to have experts examine the gun for fingerprints. Jack Rosenblum appeared none too anxious to let defense counsel or his representatives see the gun. Leibowitz explained that he would withdraw from the case if Gatti's print was on it, but the District Attorney continued to be evasive, right up to the day of the trial. This attitude confirmed Leibowitz' suspicions that Gatti had in fact been lying to him right along.

The trial opened before Judge James Garrett Wallace. Leibowitz was the attorney of record. He couldn't withdraw from the case now without permission of the court. He sought this permission and offered to return the entire fee he had received. The trial record of *People of the State of New York vs. Salvatore Gatti and Charles Sherna* reveals the following colloquy between defense counsel and the court (at the bench):

Mr. Leibowitz. I told Mr. Rosenblum two months ago that if this man's fingerprint was on the gun I would not defend him. Mr. Rosenblum said we could inspect the gun and our expert could look at it and determine whether or not Gatti's fingerprint was on it. Now, we have been trying to get a look at this gun for a long while. On Monday of this week Mr. Rosenblum made an arrangement with us to have the gun examined. We had a photographer and an expert ready, but the gun was not produced. Now, Your Honor, if this man's fingerprint is on this gun, I request to be relieved as his counsel. I cannot give my best efforts to a client who has lied to me.

Judge Wallace. I think you can. I think you are an experienced counsel who was engaged by this defendant back in October. The question as to whether or not you will represent him if the fingerprint is on the gun did not arise until some time thereafter. I think you have a moral and a legal obligation to defend this man.

Mr. Leibowitz. The defendant, on the other hand, is perfectly satisfied that I shall not try this case, as this agreement shows. (Here Leibowitz handed Judge Wallace the written agreement signed by Gatti, releasing counsel if his fingerprint was found on the gun. The jurist read the agreement.) I do not feel in conscience that I can try this case. And feeling that way . . .

Judge Wallace. Is it your theory that you never represented anybody except a defendant who was innocent, a man of your long experience at the criminal bar?

Mr. Leibowitz. I have never had a case yet where it was claimed by the prosecution that the fingerprint of my client was on the incriminating instrument. There have been cases where the witnesses have said, "That is the man"; and the defendant claimed he was not the man; and often these witnesses were proven to be mistaken

354

in their identification. But I don't know how a mistake can be made where there is a fingerprint. My information is that the fingerprint of the defendant is on that gun. Now, I do not mean to be disrespectful but I do feel that the Court should not ask a lawyer to represent a man, especially where the man's life is at stake, where the lawyer's heart is not in the case.

Judge Wallace. You are an able and experienced trial counsel, having defended a great number of persons for murder in the first degree. Moreover, I do not think that in all of the cases in which you went to the jury, that your defendant was innocent, but that you felt merely that he was entitled to a trial to the best of your ability, and I feel that you can give this man an adequate and proper defense. Therefore, I direct that you proceed with this trial on Friday.

Gatti?

The Defendant Gatti. Yes sir.

Judge Wallace. Are you satisfied to have Mr. Leibowitz try the case for you?

The Defendant Gatti. Yes.

Judge Wallace. That is all I want to know.

The trial began the next morning. Never had Leibowitz felt less sympathy for a client than he felt for Gatti; never had he given a client a more masterful defense. Understandably baffled by Judge Wallace (nine times out of ten the court grants application by dissatisfied defense counsel to withdraw from a case), annoyed at Jack Rosenblum because of his refusal to allow him access to a prosecution exhibit, he threw every bit of legal skill and energy at his command into the defense. Leibowitz, by the sheer skill of his cross-examination of identification witnesses, cast considerable doubt upon the identification of Gatti. One witness actually said, "Frankly, I couldn't take my eyes off the guns in the hands of the robbers. I never did get a good look at their faces."

Then Rosenblum produced the gun, and sure enough, it did have Gatti's print on it. Leibowitz was fighting with his back to the wall

355

now, but he did not allow the untenable position in which he found himself to discourage or anger him. He fought back with cool calculation. He didn't say that the print had been forged. He did bring out in cross-examination the fact that such a print could have been forged.

And then Salvator Gatti apparently decided that Rosenblum wasn't hustling him toward the electric chair quickly enough. He would help Rosenblum along. Without notifying Leibowitz, Gatti had decided to go on the stand, not to testify in his own behalf, but to testify for his friend Charlie Sberna. Attorney Caesar Barra called him to the stand. Gatti said that Sberna was completely innocent. He himself had been at the scene of the crime, he admitted under Barra's questioning, but he had gone there with two chance acquaintances to "collect a bill that Rudisch owed them." Leibowitz watched in fascinated horror as Gatti lied himself right into the electric chair. But Gatti wasn't lying as convincingly now as he had lied while talking to Leibowitz in the Tombs, and it appeared obvious that the jury didn't believe a word he said. By taking the stand he surrendered himself to eternity.

I have read at least one hundred of Leibowitz' summations to juries. His four-hour address to the jury on behalf of Salvatore Gatti was one of his best. He was pleading for the life of a man who had virtually admitted his guilt. He was pleading for the life of a man who had lied to him and whom he despised, but he gave this man his best. He was pleading for a cause that was lost before he arose to his feet, but the odds against him merely sharpened his arguments and increased his eloquence. He ended with a ringing plea that the jury bring in a recommendation for mercy which would stay the death penalty and make a life sentence mandatory.

The jury listened spellbound—and after fourteen hours of deliberation brought in a verdict of guilty. Judge Wallace sentenced both to the electric chair. They were both executed.

Salvatore Gatti was the only client in twenty-one years of practice Leibowitz lost to the electric chair. Was the court justified in insisting that Leibowitz continue to represent a client who had lied to him? Lawyers and judges in New York have argued that question

356

for a long time. In any case, his decision meant that the courtroom pitcher who had won 139 consecutive games was finally knocked out of the box.

4

"I want to ask you how you really feel now about the Gatti case."

Judge Leibowitz smiled. "People never forget that Fred Merkle failed to touch second in that all-important game against Chicago. They never remember his home runs. I suppose they'll remember me only for the Gatti case."

"Well, Joe Di Maggio once dropped a fly ball," I reminded him.

"I just don't believe that," the ardent Di Maggio admirer said, aghast.

"It was in August, 1946," I said. "The Yanks were playing the Browns. Dillinger hit an easy fly to center field. Joe stood there; the ball dropped into his hands and then popped out. Toots Shor and I were there that day. That Christmas we sent him a kid's book called How to Play Center Field. We never let Joe forget the one fly ball he dropped in his entire career."

"Well, they'll never let me forget the Gatti case, either," Judge Leibowitz continued. "I made a fatal mistake in that case. I believed my client. The story his mother and sister told me was so convincing and they seemed such fine, sincere people, that I was prepared to believe Gatti when I went to see him. Of course I should have known better. I learned that lesson early. When I was just a youngster at the bar, I had a penniless client accused of a petty candy store burglary. He had what seemed to me to be a perfect alibi. My client seemed innocent, as he claimed. The prosecution sprang a surprise on me. The D.A. introduced a hat into evidence, claiming that my client had dropped his hat when he had fled the scene of the crime. Although the hat fitted perfectly, the defendant's denials were so sincere that the jury brought in a not guilty verdict. I too felt that justice had been done. My client walked out of the courtroom with me. In the corridor he stopped and said, 'Now that the

357

trial is over, can I get my hat back from the District Attorney?' "

"Not all of your clients lied to you?"

"No, it was the man with a criminal record who usually lied," he said. "Take Robert Irwin. He was one of the most truthful men I ever met. In his lucid intervals he was completely honest. Perhaps you remember that he had himself committed to an insane asylum five times just because he was afraid that he might become violent and hurt someone. Irwin was quite willing to go to the chair for the murders he had committed. Poor Louis Greenfield, the pathetic Joe Scutellaro and Duncan Ladd were honest men. The great German writer Gotthold Lessing once said, 'The man who doesn't lose his mind in certain situations has no mind to lose.' These men and Laura Parr, too, lost their minds temporarily under emotional stress that was too much for them. But they never lied to me or to the court when they were on trial. The men who've been in jail before become what we call 'stir lawyers.' They're like patients who fool their doctors by pouring his medicine down the drain. In jail they pick up a bit of what they think to be legal lore. They seldom confide in their lawyers. They tell a story which they hope will convince the lawyer of their innocence. Once he is convinced, they hope he will be able to convince a jury. The psychology of the criminal is a peculiar one.

"The criminal won't tell his lawyer the truth because he suspects that the lawyer will sell him out to the police. Or he feels that if his lawyer knows that he is guilty, the lawyer won't exercise his best efforts. Salvatore Gatti was like that. After more than twenty years of experience with them I must say the criminal mind still baffles me."

"Suppose the lawyer, after talking to the defendant, realizes that he is guilty beyond doubt?" I asked. "Should he then refuse to represent him?"

"Certainly not," the Judge said. "The legal profession has a canon of ethics, which is the moral code for the lawyer. Canon No. 5 says that a lawyer is bound to undertake the defense of a person accused of a crime regardless of his personal opinion as to the guilt of the accused. If this were not so, innocent persons, victims only of sus-

358

picious circumstances, might be denied proper defense. But, in a situation like the one in which I found myself with Gatti, I do not believe that either law or ethics compelled me to remain as his counsel in view of what transpired—my client and his family had lied to me from the beginning."

5

For some years Leibowitz had been increasingly reluctant to represent underworld characters. This was not a negation or contradiction of his oft-stated belief that they had as much right to proper legal representation as did the decent citizen whom circumstances or mental instability had forced into crime. There was nothing sanctimonious about his feeling; he had not developed a holier-than-thou attitude. But the strain had become intolerable. Too much was expected of him. During his early days he had always gone joyously into legal battle, relishing the fight. Now each new case was a backbreaking chore.

In the beginning the law had been his profession, but over the years it had become his avocation as well. The law was something he lived with twenty-four hours a day, and he felt that a man who didn't have his own sense of complete dedication to the law had no right to be a lawyer. Leibowitz was a complete individualist. He never followed the methods used by Max Steuer, Clarence Darrow, or Earl Rogers (the three trial lawyers for whom he had the most respect). He had to play it his way, and his way was to play it alone. The newspapers thought of him as a legal magician; lawyers and jurists (rather belatedly) realized that it was his sound knowledge of law, his intense and thorough preparation for a trial and his dramatic way of presenting his case in court that were responsible for his success.

But now the pace was beginning to tell even on the healthy, dynamic Leibowitz. He seldom slept more than an hour or two a day during a difficult trial. He used to envy his colleagues of the civil courts. They could lose a case, or a dozen cases, and it would not harm their professional standing a bit. He mustn't lose; he dare not take a trial casually. Every district attorney in New York hoped to be the one to beat Leibowitz in a major case.

To Leibowitz the worst time during a trial were those hours when the jury was out pondering the evidence. To him these hours were purgatory. The jury considering the guilt or innocence of Max Becker, charged with the murder of the principal keeper during the convict break of Auburn Prison in 1929, was out twenty-three and a half hours, and Leibowitz paced the corridors of the courthouse that entire time. When the jury came in and its foreman called, "Not guilty," the defendant Becker merely smiled. He had expected that Leibowitz would get him off. Leibowitz didn't smile. The color drained from his ruddy face and he toppled over in a dead faint. He was in bed for a week recuperating from the strain of that one. Every time he went into a courtroom he looked enviously at the judge. It didn't matter to the judge what the jury did. The judge could go home at night, forget the case and get a good night's sleep. Leibowitz couldn't.

He acquitted such unsavory characters as Harry Stein (the State said he murdered the flaming-haired courtesan, Vivian Gordon), Pittsburgh Phil Strauss, Ben Siegel (whom the newspapers but no one else called "Buggsy"), Abe Reles, Buggsy Goldstein and dozens of others. To Leibowitz these for the most part were "routine" cases. A reading of the trial records reveals nothing interesting enough to warrant their detailed inclusion in these pages. They were marked neither by high drama nor by interesting legal complexities. They wouldn't be worth mention except that the defendants were considered by the newspapers to be public enemies of prominence, and the trials received wide publicity.

6

One night in 1939, just after the dinner dishes had been cleared away, the doorbell rang and the maid said that there were three men to see Mr. Leibowitz.

"The picture begins at eight-thirty, Sam," Belle Leibowitz warned, "and we don't want to be late."

"I'll get rid of them quickly," he said. He ushered the three men to the library. Belle went into the bedroom to finish those inevitable last-minute touches to hair and make-up which are responsible for making wives late for theatre and moving picture the world over. But this time it wasn't her fault that they missed the opening of the film. She heard the men talking.

"Lepke wants you to defend him," she heard. Belle Leibowitz had never heard of Lepke. But she'd heard of Cary Grant and she knew that Cary's picture would be starting in about twenty minutes, and she wished that her husband would get rid of his three visitors.

"I don't want it," she heard her husband say. "I'm just not interested. Why, there are a dozen lawyers around who will be happy to take the case and do a good job, too."

"But Lepke only wants you," she heard. "Won't have anyone else. You can name your fee."

"Not interested," she heard, "and besides, Mrs. Leibowitz and I have a date to go to the movies."

This, Belle Leibowitz thought, was her cue. She walked to the doorway of the library, stood for a moment and then gasped. One of the men had opened a brief case, had up-ended it and dumped the contents on the library table. There on that table was a stack of green bills nearly a foot high.

"There's two hundred and fifty grand, Counselor," the man said. "A quarter of a million bucks. It's yours if you take the case. Win, lose or draw, it's yours."

She saw her husband look at the library clock. It was eight-thirty. "I told you I had a date with my wife," he said, smiling. "Put the money away. I'm just not interested."

Five minutes later she and her husband were hurrying to see Cary Grant.

"Who is Lepke?" she asked.

"The papers say he's the boss man of a gang," he said. "He's been indicted for murder."

"Is he guilty?"

361

"I have no idea," he said indifferently. "As a lawyer, I've defended plenty of men like Lepke. Let someone else defend them from now on. It's a tough, grueling game and I'm a little tired. Oh, I get a kick out of freeing a Louis Greenfield or a Joseph Scutellaro or those Scottsboro kids. But . . ."

"I know," she smiled. "You want to be on the other side of the bench."

He laughed. "Well, that isn't such a bad ambition, is it? Wanting to be a judge?"

"It's a good ambition," she said gravely.

7

In 1940 the Democratic party nominated Samuel S. Leibowitz as its candidate for Judge of the King's County Court. The term is fourteen years and the salary twenty-eight thousand dollars. There are no rules in the dirty game of politics, and his opponents tried to prove desperately that the candidate's role as counsel for defense in so many sensational criminal cases had unfitted him for a judicial post.

"Elect Leibowitz and he'll open the doors of the jails," his political opponents screamed. "He'll turn loose every crook who comes before him."

His opponents submitted his private and professional life to microscopic scrutiny. They seized with glee on the fact that back in 1931 he had been indicted for conspiracy and subornation of perjury.

This was an aftermath of his defense of some of the vice cops standing trial in police departmental hearings. The evidence against them was for the most part predicated on testimony given by a professional stool pigeon named Chile Mapocha Acuna. The man with the name just made for writers of limericks had another trade. He was also a professional procurer, whose modest fee for bringing customers to the girls he represented was one dollar a customer, and he testified that the accused policemen were silent partners and financial beneficiaries of his activities. In defending the cops, Leibowitz had utterly destroyed Acuna's credibility by proving his character. One of the witnesses who appeared against Acuna was a prostitute named Eva Esperanza Mackay.

The relationship between Acuna and Eva was a beautiful one, based not only on mutual affection but on a common enthusiasm for the fruits of free enterprise. Eva had something to sell; her lover was a fine salesman. But Eva was a jealous girl, and when she found that Chile Mapocha Acuna occasionally visited her professional colleagues for personal rather than professional reasons, her touching affection for the procurer turned to hatred, and she severed all relations with him. He had boasted of his influence with the cops, but this hadn't prevented Eva from having been arrested and convicted as a prostitute six times. Of course, things like that reflected on a girl's character, and she blamed Chile for not having kept her out of the clutches of the law. In addition, she found that Chile often sent choice clients to competitors, a breach of ethics she found it difficult to overlook.

Out of a clear blue sky she appeared at the hearing as a defense witness. She was very glad to testify as to the character of Chile Mapocha Acuna. She told of how he had inducted her into the business of prostitution, of how he had trained her and of the financial arrangements they had made; he was to get a one-dollar commission for every sale he made, and because Eva was such an industrious, hard-working girl, this added up to a tidy annual sum. When Eva was through, no one on earth would have believed anything that Chile said.

Chile was furious at Leibowitz for having exposed him. As he left the courtroom, after being torn to pieces by the ruthless cross-examination, he exploded in voluble Spanish. He swore that he would "get even." A reporter who was linguistically literate heard his outbursts and passed the threats on to the lawyer, who promptly forgot them.

But Chile Mapocha Acuna never lost his feeling of resentment. He was an ingratiating, persuasive man, and somehow or other he managed to resell himself to Eva Esperanza Mackay. Once more she succumbed to the fascination of his Latin charms. He convinced her

363

that their lovers' tiff had been nothing but a misunderstanding. He convinced her that she could earn nice money by repudiating her previous testimony. The newspapers would pay for such a story. One paper promised to use her story if she would first go to the D.A. with it. Chile and Eva resumed both personal and business relationships.

Several months after the trial of the cops, Chile and Eva appeared at the offices of William F. X. Geoghan, District Attorney of Brooklyn, chaperoned by a reporter. Eva had something she wanted to reveal to the District Attorney. The D.A. listened with attentive ears. She had lied about Chile Acuna, she said now, and her conscience had been bothering her ever since. She had been angry at him and she had branded him as a procurer just to get even with him. He had never been her procurer. He had merely been her boy friend, she said coyly, and her outburst against him had been the result of a lovers' quarrel. And anyhow, it hadn't been her idea at all to brand Acuna as a procurer, she said; it was that lawyer who suggested that she do it and she, like a silly little fool, had told the lies he had put in her mouth.

"What lawyer told you to lie?" Geoghan demanded.

"Mr. Leibowitz," she faltered, with downcast eyes.

And Geoghan eventually secured an indictment against Leibowitz from the Grand Jury. No one in courthouse circles ever thought for a moment that Geoghan intended ever to bring the case to trial. No one ever dreamed that anyone would be foolish enough to go into court with only a discredited procurer and stool pigeon and a six-times convicted prostitute as his witnesses.

Geoghan had never won a major legal victory over Leibowitz. More able legal minds were convinced that Geoghan would only make himself ridiculous in the eyes of the public and of his colleagues if he persisted in pressing the indictment. One day he appeared before Judge Algeron I. Nova. It was to ask that the indictment be dismissed.

"The case is of unusual importance because the defendant happens to be a well-known criminal lawyer. Character is so easily destroyed that we should be quite zealous to see that the quality of testimony produced against a lawyer is the type and kind that will be believed," the court said.

"Lawyers who for years and years have built up a good reputation will never be safe if it is our law that an unscrupulous witness can walk in and say, 'The lawyer told me to say that.' To ruin and stain a lawyer's reputation, ruin his family life, take away his right to practice upon the word alone, so to speak, of an admitted disreputable prostitute, is carrying it a bit too far.

"I have never known Mr. Leibowitz to do a thing that was not honorable and decent as a lawyer. But it is because of my reading of the testimony before the Grand Jury that I know I could never personally justify the finding of the indictment.

"I am happy in the opportunity that comes to me to dismiss the indictment, and I so do direct that the indictment be dismissed."

That fiasco gave small comfort to those who opposed the election of Leibowitz. They searched his record thoroughly and were unable to find a single incident which they could use against him. Leibowitz was elected by a plurality of nearly 400,000 votes, the largest ever given to a candidate running for local office in Brooklyn.

8

On January 6, 1941, Samuel S. Leibowitz was inducted as a judge of the Kings County Court. He left his home in Brooklyn early that morning, driving his own car. He was a supremely happy and contented man. Twenty-one years of battling in the criminal courts had tired him. Now he could to some extent relax and watch other lawyers do the fighting. He drove along, his mind occupied with pleasant thoughts of the future. His car followed the well-remembered route it had traveled for so many years. It passed right by the big, white Central Court Building where the induction was to take place. It crossed the Brooklyn Bridge, turned south and stopped in front of 225 Broadway. Leibowitz stepped out, entered the building, said "Hello" to the elevator man and was taken up to the forty-second floor. There was his name on the office door. He opened the door and blinked with astonishment. There wasn't a stick of furniture left in the suite of offices.

In a moment his mind jumped back to reality. His place was over in Brooklyn at the courthouse. He looked at his watch. Well, he still had plenty of time. Habit had led him here to his old office. He walked to the window and looked down on the Battery and beyond to the harbor. There on Bedloes Island stood the Lady of Liberty. Back in 1897, the good ship *Kensington* had crawled into the harbor, had slid by that statue and had nosed up the North River. His mother and father had been passengers on the little ship and he, their four-year-old son, had been with them.

He turned from the window to look around the bare office. It was haunted by a thousand memories. Anna Hauptmann, wife of the man who kidnapped and murdered the Lindbergh child, had come here to plead with him to save her husband from the electric chair. The mother of Salvatore Gatti had cried miserably here and had protested her son's innocence to such good effect that Leibowitz had taken on the hopeless job of trying to clear him. Poor, grief-stricken Anna Greenfield had sat here before his desk asking him to defend her husband, who had admittedly killed their son with chloroform. And that pleasant, intelligent school-teacher . . . what was her name? Oh yes, Mrs. John Barry Coughlin. Her husband was in jail waiting sentence. Could he help her? Somewhere or other she and her husband were now enjoying the lives of free and useful citizens because he had been able to help her; had been able to prove, as he had proven many times, that the law was capable of error. Here in this office he had mapped the defense of the Scottsboro boys. Here—all the others—

The sharp ring of the phone lying on the bare cement floor in the corner cut through his reverie. He had completely forgotten to notify the telephone company that he had given up the office. His hand reached out to pick up the receiver, and he noticed that the watch on his wrist read ten o'clock. At ten-thirty he would be inducted as judge. He dropped his hand, looked once rather regretfully at the ringing phone and then hurried out of the office. He turned back just once and was startled to see that *Samuel S. Leibowitz, Attor-*

ney-at-Law was still on the door. Attached to his key ring was a small penknife. He took out the knife, opened the blade and scratched the name off the door. It took some time to do that. Just as he finished he heard the phone ringing again. The temptation to rush into the office and pick up that receiver was almost overwhelming, but he resisted it. He pushed the button for the elevator. As it stopped the phone stopped too. The elevator shot down to street level. Leibowitz sensed a feeling of relief when he was out of the building. It was all behind him now. Within twenty minutes he would be a judge. If he had answered that phone, who knows? The story told by the man or woman at the other end might have been so appealing that . . . He shook his head to dismiss such thoughts, climbed behind the wheel of his car, and headed for the Central Court Building in Brooklyn.

The car threaded its way through the busy down-town traffic and over the bridge to the courthouse in Brooklyn. He entered the elevator marked *Judges Only,* passed by the office where fresh new lettering on the glass door read *Chambers of Judge Leibowitz,* and went into the huge library. The other four judges comprising the County Court were waiting for him. Judge Franklin Taylor, Senior Judge of the Court, slipped the black silk robe around his shoulders and then led the way to the Part I Courtroom.

The courtroom was packed to the doors with judges, district attorneys, bar association officers, members of the clergy, Zionists, dignitaries of the Masonic and Pythian orders, and officials of charitable, social and civic organizations with which the new jurist had been identified over the years. There were also Negro leaders, who by their presence were thanking him for his work in the Scottsboro case; and his family and friends.

Five huge leather chairs had been placed behind the bench. The sound of the gavel echoed through the hushed courtroom. The entire assemblage arose as the judges took their places. The new judge sat in the middle, flanked by his colleagues. Each of them in turn arose to pay tribute to the man who had fought in so many celebrated cases before his court.

"You come here," Judge John J. Fitzgerald said, "with an equipment that few judges have had prior to their elevation to the bench.

367

You were born the year I was admitted to the bar. It was Socrates, not exactly a contemporary of mine, who said, 'Four things belong to a judge; to hear courteously; to answer wisely; to consider soberly and to decide impartially.' Today we add one more qualification. It is desirable that a judge know some law. You have all of these attributes."

Judge Franklin Taylor presented a gavel and said, "You have been Samuel Leibowitz, the great lawyer. You will be Samuel Leibowitz, the great judge." Judge George W. Martin and Judge Peter J. Brancato also paid their respects. The District Attorney of Kings County stepped before the bench and asked to be heard. He was soon to become Mayor William O'Dwyer, but in 1941 he was the fighting D.A. of Brooklyn.

"It is a great honor for me," O'Dwyer said, "personally and as District Attorney to join in this welcome to our new judge. I know that this is the court where the criminal who sets his hand against the community comes to be tried, and even at his worst, he has certain rights, one of which is the right to a fair trial. Because of your experience I know that you will be zealous in safeguarding those rights for the defendants who will appear before you. I can only say . . . good luck, Judge."

And then the new Judge arose. To his amazement he found that his brow was moist and that the palms of his hands were sweating. He cleared his throat, swallowed a couple of times. It wasn't like him to be nervous in a courtroom. The last time he'd really been nervous was that never-to-be-forgotten day when he appeared for the first time to defend a skid-row character named Harry Patterson. But that was twenty-one years ago. What made him nervous now? Was it the weight of the robe that hung from his shoulders?

"It is the first time in many years I have been at a loss for words in a courtroom," he said in a low, faltering voice. "I am deeply moved by the kind sentiments expressed here this morning. My only regret is that my parents did not live to hear them spoken. They brought me here, an immigrant boy, hoping that I would have the chance that would have been denied me in their native Roumania. This glorious country of ours gave me that chance. I am grateful.

368

My years in this very courtroom have taught me that the chief duty of the judge is to accord the litigants a fair trial, to the end that the innocent shall be freed and the guilty convicted, that the hardened criminal be segregated so that society may be protected; that to the unfortunate, who can be reclaimed, be extended the merciful and helping hand of Justice. I am awed by the responsibility that is mine, for I realize how weak are they who sit in judgment upon their fellow human beings. I pray that God will help me in the performance of my task."

He sat down. The other judges left the bench and went to their respective courtrooms. District Attorney O'Dwyer smiled to the Judge, warmly congratulated Belle Leibowitz and the children, and left for his office. Judge Leibowitz picked up the gavel that lay on the bench. For a moment he hesitated, then gently laid it back. He slipped his hand inside his robe, withdrew a pencil from his vest pocket and tapped with it lightly on the bench. Assistant District Attorney James A. McGough approached.

"Your Honor," he said, "I move for trial the case of *The People of the State of New York against Herbert Brown*. The indictment charges first-degree manslaughter."

Judge Leibowitz nodded to George Leonard, Clerk of the Court. "Mr. Clerk," he said briskly, "impanel a jury . . ."

And so a judge was born.

14. THE BLACK ROBE

Give then thy servant an understanding heart, where-
with to judge Thy people, that I may discern between
good and evil."

KING SOLOMON

1

Aristotle said that the Athenian statesman Solon wrote his famous
Code in obscure language so that many lawsuits would result, and
thus give the State ample opportunity to exercise and increase its authority over the citizens through frequent adjudication. The Penal
Code which guides the jurist who presides over a criminal court today is neither obscure nor is its purpose to add to the complexities
of dispensing justice. Penal laws are simple, direct and easily understood, and the uninformed might think that they made the task
of a judge a sinecure.

But however uncomplicated the statutes, there is nothing uncomplicated about the defendants who come to court because they have
violated them. Theoretically, things should be black or white in the
courtroom. But actually it doesn't always work out that way; not
when you are dealing with flesh and blood—with the life or liberty
of a human being, and with the safety of the community.

In the courtroom presided over by Judge Leibowitz there are two
doors. One leads to the corridor and to freedom; the other leads to
imprisonment and sometimes to death. On sentence day, convicted defendants stand in front of the bench and the Judge has to decide
which door each defendant will use when he leaves the courtroom.
The power he has been given is awesome. Only in rare cases does
the decision of a jury make a sentence mandatory. Usually the

Judge has a wide latitude. He asks himself just one question, "What is justice in this case?"

In 1890, Robert Ingersoll delivered an address before the New York State Bar Association which has become a classic treatise on the subject of justice and punishment.

"All nations," he declared, "seem to have had supreme confidence in the deterrent power of threatened and inflicted pain. They have regarded punishment as the shortest road to reformation. Imprisonment, torture and death constitute a trinity under whose protection society might feel secure. Nations have relied on confiscation and degradation, on maimings, whippings and brandings. The chamber of torture was always connected with the courts. The ingenuity of man was exhausted in the construction of instruments that would surely rend the most sensitive nerve. But curiously enough, the fact is that no matter how severe and painful the punishment was—crime increased."

It is as true today as when Ingersoll spoke, that, usually, punishment is no deterrent to crime. To some slight extent society has recognized this. We no longer find the rack, the hot iron or the wheel in our prisons. Less than a century ago the penalty in England for committing any one of two hundred crimes was death. Today, in general, we reserve the supreme penalty for the two major crimes; murder and treason. (In some parts of the United States rape is also punishable by death.)

"We have made some progress," Judge Leibowitz says, in discussing the question of punishment. "Physical torture is a thing of the past; even the silence rule, the lock-step, the degrading prison stripes and the shaven heads are (except in a few communities) now happily outlawed. But we still throw the first offender and the unregenerate criminal into the same prison yard. The experience of any judge is that only in very rare cases does prison ever reform a man. In most cases he emerges more depraved and antisocial than when he was first put behind bars. Our probation system does its best to rehabilitate those who can be salvaged, but what can society do except to cage the hardened criminal who has made a profession of crime? Society does this merely as a matter of self-defense.

371

"You sit there on the bench," the Judge continued, "and they parade before you; the vicious, the frightened juvenile, the degenerate, the cold-blooded criminal, the moral cripple, the spiritual consumptive. You have the frightening power of life and death over these men and women. What is justice in this case? You ask yourself that a dozen times each week. Which door will you open to this defendant?"

Put yourself in the place of the judge. What would you have done, for instance, in the case of Tony Tichon?

2

Anthony Tichon gloried in the nickname of Tough Tony. The name had not been given carelessly; he had really earned it. Before his sixteenth birthday he had made three command appearances in the Children's Court, and was known to the probation officers as a lad who had taken on juvenile delinquency not only as a profession but as an avocation. He seemed to enjoy lawbreaking as other boys enjoyed baseball. When he was finally sent to reform school (it is called the Children's Village), he found that he didn't like it. He expressed his contempt for the institution by escaping not once but four times.

During the next nine years he spent considerable time in institutions from which escape was more difficult. Sing Sing he found especially confining, but unable to escape, he donned his best behavior and after five years of state hospitality he was paroled. Late in 1941, he and two companions, Jerry Mantesta and Frank Nazurek (alias Bruno Perry), robbed a poolroom owned by Benjamin Kleinman. Their loot was disappointing, for none of the half-dozen pool players present was very affluent. But they got a few dollars in currency, several pawn tickets and some jewelry. They made a clean getaway in a stolen car.

The victims identified the three men from police pictures. A few days later Mantesta and Nazurek were picked up. Mantesta said that he was on his way to meet his pal, Tough Tony, and Detective

Joseph Healy said he'd like to go along for the ride. Mantesta at the moment was behind the wheel of a lovely new Nash sedan which the three men had appropriated and had used in their getaway.

When Tough Tony saw that his friend Mantesta was accompanied by a stocky, grim-faced man, he deduced that this might be the law, so with commendable alacrity he ran. In his haste he ran through a plate-glass window and into a shop. He dashed into the back yard and tried to climb a fence, but Detective Healy was hot on his trail with his gun blazing. A bullet lodged in the spine of Tough Tony and he dropped to the ground. He was taken to the Kings County Hospital in serious condition.

Mantesta and Nazurek were tried and sentenced. It was several months before Tony Tichon could answer the charge of robbery. He was carried into court on a stretcher, and doctors testified that he had completely lost the use of his legs. Tough Tony, they said, would be bedridden, a helpless invalid, for the rest of his life. Tony admitted his guilt. Now the Judge had to sentence him.

Judge Leibowitz looked at the record that lay on the bench. It was evident that Tough Tony had never done a day's work in his life (except while in prison). He was on his record an unregenerate criminal. The investigation report said, "His whole career seems to have been characterized by wild, unruly and reckless behavior, one of the manifestations of which was a complete disregard for law and order, or any of its responsibilities. Early in life he became acquainted with a tough crowd, and he seems to have associated only with holdup men, racketeers, racetrack bettors; and frequented places where such characters are generally found. He is known to have carried a gun as a matter of habit, and in general earned himself the appellation of 'Tough Tony.' Even in the hospital he was uncooperative, abusive and insulting to the physicians and nurses to such an extent that he had to be transferred to the Penitentiary Hospital on Rikers Island."

Looking at his record of convictions, Judge Leibowitz knew that the mandatory ten-to-twenty-year sentence was entirely just. Then he read on. He smiled a bit as he read what Chief Probation Officer

373

Edmond Fitzgerald had to say of Tough Tony. He had spent a great deal of time with the paralyzed defendant and he had written:

He attributes his final downfall to his "girl friend." He said that when he came out of prison, he had not seen a girl for so long that his head was turned and he became "crazy about her." She had a poor reputation for chastity, he says, but he was very devoted to her. Her demands for money and entertainment, he says, were insatiable and he spent most of his rather low salary on her weekly. He gave no money to the family, his mother exempting him from this obligation until he could make more. However, he was unable to earn enough and says that it was for this reason that he went out on holdups.

It was just like Fitz, the Judge reflected, to find something good to say of even such a worthless specimen of humanity as Tony Tichon. Judge Leibowitz looked down at the defendant, and despite himself he felt a twinge of sympathy. The stretcher had been placed on the table usually reserved for defense counsel. The defendant appeared to be nothing but a parchment-covered skeleton. His cheeks were hollow and his clawlike hands clutched nervously at the gray blanket that covered him. Benjamin Schifter, his counsel, said, "Your Honor, before you sentence the defendant, will you hear him? He wants to say something to you, but unfortunately his voice will not carry to the bench."

"I'll come down," the Judge said, and he descended from the bench to stand alongside the stretcher.

Tony Tichon whispered, "Judge, I'm not looking for sympathy. I committed the crime and deserve to be punished. I'm not deserving of sympathy. But I would like to know if there is any possible way the court can send me to a hospital for an operation. I'm a young fellow, Judge, only twenty-seven. I don't want to go on like this, only half alive."

The court record shows the conversation between Judge Leibowitz and the defendant to be as follows:

The Court. You will get the best of medical attention in the hospital up in Sing Sing. That is the only place where I can send you.

You see, you pleaded guilty of robbery in the third degree, and with your criminal record the sentence is mandatory.

The Defendant. Yes.

The Court. I am taking into consideration that God has visited upon you a punishment which no judge could inflict. You are paralyzed, you are suffering pain and discomfort. You have ruined your life —but you have ruined it yourself, by your own conduct. I am not here to lecture you. You have my sympathy, because no matter how bad you have been in the past, you are still a human being and you are now suffering the tortures of hell. I am thinking of the hundreds of thousands of other kids in this country, who read dime novels and look at moving pictures which glorify gangsters; kids who frequent poolrooms and who look up to a man with a gun in his hand as a hero. Now you have come straight face to face with the whole situation. Let me ask you this: If you had a chance to have all of these young kids that go and do these crazy things with guns—if you had a chance to speak to them in this courtroom . . .

The Defendant. I only hope that some kids could just take a look at me now. What I have learned in seven months on my back, twenty years could not have taught me. I thought I could get away with anything; I was Tough Tony; I thought I was a smart guy; I had the impression I was too smart for anybody else. I was brought up in a neighborhood where 90 per cent of my friends were dishonest. I am not blaming that. It is my own fault. I came from a very good family. There is no one dishonest in it. I ruined my whole life. I only hope that half of those school kids in my neighborhood could just see Tough Tony now. This could teach them more than any twenty-year or sixty-year sentence.

The Court. Well, Tony, I think you may have learned your lesson. I don't think that these are crocodile tears you are shedding. I think they are honest tears. I promise you that this court will do all in its power to see that you get the best of medical attention. I will communicate personally with the Warden of Sing Sing and ask him to extend to you every possible consideration, and if nec-

375

essary the finest medical experts in the country will be enlisted to help you.

The Defendant. I hear a lot of fellows speak of how tough you are supposed to be with criminals, but you've just spoken to me as though I was a human being. If I could only live my life over again, I would never ruin it, never ruin my family. I would rather be dead than be what I am today.

The Court. You have a record and I have to send you away for a long time. The law gives me no alternative. But what can a judge do with men who come before him with long records? I don't mean men who commit petty crimes. I mean stickups with a gun. You know how itchy the finger is on that trigger when you are pointing it at another human being. You know how easy it is to snuff out his life. What else can a judge do, except to be tough with tough people?

The Defendant. No, there isn't anything else, because a person should know when he commits a crime like that, he is going to be arrested, that he is going to be punished.

The Court. I am going to impose the minimum sentence.

The Defendant. My brother is in the Army. My mother is still alive. What I am afraid of, Your Honor, is that if I was to lose my mother while I am up there, nobody outside would take care of me when I get out. Nobody would give me a job. I'll have no place to live. And my mother is old now. Is there a possibility for me, after I do about six years, to get some kind of clemency so I can go home to my family? Honest, Your Honor, I am not trying to look for sympathy. It went through my mind many times, the thought of trying to kill myself, because I cannot go through life like this. I was a wonderful swimmer and dancer. Now I can't even sit up.

The Court. Tony, feel that you have a friend in me. Where a man shows a real effort to be good and decent and fine, even though he has sinned in the past and sinned most miserably against society, one would be less than human if he did not try to help him reclaim himself, to become a God-fearing man, a decent, law-abiding citizen. After a few years, I will do all I can to help you. Of course, that all depends on investigation and how the authorities feel about it. But you write to me.

To Assistant District Attorney John E. Cone: Mr. Cone, would it be agreeable to you if the Court reduced this plea to attempted robbery in the third degree, so that I may impose a lower sentence?

Mr. Cone. Absolutely, Your Honor. I have never seen a sight like this before and I feel that certainly we are well within our rights in granting clemency here.

The Court. Mr. Clerk, go through the procedure.

The Clerk. The original plea is withdrawn and a plea of not guilty entered?

Mr. Schifter (defense attorney). For the record, the defendant respectfully asks for leave to withdraw his plea of guilty of robbery in the third degree and for leave to interpose a plea of guilty of attempted robbery in the third degree.

Mr. Cone. That plea is consented to by the District Attorney in view of the circumstances which have been presented here today.

The Clerk. Do you desire to plead guilty of attempted robbery in the third degree?

The Defendant. Yes, sir.

The Court (To the defendant). Now, you see how people are? People have hearts, people are decent, District Attorneys and police and everybody else want to be as kind to a fellow human being as they can possibly be. It is time that we practice some of the things that we preach about in our churches and synagogues. It is high time that the peoples of the world practice a little more Christianity, a little more Judaism. Tony, I am going to cut the original sentence in half for you.

The Defendant. Thank you.

The Court. I sentence you to five to ten years instead of ten to twenty years.

The Defendant. Before I leave I want you to know that anything I told you really did come from my heart. I cannot explain it. I cannot use good language or anything like that. I really appreciate it as far as a human being could possibly do. People like me are

377

scared to come in front of a judge like you. I hear a lot of inmates speak how hard you are on guys with records, and how I
would never get a break or anything in front of you. I just cannot
use words right to tell you what I mean. I really appreciate everything you done for me.

The Court. All right, Tony. God bless you.

The Defendant. Thank you, Your Honor.

Tears were rolling down the emaciated cheeks of Tough Tony
Tichon as attendants lifted the stretcher from the table and carried
him out of the courtroom. Fitzgerald had been absolutely right,
the Judge felt. This poor, crippled creature had somehow been given
the grace to renounce his life of crime. During the following two
years Judge Liebowitz often thought of the physical wreck he had
been forced to jail.

One day he received a letter from the Fletcher General Hospital
in Cambridge, Ohio, from a returned veteran, Private Alex Tichon,
who had been wounded in Italy. He wrote:

My brother, Tony Tichon, whom you sentenced to Sing Sing, is
now an incurable cripple. Judge, I know you gave my brother a lot of
consideration, you are a humane and understanding judge. I can only
think of the men I saw wounded at Salerno and other battlefields and
the agony they went through. My brother didn't receive his wounds on
a battlefield, but he is suffering just as much; he is just a mangled
piece of humanity. If you could get Tony out I would have him live
with my mother and me and take good care of him. The highest court
of Our Lord has imposed a severe enough sentence on him.

But there was nothing that the Judge could do. Shortly after receiving the letter he had a caller, the Reverend Bernard M. Martin,
Chaplain of Sing Sing, and Father Martin had come to talk about
Tony Tichon. He said that he saw a great deal of Tony in the hospital ward at Sing Sing. Father Martin was not a man to be fooled by
the usual protestations of reform made by criminals. He had had too
many disillusioning experiences with convicts at the big jail. But Tony
was one man in whom he completely believed.

"I agree with you, Father," the Judge said. "I felt that he had really reformed. But the law gave me no discretion. I had to impose the five-to-ten-year sentence."

"You had to impose that because of his record?"

Judge Leibowitz nodded. "He had been convicted of a felony before, Father."

"But, Judge," the priest explained eagerly, "I have done some investigating. I have found that when he was convicted of that previous felony he was not represented by counsel. The records themselves show that. If that conviction could be voided, Tony would not have had it on his record and you could have given him a lighter sentence."

"That's true," the Judge nodded. "Now I want to help that poor devil just as much as you do. Here's the way it has to be done, according to law. I know that Tony is penniless and can't afford counsel. I shall therefore assign former Judge Leo Healy to take the necessary legal action. If the facts are as you say, I can then legally adjust the sentence I gave Tony."

The legal proceedings were gone through. Leo Healy gave generously of his time. Judge Leibowitz then changed Tony's sentence to a two-year term. Because he had already served two years, he left the courtroom, this time a free man. His reformation seemed complete. In prison he had gained weight and his cheeks were no longer hollow. But he was still paralyzed, still confined to a wheel chair. He would never walk again. But he said he would get a job; and meanwhile his brother would take care of him. Tony was tearful in his protestations of gratitude.

And so a reclaimed man was returned to society. Everyone felt good about it. Jack Cone was pleased by the reform of Tough Tony. Father Martin was delighted that he had helped pluck a burning brand from the fire and that Tony would henceforth walk with God. Judge Leibowitz felt best of all. The case of Tony Tichon reaffirmed one's faith in human decency. Fundamentally, man wanted to be good; sometimes a man needed a severe jolt, as in the case of Tony Tichon.

A year later, a dock worker named Tony Tichon was arrested for the holdup of a sailor. They lodged Tony in the Tombs to await

379

trial. One morning the guard found Tony hanging by the neck from the cell door. He was cut down and revived. In the meantime, three murderous waterfront gangsters were arrested for "rubbing out" a competitor. Tony appeared as a State's witness against them. They were sent to the electric chair and executed. Tony escaped prosecution because he had turned State's evidence. It was the same Tony, as tough as ever. Miraculously, he had recovered the use of his legs. Not so miraculously, he had disavowed the fine sentiments of reform which the Judge, the District Attorney and Father Martin had believed. Today? Tony is still around. Perhaps you'll be hearing of him again some day. Will Judge Leibowitz see him again—in his courtroom?

3

A judge is apt to be soured by his experiences with a Tony Tichon. And then he meets a man like William Samet. There was nothing very impressive about William Samet that day in December 1926, when he stood before Judge Adel in Queens County Court and heard himself castigated as a worthless, nineteen-year-old habitual criminal. He had been convicted four times of felony, and a sentence of life imprisonment was mandatory. "Life imprisonment" doesn't actually mean what it says. After twenty years a man receiving such a sentence is eligible for parole. A fifth crime was charged to Samet in Brooklyn. Judge Adel did not press it. If Samet was ever released on parole, he would have to face that one too.

He was paroled in 1948, after spending twenty years in Dannemora, and he came before Judge Leibowitz on the old indictment charging that he had robbed a grocery store of twenty-five dollars. Judge Leibowitz read his old record: burglary in Chicago, burglary in Texas, arson in New York, burglary in New York. Then he looked down at the defendant. He received a shock. William Samet was not the gray-faced, emaciated, shifty-eyed individual one might expect him to be after spending twenty years in Dannemora. At thirty-nine, Samet was tall, with dark hair graying slightly at the temples. He stood erect, looking calmly into the Judge's eyes. He might just as well have been a young business executive about to ask the Judge to postpone his jury service for a month. The Judge gazed at him in astonishment. He asked him a few questions. It developed that Samet (who had never gone above the sixth grade at school) had educated himself at Dannemora. He had become an accomplished painter and a musician.

"How is it," the Judge asked, "that a man of your background has emerged after twenty years of prison so cultured and so poised?"

"By study and constant reading, Your Honor," Samet said quietly. "I've come to the conclusion that one who goes out and struggles for a living is a real man. Any fool can go out with a gun and commit a holdup."

"How did you happen to take up painting?" the Judge asked.

"We have a wonderful man at Dannemora, Judge," Samet said. "Father Ambrose Hyland, our Chaplain. I'd been there a few years when I discovered that I could draw. It came to me naturally. I sketched a lot just to pass the time. One day I was drawing a woman's head when Father Hyland passed my cell. He saw what I was doing. He told me that he was looking for a couple of men to work on stained-glass windows for his new chapel; it was called the Church of the Good Thief. Father Hyland got a real expert to come to Dannemora to teach me the technique. Once I had mastered it, I went to work on the stained-glass windows."

Assistant District Attorney Maxwell Lustig, who was in court to present the indictment, nodded. "May I say a word, Your Honor? Everything he says is true. I have discussed this man with Father Hyland and prison officials and I know that in addition to mastering two musical instruments, and learning to paint, he has become a sculptor of ability. When I looked at the written record of this case I said to myself, 'On his record of convictions, he is entitled to no consideration.' But then I met him and dug into the well of his mind and I had the same reaction you have. He comes from a decent family. His mother and sister are here in court today. He is only thirty-nine, and I do not think he will ever again commit a crime."

"I agree," the Judge nodded. "Now if you don't mind, I'd like to ask you some questions, Samet. I wonder often about the curative effects of prison life."

Samet replied, "I believe a man, in order to change, must be in prison for at least ten years. Those who serve terms of less than that become repeaters. They return all their lives for sentences of two, five, or ten or more years. Of the seventeen hundred prisoners at Dannemora I believe those who have served sentences of ten years or more include a great many who are rehabilitated and could well be turned loose. I would not accept responsibility for those who have served less than ten years."

Judge Leibowitz asked Samet what he thought of the use of psychiatry in the treatment of prisoners.

"I believe psychiatry at present is in an experimental rather than a practical stage," said Samet. "I believe it is a noble idea and should be developed."

"Tell me, if you had the power," Judge Leibowitz asked, "how many of the 1750 prisoners at Dannemora would you release right now?"

"Not more than three hundred," the man in front of the bench said promptly.

"The late Warden Lawes of Sing Sing had a theory that a prison should be like a hospital," the Judge went on. "You do not confine a patient to a hospital for a specified term of say ten years. You send him to a hospital until he is cured. Warden Lawes said that we should sentence men to prison in the same manner."

Samet shook his head. "I wouldn't be that lenient. I don't know if there are officials capable of judging when a man has sincerely reformed. Criminals are good at fooling people, but I do think the present parole system works out pretty well."

For nearly an hour the defendant, District Attorney and Judge discussed prisons and the mentality of criminals, and the best way to rehabilitate lawbreakers. Samet was brilliant in his analysis of the criminal mind, and he gave practical suggestions as to prison reform.

"If this man is really on the level, as he appears to be," the Judge said to the District Attorney, "he might make a good warden of a state prison. He seems to understand the whole problem of prison life and the rehabilitation of men so well. Now, in the usual course of events, having already served twenty years in prison, I would give the defendant a suspended sentence. But if the District Attorney does not object, I would like to dismiss this indictment entirely so that he can start life anew—with a clean slate."

"The District Attorney has no objection," Lustig said.

"Samet, when you leave this courtroom," the Judge said, "you may be sure every decent person in this community wants to help you if you are decent yourself. More power to you, Samet. I hope that you'll lead a clean, useful life. You are discharged."

William Samet walked to where his mother and sister sat. His face was alight with happiness. He embraced these two loyal women who had kept their faith in him during those long twenty years. But he was only thirty-nine. He had plenty of time to make everything up to them, he told reporters at the press table. What would he do? Well, he might open a small art shop. He'd sell artists' supplies and paint a little himself. He might even give lessons. But above all, he hoped to be given a chance to speak to groups of young men; to give them the benefit of his experience. He wanted to show the kids that a life of crime didn't pay. Why, he'd figured out just how much he had made during his brief career as a criminal. Spread over the twenty years he had served, it came to three-quarters of a cent a day. Finally, erect, clear-eyed, smiling, Samet walked off with his mother and sister on each side of him, beaming proudly.

Less than a year later Judge Leibowitz picked up his morning newspaper. Staring at him was a headline, "Forty-eight State Dragnet for Bandit Samet." Samet, at the point of a sub-Thompson machine gun, had held up a bank in Tulsa, Oklahoma. He had been wounded by police. Taken to a doctor's office for medical attention, he had escaped. A few weeks later he was recaptured. The prison physicians had to amputate his left arm, which had been shot to pieces in a duel with the officers. Now he is serving a life sentence in an Oklahoma prison.

4

If you're a judge, how do you keep from becoming a complete cynic? How do you retain any faith in all mankind? How do you keep from looking with jaundiced eyes at every man who stands before you pleading for "just one more chance"? You have been fooled by Tony Tichon, a William Samet and a dozen others. What is it that makes jurists continue to listen with sympathy to pleas made by convicted defendants?

Perhaps it's because of boys like Jerry Czeszik. In 1941, Jerry was eighteen, working as a messenger boy. His employers liked him and gave him additional responsibilities, and as their trust grew, they sent him to the bank to pick up the payrolls. They didn't pay him much, but they told him he had a future with the firm.

Then one day Jerry's employers were horrified to read in the papers that Jerry and two older companions had held up a store, had fatally injured the owner, and had been arrested on a charge of murder. Jerry and his two companions in crime were arraigned before Judge Leibowitz. Jerry seemed to have nothing in common with the two criminals with whom he had been arrested. They were neighborhood hoodlums; he had been a hard-working, decent boy who had no police record at all.

Bit by bit, Jerry's story was pieced together. With no little sacrifice of personal pleasure, Jerry had managed to save enough money to buy an ancient jalopy. In his neighborhood, ownership of a car of even such ancient vintage made Jerry an outstanding individual. His two companions had sought him out, flattered him with their attentions, and Jerry had accepted them as friends. He often took them out for rides. One day they suggested they had found a shop which was an easy "take." Jerry would hear none of it at first, but his companions said, "Don't be yellow. Do you want to run out on us guys?" In a moment of weakness—of sheer madness, he later realized—Jerry succumbed. He agreed to drive them to the shop if there were no "rough stuff." His companions assured him it was a "cinch." He drove them to the scene and waited in his car, while his companions

384

entered the shop. Jerry heard the sound of a shot and then his two friends burst from the store, hurled themselves into the car and told Jerry to get going fast. He did. He turned the next corner on two wheels and his car brushed the side of a truck. The three in the car were momentarily dazed, when a policeman, who happened to be within a hundred feet of the accident, nabbed them. They offered no resistance.

The two older men, both of whom had criminal records, were sentenced to life terms, but Judge Leibowitz hesitated to impose such a drastic sentence upon young Jerry.

The Judge had Jerry brought to his chambers. He questioned him for two hours. The boy was absolutely crushed. This could either be a manifestation of the consciousness of guilt, or the natural despair of a lad who had made his first mistake. Which was it? The Judge called the prosecutor into the conference. "Listen, Frank," said the Judge, "I'm convinced we're dealing with a good kid whose friends got him into a tough spot. You know the score. The kid had to run with the herd. It was either go along or be marked yellow. Why not give him a break? He certainly deserves more consideration than the other two 'hoods.'" The prosecutor listened to the story and was convinced. He agreed to allow the lad to plead to a lesser degree of homicide, and the Judge then sentenced him to a minimum term of four years.

Two and a half years later, with time off for good behavior, Jerry walked out of prison. He immediately went to the Judge's chambers. He was twenty-one now; strangely, prison life had not hurt him. He wanted help from the Judge. What help? He wanted to enlist in a combat outfit, and was afraid his prison record would bar him. Judge Leibowitz made a phone call to an understanding general he knew, and, within a matter of weeks, Jerry was on his way to war. He served with distinction, was wounded in action, and when he was mustered out because of his wounds, he went to see the Judge again, this time to show him the bronze battle star and Purple Heart medal he had received. He already had a job, he told the Judge.

That was in 1944. He said to Judge Leibowitz, "You could have

385

sentenced me to a long stretch in jail. My life would have been ended. The way I figure it, Judge, you gave me my life back. There's only one way I can think of to show my appreciation."

"What's that?" the Judge smiled.

"You'll see," said Jerry solemnly. The day before the next Christmas, Jerry appeared at the Judge's chambers. He carried a box of cigars with him, as a present to the jurist. Judge Leibowitz is a sentimental man, and was deeply affected by this visit.

"While I was in the Army hospital in France," Jerry explained, "I read an article in Leonard Lyons' column in an old copy of the *N.Y. Post*. It was about you. Lyons said that you defended 140 men and women for murder while you were a lawyer. You lost only one case to the chair, yet you never got as much as a Christmas card from one of them. I made up my mind then that as long as I live, I'll bring you a Christmas card every Christmas Eve. My Christmas card is in this box of cigars."

Every Christmas Eve, Jerry calls at the Judge's chambers with his Christmas card. Last Christmas he arrived in a new truck, accompanied by a brand-new wife. He proudly announced it was his own truck. Now he was in business for himself. At twenty-seven, he was secure, facing the future with calm confidence. Judge Leibowitz would bet his life on Jerry. One Jerry can make you forget a dozen Tony Tichons and William Samets.

5

If you live on Long Island, it may be that you buy your gasoline from Mike Adalna. Back in 1936, as a lawyer, Judge Leibowitz defended Mike on a murder charge. There was no conflict as to the facts—Mike Adalna had admittedly killed a man. He had broken into a store to steal food, and when confronted by the owner a struggle had taken place. The owner had a very bad heart, and when Mike hit him he fell dead. In the depression period, Mike, unemployed, was hard put to keep body and soul together. Leibowitz convinced the D. A. that his client was entitled to some leniency and the Judge let Mike off with a prison term.

One blustery, snow-swept night in January 1945, the bell rang at the home of Judge Leibowitz. A shivering, poorly clothed man was shown in. It was Mike. He had been released from State Prison just six weeks before. His cheeks were hollow, his shoulders sagged, his eyes were dull, almost lifeless.

"I came to see you, Judge," he said, "because I'm up against it, just as I was that night in 1936 when I broke into that grocery store. If you don't help me, I'm afraid I'll have to do the same thing all over again."

The Judge led him to the kitchen. He fed him and then listened to Mike's story.

"For six weeks I've walked the pavements trying to land a job," the sallow-faced ex-convict said. "They always ask for references. The only reference I got is from the warden, and the best he can say is that I got time off for good behavior. I've answered a hundred want ads and got nowhere. I haven't a cent in my pocket. I walked thirteen miles from the Bowery to get here tonight. If you don't believe me, take a look at these."

He lifted up one foot—then the other. The shoes were soaked through from the wet snow. There was a hole in the bottom of each shoe. The socks had been worn through and the flesh that peeked through the holes was raw.

"If you don't get me a job," he said quietly, unemotionally, "I'm going to get a piece of lead pipe and dump the first man I see who looks like he has ten bucks in his pocket. I'm not a crook at heart, but Jesus, what must a guy do that wants to go straight?"

"Did they teach you a trade in prison?"

"Two trades," the ex-convict laughed sardonically. "Broom-making and shoemaking. Do you know how many broom factories there is in New York? Exactly three. Look in your classified phone directory and you'll find them listed. And they have all the help they want."

"And shoemaking?" the Judge asked.

"Shoemaking?" Again the man laughed. "The machines we used in prison were out of date twenty years ago. I found one factory that might have taken a Brodie on me. Sure I said I could run their machine. But when I took one look at the modern machines they have, I knew I was licked. I didn't know one end of it from the other. And they didn't have time to teach me. It's up to you, Judge. Either get me a job or I'll have to go back to steal, maybe kill, before this night is over."

"If I get you a job, I have no assurance that you won't go back to crime within a week," the Judge said thoughtfully.

Mike shrugged his thin shoulders. "That's right," he said calmly. "But remember, the only time I broke the law was when I was hungry."

"Okay, I'll try," the Judge said slowly. "Wait here a few minutes."

He went to his library and phoned a friend who owned a string of Long Island gasoline stations. He knew him well enough to tell him the whole story.

"But, Judge, I don't need any help at the moment," he protested.

"But this man does need help at the moment," the Judge said grimly. "You may save this poor devil's life by putting him to work."

"If you put it that way," the owner of the gasoline stations sighed, "I guess I've got to go along."

The Judge went to his bedroom and found some warm socks and a pair of serviceable shoes. They fitted Mike pretty well. Mike went to work the next morning. Two years later, his boss expanded his business. He opened another filling station, put Mike in charge of it and gave him a percentage of the profits. In 1947, new cars began to flood the highways. Mike decided to open a filling station of his own. He'd saved his money and his boss made him a substantial loan. Today? If you live on Long Island it may be that you buy your gasoline and oil from Mike Adalna. He now owns four prosperous stations of his own. He employs twenty-two men. None of them knows his past history. To them he is merely a decent, not too exacting boss with only one idiosyncrasy. He's a little odd on the subject of shoes, they say. As usual, last Christmas he gave two pairs of shoes to each of his twenty-two employees. And he sent a pair of shoes to Judge Leibowitz—to give to a needy defendant.

388

Will the Judge bet on Mike? He'll bet his life on him. The eternal question in that courtroom is: What is justice in this case? If a judge can answer that question correctly most of the time, he is conforming to the highest tradition of American jurisprudence.

6

There is nothing that causes Judges as much mental torture as the problem of the young bandit who has been caught and who faces a long prison term. Nearly every day, kids of sixteen to nineteen are led into Part One of the County Court charged with felony. These are the cases that cause judges sleepless nights. What can be done with such a defendant? Happily, in the case of minors, the law is elastic. If a judge really thinks that a boy can be reformed, he can give him a suspended sentence and put him on probation. He can find a job for him, keep in touch with him, advise him and sometimes he has the satisfying experience of seeing such a boy turn out all right.

One morning Judge Leibowitz looked down from the bench in amazement. A boy with cherubic features and curly golden hair, who looked about twelve, was standing there. He was Joseph Kaschan, and he had confessed to taking part in ten armed robberies. He was sixteen. He had started his criminal career at eight, pilfering from schoolmates. He had been in and out of reform schools half a dozen times.

"Do you want a lawyer, son?" Judge Leibowitz asked.

"Naw," the boy said in a surly tone. "Phooey! A lawyer won't do me no good. I'm guilty, all right."

"Where did you get the gun you used in these holdups?"

"I found it on the sidewalk," the boy sneered.

"You need a lawyer, son. I'm appointing attorney Benjamin Spector to defend you."

Attorney Spector was in the courtroom waiting to represent another client. He walked toward the lad. "Get away from me," Joseph snarled. "How do I know you ain't a cop or a D.A.? I'm guilty, see, and I don't want no lawyer."

"Do you know what you're facing?" Judge Leibowitz asked. "With your record you face a possible forty-year term."

"Yeah? So what?" the boy said. "I'll get out some day."

After much persuasion he conferred with the attorney. Joseph pleaded guilty, and following the custom of the criminal court, his case was turned over to the Probation Department. Assistant Chief Probation Officer Joseph Shelley was assigned to dig into the life history of Joseph Kaschan. His beautifully written report covering twenty pages was put on the Judge's desk.

Joseph had been lodged in the Raymond Street Jail. He had simulated suicide twice. He had written a "suicide" note saying that he wanted to die because he had just heard that his "great friend Al Capone" was mortally ill. He told other inmates at the jail to call him "Baby Face." The mature criminals at the jail laughed at the youngster and this infuriated him. It was obvious to Joe Shelley that the boy had a decided "big shot" complex. His hero was Humphrey Bogart of the films, and he tried to imitate the mannerisms and the voice of the film star. When he had appeared in court the newspapers had taken pictures of him. He had cut these out and was very proud of them.

The Essex County (New Jersey) Probation Department reported that the boy's delinquent tendencies "were nurtured in the soil of parental inadequacies." He spent much time away from home, staying with chance acquaintances he picked up. More than once he had spent the night with homosexuals. He had absolutely no abnormal sexual tendencies himself, but played the passive role with homosexuals for the sake of a night's lodging or a dollar or two. He felt no revulsion for his actions at all. To him it was merely a way of picking up movie money. He spent a great deal of time watching gangster pictures. Try as Shelley might, he couldn't find any extenuating circumstances to mitigate the guilt of the lad.

Those who came in contact with Kaschan had the following to say:

Sister: "He was born that way."

Teacher: "He is beyond reform at any stage; he is a rotter through and through."

Principal: "He is a deceptive and chronic liar, the slickest-tongued fellow I ever knew. He is destined to be a notorious criminal."

Policeman: "At eight years, there goes a cop killer."

Psychologist: "He is a miniature gangster."

Psychiatrist: "Has high intelligence quotient, but is absolutely incorrigible, beyond reclaim; he is not insane, but his moral sense is atrophied."

Post Office Inspector (who questioned him about stealing from the mails): "He is a very dangerous boy and will try to shoot his way out of any difficulty; he puts on a nice act on occasions, but I wouldn't turn my back on him for anything."

Father Flanagan of Boys' Town: "I will not consider taking him in under any circumstances. Boys' Town is intended for boys who are homeless and not for criminals of this type."

"On the surface," Shelley wrote in his report, "the defendant seems a stable and likable person, but underneath, when studied enough, it can be seen that he is living within a world of his own in which he thinks that as a gangster he has a rendezvous with destiny. Those who have known the defendant intimately over a period of years are of the unanimous opinion that the defendant has none of the stuff of reformation. Never before have we come across so confirmed a criminal of such immature years. He has confessed to ten armed robberies and scores of burglaries. Community protection is about the only thing to be considered in imposing sentence, since all approaches on the basis of reclamation and reformation have already been tried and have failed, and since it is the considered opinion of all the people who have dealt with Kaschan that he is unsalvageable."

Judge Leibowitz had the boy brought to his chambers. He strutted in, puffing on a cigarette held tightly between his lips. Then, with the contemptuous gesture of the moving-picture gangster, he flicked the ashes from the cigarette onto the Judge's gown. "Well," he muttered, "what do you want now?" The Judge hoped to find some spark within him that might be fanned by decency and kindness. But he found none. The boy was stubborn, unrepentant, arrogant. With the greatest reluctance he finally had to impose sentence on the defendant.

391

"Joseph," he said, "I sentence you to not less than twenty and not more than forty years . . ."

The boy almost tore away from the grip of the court officer. He lurched toward the bench and spat at the Judge.

"I'll get you for that, you rat," he yelled, his baby face contorted with fury. "I'll be out in three months . . ."

Judge Leibowitz didn't sleep much that night. Sending a boy away for what might amount to the rest of his natural life is not something a man can do casually—and then forget. But what was the alternative?

Five years had passed. On a cold, wintry day a car drew up at the entrance to the reformatory at Elmira, New York. The motorist was soon sitting in the office of Colonel Weaver, superintendent of the institution. Colonel Weaver lifted the telephone and said, "Have Joseph Kaschan brought to my office." Presently a guard led in the prisoner.

"Do you recognize this man?" the Colonel asked.

"Why, he's the Judge who sent me up," he blurted out.

"That's right," Judge Leibowitz said. "You're older now. The superintendent has just told me that you've been very troublesome during the entire period and that it was only recently that you have calmed down."

"Yes, sir, I know I have not been behaving myself. I know I have been raising hell," the prisoner said.

"Well," the Judge continued, "Colonel Weaver says that you've behaved pretty well lately, and as a reward he's going to let you enter the boxing tournament. Joseph, I have kept in close touch with your case through the chaplain and the prison authorities. You must realize that I had no alternative except to sentence you to twenty to forty years. The Governor always has the power to commute your sentence, if he wishes. When the time comes that you can satisfy the superintendent, the chaplain, the psychiatrist and me that you have come to your senses, and that you are a safe risk to turn back into the community, I'll go to bat for you with the Governor and see what I can do. I want you to know that you haven't been and will not be forgotten."

And then the boy broke down and wept. It was the first time since his arrest that the hard shell he had grown had cracked. He thanked the Judge, and perhaps in that moment a criminal died and a citizen was born. Perhaps?

When the prisoner had gone, Colonel Weaver turned to Judge Leibowitz and said, "By your visit you have done more to lift the morale of all of the inmates of this institution than anything that I know of. Within ten minutes, the fact that the judge who sentenced this boy had traveled more than three hundred miles to see him, will be known to every inmate here. I wish that judges came here more often, instead of merely pronouncing sentence and promptly forgetting about the human being whom they have consigned to a cell."

7

On September 17, 1940, the Brooklyn Dodgers and the Cincinnati Reds were closing out their baseball operations for the season. It was the ninth inning and Umpire Billy Stewart ruled that second baseman Pete Coscarart of the Reds had dropped the ball before making the out. The decision meant the ball game. Umpire George Magerkurth behind the plate, who was the umpire-in-chief, reversed the decision of his colleague. The game was over. The fans poured onto the field. As Magerkurth made for the dugout to go to the dressing room, a short, powerfully built young fellow jumped on his back and bore him to the ground. Then, with his knees on Magerkurth's expansive belly, he pummeled the umpire about the face until he was pulled off.

On the following day Jimmy Wood, sports columnist of the *Brooklyn Daily Eagle*, reported the incident as follows:

Pardon us for smirking, but we can't be broken up by the young fellow taking the bull by the horns yesterday out at Ebbets Field. The exuberant young man, a member of the community commonly known as "the good people of Brooklyn," may have done something no law-abiding citizen can ever do with impunity—assaulting an umpire—but he has fulfilled the secret ambition of millions of fans.

He stands today at the bar of justice and His Honor looks at him

393

gravely, wondering if he typifies the unbridled instincts of mob rule, and if His Honor has never sat out at Section M at Ebbets Field, has never nervously chewed peanuts and discarded the nut, and never pounded the back of his neighbors when Camilli or Walker batted one up against the wall, we feel for the prisoner. A sentence or heavy fine might make for a cause celebre in Flatbush. A defense committee headed by a hundred notables can be hastily organized to appeal his case. Petitions can be circulated demanding a fair trial by a jury of his peers. If Samuel Leibowitz is not elected at the next election for County Judge, he may be persuaded to fight the case to the highest tribunal of the land, to clear the fair name of the prisoner and that of Flatbush.

The prisoner is a roly-poly, weighs about 180 pounds. Magerkurth is a giant of a man, 6'3" and 250 pounds or more, with a face like Herbert Hoover, two arms like the legs of a piano, two fists as big as hams. Yet our rooter bowled him over. Virtue aroused knows no obstacles. Didn't naked fists once batter down the iron gates of the Bastille?

When the case appeared before the magistrate, Magerkurth, who had to leave on an umpiring assignment in another city, withdrew the charge and the defendant was dismissed.

On April 8, 1947, Frank Germano, a short squat individual, stood before Judge Leibowitz waiting to be sentenced on a charge of picking pockets. Assistant D.A. J. Kenneth McCabe read off his long record as a pickpocket. The Judge looked down from the bench at the prisoner.

"Your face is familiar," he said. "Haven't we met before?"

The prisoner replied, "Maybe. I'm around a good deal."

"You know," the Judge continued, "it seems to me that I've seen you in some crowd a few years ago—was it Ebbets Field?"

"Yes," the prisoner smiled. "I'm a rabid Dodger rooter."

"Aren't you the fellow who knocked down Umpire Magerkurth?"

The prisoner squared his shoulders, and with pride in his voice announced, "Yes, Your Honor, I'm the man."

"You are a professional pickpocket," the Court continued. "Certainly if we're going to have our umpires assaulted at Ebbets Field, we don't want to have pickpockets doing it. I'm firmly convinced that it wasn't the umpire's decision that prompted you to knock him down.

394

You undoubtedly had in mind to have a crowd collect and then have your partner go through their pockets. I'm going to send you to Sing Sing for a term of two and a half to five years. On Sundays you will attend ball games up there at the Big House. The umpires come from the outside, so don't you dare try to assault them. Stay in the stands and when you get out, if you get the urge to pick pockets the best advice I can give you is never leave your home unless you put on a pair of boxing gloves. Then you'll be absolutely safe from arrest. Do you promise that you will wear gloves summer and winter when you get out?"

"Yes," the defendant promised. He was then led out of the courtroom en route to Sing Sing.

8

What would you have done in the case of Joseph Reese? Joseph Reese was a member of a professional car-stealing ring. The law finally caught up with him; he was tried, found guilty and went to jail to await sentence. On sentence day, Mrs. Lucy Garrity came into court to show Judge Leibowitz a letter she had received from Reese. Did she know Reese? No, she'd never heard of him until the letter arrived. Puzzled, the Judge asked for the letter.

While languishing in jail, Reese had been reading the newspapers. The *Brooklyn Eagle* had carried a touching story about fourteen-year-old Gloria Garrity. Gloria was blind. When she was five she had fallen on a spike which had destroyed her right eye. Vision in the other eye soon failed, and Gloria would be totally blind for life. But the youngster had plenty of courage and an undisclosed gift for music. One of the public schools had a Braille-reading class in music, and Gloria's excellent work was rewarded by the winning of a scholarship in music awarded by a Long Island school. This is the story Reese read while awaiting sentence. He immediately wrote to Gloria's mother.

"If a doctor can transplant an eye from one person to another," the letter read, "I would like very much to be that other person. I

395

assure you I want nothing for myself but the happiness I'll feel if little Gloria can see again. I pray that God will recognize my willingness to do this. Believe me, I just want Gloria to see again."

The Judge looked down at the thin, boyish-looking, twenty-nine-year-old defendant. He questioned him as to his motives, and at first blush it seemed that Reese was sincere in his wish to give up an eye for the youngster.

"Your Honor," Reese said, "I just mean to do something honorable for once in my life."

He looked at the Judge steadily out of clear brown eyes.

"Men on their way to the chair have made such gestures," the Judge said. "But you only face a short prison term. You are young. You'll survive the term all right, and if you are allowed to make this sacrifice you'll emerge from prison with only one eye."

"I understand," the defendant said firmly. "I've thought it over seriously. I'm not asking for clemency or any shortening of sentence. I repeat I only want to do something decent for once. This kid deserves the eye more than I do. I never did anything good with it."

The Judge was visibly moved by the apparent sincerity of Ross. So was the mother of the child. She stood there with her eyes shining with hope. To her the offer must have seemed like a miracle.

It was not something that could be decided casually, the Judge thought. He remanded the prisoner to jail and said he'd investigate all angles of the situation. He did. He conferred with Father John Keenan, who could find no moral objection to this specific case of organic transplantation; and he was advised by Dr. Philip I. Nash, medical assistant to the District Attorney, that there was nothing "ethically wrong" in such an operation. Next, Judge Leibowitz called Reese's twenty-year-old wife for questioning. Jean Reese had married at fifteen. Now she had two children.

"Would you object if your husband gave an eye to the little girl?" the Judge asked.

"Yes, I would," she said firmly. "First of all, I believe that such a thing would be against the law of God. There is another reason. I have two children to support. I am working now, but I don't know how long I can keep my job. When my husband gets out of prison

396

he will have to support our children. One eye would be a handicap to him. He seems to think that he is a free man, but he forgets that he has a responsibility to me and to our children."

"You have told the Probation Department that you wanted nothing further to do with your husband; that you no longer loved him. Is your objection founded on love or money?"

"I don't know whether or not I still love him," the young wife said tremulously. "But . . . I still have some feeling for him. And he has such beautiful brown eyes."

Judge Leibowitz and Fitzgerald spent three weeks investigating the defendant's motives. The findings convinced the Judge that there was only one decision to be made. He called Reese in for sentence.

"Having heard all parties," he said, "and having investigated the character and past life of the defendant, I am convinced that he is not sincere and that he has sought to evade the just penalty for his misdeeds by an attempt to play upon human sympathy. The pre-sentence investigation report discloses that he is a cool, calculating and unstable criminal. He has not treated his wife and children with any of the sacrificial affection he advertises as the object of his offer. On the contrary, he has been a shabby husband and father."

Dr. E. Clifford Place, an eye specialist, then stepped forward. "Your Honor," he said, "even if the defendant's offer were accepted, I am afraid that it will serve no useful purpose for the poor blind girl. The only part of an eye which can be transplanted with success is the cornea. That is the clear, transparent, shiny part of the eyeball. This part of the eye can be transferred to another eye in a living person, providing the eye of the recipient is healthy except for an opaque cornea. Those are the limits to which eye transplantation can be carried out at the present time. Unfortunately, the retinas of the eyes of this girl are entirely destroyed and a transplantation of the cornea would have no effect."

"I'm not so sure, Reese," the Judge said to the prisoner, "when this girl's condition was published in the newspaper, that you, with your cunning, didn't find out beforehand that what you offered to do would turn out to be merely a gesture. At any rate, there is no doubt in my mind that you are just a plain faker who is trying to play upon the sympathy of the Court. You are sentenced to a two-and a-half-to-five-year term in State Prison."

9

What would you have done to Mrs. Richard Smith? Mrs. Smith, a widow, was the sole support of a thirteen-year-old daughter. The youngster was about to graduate from school and her mother was making a beautiful, white graduation dress for the occasion. No girl would wear a finer dress, she told her daughter; this was pure silk and the lace that fringed it was imported. Mrs. Smith was actually sewing on the dress when two callers arrived. They were polite and, seeing the thirteen-year-old child, merely asked if Mrs. Smith would accompany them around the corner. She told her child she'd be right back and left with the two men.

The two men were detectives, and they took her to the station house. There were witnesses who identified her as a shoplifter with a long record. Her latest theft had been that of some silk and a quantity of imported lace.

She came up before Judge Leibowitz for trial. Mrs. Smith sobbed her story to the court. She admitted her record. She admitted the theft of the silk and the lace. And she told Judge Leibowitz about her daughter. Graduation was only three days away. Her daughter did not know that the material for the dress she dreamed about had been stolen. Her daughter only knew that her mother earned her living by sewing. She would rather die than have her child know that she had ever broken the law. She swore by all that was sacred that she would never steal again. What would you have done?

The Judge caught the eye of the Assistant D.A. Joseph P. Hoey, prosecuting the case. Hoey nodded.

"Sentence is suspended, go home to your daughter. Congratulations on her graduation," Judge Leibowitz said in a husky voice.

Through her tears the woman groped her way out of the courtroom.

What would you have done in the case of Al Barrone?

Barrone was indicted for first-degree murder. The jury was selected and the actual trial began. Suddenly Barrone slipped off his jacket. The Judge noticed it but made no comment. Then Barrone took off his tie and there was still no comment from the bench. The day was cool but after all the defendant may have felt warm thinking of the seat with the electrodes up in the death house at Sing Sing. But then he slipped off his shirt, arose and, pointing at the Judge, he cried out, "Look at that white-haired bastard sitting up there!"

The Judge had to take judicial notice of that. He excused the jury and admonished Barrone's counsel to keep his client quiet. The trial proceeded. The next morning Barrone appeared in court barefooted and wrapped in a blanket. Again the Judge excused the jury to discover the reason for the strange sartorial display by the defendant. The court attendants said that Barrone had disrobed in the corridor while waiting for court to open and that efforts to make him put on his clothes had been unavailing. The court officers therefore wrapped the blanket around him, secured it with safety pins, and hustled him into the courtroom. Well, there was no reason why a defendant had to be impeccably dressed, so the Judge let it go. But now Barrone really went into his act. He stood up and in a loud voice began to yodel like a Swiss mountaineer. In vain the Judge tried to preserve order. Then Barrone switched to an earsplitting version of "Yankee Doodle."

The Judge adjourned court and summoned Dr. Gladys McDermaid, psychiatrist. Dr. McDermaid examined the defendant, talked to him at great length and told Judge Leibowitz bluntly that the man was merely feigning insanity.

The next morning the Court told Barrone that if he persisted in his conduct, he would be confined and gagged under the direct supervision of Dr. McDermaid. Barrone did persist in singing, yelling and yodeling. Again the jury was excused. Judge Leibowitz now ordered the defendant bound and gagged. Attendants put the confining strait jacket on him and gagged him. When they had finished he looked like an overstuffed Egyptian mummy. Only his eyes showed, and they glittered happily.

"You've learned some tricks while awaiting trial," Judge Leibowitz told the defendant. "You have determined to do everything you can to prevent this trial from proceeding in an orderly manner, but you are in error if you think that you are more powerful than the law. You deliberately goaded the court into gagging you in the hope that an appeal will be made on the grounds that you were kept from communicating with your lawyer, which would be a violation of your constitutional rights. Now, any time you wish to consult with your counsel, tap three times with your foot and the restraining gag will be removed."

The trial resumed. Barrone had apparently quieted down. Finally it was his turn to take the stand. The restraints were removed and he was led to the witness chair. He sat there for a moment and then lashed out with both feet at the court clerk, who was swearing him in. Then turning quickly in the witness chair, his feet almost found the silver-haired head of shorthand reporter Ralph Roberts. Back went the strait jacket and the gag. The jury was not fooled by Barrone's conduct. He was found guilty in short order, sentenced to death and was sent to Sing Sing.

It is customary to give a physical and mental examination to newly arrived prisoners at the Big House on the Hudson. The attending psychiatrist who had read of Barrone's eccentric behavior in court asked him about it.

"What the hell," the prisoner said philosophically. "Sure I was putting on an act. You can't blame a man for trying. But that damned Judge was too smart for me." As they strapped him into the electric chair, he wisecracked to one of the guards, "Give Judge Leibowitz my best."

15. SUMMATION

"Absolute perfection cannot be expected, as every human institution is in the hands of fallible, imperfect human agents."

ALBERT S. OSBORN

For seven months now I'd been making weekly visits to the Central Court Building in Brooklyn. I'd stop and listen to the cheerful chatter of Bill St. George, the blind newsdealer whose stand is in the lobby of the huge building. I'd ride up to the fifth floor in the elevator marked *Judges Only*, and from Felipo Centineo, who ran the elevator, I'd hear again and again the sad story of how his rooster had been executed by the State of New York. When Felipo talked of his dead pet, tears welled into his eyes and indignation took command of his accent so that it came out half-Brooklyn, half-Italian.

"The roost', he wake up the school teach' who live next door," Felipo would sputter. "Six o'clock is time to get up, no? He's go to Magistrate Court and the judge he maka me killa the roost'. I tell Judge Leibowitz he should bringa this school teach' to his court. But he say he no can do. He say his court is got no business with a roost'. He say, 'Felipo, *perchone non compri un cane?*' Go get a dog, he say. Always he speaks Eyetalian to me. But I no lika the dog. I lika the roost'. What goo the wife widout da husban'? What good da chick widouta da roost'?"

I'd walk into Part I, where Judge Leibowitz presided, and if the representatives of the press, Joe Kiernan and Ernest Wiener of the *Daily News*, Jean Toomey of the *Brooklyn Eagle*, Milt Honig of the *New York Times*, and Eddie Ross of *Standard News* were

401

there, I'd know the trial was worth watching. They cover the County Court in Brooklyn.

One morning we watched a very young lawyer cross-examining a prosecution witness. There were several important inconsistencies in his testimony, but the inexperienced counsel didn't seem to grasp their significance. Judge Leibowitz sat on the bench, his arms folded, and then in a quiet voice he asked, "Counselor, just to straighten something out in my own mind, may I ask the witness a few questions?" The young lawyer nodded.

Eddie Ross, an old friend, nudged me. "Watch him go to work on this liar."

Quietly, almost casually, Judge Leibowitz asked the witness to repeat some of his answers. He asked a dozen questions "just to straighten things out" in his own mind, and by now the witness was an unhappy, desperate man whose answers revealed that he was either horribly mistaken or was fabricating his testimony. Then the Judge nodded toward counsel. "You may resume now."

Court was finally recessed and Ross, who has covered the court during the nine years Judge Leibowitz has been on the bench, talked about the change in the Judge. "When he first came here," Ross said, "he was like a great ball player who becomes a manager. The former ball player expects his players to display the perfection he once showed, and he is impatient with mediocrity. The Judge was like that at first. But he's mellowed. You saw how he helped that young fellow out. That kid lawyer learned something during those few minutes. He had a chance to see how a real master cross-examines."

When court reconvened, there was a knock on the courtroom door and an officer ushered in the twenty-three men and women of the Grand Jury panel. This was arraignment day, and the Grand Jury presented the indictments it had voted during the preceding week. Judge Leibowitz bowed to the grand jurors as they took their seats in their accustomed places, and Clerk Leonard called the indicted defendants to the bar for pleading.

A steady stream of men and women filed before the bench. The routine seldom varied.

"What is your name?"

"John Black."

"You have been indicted for the crime of burglary in the first degree. Have you a lawyer?"

"No."

"Have you money to retain a lawyer?"

"No."

"Do you wish the court to assign a lawyer to represent you without charge?"

"Yes."

"The court assigns Mr. Richard Fillmore," the Judge said.

"How do you plead?" the clerk broke in.

"Not guilty," said the defendant.

"On the question of bail . . ." the Judge addressed the prosecutor. Assistant D.A. Moorhead, Chief of the Indictment Bureau, looked up and gave the Judge a brief synopsis of the facts of the crime. From his desk the Judge then picked up a yellow slip containing the defendant's police record; then he announced the amount of bail that would be required should the defendant seek freedom pending trial. The defendant was removed and another immediately took his place as the clerk called out the name on the next indictment.

Judge Leibowitz had disposed of more than forty arraignments when a big hulk of a man, his face marred by a newly healed scar that ran from his left cheekbone to his chin, stood before the bench. His eyes were half closed and his whole demeanor suggested surly resignation to his fate. District Attorney Miles F. McDonald himself presented the facts. Reading from the indictment he said that the defendant Jones had broken into the home of a woman neighbor at night with intent to rob. The woman had awakened and surprised the intruder. He had then attempted to choke her.

"The indictment charges robbery and assault, Your Honor," the D.A. said. "I request that the defendant be held in fifty-thousand-dollars bail."

"How do you plead?"

"Not guilty."

The Judge picked up the yellow slip of paper. "Let's see now," the Judge said. "You first appeared in Juvenile Court when you were fifteen. Since then you've been charged with crime, twelve times; everything from petty larceny to manslaughter. You've been convicted four times, and you've spent ten years behind bars. Bail is fixed at fifty thousand dollars. Have you got a lawyer?"

"I got no money to pay a lawyer," the defendant said.

"You need a good lawyer," the Judge said. "I'm going to appoint the best defense lawyer I know to represent you, without pay."

Judge Leibowitz mentioned the name of a former district attorney now practicing. The eyes of the defendant flicked open in surprise and gratitude. That was the final case on the calendar. Ralph Roberts, the court reporter, noted the name of the lawyer in his record.

The Judge arose and said, "This court stands adjourned until ten o'clock tomorrow morning." The clerk cried out, "All rise, please," and the Judge, closely followed by white-haired John Sullivan, his personal attendant, hurried through the door to the left of the bench. I went after him. The corridors were crowded with witnesses, lawyers, spectators. Sullivan was ahead of the Judge now, crying, "One side, please." Judge Leibowitz is a tall, long-striding man, and now his robe was flapping loosely behind him. He walked into his chambers, a suite of three offices. He nodded to secretary Tina Metz, who was typing busily in the outer room. As he entered his private office, John Sullivan slipped the robe from his shoulders and then handed Judge Leibowitz his pipe. The jurist sat down at his big mahogany desk and lit his pipe. Murray Pearlman, his legal secretary, came in and said, "There's an order on your desk to sign in the case of *People vs. Farmer.*" The Judge nodded, leaned back in his chair, puffed contentedly on his pipe and looked inquiringly at me.

"Why did you assign one of the best lawyers in New York to defend that rat, Jones?" I blurted out. "He's obviously guilty, and it seems to me you're wasting the time of a busy, important lawyer . . ."

"Wait a minute." The Judge looked amused. "How do you know that man Jones is guilty? Have you heard a single bit of evidence against him? Have you heard his side of the case? Have you for-

404

gotten the basic premise of our law, that a man is presumed innocent until proven guilty? I know nothing about that man except that he has been indicted; the District Attorney presented certain evidence to the Grand Jury, and that body thought the evidence convincing enough to indict him. But an indictment is merely an accusation; it doesn't prove that a man is guilty."

"I doubt if the best lawyer in the world could do anything for that character, Jones," I persisted.

"You should go over to the City Hospital on Welfare Island sometime," the Judge said. "There you'll see hundreds of penniless patients. They can't afford the services of even the youngest, most inexperienced doctor. Go into the operating room there, as I have. There you'll see the finest surgeons in New York operating on these patients and doing it gratis. Suppose you saw a patient with a terrible brain tumor so serious that he only had a hundred-to-one chance of survival? Wouldn't you be shocked if they handed a drill to a kid just out of medical school and told him to operate?"

"I don't get the point, Judge."

"That wretch we saw up in the courtroom is in the position of a charity patient with a brain tumor," he said. "His illness isn't medical—it's legal. He may be suffering from moral syphilis; his record indicates that. He's in a desperate position. If found guilty, he faces a forty-year prison sentence. It would be morally reprehensible for me to appoint some inexperienced lawyer to represent him. He needs the best counsel possible, just as a desperately ill charity patient needs' the best surgeon possible. Now he may come up before me. He'll be represented by a capable trial lawyer and when the trial is over I will know that every legal precaution has been taken to guard his rights; to see to it there was no false or mistaken testimony presented against him; the lawyer I appointed would soon expose any witnesses who lied or who were honestly mistaken. I will then be satisfied that Jones had his day in court and was given every opportunity to refute the charges made against him. If the jury says he is guilty and Fitz's men have gone over the case, I can pronounce sentence with a clear conscience.

"Suppose I appointed some inexperienced youngster to defend

405

Jones," he went on. "He will be opposed by the District Attorney who has at his beck and call, not only a large and capable staff of assistants and investigators, but also the Police Department of the city —eighteen thousand men. The young lawyer will have no resources except a theoretical knowledge of law gained at law school.

"Under our system today," his pipe was going good now, "any law school graduate who has passed his state bar examination and has received his license, has the absolute right to defend a client without reference to his competence. To assign an inexperienced youngster to defend a man like Jones, for instance, is as absurd, and as cruel, as it would be to assign a brand-new medical school graduate to operate on the brain of a penniless charity patient. That's why I appointed the lawyer I did. He's a busy man, but he has the same sense of responsibility to his profession that a great doctor has."

"I seldom see the better criminal lawyers taking on penniless defendants," I said.

"Unfortunately, that's true," he frowned. "The eminent doctor can regulate his calendar. He can give one day a week or certain hours on certain days to charity work. But if I assign a prominent lawyer to defend a man accused of manslaughter, for instance, he can in all sincerity say to me, 'This trial may last three weeks. I cannot afford to give three weeks to a charity case. I have several other cases pending, and if I represent your defendant I'll have to withdraw from the others.' That's the difference between the problem confronting the doctor and lawyer."

"What's the answer to this condition?"

"We need a Public Defender," Judge Leibowitz said. "The State prosecutes a man; that man, the law says, is presumed to be innocent —why should it not defend him? Defense of a person accused of crime should not be the burden of a privately financed legal aid society. It should be a public function. The Public Defender should be a trial lawyer of experience whose standing is just as high as that of a district attorney, and he should have well-paid assistants, just as the District Attorney's office has well-paid and experienced assistants. A poverty-stricken defendant could go to such a Public Defender and be assured of getting the same skillful, legal representation that the prosecution

406

gets from its district attorney and his staff. The establishment of the office of Public Defender would be no threat to free enterprise for the legal profession. It would work no economic hardship on the lawyers of a community, for obviously only the penniless defendant would be permitted to take advantage of such an office."

"Would it be possible to obtain a really first-rate man for the office?"

"Of course it would," Judge Leibowitz said emphatically. "His staff could consist of experienced men plus some of the brightest law school graduates. Here, the novice would serve his apprenticeship in the criminal law just as a graduate of a medical school serves his internship in medicine, and, under the supervision of experienced men, he would mature to the point where one would feel justified in putting the fate of a defendant in his hands. The worth of a Public Defender has been proven in Chicago, St. Louis, San Francisco, Los Angeles and throughout the states of Rhode Island and Connecticut, as well as other communities."

2

"Since this is what you judges and lawyers would call 'summation of the case,' there are several questions I'd like to resolve. Tell me, Judge, how does the present-day criminal lawyer compare with the lawyer of yesterday?"

"Without even considering the great masters of the criminal bar of the nineteenth century, I am sorry to see the modern defense lawyers of eminence like the Darrows, Steuers and Littletons rapidly disappearing from the criminal courtrooms of America, with few to take their places."

"What's the reason?"

"Well, first, there is much more money to be made in almost any other branch of the law. Second, the criminal law is undoubtedly the most back-breaking branch of the profession and demands trial court talent of the first order. Third, the young lawyer is discouraged from entering this field of the law.

"I've already told you how the public mind has been poisoned against the criminal lawyer; how the newspapers, magazines, movies, radio, and now television, have distorted the picture of the real defense counsel and have twisted him into an odious lawyer criminal. If that were not sufficient to discourage the youngster, the law schools add their nod of disdain.

"To begin with, the student is drowned in a sea of lawbooks. True, the object of the good school is not merely to cram his head full of a thousand and one little rules of law, but so to discipline the student's mind that when a problem is presented to him by a client, he will think it out in a lawyer-like manner. This, the law schools have accomplished to a reasonably fair degree.

"But no real effort has been made by the school to prepare the student to actually practice his profession—certainly not to step into either a civil or criminal trial courtroom. In fact, the whisper has filtered out of the faculty rooms of many leading law schools that criminal law (except for the few law lectures which the professor delivers during the two-or three-day-per-week, one-semester course) is to be avoided and the criminal courts shunned as one would a pestilence.

"Quent, I cannot for the life of me understand such an attitude. The student is regaled with lofty polemics on the sanctity of human life and liberty. He is charged about his sacred mission as a minister of justice, to fight wholeheartedly for the protection and preservation of these basic rights. Are not the criminal courtrooms of our nation the battlefields where these rights are to be protected? Yet, with a wink and an aside, the student is cautioned to keep his distance from these courtrooms—lest he, Heaven forbid, rub shoulders with unsavory characters and be contaminated by those who 'resort to the use of immoral tactics,' as a famous Harvard professor has recently termed it."

"Judge, how do lawyers themselves feel about the practice of criminal law?"

The Judge laughed out loud. "This misapprehension has also infected many members of the bar, who either never see the inside of a courtroom, or who practice in the rarefied atmosphere of the civil courtrooms and who peer down their noses at the criminal lawyer with that deprecating look that a parent usually reserves for the errant child."

"Then Judge, you believe the law student should be encouraged to enter criminal law practice?"

"I do indeed! And the law schools could certainly do a better job in training students for life in the courtroom. Remember that a trial, especially in a criminal court, is more of a fact suit than a law suit. The troublesome problem confronting the court and jury is not so much *what the law is*, as *what happened*. 'Did he steal?' 'Did he assault?' 'Did he commit arson?' 'Did he kill, and under what circumstances?'

"The law schools make no attempt whatever to teach the student how to garner the necessary facts in the preparation of a case for trial. All that they crowd into the students' heads are abstract legal principles. Each law school should inaugurate what might be called, for want of a better name, a 'Department of the Facts.' This suggestion is not my brainchild. Judge Jerome Frank, in his recent, brilliant work entitled *Courts on Trial*, writes about a 'Chair of Facts,' which he urges as a vital necessity in our law schools."

"How would that work?" I asked.

"Well," the Judge said thoughtfully, "the school should have a legal clinic. A few selected and typical civil and criminal cases would be handled for the poor of the community. The professor, himself a lawyer admitted to practice, would take charge of these cases and with his group of students, observing and working with him, he would prepare and try these cases in court.

"The so-called *moot court* trial, now in vogue in the law schools, can never be as effective as a trial of a 'live' case. The moot court trial is merely a 'mock trial' at best and it often takes on Gilbert and Sullivan aspects.

"In the legal clinic, the young future lawyer would at least receive practical training similar to that of his brother in the medical school. The medical student is taught to apply what he learns from his books and his classroom lectures in the laboratory, with its microscopes and specimens, the dissecting room, with its human ca-

409

davers, the out-patient clinics with its myriads of live patients and the hospital wards and operating rooms. The young doctor in the operating room begins by handing instruments to the surgeon. He then advances to the point where he is allowed to take a few sutures. And always he is learning by watching and listening to the experienced surgeon. Finally he is allowed to perform a few simple operations, still under the eye of the established surgeon, and gradually, as his skill increases, he is given more serious operations to perform. All this takes years, and finally the young doctor is qualified. No such training is provided for the law student.

"There are six famous law schools in New York City, all of them a short distance from the largest court system in the world, federal, state and municipal. Do any of the professors take their students to these courtrooms—laboratories where the abstract principles of law they teach in their schools are applied in actual 'live' cases?

"In my nine years on the bench I have yet to have the privilege of welcoming such a delegation in my courtroom."

3

"You've been talking about changes in the law schools, Judge," I said. "But you've said very little about the police. During the past few months in your court, I've seen at least a dozen confessions repudiated by defendants. These confessions had been made to detectives at police stations. Many of them did not stand up in court."

"Confessions obtained by duress may be a part of the judicial system of Russia, but they have no place in a democracy," he said.

"But," I asked, "what about the third degree that still continues?"

"To show that democracy works all the time our police should use the third degree none of the time. The third degree is always a trespass on personal liberty and a discredit to public justice. The police themselves should be the most law-abiding of citizens and our station houses refuges from violence. Too many police make 'short cuts' instead of thorough investigations. But these 'short cuts' don't always stand up in court. Extorted confessions are often repudiated and juries acquit because they don't believe their own police. Since the policeman is our first line of judicial defense in the community, he should always move in an atmosphere of justice, never under a cloud of suspicion."

4

"It seems to me, Judge, that a jury is as unpredictable as a first-night theatre audience," I said. "And their verdict is often as difficult to understand. I've seen first-night audiences applaud a bad play hysterically, and I've seen such audiences sit on their hands at a fine play."

"Jurors are human, and nothing human is infallible. But name a better system for determining the truth or falsity of a given set of facts," Judge Leibowitz challenged.

"Why then do juries make so many mistakes?"

"Do they?" Judge Leibowitz asked. "I don't suppose you read the *American Bar Association Journal* regularly?"

"I don't suppose I do," I admitted.

"I commend a recent article it published, written by Judge Richard Hartshorne, of Newark, New Jersey," he said. "During the past twelve years he presided over 523 civil and criminal jury trials. He made a study of their verdicts. Each time a jury went out, he himself voted and recorded his private vote in his notes. He found that he agreed with the verdict in 437 out of the 523 cases. In eighteen of the verdicts with which he didn't agree, he felt that doubt was so manifest that he might well have been wrong and the jury right. Mathematically speaking, Judge Hartshorne came to the conclusion that the jury was right 89 per cent of the time in criminal cases and 85 per cent right in civil cases. Judge Hartshorne summed up his findings by saying, 'The jury system results, on the whole, in realistic justice.'" And Judge Leibowitz concluded, "If our courts can generally provide realistic justice, they justify themselves and the system under which they operate."

"Even those statistics show that there is an error of about 10 per cent in criminal cases," I suggested.

Judge Leibowitz interrupted. "Again, Quent, you're assuming something that's not necessarily a fact. Who can say with certainty that the jury was wrong in the 10 per cent of the cases where their verdict disagreed with the opinion of the judge—and that the judge was right?

"There has been so much talk about the superiority of a judge as a trier of the facts over the twelve 'good men and true' in the jury box. But we have criminal courts here in the city of New York where defendants are tried before judges instead of juries. The Court of Special Sessions tries misdemeanor cases. It has the power to sentence a defendant to the penitentiary where he may be imprisoned for three years. Three judges sit at the trial of each case. Yet, the instances are numerous, where two of the judges will vote 'guilty' and the third judge will vote 'innocent.' On the basis of the decision of the two, he may then be sent off to prison. Who is there to say that the two judges decided correctly and that the one in minority was in error? Here we have trained men, in judicial gowns, disagreeing on pure questions of fact which determine a defendant's guilt or innocence. What justification is there for criticizing a jury whose verdict, to be legal, at least must be unanimous?

"But, of course, jurors, like judges, are only human beings. They are not infallible. A jury is composed of twelve minds, twelve hearts, twelve sets of emotions, and if these can emerge with the right answer even 90 per cent of the time, we should consider ourselves fairly fortunate. Take the case of doctors. No one can tell how many mistakes the medical profession makes, and theirs is a science."

"If the personnel of a jury could be improved, wouldn't their errors be fewer?" I asked.

"Of course," he snapped. "But many intelligent, decent citizens, who gladly put on uniforms in time of war, who scrupulously uphold the law, who give generously of their time and money to community charities, who bring up their kids to believe in the best American traditions, manage to dodge jury service. It is a blind spot in the Americanism of the average American."

"Can't the court force such men to serve?"

"Yes, indeed, and it is the duty of the presiding judge to do so.

While in our court the judges are liberal in postponing a juror's service to some period when it will be convenient for him to serve, we rarely excuse a juror outright unless it is for legal cause."

5

"It seems to me," I suggested, "that there is an awfully large margin for error in the courtroom. This margin for error is the result of human frailties. So many intangible factors are involved in a criminal trial, it seems a wonder that justice is ever done. Can't science do anything to insure that the real facts emerge in every trial?"

"Of course," the Judge said. "If the law would only recognize the value of science. Take the lie detector, for instance. The court cannot take judicial cognizance of the results of a 'lie test.' A recent New York Court of Appeals decision dealt with evidence sought to be obtained by use of the lie detector. This decision bears careful study by lawyers who are interested in this subject."

The Judge pressed a finger on a button on his desk. John Sullivan appeared.

"John," the Judge said, "will you fetch Volume 279 of the *N.Y. Reports*."

Sullivan left the room and soon returned with the lawbook. Turning to page 204, the Judge said, "Here is what the case of *People vs. Forte* was about. The accused was convicted by the verdict of the jury. Defense counsel asked that the case be reopened and that the defendant be taken to the psychological laboratory at Fordham University to be examined under the pathometer, the technical name for the 'lie detector.' Judge O'Brien in this Forte case decision says that the trial court could not take judicial notice that the instrument was or was not effective for the purpose of determining the truth. 'The record,' Judge O'Brien says, 'is devoid of evidence tending to show a general scientific recognition that the pathometer possesses efficacy. Until such a fact is demonstrated by qualified experts in respect to the lie detector, we cannot hold that error was committed in refusing to allow defendant to experiment with it.'

413

"The prosecution and police rely heavily on science to convict," I said. "I've seen the police laboratory, and it's magnificent. But I never see a trial lawyer using the latest scientific aids."

"You're right," he said. "The police call the application of physical science to the investigation of crime 'criminalistics.' When evidence emerging from the laboratory is introduced in the courtroom, we call it forensic science. The science is founded on the basic principles of chemistry, physics and biology, and I believe the New York police force leads the world in this type of work. The usual court appointed lawyer, because of lack of funds, must ignore science in evaluating the story told him by his client, and in assaying the physical evidence involved in a case. For instance, consider a case where a document is a vital part of the evidence. Suppose the defendant says it is forged. The prosecution can call upon the police for an optical analysis. They have experts on microscopy, photomicrography; they can make a spectrochemical analysis. The lawyer defending paupers who can't afford experts has nothing but the word of his client as to the authenticity of the document. If the magnificent police laboratory were open to representatives of the defense as well as representatives of the prosecution, a pauper defendant would have a better chance of proving the truth of his contention."

"In short, science helps convict the guilty but seldom helps to acquit the innocent."

"That's true," he said. "Some years ago a man was murdered in New York. When the corpse was found it had a thick lock of hair grasped in one hand. The prosecution said that the hair exactly matched the hair of the defendant, and the defendant was found guilty chiefly on that evidence. Later the real murderer confessed the crime. He said he had obtained the hair from the suspect's comb and had planted it on the corpse. Had the defense lawyer in the case been alert, he would have hired a laboratory technician who could have demonstrated from an examination of the root ends of the hair that this hair had not been pulled from the hand of the suspect by force. Once that was established, a closer scrutiny would have been given to the rest of the physical evidence, all of which had been similarly planted. If we had a Public Defender, he would have access to the police laboratory and be able to give the defendant the bene-fit of science. But while science used properly by defense counsel can minimize mistakes in the courtroom, yet, until we can read the hearts and minds of witnesses, there will be occasional cases of in-justice," he added.

6

"Now, Judge, that we have better police, more and better lawyers (and prosecutors, too), better juries, more science, I'd be greatly sur-prised if the next improvement you'd urge wouldn't be better judges," I said.

The Judge did not reply immediately. He refilled his pipe, lit it, put the match carefully into the ash tray, took a few slow puffs, and finally the answer came slowly and deliberately.

"Of course, we can always use better judges. But it is only fair to say that, considering our methods of selection, the judges of our criminal courts are remarkably fine, capable and hardworking men. In our country, judges are not trained for the bench. In Great Britain new judges are usually first appointed to the lower courts. There they serve their apprenticeships and, if qualified, are then promoted to the higher tribunals. Thus, the judicial office is made into a career. This results in more qualified judges, especially in the trial courts. My years of practice in the criminal courts have convinced me that the hub around which the wheel of justice revolves is the judge who presides over the trial of the accused.

"No judge worth his salt will sit quietly by and permit a timid witness who is almost scared to death in the strange courtroom atmosphere, to be bullied and browbeaten by a prosecutor or defense lawyer. I believe that a judge does not function properly as a minister of justice, by merely sitting there like a ventriloquist's dummy mum-bling 'objection sustained' and 'objection overruled.' He is there to see to it that the facts are fully and clearly developed so that the jury may make an intelligent decision in the case.

"For instance, consider the lawyer who is a bore. He is questioning a witness. He drones on and on. The judge looks over at the twelve citizens in the jury box. The eyes of juror number six, the fat man, are slowly closing. Juror number three, the nervous gentleman, is taking jerky peeks at the clock on the wall. The lady in seat number one has fixed her eye on the courtroom window. As far as she is concerned, the trial in this courtroom is a million miles away; still the bore drones interminably on and on. And a man's life or liberty may be at stake! Now surely, Quent," the Judge continued, "the man on the bench should be able to bring the proceedings back to life if he knows his business.

"Then again, justice is defeated, although not in any venal sense, when lawyers are permitted to confuse witnesses by the use of highbrow language. Here is a picture that you will see in many a courtroom: A Mike Slovak, for instance, is on the stand. The examiner proceeds in the following manner:

"On the fourteenth day of April of this year were you present at the intersection of Main Street and Third Avenue when the defendant is alleged to have perpetrated the assault upon the prosecutrix?"

"What he say?" exclaims the puzzled witness, turning to the Judge for enlightenment.

The Judge replies, "What the lawyer means, Mr. Slovak, is: Were you on the corner when the prisoner shot the lady?"

"Oh, yeah." Slovak lights up.

"Where were you prior to that occasion?" the lawyer persists.

Again Mr. Slovak stares blankly at the questioner.

"What he means," the Judge interposes, "is: Where were you before this happened?"

"Oh, yeah. I was by Mr. Flannagan in saloon."

But the lawyer from the Ivy League Campus continues:

"And, Mr. Slovak, where did you proceed subsequent to the occurrence?"

Again the Judge must rush to the rescue.

"What he means, Mr. Slovak, is: Where did you go after it happened?"

416

"Back to Mr. Flannagan in saloon," the witness offers with a smile of apology.

"Do you see what I mean, Quent? With a capable, alert judge on the bench, there will be precious few wrong verdicts in his courtroom."

"We've hardly touched on the subject of crime prevention, Judge," I said, "but I know it is high on your docket of 'reform.'"

"The libraries are filled with books on how to prevent crime," he answered. "I have a lot of ideas on the subject of crime prevention, but I'm afraid it would take another good-sized book to expound them. I think you have enough material for one book now, haven't you?"

"I hope so, Judge," I said fervently, "I hope so. One more question, Judge . . ."

"I'm sure I know what it is," he laughed. "You want to ask me if I'd do it all over again. If I could relive my life would I practice criminal law, would I eventually aim for the bench. Has my professional career given me abiding satisfaction? Am I right?"

"That's close enough, Judge," I told him.

"That's easy to answer," he said. "I would do exactly as I have done. I have not always been right; but my professional life thus far has been gratifying. As a lawyer you may be sure that it was no joy to rub shoulders with the Colls, Capones, Hauptmanns and others of their ilk—professional criminals all. Such vultures of our society were as personally repulsive to me as I am certain they would be to all decent citizens. At the same time they were facing serious charges and under our basic laws entitled to their day in court. Like all Americans, good, bad and indifferent, they were presumed to be innocent until proven guilty and, as in the case where I defended Coll, some actually were innocent. Their way of life, their abnormal personalities and their standing in the social firmament were something of less interest to me, as a lawyer, than their status as citizens entitled to representation by counsel and a fair trial. My feeling to-

417

ward such clients was very much like that of the physician toward a patient suffering from a contagious disease. The doctor uses all the skill and scientific knowledge at his command, yet takes every precaution not to become infected by the germs of his patient. The doctor cloaks himself in a white gown and doesn't remove it until his day at the office and in the hospital is over. Figuratively speaking, I made it my business to don a 'white gown' to avoid exposure to antisocial germs. The regrettable fact is that a few specialists in this field neglected to distinguish between their professional obligations and their social life and made the fatal mistake of not wearing a 'white gown' any of the time. At the end of the legal day's work they hobnobbed on intimate terms with their virulent clients and thus brought disgrace on themselves and dishonor on a noble profession. All things considered, I feel that I fulfilled my legal mission in life to the best of my abilities. The big people and the little people came to me for help and it made no difference to me what sort of opinion they held of themselves. Some were afflicted with inflated egos while others were merely battered unfortunate creatures of circumstance.

"The important thing is that the rights they represented were of greater consequence to me than the individuals themselves. All of them were part and parcel of this country of ours, and by defending them I feel that I made my own little contribution to the preservation of human rights and human freedom. After all, these are the basic ingredients of our American way of life. From some sanctimonious quarters the remark is sometimes heard that lawyers who make their livelihoods defending such characters are worthy only of condemnation. Such a holier-than-thou attitude more often than not is mere posing. Careful examination of such sentiments show them to be insincere and unrealistic and motivated by many mixed feelings, mostly destructive ones.

"As a judge I have found life just as exciting as practicing law. My present office is by no means an easy one—not when you are dealing with the lives and liberties of your fellow men and women. It is no simple thing to pronounce those words that doom a human being to a long prison term or to the death chair. Even the run-of-the-mill case fascinates me for the simple reason that all cases, both big and small, are made up of human beings. And I find the opportunities never ending for discovering flaws in our machinery of justice. While I realize it is not easy to achieve a state of perfection in any field, yet here is one in which all of us would want more nearly to approach absolute justice. My thirty years both before the bench and on the bench have been packed with thrills. They have been soul-satisfying years—these years that, professionally, I have lived in the courtroom."